Hegel, Marx and Vygotsky

Studies in Critical Social Sciences

Series Editor
David Fasenfest (*Wayne State University*)

Editorial Board
Eduardo Bonilla-Silva (*Duke University*)
Chris Chase-Dunn (*University of California-Riverside*)
William Carroll (*University of Victoria*)
Raewyn Connell (*University of Sydney*)
Kimberlé W. Crenshaw (*University of California, LA,* and *Columbia University*)
Raju Das (*York University*)
Heidi Gottfried (*Wayne State University*)
Karin Gottschall (*University of Bremen*)
Alfredo Saad-Filho (*King's College London*)
Chizuko Ueno (*University of Tokyo*)
Sylvia Walby (*Lancaster University*)

VOLUME 195

The titles published in this series are listed at *brill.com/scss*

Hegel, Marx and Vygotsky

Essays on Social Philosophy

By

Andy Blunden

BRILL

LEIDEN | BOSTON

Cover illustration: Portraits of Vygotsky, Marx, and Hegel, marxists.org. Images are in the public domain.

The Library of Congress Cataloging-in-Publication Data is available online at https://catalog.loc.gov

Typeface for the Latin, Greek, and Cyrillic scripts: "Brill". See and download: brill.com/brill-typeface.

ISSN 1573-4234
ISBN 978-90-04-46686-9 (hardback)
ISBN 978-90-04-47097-2 (e-book)

Copyright 2022 by Koninklijke Brill NV, Leiden, The Netherlands.
Koninklijke Brill NV incorporates the imprints Brill, Brill Nijhoff, Brill Hotei, Brill Schöningh, Brill Fink, Brill mentis, Vandenhoeck & Ruprecht, Böhlau Verlag and V&R Unipress.
All rights reserved. No part of this publication may be reproduced, translated, stored in a retrieval system, or transmitted in any form or by any means, electronic, mechanical, photocopying, recording or otherwise, without prior written permission from the publisher. Requests for re-use and/or translations must be addressed to Koninklijke Brill NV via brill.com or copyright.com.

This book is printed on acid-free paper and produced in a sustainable manner.

Contents

Acknowledgements XI
Analytical Contents List XII
List of Illustrations XIX

Introduction 1

1 What Is the Difference between Hegel and Marx? 7
    1 The Main Difference between Hegel and Marx Is the Times They Lived In 7
    2 The Young Marx vs. Hegel on the State 8
    3 Hegel and Marx on Universal Suffrage 11
    4 Marx and Hegel on the State 13
    5 Hegel's Misogyny 14
    6 Hegel's Failure to See the Contradiction in the Value of Commodities 14
    7 Universal Suffrage and Participatory Democracy 16
    8 In What Sense Was Hegel an Idealist? 17
    9 Turning Hegel on His Head 24
    10 Goethe, Hegel and Marx 25
    11 Summary 33

2 The Unit of Analysis and Germ Cell in Hegel, Marx and Vygotsky 34
    1 From Goethe to Marx 34
    2 Vygotsky and Activity Theory 43

3 Concrete Historicism as a Research Paradigm 61
    1 Structuralism and Abstract Historicism 61
    2 Concrete Historicism 71
    3 Conclusion 76

4 *Perezhivanie* as Human Self-Creation 78
    1 Introduction 78
    2 No Mystery 78
    3 An Experience 80
    4 Etymology 81
    5 Catharsis 82
    6 Personality 84

	7	Continuity and Discontinuity 85
	8	Unity 86
	9	Lived Experiences 88
	10	Units 88
	11	Development 89
	12	Reflection 91
	13	Examples 92
	14	Critiques 93
	15	*Perezhivaniya* on the Social-Historical Plane 94
	16	Conclusion 97
5	**Agency** 98
	1	The Domains of Self-Determination 98
	2	Free Will 100
	3	The Natural Will 101
	4	The Development of the Will in Childhood 103
	5	Self-Control 105
	6	Acquisition of Ideals 106
	7	*Perezhivaniya* 106
	8	Freedom and the State 108
	9	Voluntary Association 109
	10	Alliance Politics 110
	11	Conclusion 111
6	**Tool and Sign in Vygotsky's Development** 113
	1	*Ape, Primitive Man and Child* 114
	2	Tool and Sign in Vygotsky after 1930 128
	3	Marx, Engels, Vygotsky and the Marxist Tradition 134
	4	Conclusion 142
7	**Vygotsky's Theory of Child Development** 143
	1	The Concepts of Vygotsky's Periodisation 143
	2	Social Situation of Development 144
	3	Central Neoformation 147
	4	Lines of Development 149
	5	Age Levels 150
	6	Self-Relation and the Crisis Periods 151
	7	'Leading Activity' and Zone of Proximal Development 152

CONTENTS

8 **The Concept of Object** 156
   1 The Various Concepts of Object 156
   2 Hegel's *Objekt* and *Gegenstand* 157
   3 Objective and Universal 158
   4 Marx's Critique of Hegel and Feuerbach 159
   5 *Arbeitsgegenstand* – The Object to Be Worked Upon 161
   6 Object-Concept 165
   7 Boundary Objects 167
   8 The Object of a Project 168
   9 Conclusion 169

9 **Leontyev's Activity Theory and Social Theory** 171
   1 Objects and Activities in Leontyev's Activity Theory 172
   2 Leontyev's Theory of the Personality 190
   3 A 'Project' as an Activity 193

10 **Fedor Vasilyuk's Psychology of Life-Projects** 195
   1 *Otnosheniye* (отношение) 196
   2 The Lifeworld (жизненный мир) 197
   3 *Perezhivanie* (переживание) 199
   4 Types of *perezhivanie* 199
   5 Social Theory 201

11 **The Invention of Nicaraguan Sign Language** 203
   1 Introduction 203
   2 Vygotsky on the Ideal Form 205
   3 Deaf Children in Nicaragua 207
   4 The Effect of the 1979 Revolution 208
   5 APRIAS (Association to Help and Integrate the Deaf) 211
   6 Was ANSNIC Acting Alone? 213
   7 Minimal Conditions for Acquisition of a Sign Language 215
   8 In What Sense May the Case of NSL Be Generalised? 216
   9 The Development of Language Communities 219
   10 Goldin-Meadow on the Structure of Personal Sign 220
   11 Conclusion 225

12 **Language in Human Evolution** 226
   1 The Co-evolution of Animal Behaviour and Biology 226
   2 Bipedalism 227
   3 Delayed Gratification 231

	4	Voluntary Control and Conscious Awareness 235
	5	Speech 238
	6	Conclusions 244
13	**Power, Activity and Human Flourishing** 245	
	1	Collaborative Project as a Unit of Social Life 245
	2	The Abuse of Power 248
	3	The Human Subject 256
	4	Political Economy 257
14	**Vaccine Hesitancy** 259	
	1	Risk Culture and Healthism 260
	2	Trust 261
	3	The 'VH Compass' 262
	4	Conclusion 275
	5	Postscript 2020 276
15	**Something Worth Dying For?** 278	
	1	Foreign fighters 278
	2	Who Wants to Be a Foreign Fighter? 283
	3	Conclusion 289
16	***Capital* and the *Urpraxis* of Socialism** 291	
	0	Preliminaries 291
	1	Goethe, Hegel, Marx, Vygotsky 292
	2	Projects and Solidarity 294
17	**Virtue and Utopia** 300	
	1	Internal Goods 301
	2	Problems with MacIntyre's Virtue Ethics 303
	3	Consequentialism and Deontology 305
	4	Virtue Ethics 305
	5	Practical Anarchism and Virtue Ethics 307
	6	Goals and Motives 309
	7	Ethics and Utopia 310
	8	The Virtues of Practices 312
	9	Summary 315
	10	The Question of Delegation and Hierarchy 315
	11	Conclusion 316

18 The Origins of Collective Decision Making (Synopsis) 317
1. The Question 317
2. Research Methodology 318
3. Collective Decisions without Voting 319
4. Counsel 320
5. Where Did Majority Come From? 321
6. Origins of Majority 322
7. The Development of Majoritarianism 323
8. Crisis of Majoritarianism 325
9. The Quakers and Consensus 325
10. Myles Horton and Consensus in SNCC 327
11. James Lawson and Consensus in SNCC 328
12. Women Strike for Peace 329
13. 1968 and After 330
14. Conclusion 330
15. Postscript 331

19 False Heroes and Villains 333
1. Villains and False Heroes 333
2. John Howard 335
3. The Right-Wing Populist Narrative 336
4. An Alternative Left-Wing Narrative 337

20 Amartya Sen on Critical Voice and Social Choice Theory 339
1. The Critique of Distributive Justice 339
2. Amartya Sen 339
3. Human Needs and Social Justice 341
4. Utilitarianism and Positivism 347
5. Utilitarianism and the Real Ethic of Bourgeois Society 348
6. Sen's Critique of Social Choice Theory 349
7. Conclusion 353

21 Comments on 'Social Capital' 355

22 Nancy Fraser on Welfare Dependency 360
1. Pre-Capitalist Society 361
2. Wage Labour 362
3. Domestic Labour 364
4. Public Assistance 366
5. Universal and Targeted Benefits 367

　　　　6　Dependency as a Personality Trait　368
　　　　7　Building Capacity vs. Philanthropy　369
　　　　8　The Ideology of Self-Help　371

23　**Anthony Giddens on Structuration**　374
　　　　1　The Knowledgeability of Social Actors　376
　　　　2　Routines　378
　　　　3　Practical Consciousness　379
　　　　4　Concepts and Motives　381
　　　　5　Unintended Consequences and Conceptual Development　383
　　　　6　Institutions and Social Movements　385
　　　　7　Conclusion　385

24　**Bourdieu on Status, Class and Culture**　387
　　　　1　Capital　388
　　　　2　Field and Habitus　390
　　　　3　Class and Habitus　391
　　　　4　Cultural Capital and Educational Capital　392
　　　　5　Social Capital, Body Capital, Linguistic Capital, Political Capital　394
　　　　6　Cultural Relativism　394
　　　　7　Idealism　396
　　　　8　Political Opinion Formation　397
　　　　9　Systems of Status Subordination　397
　　　　10　Social Capital Theory　398
　　　　11　Axel Honneth's Criticism of Bourdieu　399
　　　　12　Subjectivity　400
　　　　13　Conclusion　400

25　**The Coronavirus Pandemic Is a World *Perezhivanie***　402

26　**As of 2020, the American Century Is Over**　407

　　References　415
　　Index　425

Acknowledgements

My thanks go to Carol Macdonald, Bridget Leach, Julian Williams, Deanya Schemp, Avis Ridgeway, Megan Anakin, Phil Edwards, Jeremy Dixon, Anne-Thérèse Arstorp, Shannon Brincat and Helen Harper who read draft chapters and gave me feedback and made corrections. Every one of these friends gifted me new insights and improved my writing in a unique way. Thanks also to all the members of the Hegel Reading Group who have helped me develop my understanding of Hegel by reading and discussing Hegel line by line over the past seven years, including Darren Roso, Sadia Schneider, Peter Green, Emma Black, Sarah Bacaller and Maria Nicholas.

My thanks also go to David Fasenfest for his support for my publishing in this series over the past decade. Our collaboration began in February 2009 when I was looking for somewhere to publish an article which had been rejected by an academic journal. I sent David a synopsis and asked for advice about word length to submit to his journal and he replied "90,000 words."

My thanks also to Mike Cole who has encouraged, mentored and inspired me since I first mistook him for some kind of bot which answered any question that I sent to the listserv xmca back in 1999.

Analytical Contents List

Introduction

The circumstances that led me to the nexus of Hegel, Marx and Vygotsky are outlined, with an overview of the contents of this volume. I conclude with a brief survey of the present historical conjuncture.

1   What Is the Difference between Hegel and Marx?

This article was written in February 2020 and has been translated into Spanish, Portuguese and Italian. It draws on material from my *Hegel for Social Movements* to review the vexed question of the relation between Marx and Hegel. I base my observations on what Marx wrote on various philosophical, methodological and political issues rather than what he himself said about his relation to Hegel, which are generally polemical and misleading. Nor do I rely on what Engels said in the course of popularising Marx's ideas for 19th century socialists.

2   The Unit of Analysis and Germ Cell in Hegel, Marx and Vygotsky

This article was written in August 2020, for Deakin University's CHARR reading group. It is shown how the concepts of unit of analysis and germ cell originated with Herder and Goethe, and were formulated systematically by Hegel. The idea was key to Marx's *Capital* and became the central concept in Vygotsky's cultural psychology. The activity theorists further developed the idea in new ways. An understanding of Hegel's arcane but precise formulation is essential to understanding the idea, which can be more concretely grasped by reflecting on the wide variety of contexts in which it has been used.

3   Concrete Historicism as a Research Paradigm

An approach to the analysis of a social formation formulated in 2020 which utilises the concepts of 'concrete historicism' and 'germ cell' as elaborated by the activity theorists. The result is a logical-historical method of analysis utilising the methods of Hegel's *Logic* and Marx's *Capital* which can be deployed for the solution of problems in the social and political domain. The article was written as the theoretical introduction for a collaborative study of the political crisis in a specific country.

4   *Perezhivanie* as Human Self-Creation

An earlier version of this article, focusing on psychological aspects of *perezhivanie* alone was published in *Mind, Culture, and Activity* in November 2016. Here an outline is suggested for how the word *perezhivanie* can be appropriated from Russian psychology in general and Vygotskian psychology in particular, as a concept for Anglophone psychology, drawing on cognate concepts from Freud, Winnicott, Dewey, Kübler-Ross, Stanislavskii, et al. It is further outlined how the concept can play a key role in social theory where individual life-projects are tied up with the fate of broader movements of social transformation.

5   Agency

This article was written in 2020 in response to the term 'agency' having become ubiquitous in academic writing. In this critical overview, nine distinct domains are considered in which 'agency' refers to a unique phenomenon, each requiring an appropriate unit of analysis in order to be grasped concretely.

6   Tool and Sign in Vygotsky's Development

Vygotsky's views on tools and signs are elaborated in this chapter by comparing his early anthropological writings with his later works. It is argued that the relations between these concepts underlie ideological tensions which persist across the human sciences to this day. In the end, Vygotsky discovered what was before his eyes in the first place: *speech*, which originated at the same time as labour and in close connection with it. It was the production and use of tools in labour, *in combination with speech* which created the human species.

7   Vygotsky's Theory of Child Development

In this talk presented at the University of Witwatersrand in Johannesburg in 2011, I present in broad outline how Vygotsky sees child development in terms of a series of culturally determined periods of gradual development punctuated by periods of crisis.

8   The Concept of Object

This review of the various usages of the word 'object', especially by Hegel, Marx, A.N. Leontyev and Y. Engeström, was written in 2015. It includes a short etymology, discussion of the problem of translation between Russian, German and English, and an elaboration of the meaning of 'object' determined for use in a version of activity theory alongside 'project'.

9   Leontyev's Activity Theory and Social Theory

Leontyev's construction of the foundations of activity theory is critically reviewed, highlighting his original innovations in the study of human action as well as his limitations, which, in general, flowed from his living in the restricted social conditions of Stalin's Soviet Union. Leontyev's theory of the personality is then outlined, demonstrating its importance for social theory despite some limitations with respect to psychological application.

10   Fedor Vasilyuk's Psychology of Life-Projects

This is my short review of Fedor Vasilyuk's 'Psychology of *Perezhivanie*' written in 2015. In further developing Leontyev's theory of the personality, Vasilyuk added new insights to the concept of *perezhivanie* in showing how the development of personality during adult life is tied up with the person's participation in projects in the wider social world and the fate of those projects. It is shown that a social formation and the personality of an individual belonging to that social formation are composed of the same units.

11   The Invention of Nicaraguan Sign Language

This article was written in 2014, in response to the urban myth to the effect that a new sign language in Nicaragua had been created by illiterate deaf children without any adult assistance during the 1980s. It is shown that this report is false, and the conditions under which Nicaraguan Sign Language was invented are reconstructed. It is shown that a new language can develop only thanks to a project in which a community promotes its own aims.

12 Language in Human Evolution

A number of principles are formulated which constrain theories of the origins of speech and language, and their place in human evolution. In addition, some plausible speculations are offered. The article does not bring any new empirical evidence to the problem of human origins, but rather aims to limit possible theories by a series of principles which have a logical rather than an empirical foundation. The article concludes with the suggestion that the key activity which led to the formation of the hominid line was carry things back to camp.

13 Power, Activity and Human Flourishing

This study of the notion of power and human flourishing was first published in 2013 and subsequently translated into Portuguese and Spanish. The article also contains a sketch of the basis for choosing 'projects' as units for social theory.

14 Vaccine Hesitancy

An abridged version of this article was published in Australia in April 2015, before Donald Trump ushered us into the 'post-truth era'. The Australian government had become alarmed that vaccination rates of children under five years had fallen to 92%. Prime Minister Tony Abbott proposed to withhold welfare payments of up to $2100 per child and bar unvaccinated children from access to childcare, leading to widespread discussion in the media.

At the time of editing for this volume (August 2020), the vaccination rate at five years is 95% and approximately 50% of the population has received the seasonal flu vaccine. Vaccination has become a more contentious issue than it was in 2015, and distrust of authority more pervasive, so I have added a postscript to deal briefly with the new significance of vaccine hesitancy in the light of the COVID pandemic.

15 Something Worth Dying For?

An abridged version of this article was published in April 2015 at a time when the government of Tony Abbott was legislating to prevent Australian citizens suspected of involvement in Middle Eastern conflicts from returning to Australia. There was widespread debate about the legality of such a move and the extent of the danger to the public posed by returning foreign fighters.

16   *Capital* and the *Urpraxis* of Socialism

This is the text of a talk at the 'Marx 2.0' Symposium, Sydney 22–23 February 2018. The aim of the talk was to justify and present a concept of Socialism grounded in the political and theoretical work of Karl Marx which can withstand the ever-changing social conditions which have unfolded since the 1840s.

17   Virtue and Utopia

This is a review of Benjamin Franks' *Anarchism and the Virtues*. The article includes an appropriation of MacIntyre's virtue ethics, introduces the concept of 'virtuous social practices' and examines the basis for collaboration between anarchists and Marxists by means of an agreement on the ethics of collaboration.

18   The Origins of Collective Decision Making (Synopsis)

This article is a synopsis of my 2015 book *Origins of Collective Decision Making*. It was intended as a contribution to intense discussion on the Left at the time about the respective merits of different modes of decision making, including misleading origins myths. Because a group of people making a collective decision is the germ cell and unit of political life, this study provides a foundation for a more far-reaching analysis of political life.

19   False Heroes and Villains

This short article was written in 2005, in the last years of the socially conservative and neoliberal government of John Howard which had been in power since 1996. It is the only occasion on which I have drawn on the narrative theory of Vladimir Propp. It confronts problems facing everyone under socially conservative economically liberal governments from the USA to Russia.

In 2005, 'social conservatism' did not include climate change denial or anti-science conspiracy theories. The amalgam of reckless disregard for the natural conditions for human life with social conservatism in the USA and Australia has created new problems.

20   Amartya Sen on Critical Voice and Social Choice Theory

This review of Amartya Sen's work was written in 2004. It prefigures ideas which would later become themes of my work. The review takes the form of an imminent critique which in turn casts Sen's work as an immanent critique of distributive justice and welfare economics. It traces the unfolding of Sen's ideas in terms of the search for a unit of analysis for distributive justice – 'what it is which is to be fairly distributed'. The development is complete when Sen achieves an identity between distributive and recognitive justice.

21   Comments on 'Social Capital'

An abridged version of this article was published in June 2004, at a time when the concept of 'social capital' was being widely discussed. I conclude that the concept is being used to highlight real problems in the development of neoliberal capitalism, but to cast it as a form of capital is misconceived. This article is the first in which I used the concept of 'project'.

22   Nancy Fraser on Welfare Dependency

A version of this article was written in September 2004 at a time when conservative politicians in Australia were at war with the welfare community over 'welfare dependency'. Having now seen the pandemic close down whole sections of the economy, the old 'dole bludger' assumptions can no longer drive the welfare discourse as they once did, but the underlying problems have returned in intensified form. My article draws critically on Nancy Fraser's post-structurally inclined Marxism. While I still used the term 'subject', this is one of the first instances of me using the concept of 'project'.

23   Anthony Giddens on Structuration

This review of Anthony Giddens' epoch-making book was written in 2016 as an appreciation of his critique of functionalism and structuralism. I point to the difficulty for a sociological theory to transcend these theories if it lacks an adequate theory of psychology, such as Vygotsky's cultural psychology and activity theory.

24 Bourdieu on Status, Class and Culture

This review of Bourdieu's theory of the class structure of capitalism in terms of different kinds of capital – economic, cultural, social, etc. – was written in May 2004. Bourdieu's insights are appreciated but the structuralist form of the theory is criticised.

25 The Coronavirus Pandemic Is a World *Perezhivanie*

This article was published on the web on 13 April 2020 as the death toll from the pandemic reached its first peak. Its aim was to demonstrate how the concept of *perezhivanie* can be used to understand the development of the world system through periods of crisis separating periods of relatively gradual adjustment.

26 As of 2020, the American Century Is Over

This article was written in April 2020, with the US election still seven months away. The claim was by no means unique but allowed me to review the condition and history of USA as it ceded its position of world hegemony in the midst of a global pandemic and ushered in a new epoch of world history.

Illustrations

Figures

1   The germ cell of cultural development   44
2   The codevelopment of thinking and speech   48
3   Mediation in Activity Theory   185
4   The VH Compass   260

Table

1   Periods of crisis in child development   152

Introduction

About 20 years ago, as I approached retirement, I reflected on a lifetime in the peace movement, Trotskyist movement and trade unions. The world was now very different from how it had been when I first committed myself to these projects. Things were better in some ways, but the political projects which had been my life were now marginalised, and along with my working life, did not seem to have much of a future. I regretted nothing, but all the work still remained to be done.

Since Marx's death in 1883, the labour process had been completely transformed, and not only in the advanced capitalist countries, but everywhere. As the labour process had changed, so the working class had been transformed. Although it remained the case that the industrial working class was indispensable to the overthrow of capital, this class was no longer the socially or politically progressive class. Indeed, the industrial working class had been completely gutted. All the old categories had to be reconstructed. This was an immense task, and I became acutely aware that Marxism as I knew it was not up to the task.

I had already spent a number of years studying the history of communism from 1917 to the collapse of the USSR in 1991. Now events conspired to oblige me to renew my study of Hegel and deepen my understanding of Marx as a volunteer in the Marxists Internet Archive. At the same moment I was introduced to Vygotsky through my work at the University of Melbourne.

I soon became convinced that a Hegelian reading of Marx mediated by Vygotsky offered the possibility for a renewal of Marxism. At an earlier historical moment of the same kind, Max Horkheimer had observed:

> The economic appears as the comprehensive and primary category, but recognising its conditionedness, investigating the mediating processes themselves, and thus also grasping the results, depend upon psychological work.
>
> 1932, p. 125

But, alas, the currents in psychology to which the Frankfurt School had turned were inadequate to the task they set for it. Although Vygotsky and the activity theorists were psychologists, it was not their psychology which interested me so much. The philosophical foundations which had been worked out by Vygotsky in the late 1920s and early 1930s provided the basis for a truly interdisciplinary theory of human activity, equally valid in the disciplines of psychology or social theory. This meant that social theorists could collaborate with psychologists, each working in the domains for which they were qualified and experienced, but using the same set of concepts, which would allow for insights to freely flow from one domain to the other.

The 19th century had bequeathed us two psychologies: one based on introspection and the study of the cultural products which realistically described the full breadth of the human condition but lacked any scientific explanation of our psychic life, and the other, 'brass instrument psychology' and behaviourism, which explained the minutiae of nervous reactions but could describe nothing more than trivialities about real human life. What was required was a unification of descriptive and explanatory psychology (Vygotsky, 1928b, p. 302).

Vygotsky's insight came from his unique reading of Marx's *Capital* in terms of Marx's identification of the 'germ cell' or 'unit of analysis' of bourgeois society, viz., the commodity relation, from which all the phenomena of capitalist economic life could be unfolded by synthetic cognition. "Psychology is in need of its own *Das Kapital*," wrote Vygotsky (*op. cit.*, p. 330). The problem of finding a starting point for a general psychology was then reduced to that of identifying what Hegel had called 'the One', that 'concrete simple something' which could be taken as a unit of analysis for the study of psychology.

Vygotsky solved this problem in a way which unified 'objective psychology' and 'subjective psychology', and allowed the full breadth of cultural phenomena to be studied in laboratory conditions. He also showed how the study of consciousness could be made into an objective science, rather than denying its existence as Behaviourism had, or relying on introspection as subjective psychology had. The unit of analysis for a general psychology entailed introducing an artefact (sign or tool) taken from the cultural world into the relation between subject and object. In each case, the subject apprehended the object *immediately* and simultaneously as *mediated* by the cultural artefact. Thus, the entire world of human culture generated from outside the subject's horizons was introduced into the subject's relation to the object or person before them.

Importantly, Vygotsky insisted on the distinction between units: on the one hand, sign-mediated actions, which opened the way for the study of the intellect, attention, self-control, etc., and on the other hand, tool-mediated actions, which shed light on a wider field of psychological activity, including social systems in particular. In the course of his short career in psychology, Vygotsky determined three other units: defect-compensation for the study of disability; social situation of development for the study of child development; and *perezhivanie* for the study of personality development. Like Einstein, Vygotsky revolutionised not one but five domains of science in his chosen discipline.

After his death in 1934, his work was suppressed, and was largely unknown in the West until 1978, when *Mind in Society* was published.

Although it admittedly took me 20 years, I eventually identified Hegel's explanation of how this method based on 'the One' (Hegel, 1831, §96) works in the *Encyclopaedia*, that is, the identification of a 'concrete simple something' (Hegel, 1816, p. 801, S 779). I had long ago recognised this method in Hegel, however, simply by observing the structure of all his books. I had also known how Marx had appropriated this method in *Capital*, not only in the use of the commodity relation, C–M–C, as the unit of the market, but also M–C–M', as the unit of capital, the capitalist firm. So it seemed to me that I had grasped, at the most fundamental level, the common theme in how these three thinkers went about the work they had set themselves.

At the same time, I found that no one among Vygotsky's followers understood this, and there was utter confusion about the meaning of 'unit of analysis'. Equally, no Hegel scholar that I had come across had understood the immense significance of these passages in which Hegel described with precision how he constructed the *Encyclopaedia*, and no Marxist-Hegelian had correctly identified the relation between Hegel's *Logic* and Marx's *Capital*. I was on my own.

Although it has taken me 20 years to gain these insights, mostly withdrawn from work and political activity and outside of the academy, from the beginning I had set my task to convince Vygotskyists to study Hegel and convince Marxists to study Vygotsky. In the meantime, by reading Hegel, not so much in the context of German Idealism, but in the light of today's problems, I hoped to get an audience for my reading of Hegel amongst Hegel scholars.

Suffice it to say, that I still have much to do if I am to succeed in any of these projects.

∴

The essays collected in this volume have been written over the past 16 years. The first five were written quite recently and represent my current thinking on the crucial philosophical questions at the centre of my work. The second group of five essays covers my critical appropriation of three Soviet psychologists – Lev Vygotsky, A.N. Leontyev and Fedor Vasilyuk. The next group of five essays are explorations in diverse domains of enquiry in which I am not really qualified to speak, but which gave me the opportunity to test out the value of what I was doing as an interdisciplinary exercise. Then I have three essays, beginning with my talk on the *Urpraxis* of Socialism, which set out ethical-political principles so far as is possible at this utterly indeterminate juncture in world history. Finally, I review the ideas of a diverse group of writers: Alasdair

MacIntyre, Vladimir Propp, Amartya Sen, Robert Putnam et al. on 'social capital', Nancy Fraser, Anthony Giddens and Pierre Bourdieu, all with the aim of appropriating insights for the building of an interdisciplinary theory of social life. The last two were written in April 2020 with my reflections on the conjuncture as the world was gripped by the COVID-19 pandemic.

The pandemic is not a transient event. It is a feature of a world in which eight billion human beings live cheek-by-jowl with nature, and move people and goods freely across global networks at supersonic speed. In the past decade Swine flu, Ebola, Zika virus, MERS and COVID-19 spread across these networks, and as I write, COVID continues to mutate. In the past, great pandemics have come in the wake of wars and colonial invasions. The Plague of Justinian triggered the decline of the Byzantine Empire, the Black Death the decline of feudalism in Europe, and the Great Plague in London the end of absolute monarchy in England. COVID-19 marks the end of open borders for the global middle class as well as for the masses left to endure life where there is no functioning state at all, thanks to economic pillaging, US invasions and sectarian conflict.

For 30 years, triumphant neoliberal leaders have preached the incapacity of government and the need to hand over every social function to the market. When the pandemic struck, capital came running to the state with its begging bowl. Even after a generation of evisceration by outsourcing and privatisation had stripped the civil service of expertise, corporate memory, and self-confidence, the state was still the only entity capable of managing the impact of the pandemic. All efforts to privatise the response to the pandemic ended in disaster.

In many cases these governments were led by incompetent leaders elected on delusional programs and incapable of managing the pandemic with anything resembling rationality. In particular, the USA and the UK, the great capitalist powers of the past century, have suffered the highest death rates while sending their once-dominant economies into decline. The signal failure of these governments where there are longstanding functional electoral systems is hardly surprising, given their ceding of hegemony over public communication to Rupert Murdoch. The great hopes for a democratic utopia – the internet and social media – has turned out to be vehicles for hatred and misinformation managed by a small number of global companies, creaming the unpaid labour off their users' outrage and sucking advertising revenue from independent journalism.

And alongside all this is China, which does not suffer from the delusions of small government or the diktat of Fox News, where *laissez faire* is a foreign language and the government leaders are supremely rational if nothing else.

China, already the second largest market in the world, is rapidly becoming the pre-eminent economic world power. But Hong Kong has made it abundantly clear that China does not offer an alternate model for life in the 21st century for anyone who can avoid it.

The key word is 'trust'. When trust networks increasingly mirror political allegiances and extend hardly further than immediate friends and family, conspiracy theories flourish and communities fragment. The extreme concentration of capital and the evisceration of the public sector reflected in near-zero interest rates co-existing with huge rates of profit for a few large corporations and escalating property prices have extinguished most opportunities for meso-level collaborative projects, whether public or private. Local sports clubs need sponsors if they are to pay for their insurance. People tend to only trust people with whom they have some kind of collaborative relationship, and this has reduced the horizons of trust to extremely limited circles. Meanwhile, modern technique has made instantaneous communication across global networks available to almost everyone. Fluid communication without trust is a huge contradiction, one which can only be restored by a strengthening of public life at levels in between the household and the global.

At the time of writing, the only states which have shown themselves capable of maintaining a viable and rational way of life through this pandemic have been those developed nations and sub-national states in the Western Pacific with populations small enough that their leaders are close to their people and in a position to control their borders with strict quarantine measures, to the extent they do not have an underclass in their midst, excluded from the benefits enjoyed by the majority, where disease can incubate. All the nations and states I have in mind are trading nations firmly locked into global supply chains, and capable of providing a standard of living for their people. The Federal government in Australia is led by a corrupt Evangelical Christian, close to QAnon, hostage to fossil fuel interests, who has used the pandemic to attack the universities, the arts and the precariat. Nonetheless, the collaboration of state governments, including those with conservative leadership, managed to suppress the virus and avoided economic collapse.

The dream of the EU as a fully integrated superstate is over. The adoption of the Euro made any measure of political autonomy for Eurozone member states impossible, as evidenced by the tragedy of Greece. This model of development is not viable. All great states have their rust belts, and the market and the large nation-state equalise cultures which are essentially incommensurable. World trade and global cultural activity and communication has to be able co-exist with relatively localised political autonomy. Otherwise, it is impossible for ordinary working people to control the conditions of their own lives.

As I despatch this text to the publisher in January 2021, the American Century is over and the world is undergoing a *perezhivanie* which entails a complete reorganisation of the parts into a new whole and a transformation of the parts. But how this reformation of the world will unfold is at this moment *utterly indeterminate*. It is up for grabs. Truisms of the past have been shattered. The climate crisis however means that the world has no room for double guessing the way forward. Nature has set us the imperatives, but only decisive human action can maintain the conditions for human life on Earth. The future is indeterminate but surely the experience of the Trump presidency has proved that an interdisciplinary social and psychological theory is needed to understand the present moment. While I refuse to make predictions about the future, I remain convinced that the approach sketched in the pages which follow has the elements needed for an analysis as the next century unfolds.

CHAPTER 1

What Is the Difference between Hegel and Marx?

1 The Main Difference between Hegel and Marx Is the Times They Lived In

The philosophical difference between Hegel and Marx is a topic which has been hotly disputed for over a century. The differences between the philosophical approaches of Hegel and Marx will be dealt with in detail later on, but the essential difference between Marx and Hegel is the times they lived in.

Given the economic, social and cultural peculiarities of Germany in Hegel's day there was some basis for Hegel to believe that it would be through *philosophy* that Germany could modernise itself. Today, this stands clearly exposed as an 'idealist' position – to believe that an economic, social and cultural transformation could be achieved via a philosophical revolution, rather than the other way around. But this does not invalidate the choice Hegel made in his day. After Hegel's death in 1831, his students did draw the revolutionary conclusions that were implicit in their teacher's philosophy. Hegelianism spilt over the walls of the academy as his students popularised his teachings and translated them into the language of politics – or more correctly, translated politics into the language of Hegelian philosophy. In 1841, the Prussian government moved to "expunge the dragon's seed of Hegelian pantheism" from the minds of Prussian youth. The newly appointed Minister for Culture mobilised Friedrich Schelling (the last surviving representative of German Idealism, and now a conservative) to come to Berlin and do the job. His lecture in December 1841 was attended by Engels, Bakunin, Kierkegaard and notables from all over Europe but manifestly failed to quell the spread of radical ideas and revolutionary agitation which embraced Hegelian philosophy.

It is a remarkable fact that almost all the revolutionaries of the 19th and 20th centuries were either students of Hegel, Hegelians of the second or third philosophical generation or influenced by other figures of German Philosophy of the time – Kant, Fichte and Schelling, but above all Hegel – whether in the form of Marxism or other critical philosophical currents. So Hegel was not entirely mistaken in his belief in the political power of philosophy.

By the time that Marx resigned the editorship of the *Rheinische Zeitung* in 1843, France had been rocked by a series of working-class revolts and Paris was seething with revolutionary ferment, the English working class had constructed the first working class political party in history (the National Charter

Association) and were challenging bourgeois rule in Britain, and an advanced industrial working class was emerging in Germany. It was now obvious that change would come to Europe through the political struggle of the *industrial working class*. Capitalist development was disrupting all the old relations and it was going to be the industrial working class who would lead the transformation. Furthermore, the leaders of the labour movement were not just demanding inclusion in or reform of the state, or even aiming to replace the government with one of their own, but to *smash* the state. This was something unimaginable in Hegel's day.

On reflection, it will be seen that all the political and philosophical differences between Marx and Hegel arise from the changes which took place in Europe in the interval between Hegel's last years and Marx's entry into radical political activity. This began with the first proletarian uprising in Paris in 1831, the year of Hegel's death, when Marx was 12 years old.

The differences between Marx and Hegel are of two kinds. Firstly, there is their political differences, and secondly their philosophical differences. Marx's political differences with Hegel are shown in his polemic against Hegel in *Critique of Hegel's Philosophy of Right*. In assessing this polemic, it must be taken into account that Marx had not yet formulated his own distinctive political and philosophical view. Over the following 40 years, Marx's views became more distinctive.

Marx's theoretical differences with Hegel have to be divined from a study of his economic and social analysis and cannot be based on Marx's own declarations on his relation to Hegel, since these are polemical in nature and cannot be relied upon. To bring out the philosophical differences between these two writers, I will outline the real differences between materialism and idealism, a problem far more multifaceted than usually imagined. Finally, I will look at Marx and Hegel in the context of a more extended philosophical and methodological genealogy so as to formulate a position appropriate for our times which draws upon the strengths of both bodies of work.

2   The Young Marx vs. Hegel on the State

In the Spring of 1843, the young Karl Marx made critical notes on the section of Hegel's *Philosophy of Right* on the State (although he references earlier sections in the course of his commentary), abandoning the work in disgust at §313, as Hegel sails off into speculations about the course of World History.

At this point in his life, Marx read Hegel as a Feuerbachian – that is, he criticised Hegel for inverting the subject-predicate relationship, and much of his commentary is a rather tiresome ridicule of Hegel's idealistic forms of argument and expression. Marx regarded almost everything Hegel said as a rationalisation of the status quo. The criticisms he made which are worth taking particular note of are as follows.

Marx observes how in Hegel's scheme, the State reinforces already existing hierarchy and privilege in civil society and further that there is a 'civil society' within the civil service:

> The *corporations*[1] are the materialism of the bureaucracy, and the bureaucracy is the *spiritualism* of the corporations. The corporation is the bureaucracy of civil society, and the bureaucracy is the corporation of the state. In actuality, the bureaucracy as civil society of the state is opposed to the state of civil society, the corporations. Where the bureaucracy is to become a new principle, where the universal interest of the state begins to become explicitly a singular and thereby a real interest, it struggles against the corporations as every consequence struggles against the existence of its premises. On the other hand once the real life of the state awakens and civil society frees itself from the corporations out of its inherent rational impulse, the bureaucracy seeks to restore them; for as soon as the state of civil society falls so too does the civil society of the state.
>
> MARX, 1843, p. 45

This passage is followed by an extended criticism of bureaucratism and hierarchy, upon which Hegel relied for the rationality of the State – the civil servant "is like a hammer *vis-à-vis* those below, he is like an anvil in relation to those above" (Marx, p. 53). And the civil servant's "office is indeed his substantial situation and his bread and butter. Fine, except that Hegel sets direct education in thought and ethical conduct against the mechanism of bureaucratic knowledge and work. The man within the civil servant is supposed to secure the civil servant against himself" (p. 53). In other words, Marx thinks that Hegel's belief in the progressive role of the civil service is an idealistic delusion – all forms of bureaucracy and hierarchy lead to oppression.

Marx criticises the mediating role Hegel assigns to the Estates:[2]

---

1 The 'corporations' refer to the artisanal and commercial guilds, town councils, etc. of medieval society, which Hegel believed should be resurrected as part of the self-governance of civil society.
2 The 'estates' refer to the medieval institutions representing social classes in the political sphere. As Hegel saw it, the landed aristocracy represented all rural people, and the bourgeois elite represented the townspeople in the respective estates. They were precursors of

> The Estates preserve the state from the unorganised aggregate only through the disorganisation of this very aggregate.
>
> At the same time, however, the mediation of the Estates is to prevent the isolation of the particular interests of persons, societies and corporations. This they achieve, first, by coming to an understanding with the interest of the state and, second, by being themselves the political isolation of these particular interests, this isolation as political act, in that through them these isolated interests achieve the rank of the universal.
>
> Finally, the Estates are to mediate against the isolation of the power of the crown as an extreme (which otherwise might seem a mere arbitrary tyranny). This is correct in so far as the principle of the power of the crown (arbitrary will) is limited by means of the Estates, at least can operate only in fetters, and in so far as the Estates themselves become a partaker and accessory of the power of the crown.
>
> *op. cit.*, p. 68

Marx claims that this arrangement is aimed at *preventing* the people from forming an organised will, rather than at giving the people a means of *expressing* that will – participation in government transforms the political party from an instrument for the representation of the people into a means for control of the people by the state.

Marx rejects with contempt Hegel's 'deduction' of primogeniture and monarchy:

> Hegel has accomplished the masterpiece: he has developed peerage by birthright, wealth by inheritance, etc. etc., this support of the throne and society, on top of the absolute Idea.
>
> *op. cit.*, p. 74

and further rejects Hegel's dismissal of a 'representative constitution', i.e., universal suffrage. In considering the complex mediations Hegel creates between the various civil powers, Marx comments in exasperation:

> The sovereign, then, had to be the middle term in the legislature between the executive and the Estates; but, of course, the executive is the middle term between him and the Estates, and the Estates between him and civil

---

today's political parties. The same German word, *Stände*, is used for both classes and estates. But *Klassen* are also classes, and it is clear from the context when *Stände* means estates and not classes.

society. How is he to mediate between what he himself needs as a mean lest his own existence become a one-sided extreme? Now the complete absurdity of these extremes, which interchangeably play now the part of the extreme and now the part of the mean, becomes apparent. They are like Janus with two-faced heads, which now show themselves from the front and now from the back, with a diverse character at either side. What was first intended to be the mean between two extremes now itself occurs as an extreme; and the other of the two extremes, which had just been mediated by it, now intervenes as an extreme (because of its *distinction* from the other extreme) between its extreme and its mean. This is a kind of mutual reconciliation society. ... It is like the story of the man and wife who quarrelled and the doctor who wished to mediate between them, whereupon the wife soon had to step between the doctor and her husband, and then the husband between his wife and the doctor.

op. cit., p. 87

In the course of a long diatribe against Hegel's obsession with mediation, Marx says:

Actual extremes cannot be mediated with each other precisely because they are actual extremes. But neither are they in need of mediation, because they are opposed in essence. They have nothing in common with one another; they neither need nor complement one another. The one does not carry in its womb the yearning, the need, the anticipation of the other.

op. cit., p. 88

This of course cannot be squared with Marx's later views on the bourgeoisie and the proletariat, but its political meaning is clear: the domination of the proletariat by the bourgeoisie does not need to be *mediated*, but *overthrown*, and the state is not in fact a mediator, but an instrument wielded by one party against the other. This is the essential political difference between Marx and Hegel.

3   Hegel and Marx on Universal Suffrage

Hegel argues consistently for highly mediated forms of representation and against universal suffrage. Marx responds by pointing out that Hegel's valid criticism of universal suffrage is avoiding the main question:

> The question whether all as individuals should share in deliberating and deciding on political matters of general concern is a question that arises from the separation of the political state and civil society.
>
> *op. cit.*, p. 118

and

> It is not a question of whether civil society should exercise legislative power through deputies or through all as individuals. Rather, it is a question of the extension and greatest possible universalisation of voting, of active as well as passive suffrage. This is the real point of dispute in the matter of political reform, in France as well as in England.
>
> *op. cit.*, p. 120

Marx does not proffer solutions to this problem but makes an extended criticism of Hegel which brings out the contradictions entailed in Hegel's collegiate model of representative politics. Elsewhere, Marx points out that in France, universal suffrage had been used against the urban working class by utilising the weight of the peasantry, whereas in Britain universal suffrage was the central demand of the emergent working class. Still, without meeting the problems raised by Marx, Hegel makes a prescient argument against universal suffrage.

> As for popular suffrage, it may be further remarked that especially in large states it leads inevitably to electoral indifference, since the casting of a single vote is of no significance where there is a multitude of electors. Even if a voting qualification is highly valued and esteemed by those who are entitled to it, they still do not enter the polling booth. Thus the result of an institution of this kind is more likely to be the opposite of what was intended; election actually falls into the power of a few, of a caucus, and so of the particular and contingent interest which is precisely what was to have been neutralised.
>
> HEGEL, 1821, §311 n.

Marx did not have the answer to this problem in advance but had to wait for the working class itself to show its way forward in the Paris Commune of 1871. And Marx was prepared to wait for the social process itself to point the way, rather than speculate.

According to Hegel, the deputies in the Legislature represent the various social and economic branches of society, and the electorate must not be seen as an agglomeration of atoms (Hegel, 1821, §311). Deputies should represent the various real interest groups in society and give them equal weight. Universal suffrage on the contrary requires every individual to cast their vote privately, as an isolated atom. Hegel anticipates the preference of the workers' movement, noted by Marx, for delegates to the legislature to be selected from real workplace or local community organisations, such as Soviets.

Hegel believes that the public must be educated in national affairs, and he sees the assemblies of the Estates as the means of achieving this, while political discussion "at his fireside with his wife and his friends" can never go beyond "building castles in the sky" (Hegel, 1821, §315ad). *Participation* in assemblies is essential for political education, and this can only be achieved in the bodies mediating between the real associations of civil society and the Legislature.

'Public opinion' is the name given to "individuals ... in their having and expressing their own private judgments, opinions, and recommendations on affairs of state" (Hegel, 1821, §316). Public opinion is therefore "a repository of genuine needs and correct tendencies of common life" but "infected by all the accidents of opinion, by its ignorance and perversity, by its mistakes and falsity of judgment," and Hegel quotes Goethe:

> the masses are respectable hands at fighting, but miserable hands at judging.
> HEGEL, 1821, §317n

In his preference for participatory democracy mediated by political parties and work-based organisations, Hegel is close to the positions of modern socialism. He is sharply at odds with socialism in imagining that the elite can 'represent' the *hoi poloi* in their branch of the economy.

4 Marx and Hegel on the State

Hegel's *Philosophy of Right* is a flawed work, but nonetheless a project which was exemplary in its intent and method. Hegel's critical-logical reconstruction of a constitutional monarchy was intended to function as a reform program, directed against the reactionary absolute monarchy which ruled Prussia at the time. As a philosophical treatise, the *Philosophy of Right* would have enduring significance. It is just such a critical-logical reconstruction which any social change activist should be interested in making today.

Much has changed since the book was written in 1821. In particular, the main axis of the class struggle is no longer that between the landed aristocracy and the urban bourgeoisie (though the contradiction between rural and urban communities persists), but between a globalised working class and a bourgeoisie enjoying a formerly unimaginable concentration of wealth and international organisation.

Whereas Hegel could see the state as an arena mediating the struggle for dominance in civil society, most of us today, like Marx, take it that the dominant class in civil society (now the bourgeoisie) *wields* the state as an instrument for the suppression of both organised and spontaneous revolt against capitalist exploitation. The ground was already shifting when Hegel died in 1831, and it is now more than 135 years since the death of Marx, and the nature of the labour process and therefore of the working class has also changed enormously.

The fundamental idea of Hegel's book, as set out in the Preface, remains, to my mind, utterly convincing – we have to understand what in the existing state of political affairs is rational, i.e., historically necessary and therefore in that specific sense progressive, and understand what in the existing state is irrational and deserves to perish. Marx would heartily agree with this approach. Let us review some of Hegel's major political errors from a Marxist standpoint.

5   Hegel's Misogyny

The highly misogynistic 'deduction' of the place of women in society is a pointer to the dangers of taking any social phenomenon to be *natural* and of ignoring the *protests* of those who are suffering injustice. All social and historical phenomena are constructed by human activity and can be made otherwise than how they are. Hegel's misogyny is one of those instances where Hegel did not listen to his own advice. Everything is as it is for intelligible, social, cultural or political reasons. By the time Marx was writing his mature works, thanks to the struggle of the early feminists and anthropological research, it was well-established that gender differences were social constructs, and Marx understood what Hegel failed to learn from close female associates who were strong feminists and *must* have challenged him.

6   Hegel's Failure to See the Contradiction in the Value of Commodities

Hegel was fully cognisant of the growing contradictions generated by the market, but whereas Marx was able to reveal the ground of these contradictions in the commodity form of value, Hegel stopped short of analysing the contradiction which his own analysis exposed.

Hegel had already derived the concept of 'value' in the section on Property, specifically under Use, so that value was taken as a measure of the usefulness of a commodity. Although he saw the value of a product as *conditional* upon the capacity to exchange it, he did not see that value is quantitatively *determined* in exchange. Similarly, in this section, Hegel says (1821, §196) that it is labour which confers value on products of nature and that "it is products of human effort which man consumes," so value is conditional upon the object being a product of labour. He still saw the *measure* of value as determined solely by utility and failed to see the contradiction between use value and exchange-value. Hegel recognised the system of needs and labour as a process of real abstraction and real measure, but he did not deploy what he developed in that part of his Logic to reveal the dynamics of bourgeois society. This Marx did.

The superficiality of Hegel's treatment of economic value was exposed by Marx. The contradictions of bourgeois society which generated ever increasing inequality of wealth were staring Hegel in the face, but all Hegel could do was describe and bemoan them. Marx showed how these pathologies were rooted in the process of valorisation.

It cost the Women's Liberation Movement the lifework of thousands of feminists in the mid-20th century to finally expose the social roots of women's oppression. The critique of political economy was Marx's life work, and he wrote in the context of fully developed capitalism in Britain and a powerful movement of industrial workers across Europe. The critical resolution of problems like the oppression of women or the exploitation of wage labour is not a task which can be done in an off-hand manner through the reflections of a single writer. Hegel's real accomplishment was his Logic, and it is this work which is truly enduring in a way his relatively superficial treatment of many of the social problems which came up in *The Philosophy of Right* will never be.

Hegel is fully aware of the expanding and revolutionary effect of the market economy (essentially the bourgeois labour process) on the state and social life as a whole, but he accepted the creed of the political economists that in the market "self-seeking turns into a contribution to the satisfaction of the needs of others" (1821, §199). Participation in civil society develops the habit of work and fosters an infinite range of skills, and a growing understanding of 'how the world works'. But the division of labour makes the labour of each individual less and less complex and makes people more and more dependent on one another.

the abstraction of one man's production from another's makes labour more and more mechanical, until finally man is able to step aside and install machines in his place.

HEGEL, 1821, §198

Hegel explored and rejected a number of solutions to this growing social problem – philanthropy, a social minimum income guaranteed by the state, job creation schemes, and particularly emigration to the colonies, but he also rejected out of hand the option of common ownership of the means of production (§46). Hegel failed to see that when the means of production are entirely social in character, the basic emancipatory role of private property cannot be extended from ownership of one's body, one's home and personal effects and the tools of one's trade to social means of production used in common by thousands. Hegel proved that the air and water cannot be private property, but he failed to see that by the same logic, nor can the social means of production.

7 Universal Suffrage and Participatory Democracy

The demand for universal suffrage had been sprouting from the soil of early modern society at least since the English Revolution of the 1640s, but Hegel set it aside as 'building castles in the sky', along with the demand for women's emancipation and cries against the exploitation of wage labour. But surely, we now know that such demands are the harbingers of great social struggles to come. Hegel failed to see that utopian aspirations are not necessarily castles in the sky summoned up in fireside chats, but the product of real social and historical processes and may point to events yet to fully manifest themselves.

The 'right to vote' is understood nowadays as a right which extends to every *person*. In Hegel's terms, it is like personal autonomy. But clearly it is part of the state, not abstract right or civil society. But unlike the kind of 'rights' for which civil society is responsible, the right to vote is not an 'individual right' – dependent on a person's circumstances and economic exigencies – but a 'universal right'. In the structure of the *Philosophy of Right*, a universal right for participation in the state is a contradiction in terms. Notwithstanding all the criticisms which Hegel made of universal suffrage, criticisms which have been largely shared by Marxists, and if the opinion polls are to be believed, are nowadays shared by the majority of voters themselves, it is impossible to conceive of a truly democratic republic which does not include, as a marker of citizenship, a universal right to vote.

It matters not that universal suffrage is used, alongside private ownership of the means of communication and the means of production, to manipulate the mass of the population and perpetuate systems of exploitation. As Marx put it (1843) "it is a question of the extension and greatest possible universalisation of voting, of active as well as passive suffrage," and in the *Communist Manifesto* (1848): "the first step in the revolution by the working class is to raise the proletariat to the position of ruling class to win the battle of democracy."

Hegel also presaged Marx's conception of the withering away of the state. Hegel showed us how the political role of the Crown *withers away* from the status of Chief Executive and Commander-in-chief, to being a jumped-up clerical officer who signs documents and officiates at ceremonies, a living symbol with no executive function, as the state becomes more mature and stable and the cultural level of the masses rises. The same notion applies to all the institutions of state. Universal suffrage cannot be abolished (other than to usher in a despot), but must be *transcended*.

8   In What Sense Was Hegel an Idealist?

Almost any treatment of the Marx-Hegel relation hinges on a characterisation of materialism versus idealism. This can be deceptive, because the difference cannot be adequately defined along a single axis.

8.1   *Hegel Described Himself as an Idealist*

Hegel was the final product of the philosophical movement known as 'German Idealism', which arose in Germany in response to Immanuel Kant's Critical Philosophy. Kant had aimed to resolve the impasse between largely British Empiricism and largely French Rationalism. These philosophical currents were driven by problems which had arisen from the rapid development of natural science since Galileo, chiefly the sources and limits of human knowledge of nature and the nature of reality. Kant had proposed that a thing existed 'in itself' but human beings could have knowledge only of phenomena, i.e., appearances, while the nature of the thing-in-itself remained beyond experience and unknowable. Kant's approach generated many troubling dualisms and contradictions, and the German Idealists attempted to resolve these contradictions by focusing on *forms of knowledge*, rather than by speculating on the nature of a reality outside of human practice, which was the preserve of the Materialists.

Hegel put it this way:

> The proposition that the finite is ideal constitutes Idealism. The idealism of philosophy consists in nothing else than in recognising that the finite has no veritable being. Every philosophy is essentially an idealism or at least has idealism for its principle, and the question then is only how far this principle is actually carried out. ... A philosophy which ascribed veritable, ultimate, absolute being to finite existence as such, would not deserve the name of philosophy; the principles of ancient or modern philosophies, water, or matter, or atoms are *thoughts,* universals, ideal entities, not things as they immediately present themselves to us, ... in fact what is, is only *the one concrete whole* from which the moments are inseparable.
> HEGEL, 1816, §316

So the archetypal materialists were the ancient Greek Atomists – everything, including human life, was the result of interactions between atoms. Modern materialism, which arose *after* Hegel, has a broader concept of material reality which is inclusive of *social relations*, but earlier materialists tended to be blind to the social formation of knowledge and consciousness.

It was the Idealists, Hegel in particular, who discovered the *social character* of consciousness and knowledge, not the materialists. However, the idealists did not make forms of practice explicitly the subject matter of their systems; rather they took the 'shadows' of real activity – logical categories, concepts, ideas, etc., as their subject matter, thus justifying their description as 'Idealists'. A critical reading of Hegel will show however that *content* of these ideal forms is *forms of human activity*.

Not all forms of idealism are the same. In particular, Hegel distinguished between *subjective* idealists like Bishop Berkeley, and objective idealists, such as himself and Schelling. That is, for Hegel, thought forms were not chimera existing only in the imagination, but existed *objectively*, implicit in activity and material culture, independently of any single individual, and which individuals acquired in the course of their activity. Marx would surely agree.

8.2 Hegel Emphasised the Active Side Rather Than Passive Contemplation

The very first expression of Marxism – Thesis 1 of Marx's *Theses on Feuerbach* – is referring to Hegel in particular when it speaks of 'idealism':

> The main defect of all hitherto-existing materialism – that of Feuerbach included – is that the Object, actuality, sensuousness, are conceived only in the form of the object, or of contemplation, but not as human

sensuous activity, practice, not subjectively. Hence it happened that the active side, in opposition to materialism, was developed by idealism – but only abstractly, since, of course, idealism does not know real, sensuous activity as such. Feuerbach wants sensuous objects, differentiated from thought-objects, but he does not conceive human activity itself as objective activity. ...
MARX, 1845

Not only did the Idealists see perception as an *active* process, they also saw the interpretation of one's experience, how you conceived of and reacted to a situation, as itself an active process. The contrast with the materialist attitude to the social formation of human beings is set out in Thesis 3:

The materialist doctrine that men are products of circumstances and upbringing, and that, therefore, changed men are products of changed circumstances and changed upbringing, forgets that it is men who change circumstances and that the educator must himself be educated. Hence this doctrine is bound to divide society into two parts, one of which is superior to society. ...
op. cit.

On the other hand, we see that Marx lambasted the philosophers (i.e., Hegel) for merely *interpreting* the world rather than seeking to change it (the *purpose* of doing philosophy), partly because "idealism does not know real, sensuous activity as such," being concerned with ideas rather than actions – the shadows rather than the object itself. So Marx presents us with the contradiction that it is the *idealists* who based themselves on the struggle to change reality as the source of knowledge of reality, rather than passive contemplation of reality like the materialists. But like all professional philosophers, they merely 'interpreted' the world, rather than acting to change it.

But but on balance, Marx's *Theses on Feuerbach* is a *defence* of Hegel's idealism.

8.3   *Hegel Took the Social Elite to Be the Agents of Change*
Having witnessed social change in Britain thanks to industrialisation, and in France thanks to the guillotine, Hegel looked forward to a less traumatic and chaotic revolution in Germany which would be led by the social elite – philosophy professors, enlightened monarchs and a meritocratic civil service – rather than the blind destruction wrought by mobs and factory owners. Although he supported the right of slaves and oppressed nations to throw off their

oppressors, he wanted his native Germany to achieve modernity through the perfection of a state which would guarantee the freedoms of its citizens. He saw states as guarantors of freedom, not instruments of oppression (*true* states were not oppressive, as deformed or immature states or foreign occupiers might be) and was resolutely opposed to destructive, revolutionary methods of achieving social progress. He regarded the poor and working class as incapable of being agents of social progress other than through their gradual education – their misery was a *social problem* which could be solved only by the intervention of the enlightened elite.

When a work process is improved should we credit the employer who owns the improved method, or should we credit the workers who carry out the improved technique? Did Hadrian really build Hadrian's Wall? When a social problem is solved by the passing of a new law, do we credit the parliamentarians who passed the new law, or the social movement which demanded the change? Do we get to a better world by (at least some) people forming an image of that better world and then fighting for it, or does the better world arise out of contradictions inherent in the present state of affairs which drive people into actions irrespective of whether or not they can foresee the outcome? We call those people 'idealists' who think that the social class whose business is plans and ideas are the agents of change, be they agitators or princes, rather than the masses who act out those ideas. We call those people 'materialists' who see social change arising directly out of the conditions of life with ordinary people as its (generally) unconscious agents. Recall *Thesis 5* quoted above: if, as materialists, we see people as products of their social conditions then we reduce them to passive objects of change, leaving consciousness of change to the intelligentsia or the Party.

Hegel and the Idealists erred on the side of change-from-above, but exclusive focus on change-from-below is equally mistaken because it makes the people passive objects of structural forces beyond their control.

8.4 *Hegel Believed That Institutions Tend to Be True to Their Concept*

Anyone will recognise that over the years automobiles have come to better accord with their concept than they used to, conveying passengers to their desired destination in comfort without breaking down. Likewise, since they were first invented in 1908, washing machines have become more and more likely to wash your clothes and not wreck them. Hegel believed that this idea, which has been called 'normative essentialism' (see Blunden, 2016b), applies to social institutions as well as useful artefacts, and is crucial to his social philosophy.

Although states *originate* in violence, according to Hegel, the *concept* of the state is Freedom – freedom from crime, famine and outside attack, freedom for personal development and the enjoyment of culture. That is to say, a worthwhile concept, once it comes into being, will tend to realise itself in increasingly perfect forms and only falls into crisis when the practice no longer makes sense. In this way, Hegel saw the logic of ideas and concepts as the driving force in history. Marx responded:

> *History* does *nothing*, it 'possesses *no* immense wealth', it 'wages *no* battles'. It is *man*, real, living man who does all that, who possesses and fights; "history" is not, as it were, a person apart, using man as a means to achieve *its own* aims; history is *nothing but* the activity of man pursuing his aims.
> MARX, 1845b

Marx here is expressing a materialist position, in which people are not to be seen as captive of ideals but real actors. But if Marx is not to be accused of voluntarism, we must take account of his aphorism:

> Men make their own history, but they do not make it as they please; they do not make it under self-selected circumstances, but under circumstances existing already, given and transmitted from the past. The tradition of all dead generations weighs like a nightmare on the brains of the living.
> MARX, 1852

That which is "transmitted from the past" – the institutions, techniques, resources, symbols and beliefs, the norms built up by a people over centuries – unfold in a way ably described by Hegel with his dialectical idealist philosophy. But how people *make use of* those conditions is not always logical. People do not always do what they are supposed to do, so to speak, so Marx's insistence that the realisation of an idea is a matter of *struggle* is an important *corrective* to the idealist vision of history unfolding according to intelligible, rational principles. The fact remains however that Hegel's idealism is a powerful principle of historical development and historically it has always been the idealists who have emphasised human agency in social change.

8.5   *Hegel Minimised the Effect of Mundane Relations on Institutions*
As discussed above, in his *Philosophy of Right*, Hegel is sometimes unbelievably naïve. He thinks that the civil service is a meritocracy which serves the

public good, and never considers that civil servants look out for themselves like everyone else. It doesn't matter to him how judges are appointed or from what social class they are drawn, because it is their concept to apply the law to individual cases, not to further their own class interest or political agenda. The fact that the constitutional monarch, as the traditional owner of the land, is an extremely wealthy person does not cause Hegel to suspect that their judgment might be prejudiced by their wealth.

Marx ridicules this idealism, commenting wryly: "The man within the civil servant is supposed to secure the civil servant against himself" (Marx, 1843, p. 53), noting that a 'civil society' necessarily operates *within* the civil service. Hegel seems to think that officials will act according to their job description, and Marx does not believe this. Everyone knows that the remuneration structure determines an employee's actions far more effectively than the organisation's mission statement. Likewise, if you pay a news site per click, then you'll get an outrage and titillation generator, not a news site.

In the USA people seem to accept that Supreme Court judges act according to their own political agenda, and that lower courts can be relied upon to discriminate against African Americans. However, in most developed countries, despite the fact that judges are invariably drawn from the most privileged section of society, the law is generally developing and applied in a rational fashion worthy of being written up in the law books, rather than being naked expressions of class prejudice. What is more, when decisions are made which *are* expressions of naked class prejudice, there is public outrage, appeals and political pressure, and even if it takes centuries, there is some merit in the aphorism: "The truth will out." In the long run, Hegel's idealism in this sense often turns out to have more merit than a cynical materialism would suggest.

For example, if you accept the climate science consensus, you must be an idealist, because an idealist thinks that Science, as an institution acting according to its concept, promotes true scientific knowledge. The cynical materialist, on the other hand, believes that scientists are motivated by the need to publish, get promoted, etc., and consequently are captives of corporate and bureaucratic interests, and the scientific consensus is not to be believed.

8.6 *Hegel Overestimated Speculative Reason Relative to Social Process Itself*

Hegel first published his *Encyclopædia of the Philosophical Sciences* in 1817. In this monumental work he aimed to prefigure (among other things), in outline, the entire development of natural science. But natural science did not progress by the writing of ever more perfect and comprehensive encyclopaedias. Rather, individuals and groups beavered away separately on narrowly defined problems, all the while lacking any sophisticated view of the whole, and gradually, over the decades, the separate strands more and more came into contact with one another, and over time, through a seemingly objective social process, viable, overall, interdisciplinary visions began to emerge.

Each strand of research has been influenced by the discoveries and theories and the techniques and tools produced by the others. The scope and complexity and interconnectedness of human activity developed further and further, throwing up new insights, new techniques, new theories, new forms of experiment, new possibilities endlessly, way beyond the capacity of a single mind to plan or predict. Every insight, every discovery is the product of a human mind, but the process as a whole is a gigantic worldwide social process. At each moment, the latest discovery to come out of the endless unfolding of human practice is intelligible in the light of what has gone before, what has already been discovered. But who can tell what the next discovery will be?

When Marx wrote the *Communist Manifesto,* he left many questions unresolved. One of these was the question of whether the workers' movement could seize state power and how they would use that power. Marx did not attempt to work this out in advance. He had to wait until the Paris Commune demonstrated what the workers' movement would do. He then amended the Manifesto accordingly – adding to the 1872 Preface to the *Manifesto* the words: "One thing especially was proved by the Commune, viz., that 'the working class cannot simply lay hold of the ready-made state machinery and wield it for its own purposes'."

Likewise, in the writing of *Capital,* Marx took as his starting point the simplest social form in which value was manifested, the exchange of commodities. Living in England, at that time the most advanced capitalist country, it was possible to *observe* the entire unfolding of the value relation from practice of exchanging commodities. He could make the development of capital intelligible by means of his analysis of exchange, but he made only the most general and qualified predictions of where it was headed based on his clear view of where it was at the moment. He could not predict the shape of the successive transformations of capital which would flow through the economy after his death, and Marx knew this.[3]

---

3 Marx did make a couple of qualified speculations in *Capital,* viz., that the concentration of capital in a few hands would ultimately lead to expropriation of capital, and that there was a tendency of the rate of profit to fall as a proportion of total investment. Also, in his private correspondence, he was an inveterate optimist. But the essence of his scientific work was to avoid speculation.

But compare Marx's analysis with Hegel's naïve analysis of value mentioned above.

As an Idealist, Hegel falsely believed that Logic would allow him to foresee what was as yet outside social experience. He was writing in 1817, before the microscope, Darwin's discoveries, the Michelson-Morley experiment and the burgeoning of natural scientific investigation during the 19th century. It is obvious to us that the project of the *Encyclopaedia* was untenable, even granting that the *Encyclopaedia* is in large measure merely a systematisation of scientific knowledge as it was at his time, and not wholesale speculation. Only the social process itself as a whole can work out and reveal the real content of a concept. The real content of a concept is available to the theorist to the extent that they can observe and make intelligible what exists or is already at least in the process of formation.

This is the difference between Idealism and Materialism in terms of scientific method.

9 Turning Hegel on His Head

Marx's aphorism is valid:

> My dialectic method is not only different from the Hegelian, but is its direct opposite. ... With him it is standing on its head. It must be turned right side up again.
> MARX, 1873

But without explanation, it is rather unhelpful for *understanding*, let alone *using* Marx's dialectic. Consider this criticism which Marx aimed at Hegel:

> The totality as it appears in the head, as a totality of thoughts, is a product of a thinking head, which appropriates the world in the only way it can, a way different from the artistic, religious, practical and mental appropriation of this world. The real subject retains its autonomous existence outside the head just as before; namely as long as the head's conduct is merely speculative, merely theoretical. Hence, in the theoretical method, too, the subject, society, must always be kept in mind as the presupposition.
> MARX, 1858, p. 101

The "real subject" is social practice. A form of social practice cannot be observed and made intelligible by a theoretician until it *has come into being*. The progress of knowledge has the appearance of an accomplishment of thinking, but in fact it is the *real* progress of *social practice*, subsequently '*reflected*' in the theories of successive philosophers. Practical intervention into social practice rather than 'reflection' offers a wider scope for understanding a natural or social phenomenon, however.

Now this is implicit in Hegel's advice in the Preface to *The Philosophy of Right* about the Owl of Minerva taking flight only at dusk, but Marx takes this advice *seriously*, whereas Hegel was all too inclined to believe that the *intellectual elite* of society (including himself) could use speculative logic to theorise in advance of the real development. Hegel's idealism is also reflected in the fact that Hegel always looked to the intellectual and social elite to *solve* social problems and regarded the masses as a more or less destructive force of nature, whereas Marx on the other hand looked to the workers' movement as the vehicle of social progress. This orientation to the 'earth' rather than the 'stars' is how I interpret "turning Hegel right side up again."

Concepts are forms of activity and Hegel's 'Spirit' can be interpreted as *human activity*. The paragraph from Marx just quoted shows that this is the position which Marx took. There is much in Hegel's writing that makes it hard to believe that Hegel did not *also* see it this way, but whatever may have been in his head he always wrote as if it were the spiritual entities which were the primary component and human actions merely derivative realisations. Indeed, his whole style of writing can be described as 'idealistic'. However, ideas and activity are inseparable and any theory which bases itself on one and not the other is untenable.

The way I'd like to explain the relation between Marx and Hegel is to mediate the relation between them with Goethe's 'Romantic Science'.

10 Goethe, Hegel and Marx

During his Italian Journey (1787) and in correspondence with his friend Johann Gottfried Herder, the great naturalist and poet, Johann Wolfgang von Goethe, arrived at the concept of *Urphänomen* by observing the variation of plants at different altitudes and latitudes. Each plant, he believed, was a realisation according to conditions, of an underlying form which he called the *Urpflanze*. This idea was inspired by Herder's *Schwerpunkt* – the 'strong point' of a people, their defining experience or industry, which (in Marx's words) "is a general illumination which bathes all other colours and modifies their particularity" (Marx, 1858, p. 107; cf. Herder, 1774).

The *Urphänomen* was the simplest particular instance of a complex process or organism which exhibited the essential features of the whole. Thus in one simple, sensuously perceived instance, one could grasp the whole as a *Gestalt* and this *Urphänomen* would provide the starting point for a whole science. Both Hegel and Goethe died shortly before microscopes developed sufficient power to reveal the microstructure of plants and animals and the *cell* was discovered. Goethe could never have imagined what the microscope would reveal, but the *Urphänomen* anticipated the cell, which, alongside evolution by natural selection, laid the foundation of modern biology.

Hegel explicitly credited Goethe with this discovery as the inspiration for his own method which begins from the One, the simplest concrete something, the 'germ cell', which provides a science with its starting point, given to it from outside the science itself. As is well known, the Logic begins from Being, but this turns out to be Nothing, and therefore Becoming, but Something (*Dasein*) has to become and when grasped in its immediacy this is the One, the unit. This One is the real starting point of the unfolding process. For Hegel, this 'Urconcept' cannot be the product of intellectual intuition as it was for Goethe's 'delicate empiricism', but on the contrary was a product of critical thinking. Hegel built his entire system on this idea of the logical unfolding of a concrete science from a simple abstract 'Urconcept' (this is my term, not Hegel's). Hegel outlined this method in the section entitled *Cognition* in the *Science of Logic*.

For Marx, the starting point was not a concept, but an elementary form of social practice, an *Urpraxis* (again, that's my term, not Marx's). Marx's philosophical journey leading up to his critical appropriation of Hegel's Logic exhibited in *Capital* (1867) began with *Theses on Feuerbach* (1845).

10.1 *Activity and Concepts*

In the very first words which belong to his mature views, Marx (1845) criticises philosophical materialism for accepting the standpoint of natural science: that of an observer contemplating an independently existing object. Objects exist, distinct from thought; however, it is only thanks to 'practical-critical' activity that the object is perceived and reconstructed in thought. Marx explicitly substituted systems of *social practice*, social formations, for Hegel's *Gestalten des Bewußtseins* (formations of consciousness), real activities rather than their shadows. Concepts were to be understood in the first place as specific forms of activity, not simply as the product of theoreticians. Theoreticians can only study what is to be found already in social practice, implicitly or potentially, if not explicitly. Hegel lost sight of this. He mistakenly took social progress to be the work of theoreticians. His *Logic* retains its validity, provided that concepts are interpreted as forms of practical activity, and only derivatively as subjective thought-forms or figures of categorical logic.

10.2   *The Method of Political Economy*

In the *Grundrisse* (1858), Marx explained how the structure of *Capital* is related to the *Logic* in the passage known as 'The Method of Political Economy'. He outlines how the history of any science is made up of two phases as follows:

> It seems to be correct to begin with the real and the concrete, with the real precondition, thus to begin, in economics, with e.g. the population, … However, on closer examination this proves false. The population is an abstraction if I leave out, for example, the classes of which it is composed … Thus, if I were to begin with the population, this would be a chaotic conception of the whole, and I would then, by means of further determination, move analytically towards ever more simple concepts, from the imagined concrete towards ever thinner abstractions until I had arrived at the simplest determinations.
>
>   p. 100

and then:

> From there the journey would have to be retraced until I had finally arrived at the population again, but this time not as the chaotic conception of a whole, but as a rich totality of many determinations and relations. …
>
> The concrete is concrete because it is the concentration of many determinations, hence unity of the diverse. It appears in the process of thinking, therefore, as a process of concentration, as a result, not as a point of departure, even though it is the point of departure in reality and hence also the point of departure for observation and conception. Along the first path the full conception was evaporated to yield an abstract determination; along the second, the abstract determinations lead towards a reproduction of the concrete by way of thought.
>
>   loc. cit.

This passage describes the structure of Hegel's *Logic*. The starting point of a science is the mass of measures abstracted from the flow of economic reporting. This phase is represented in Hegel's Doctrine of Being, a phase of observation and measurement which precedes scientific reflection as such. The journey begins when these measurements are worked over, reflected on and worked up into patterns and laws and a theoretical description of the data. This first phase of the development of a science (Marx: "the path historically followed by economics at the time of its origins," p. 100) is complete when it arrives at the 'simplest determination', the singular entity which exhibits the essential relations of the whole process – value. This first phase is accomplished in the history of the science by means of *immanent critique* of the concepts abstracted from Being and is represented by Hegel in the Doctrine of Essence.

The second phase is reconstructing the whole, now not as a chaotic conception, but as a systematic whole, a whole which exhibits in developed form the essential features with which we are familiar in the unit from which we began the reconstruction. This second phase – *systematic dialectic* (Marx: "obviously the scientifically correct method," p. 101) is represented by Hegel in the Doctrine of the Concept. For Marx, this *Urphänomen* would be not a phenomenon or a concept, but an interaction observable in social practice, a familiar social act which we can viscerally understand, an *Urpraxis*. In the case of political economy, this turned out to be the act of exchanging commodities. In each stage of the reconstruction, the concepts logically derived from the *Urpraxis* are validated by their objective existence in social practice. The resulting concrete reconstruction differs from the data with which the analysis began because it is a *systematic whole* rather than a mere aggregate of abstract qualities.

Marx realised this plan of work, his own part in the history of political economy, through many years of immanent critique of the rival theories of political economy, followed by a systematic reconstruction of bourgeois society in *Capital*.

10.3 The Commodity

By beginning *Capital* with the analysis of the commodity, Marx continues the legacy of Goethe and Hegel. In the first Preface to *Capital*, where Marx is talking about the problem of value in political economy, he says:

> In the analysis of economic forms, moreover, neither microscopes nor chemical reagents are of use. The force of abstraction must replace both. But in bourgeois society, the commodity form of the product of labour – or value-form of the commodity – is the economic cell-form.
>   1867, p. 8

Marx's use of the metaphor of 'cell' cannot fail to remind us of Goethe's *Urphänomen*, which the science of biology realised in the cell. The first chapter is devoted to an exposition of the commodity relation. Marx derived the concepts of value in the first three chapters of *Capital*, unfolding from the exchange of commodities, the concepts of Quality, Quantity and Measure, paralleling the first book of Hegel's *Logic*. By beginning with the commodity – the concrete simple something which is the unit of economic activity – and then unfolding from this concept a concrete conception of value in bourgeois society, Marx followed the structure which Hegel used in of *all* sections of the *Encyclopaedia*.

According to Hegel, this One from which the science is to be unfolded must be a *concrete* concept, by which Hegel meant that it must be the unity of distinct determinations. Marx took the commodity relation to be the unity of two independent lines of action represented by two forms of value: the use-value of the commodity entailed in a specific *kind* of labour and realised in the consumption of the object (its social quality), and the exchange-value of the commodity entailed in the production of the object and realised in the market (its social quantity). The partial homology between the categories of Hegel's Ontology and the early chapters of *Capital* reflects the fact that money has been doing the work of reducing all the products of human labour to a single measure, carrying out the work of logic, but as *a real social process*, rather than as an intellectual exercise. Given the social nature of Hegel's categorical logic, it is to be expected that the categories of the logic should have a real existence in corresponding social processes. However, I do not accept the suggestion by Chris Arthur (2015), that this homology is a result of Hegel's study of the British political economists. It was the Soviet philosopher Ilyenkov who highlighted this process of *objective abstraction* in his works on *Capital* (1960) and the ideal (1977), which is the basis for this homology. Hegel's own critique of political economy turned out to be rather fatuous.

10.4   Unit and Germ Cell

It might strike us as odd to begin from commodity exchange, rather than buying and selling. Although, as Marx says in the opening words of *Capital*: "The wealth of those societies in which the capitalist mode of production prevails, presents itself as 'an immense accumulation of commodities'," exchange of commodities is a rare occurrence in modern bourgeois society.

The third section of Chapter 1 shows the historical genesis of exchange from its earliest appearance in exchanges between tribal peoples, leading up to the use of gold as a universal equivalent and later the issuing of paper money by states. In this way, he showed that money is *essentially* a commodity and that wage-labour is a commodity bought and sold on the labour market and used by capitalist purchasers.

This exhibits one of the aspects of the *Urpraxis* to which I drew attention above. The *Urpraxis* arises from problems at a lower level of development (trade in pre-modern societies). But with the formation of the self-reproducing *Gestalt* (a bourgeois economic formation) which it generates, the *Urpraxis* itself goes through a series of transformations (ultimately the various forms of capital).

10.5   The *Urpraxis* Is the 'Simplest Social Form'

In his *Notes on Adolph Wagner* (1881, p. 544) Marx says:

> I do not proceed from the 'concept of value' ... What I proceed from is the simplest social form in which the product of labour presents itself in contemporary society, and this is the '*commodity*'.

This is the same as when Hegel takes *private property* as the *simplest social form* of Freedom and makes it the starting point of *The Philosophy of Right*. Just as private property leads to the State, commodity exchange leads to capital, but in both cases the book does not begin with a concept of its subject matter, but of its underlying substance.

The commodity is a *form* of value, but 'value' is an intangible, neither 'a geometrical, a chemical, or any other natural property' (Marx, 1867, p. 47) – it is a suprasensible, i.e., *social*, quality of a commodity. Value is in fact an artefact-mediated *social relation* which can therefore only be grasped *conceptually*. Nonetheless, the commodity is a form of value which, thanks to everyday experience, *can be grasped viscerally*. This means that the critique of the concept of commodity works upon relations which can be grasped viscerally by reader and writer alike. By beginning with the (concept of) commodity Marx mobilises the readers' visceral understanding of commodities, as he leads us through each successive relation. So long as that relation exists in social practice, then not only is the writer's intuition validated by the *existence* of that relation, but it also allows the reader to securely grasp and verify the logical exposition.

Marx's decision to begin not with 'value' but with the 'commodity' illustrates Marx's debt to Goethe's 'delicate empiricism' and is crucial for his praxis implementation of Hegel's *Logic*.

I am not aware of any evidence that Marx even knew about Goethe's *Urphänomen*, far less set about appropriating it. If any philosopher is the proximate source of Marx's philosophical turn to praxis, then it would be the follower of Gottlob Fichte, Moses Hess (1843), with whom Marx was working at the time he wrote *Theses on Feuerbach*. Also, much of what Marx had to say about Hegel is far from complimentary. The triadic relationship between these three holistic thinkers, Goethe, Hegel and Marx, is real notwithstanding that Marx never set out to make any kind of triad. In the 19th century, all Germans, Hegel and Marx included, were raised in the long shadow of Goethe, whose impact on German culture cannot be overstated. However, Goethe's natural scientific ideas were probably the least known of his ideas, and were widely discredited by mid-century. But the impact of Goethe (whom Marx listed alongside Dante and Shakespeare as his favourite poet) is undeniable.

Both Goethe and Hegel were one-sided in their method; the further development of science and culture, made it possible for Marx to transcend both Goethe's Empiricism and Hegel's Idealism.

Further, by making the *Urphänomen* of his science a *real* act of social practice, not an *imagined* social practice, but one whose norms had already been produced by the development of bourgeois society and could be the subject of observation and intervention, Marx turned Hegel's version of the *Urphänomen* inside out, recovering an important element of Goethe's *Urphänomen*.

10.6 'Everything' vs. a Gestalt

In Marx's view, bourgeois society was essentially a marketplace. But Marx did not believe he could explain *everything* about the modern world on the basis of the commodity relation. The state and family life were not (yet) marketplaces.

Marx was drawn into political activity by his outrage at press censorship, inequality, aristocratic privilege and the slow progress of liberal reform in Germany, but he came to see that it was not the nobility or the state, which was at the root of these social problems, but the *market*. By taking an exchange of commodities as the *unit of analysis* (Vygotsky, 1934), he had chosen a unit which already contained what he saw as essential to bourgeois society. Thus, the complex whole which Marx reconstructed was to be taken as just thousands and thousands of commodity exchanges – bourgeois society. *Capital* provided a concrete analysis of how the production of commodities leads to the exploitation of wage labour on one side and the accumulation of surplus value on the other – but he did not pretend to provide an analysis of the family, the state and world history.

Hegel, by contrast, took private property (rather than *exchange* of property) as the germ cell of Freedom, and claimed to unfold from private property the *entirety* of the state and world history. Marx's aims were rightly more modest.

10.7 Commodity and Capital

But *Capital* is a book about capital, not about simple commodity production. In Part I of the book, the first three chapters, Marx analyses the circulation of commodities and money, but from this analysis he demonstrates the emergence of a *new* relation, that of capital, a new type of commodity. C–M–C (selling a commodity in order to buy another commodity) engenders M–C–M' (buying a commodity in order to sell it at a profit). Thus Marx derives a *new* 'molar'[4] unit of analysis, a second *Urpraxis* – the capitalist company or unit of capital, marking the emergence of modern forms of capital. Beginning from Chapter 4, Marx unfolds from this second *Urpraxis* a dialectical exposition of the movement of capital, which takes up the remainder of the three-volume work.

This theme in holistic science, where there is both a molecular unit or *Urphänomen* (cell, quality, commodity, ...) and a molar unit (organism, concept, capital, ...) was first identified by the Soviet activity theorist, A.N. Leontyev (1981). It is actually the molar unit which is the subject matter of the study, the key to understanding of which lies in the molecular unit. In Hegel's *Logic*, the first volume (Objective Logic) begins with the One, and the Second Volume (Subjective Logic) begins with the Concept. What homology is there between the Subjective Logic and the succeeding chapters of *Capital*? Very little. The very general homology which can be found arises from homology between the subject matters (accumulation, competition). It can be argued that the formation of a uniform rate of profit across an economy, despite an organic composition of capital which varies from firm to firm, has a very general homology with the formation of the Idea from abstract concepts in Hegel's Concept Logic. But in any case, the homology arises from parallels in the subject matter itself, based on money as a real abstraction of human labour, not from Marx emulating Hegel. The structure of *Capital* is not a mirror of any work of Hegel's. The concepts of political economy unfold according to their own logic, and it would be a mistake to try and match *Capital* concept-for-concept with any of Hegel's books.

In summary, there are two phases in the formation of a science (the two volumes of Hegel's *Logic*, the two processes outlined in Marx's *Method of Political Economy*). Firstly, a protracted period leading up to the point when a theorist has the abstract starting point (*Urphänomen*) for the science properly so called, and then the concretisation of that abstract concept in the development of the science. Equally there are two phases in the *formation* of a social formation like capitalism: first the protracted period of history leading up to the point when its germ cell emerges, followed by the concretisation and universalisation of

---

4 'Molar unit' comes from chemistry, where it means that quantity of a substance which contains as many molecules as 12 gm of carbon-12, i.e., 6×10^{23} molecules.

that concept, entailing the transformation of all other relations in the social formation, and their subsumption under that one universal relation.

Hegel did not discover the *Urphänomen* – he appropriated it from the poet-naturalist John Wolfgang von Goethe and turned it inside out. It provided the abstract beginning of his philosophy, and each of the sciences he worked out began with a concrete simple something appropriated from the preceding science. This was the same idea which the communist Marx appropriated from the idealist philosopher, Hegel, and made the starting point for his critique of capital.

11   Summary

For Marx as for Hegel, a concept is a (normative) form of social practice, but whereas Hegel suffered from the illusion that a theorist could unfold from a conceptual ideal everything that was implicit within it, Marx consistently held to the view that the logical development had to follow the development of social practice at every stage, making intelligible what was manifested in social practice. Like Hegel, Marx took a concrete simple something as the starting point of his analysis, in the case of *Capital*, a discrete *artefact-mediated action*, rather than an abstract universal like 'value'.

Marx took the same approach in his study of the workers' movement in their struggle for state power, amending the *Manifesto of the Communist Party* in the light of the actions of the workers' movement in the Paris Commune. He never built any socialist castles in the sky. But writing in the middle third of the 19th century, Marx had material to work with, material which was not available to Hegel in the first third of the 19th century.

CHAPTER 2

The Unit of Analysis and Germ Cell in Hegel, Marx and Vygotsky

"Psychology is in need of its own *Das Kapital*," wrote Vygotsky in 1928, observing that "the whole of *Das Kapital* is written according to this method," the method in which Marx identifies the 'cell' of bourgeois society – an exchange of commodities – and then unfolds the entire process of bourgeois society from an analysis of the contradictions within this single cell. Vygotsky was the first to grasp *Das Kapital* in this way, and his application of the method of 'analysis by units' is his most important legacy.

What Vygotsky did was to produce *one* study which would function as an exemplar for research in psychology. That one study addressed the age-old problem of the relation between thinking and speech. By solving this *one problem* in an exemplary fashion, he created a paradigm for research in all domains of psychology, and as a matter of fact, in *all* the sciences. Vygotsky in fact left us as many as *five* different exemplars of analysis by units.

But first let us reflect on the historical origins of this idea.

1 From Goethe to Marx

1.1 Origins of the Concept of "Cell" as a Method of Analysis

The idea of the 'cell' originated with Johann Gottfried Herder (1744–1803), often recognised as the founder of anthropology. In his effort to understand the differences between peoples, Herder introduced the idea of a *Schwerpunkt* ('strong point'). This idea is probably better known nowadays in its formulation by Marx: "There is in every social formation a particular branch of production which determines the position and importance of all the others ... as though light of a particular hue were cast upon everything, tingeing all other colours and modifying their specific features" (1858, p. 106–107). Herder's friend, Johann Wolfgang von Goethe (1749–1832), sought to use the idea in his study of botany during his Italian journey in 1787, to understand the continuity and differences between the plants found in different parts of the country.

Goethe came to the idea of an *Urphänomen* – not a law or principle, but a simple, archetypal phenomenon in which all the essential features of a whole complex process are manifested. In Goethe's own words:

> The *Urphänomen* is not to be regarded as a basic theorem leading to a variety of consequences, but rather as a basic manifestation enveloping the specifications of form for the beholder.
>
> 1795, p. 106

> Empirical observation must first teach us what parts are common to all animals, and how these parts differ. *The idea must govern the whole*, it must abstract the general picture in a genetic way. Once such an *Urphänomen* is established, even if only provisionally, we may test it quite adequately by applying the customary methods of comparison.
>
> 1827, p. 118

This meant that in order to understand a complex process as an integral whole or *Gestalt*, we have to identify and understand just its simplest immediately given part – a radical departure from the 'Newtonian' approach to science based on postulating intangible forces and hidden laws.

It is widely agreed that the idea which Goethe was working towards was the *cell* of an organism, but it wasn't until microscopes became powerful enough to reveal the microstructure of organisms that Schleiden and Schwann were able to formulate the cell theory of biology in 1839. The cell is the unit of analysis of biology, and alongside the organism and Darwin's idea of evolution by natural selection, constitutes the foundation of biology.

1.2   Hegel's Formulation of the Idea

The philosopher, Hegel, took up Goethe's idea and gave it a firm logical foundation in his *Science of Logic*, in which the place of the cell was now taken by the *Concept* – the simplest unit of a 'formation of consciousness'. The *Logic* describes the formation and development of concepts in three Books. Book One, the Logic of Being, describes the process in which the basic regularities are abstracted from the flow of immediate perception in the form of a mass of measures. Book Two, the Logic of Essence (or Reflection), describes the emergence of theories trying to make sense of this data, with each theory being contested by opposing theories and both then being overtaken by others, digging successively deeper, and building up a theoretical picture of the phenomenon, until ... Book Three, the Logic of the Concept, begins when, in a kind of Aha! moment, an abstract concept emerges which captures the phenomenon as a whole at its simplest and most abstract level. Beginning from this abstract concept – the 'cell', the phenomenon is then reconstructed as a *Gestalt* – an entire 'organism' – by unfolding the contradictions inherent in this cell as it interacts with other cells.

Note that each of these three phases has the form of a movement from abstract (in the sense of simple and isolated) to concrete, *and* from concrete (concrete in the sense of immediate and real) to abstract. Being: from perceptions to measures, Essence: from measures to a concept; Concept: from a simple concept (cell) up to a rich and concrete concept of the whole.

In the *last* section of the *Science of Logic* on The Idea in which Hegel outlined the method of Analytic and Synthetic Cognition, he specified how the division of the subject matter of the sciences is to be carried out according to the inner nature of the subject matter itself, rather than by some arbitrary, subjective scheme imposed from without.

Here is the key passage from the *Science of Logic*:

> The progress, proper to the Concept (*Begriff*), from universal to particular, is the basis and the possibility of a **synthetic science**, of a **system** and of **systematic cognition**. The first requisite for this is, as we have shown, that the beginning be made with the subject matter in the form of a ***universal*** (*Allgemeinen*).
>
> In the sphere of actuality, whether of nature or spirit, it is the **concrete individuality** (*die konkrete Einzelheit*) that is given to **subjective, natural cognition** as the ***prius*** (*das Erste*); but in cognition that is a ***comprehension***, at least to the extent that it has the form of the Notion for basis, the ***prius*** must be on the contrary *something simple* (*das Einfache*), something *abstracted* **from the concrete**, because in this form alone has the subject-matter the form of the **self-related universal** or of an **immediate based on the Concept**.
>
> HEGEL, 1816, p. 801, S. 779. The italics are Hegel's, the bold mine

"Prius" is a translation of the German "*der Ersten*," the first. The prius is the concept from which each science is to begin – the 'cell'. Hegel is saying that the *synthetic* phase of a science must begin with this "*something simple.*" This prescription applies to "actuality, whether of nature or spirit" – i.e., the natural and social sciences.

Hegel describes this "something simple" (*das Einfache*) as "the concrete individuality that is given to subjective, *natural* cognition." *Einzel* means 'single', so *Einzelheit* means a 'singularity'. "Natural cognition" refers to the common sense or normative perception of a process within a given social formation, prior to critical analysis or synthetic cognition.

For Hegel, 'concrete' means the intersection or unity of two distinct concepts. For example, he says (1831, §§87–88) that, whereas Being and Nothing are *abstractions*, Becoming is the first concrete concept because it is the organic unity of Being and Nothing. As an organic unity of opposites, there is an internal contradiction which is what drives development and unfolds the content of the 'concrete individuality'. The beginning is made in the Logic of Being from the One, the self-related individual determinate being (1831, §97ff.). This clarification of the initial abstraction is always necessary to make the beginning with the 'first'.

The *Erste* is the product of analytical cognition. At nodal points in the development of a science a corresponding 'simple something' is abstracted from concrete experience, and subjected to *synthetic cognition*, that is, the dialectical unfolding or reconstruction of a whole process, the whole 'circle' of the particular science. These nodal points mark out the alternation between analytical cognition and synthetic cognition.

This 'something simple' must be "*abstracted* from the concrete" by analysis. So, the beginning of a science requires the abstraction of such a concrete individuality from the whole concrete field of experience which can be made the starting point for a synthetic reconstruction of the concrete in theoretical form. This act of abstraction requires an insight into the whole process:

> analytic cognition ... starts from a *presupposed*, and therefore individual (*einzeln*), *concrete* subject matter; this may be an object already *complete in itself* for ordinary thought, or it may be a *problem*, that is to say, given only in its circumstances and conditions, but not yet disengaged from them and presented on its own account in simple self-subsistence.
> HEGEL, 1816, p. 787, S. 753

Hegel said that "the first requisite for this is, as we have shown, that the beginning be made with the subject matter in the form of a *universal*." That is, the concrete *individuality* which is the product of analysis is simultaneously *the universal*, that is to say, it is an *archetype* or 'germ cell' of the entire organism which is to be synthesised in theory. 'Concrete individuality', for Hegel, means that the cell is internally contradictory (like the exchange-value and use value of a commodity), the coincidence of two antithetical concepts which can be exhibited by analysis. It is by the unfolding of this internal, implicit contradiction, that synthetic cognition unfolds the whole circle of phenomena which make up the science in question. This process of identifying a germ cell is represented in the first volume of the Logic: Being and Essence.

Note that the "something simple" is an *individuality* and this is the difference between, for example, 'morality' and moral *actions*, or between 'art' and a *work* of art. An individuality is discrete and bounded, and not continuous or intangible; a particle rather than matter, a something rather than stuff, an action rather than activity.

According to Hegel, an exposition of the science following the path of synthetic cognition begins from this concrete individuality which is deemed to be an abstract (i.e., simple, and abstracted from its concrete circumstances) instance of the Universal – the phenomenon which is the subject matter of the whole science, and proceeds from there to the various particular forms of the universal. This phase of the science is demonstrated in the *Logic*: the *concept* of a concrete individuality is taken up and clarified. It is then subjected to immanent critique, successively surpassing its limits, exploring the particular forms implicit in it, until arriving at a contradiction which can be resolved in actuality only by the emergence of some new concrete individuality, and with that a new branch of science.

It should be noted that Hegel does not claim that the natural and human sciences can be elaborated by logic alone, without reference to observation and experiment:

> Their [the sciences'] commencement, though rational at bottom, yields to the influence of fortuitousness, when they have to bring their universal truth into contact with actual facts and the single phenomena of experience. In this region of chance and change, the adequate notion of science must yield its place to reasons or grounds of explanation.
> HEGEL, 1831, §16, S. 70

Marx went further than Hegel on this point. Marx insisted that the *synthetic* phase of the science – the development from the cell to an organism – *also* necessarily relies on observation of the development of the subject matter itself and the theorist's intervention in the subject matter, rather than merely logical critique by a philosopher. Marx explicitly states this in the *Grundrisse*:

> the movement of the categories ... is a product of a thinking head, which appropriates the world ... The real subject retains its autonomous existence outside the head just as before.
> 1858, p. 102

This is evidenced in the almost complete absence of speculation about the future in *Capital*. Further, as Lenin observed, Marx made no reference in the *Communist Manifesto* (1848) to what the working class would do if it took state power, but waited until 1871 when he was able to witness the Paris Commune to amend the *Manifesto* with a Preface on this question.

In the *Logic*, the simple concepts which mark the beginning of each book are, respectively: the One, the Thing and the Abstract Concept. These concepts are in a sense also 'simple somethings', and the development of each offers a model of synthetic science to be applied in the natural and human sciences.

1.2.1   The One

The idea of the unit is first developed in the very first section of the Logic. Hegel's philosophy begins from the abstract concept of Being. Hegel shows that this concept is empty and therefore Nothing. By the fact that Being progressed to Nothing, Hegel has derived Becoming, the "first concrete concept" (as the unity of Being and Nothing). But Becoming implies that *something* is becoming, thus deriving Determinate Being (*Dasein*). Understood in itself as distinct from some other, the *Dasein* must be One (*das Eins*), and implicit in One is that there are Many. The One is what unites the Many (continuity) but at the same time marks its discreteness (discontinuity). Hegel then unfolds the entire logic of quantitative science from this unit, the One.

The remainder of the *Encyclopaedia* demonstrates the use of 'simple somethings' which have the form of the self-related universal, including, for example:

- The first book of the Logic is 'Being', but Hegel determines the One as the concept from which the Logic is to be unfolded. He insists that the One is the presupposition for the Many, rather than just being 'one amongst many' as it is for representational thinking.
- The first book of the *Philosophy of Nature* ostensibly begins with 'Space', but much more determinate concepts are his immediate beginning: the Point, the Line, and the Surface (which encloses a space).
- The second book of the *Philosophy of Nature* nominally begins with 'Mechanics', but actually begins from the Particle. 'Organic Physics', nominally about 'Life', actually begins from an Organism.
- The three books of the *Philosophy of Subjective Spirit* are 'Soul' (a nervous system), beginning with Feelings, 'Consciousness' beginning with Sensations, and the Finite Mind.
- In the *Philosophy of Objective Spirit*, 'Abstract Right', goes through: Possession (Taking Possession, Use and Alienation); 'Contract' (Gift, Exchange and Pledge) and 'Wrong' (a Non-malicious Wrong, a Fraud and a Crime).
- 'Morality' goes through: Purpose, Goal, Means, Intention, Welfare, the Good, among others, and
- 'Ethical Life' goes through: Family, Market, Public Authorities, Corporations, and State.
- In the *Philosophy of Absolute Spirit*, Art is ostensibly about the 'shape of beauty' but begins from the Work of Art; Revealed Religion begins from

the 'Concrete Individuality' (*konkrete Einzelheit*); and Philosophy from the Syllogism.

The above include 37 examples of 'cells' used by Hegel in the various sciences he outlined. There are many more. Each topic that is taken up in the *Encyclopaedia* has the same form: after an initial clarification of the subject matter which usually presents itself as an abstraction, Hegel determined a 'simple concrete something' which is the unit or germ cell representing what is universal in the science. He then 'unfolds' this germ cell in a synthetic reconstruction of the whole science or phenomenon.

1.3   *Marx's Appropriation of Hegel*

Marx acknowledged his debt to Goethe and Hegel in the first Preface to *Capital*, where he says:

> The value-form, whose fully developed shape is the money-form, is very elementary and simple. Nevertheless, the human mind has for more than 2,000 years sought in vain to get to the bottom of it, whilst on the other hand, to the successful analysis of much more composite and complex forms, there has been at least an approximation. Why? Because the body, as an organic whole, is more easy of study than are the cells of that body. In the analysis of economic forms, moreover, neither microscopes nor chemical reagents are of use. The force of abstraction must replace both. But in bourgeois society, the commodity form of the product of labour – or value-form of the commodity – is the economic cell-form.
> 1867, p. 8

Marx further indicated his debt to Hegel's *Logic* in the famous passage of the *Grundrisse*, 'The Method of Political Economy', in which he described the history of political economy in terms of two phases: firstly, an analytical phase in which the economic data is analysed and represented in a succession of theories until arriving at the abstractions, such as 'value', from which point then, the whole phenomenon can be reconstructed synthetically.

> Along the first path the full conception was evaporated to yield an abstract determination; along the second, the abstract determinations lead towards a reproduction of the concrete by way of thought.
> 1858, p. 100

The first phase corresponds to the decades Marx spent in the *immanent critique* of the theories of political economy leading to the discovery of the 'cell'. The second phase is the *dialectical reconstruction* of political economy in *Capital*, beginning from analysis of exchange of commodities in Chapter I.

In his 'Notes on Adolph Wagner' (1881, p. 544) Marx says:

> I did not start out from the 'concept of value' ... What I start out from is the simplest social form in which the product of labour is presented in contemporary society, and this is 'the commodity'.

The commodity is a *form* of value, but 'value' is an intangible, neither 'a geometrical, a chemical, or any other natural property' (Marx, 1867, p. 47) – but a suprasensible (i.e., social) quality of commodities, and as such is unsuited for the role of cell. Value is a *social relation* which can therefore only be grasped conceptually. Nonetheless, commodity exchange is a form of value which, thanks to everyday experience, *can be grasped viscerally*. This means that the critique of the concept of commodity works upon relations which can be grasped viscerally by reader and writer alike. By beginning with the (concept of) commodity Marx mobilises the readers' visceral understanding of commodities, and as he leads us through each successive relation, so long as that relation exists in social practice, then not only is the writer's intuition validated by the *existence* of that relation, but it also allows the reader to securely grasp the logical exposition.

Marx's decision to begin not with 'value' but with the 'commodity' illustrates Marx's debt to Goethe as well as Hegel. Further, he insisted on tracing the emergence of every relation in economic life, rather than in claiming to derive them from pure logic, thus recovering the *empirical* moment in Goethe's original idea, before it was taken up as a *logical* category by Hegel.

1.3.1   The Unit of Capital

Only the Chapters I to III of *Capital* deal with simple commodity production, which Marx represented symbolically as C–M–C. That is, selling a commodity (C) you have for the money (M) to buy the commodity (C) which you need. In Chapter IV, Marx derives the first, abstract concept of *capital* which is to be the real subject matter of the book: M–C–M' – buying in order to sell at a profit. This action is the basic unit of capital and is reified as the capitalist firm. While capital is an aggregate of commodities, it is a qualitatively distinct unit of analysis. Capital accumulation gives a new direction to the development of economic life, and the remaining chapters of *Capital* represent the phase of dialectical reconstruction of the concept, equivalent to Volume Two of Hegel's Logic, the 'Concept Logic'. There never has been any such thing as a society based solely on 'simple commodity production'; the historically-first instances of commodity exchange were regulated by means other than capital. 'Simple commodity production' is an analytical abstraction, not an historical precedent.

Bourgeois economists had begun their analysis with the fact of money, confronting the mystery of how money can have value. Value is utterly intangible, and nothing about the sensuous nature of money makes it possible to understand how money can have value. The entire problem is mysterious. But even a child can understand the simple act of swapping one useful product for another (C–C), without recourse to any prior theory or abstraction. We can grasp it viscerally. This gives the writer and the reader a firm grasp of the basic process and it is easy then to explain how all the complex phenomena of money credit, capital, etc., grow out of this simple germ cell.

1.3.2 The Development of Science

Marx had been able to appropriate Hegel's method, but neither the naturalist-poet Goethe, nor the philosopher Hegel nor the communist Marx could have a significant impact on the course of natural scientific activity during the nineteenth century. How could this achievement of Classical German Philosophy be transformed into methods for the resolution of the problems in the various branches of science?

Science proceeded piecemeal, and not according to the grand plan of Hegel's *Encyclopaedia of the Philosophical Sciences*. The natural sciences were in general able to make progress by problem-solving in the separate disciplines, with occasional unexpected breakthroughs, without any overall conception guiding their work. It took almost a century from Hegel's death in 1831, through the efforts of German natural science, French social theory and American Pragmatism, before a practical, laboratory method for understanding how individual human beings appropriated the cultural practices of their time was finally accomplished by Lev Vygotsky. Vygotsky's breakthrough was thanks to his appropriation of the idea of 'unit' from Hegel and Marx, and the cultural conditions created in the wake of the Russian Revolution.

1.3.3 Hegel on Mediation and Immediacy

Before looking at how Vygotsky appropriated and used the idea of 'cell', I must recall a key concept with which Hegel framed his entire philosophy. He writes in the preface to the *Science of Logic* (1816):

> [T]here is nothing, nothing in heaven, or in nature or in mind or anywhere else which does not equally contain both immediacy and mediation, so that these two determinations reveal themselves to be unseparated and inseparable.
> HEGEL, p. 68

In the introduction to his *Encyclopaedia*, Hegel characterises the history of European philosophy in terms of a struggle between the various philosophies of *immediate* knowledge: Descartes' Rationalism, the Empiricism of the natural sciences, and Jacobi's reliance on Faith, versus Kant's philosophy which held that all knowledge is *mediated* – things in themselves cannot be objects of experience, and knowledge of them is impossible.

Hegel's entire philosophy was built on what is known to followers of Vygotsky as 'double stimulation':

> The relationship of *immediacy* and *mediation within consciousness* will have to be discussed explicitly and in detail below. At this point, it suffices to point out that, although both moments *appear* to be distinct, *neither of them* may be absent and they form an *inseparable* combination.
> HEGEL, 1831, §12n

2   Vygotsky and Activity Theory

2.1   *Vygotsky on the Method of Double Stimulation*

Until Vygotsky's breakthrough, psychology had been split between those like Helmholtz who approached psychology with 'brass instruments' as if it were a branch of the natural sciences, and those like Dilthey who studied cultural phenomena as if psychology was a branch of the 'human sciences' (see Blunden, 2012, pp. 197–221). Recognising that the mind was formed by the joint actions of physiology and culture, Wundt had even proposed that there be two separate psychologies: one carried out in the laboratory with the aid of introspection, the other through the study of literature and art. In the twentieth century, psychology was split between Behaviourists who denied the existence of consciousness and saw psychology in terms of reflexes, and 'empirical psychologists' who studied the mind by means of introspection. The 'brass instrument' methods hitherto employed in psychology laboratories were capable of investigating only the most elementary and primitive reflexes which humans have in common with other animals, while introspection was incapable of providing *objective* access to consciousness. Contra Behaviourism, human behaviour cannot be understood without reference to consciousness; but consciousness (like historical or geological processes) cannot be observed *directly*. However, consciousness mediates between physiology and behaviour, both these are objectively observable (see Vygotsky, 1924).

Vygotsky solved these problems with the experimental method of double stimulation.

The method of double stimulation was first formulated by Vygotsky in conjunction with Alexander Luria in 1928 (see Luria, 1928, and Vygotsky, 1928). An experimental subject, typically a child, would be presented with a problem, such as memorising a series of words. As they were trying to solve the problem, the researcher would present them with an artefact, such as a picture-card, to use as a means in solving the problem. In this simple scenario, we have the germ cell of cultural development and activity. In Figure 1 below:

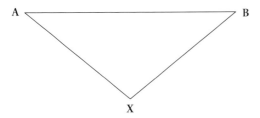

FIGURE 1   The germ cell of cultural development

A represents a person who confronts an object or problem, B, and X is a sign, an artefact introduced into the scenario by a collaborator, as a means of solving the problem. This simple germ cell captures the essential relation of people to their culture: a problem set by the social situation is solved by using an artefact (a sign in Vygotsky's experiments) drawn from the cultural environment. In the process of appropriating the use of the given artefact, the subject's psychology is enhanced by the creation of a new reflex, associating B with X. Vygotsky has set up here an extremely simple scenario, which can be sensuously experienced and therefore grasped viscerally, without the need of a pre-existing over-arching theory. But in this simple set-up we have both the immediate situation of an individual confronting a problem, and the entire cultural history of the subject's environment represented in the artefact-solution. This is a unit of analysis in which both the individual psyche and an entire cultural history are present.

The meaning of the term 'dual stimulation' is illustrated in the diagram. A is subject to two stimuli at the same time, both the object itself, $A \rightarrow B$,[1] and

---

[1] The concept of 'stimulus' implies that the arrow should be in the other direction $A \leftarrow X$, but I follow Hegel, Marx and Vygotsky in taking the *attention* to a stimulus to be an active, not a passive action by the subject.

the auxiliary stimulus, $A \to X$, which is associated with the object, $X \to B$. Thus, the subject A responds to the object B in two ways at once, the immediate perception of the object $A \to B$, and the sign $A \to X$. Each of these reactions is a perfectly natural reflex. It is the mediated reaction $A \to X \to B$, which is *socially constructed,* and which gives *meaning* to the object, B, a meaning acquired from the culture, thanks to the collaboration with the other person, in this case, the researcher. X may be an image on a card which reminds the subject of the word to be remembered, for example, or it may be a written word giving the name of the object. This idea, in which all our relations to the environment are taken to be *mediated,* is directly linked to Hegel's *dictum* (1816, §92) cited above. It is by using cultural signs and tools, to solve problems thrown up in life in collaboration with others, that people learn and become cultured citizens of their community – introducing mediating signs and other artefacts to control their interaction with their immediate environment.

Using this experimental set-up, Vygotsky was able to observe, for example, whether and how children of different ages were able to use memory-cards to improve their performance in memorising tasks, and by this means demonstrated, for example, the qualitative difference between how small children, older children and adults remember. By appropriating elements of their culture in the course of their development, people completely restructure their consciousness.

This first unit of analysis, the *sign-mediated action,* is the first germ-cell developed for psychological research by Vygotsky.

2.1.1 Word Meaning

In 1931, Vygotsky came to the conclusion that not just any sign, but *the spoken word,* was the *archetypal* cultural artefact through which people appropriated the culture of their community. After all, every physiologically able child spontaneously learns to speak while many never master literacy, and speech had emerged contemporaneously with labour (the use of tool-artefacts) in the very evolution of the human species. Signs, such as the written word, were a later invention, with writing corresponding to transition to bureaucratic class society. It was with this conviction that Vygotsky composed his last and definitive work, *Thinking and Speech* (1934).

In the first chapter of *Thinking and Speech* Vygotsky presents his only extended exposition of analysis by units, and in this instance his chosen unit was *word meaning* – a unity of speech and thinking, that is, of sound and meaning. A word is a unity of sound and meaning because a sound without a meaning is not a word and nor is a meaning without a physical sign a word – a word has to be both. Word meaning is equally a unity of generalisation and social interaction, of thinking and communication. A word is a *unit* because it is the simplest, discrete instance of such a unity.

Vygotsky was not writing as a linguist. It is a matter of indifference here whether the 'word' is a single word or actually a phrase, for example. By 'word' is meant a spoken sign for a concept. Linguistics and the related disciplines of discourse analysis, etymology, pragmatics, etc., all give further important insights for psychology, sociology, etc., and have different units of analysis. But Vygotsky's aim in this work is a general psychology, not linguistics.

The unit, word meaning, has to be understood as a *sign-mediated action*. Vygotsky insisted that word meaning is not a *subset* of the larger category of artefact-mediated actions, which would have the effect of subsuming communicative action, including speech, under labour activity. Rather, the relation between tool use and sign use is genetic. The archetype of a 'sign', according to Vygotsky is a mnemonic symbol, such as a knot in a handkerchief or a notch in a message stick, and these signs, he claimed, developed into the written word several thousand years ago. Sign-mediated actions, such as the use of written words, arose during the past few millennia as an extension of tool-mediated actions. *Speech* however arose in close connection with the development of labour in the very process of human evolution. The use of symbolic artefacts, such as writing, therefore has to be understood as something phylogenetically and ontogenetically distinct from speech which co-evolved as part of the labour process which, according to Engels (1876), drove the evolution of the human species.

In his discussion of tool use, Vygotsky distinguished between 'technical tools' and 'psychological tools'. Tools in the normal sense, technical tools, are used to operate upon matter, whereas psychological tools are used to work on the mind, and these include "language, different forms of numeration and counting, mnemotechnic techniques, algebraic symbolism, works of art, writing, schemes, diagrams, maps, blueprints, all sorts of conventional signs, etc." (Vygotsky, 1930, p. 85). Note that a 'psychological tool' is a material artefact, just like a technical tool; it is not a 'psychological entity' like a mental image or idea. Using a (technical) tool has profound psychological effects because tool use widens the scope of a person's activity, focuses their attention and expands their horizon of experience, but it does not 'work on the mind' in the direct sense as does a psychological tool. Psychological tools developed alongside of and as an extension of the development of technical tools.

It is important to emphasise that to speak, that is to say, to act with a word, is an *action*; to *mean* something, that is, word-meaning, is an action. 'Word meaning' does not refer to an entry in the dictionary, it is the action in which an intention is carried out by means of a meaningful word.

Just as Marx first analysed the commodity as early as 1843 but took until 1859 to realise that the commodity had to be taken as a *unit of analysis*, Vygotsky pointed to the importance of analysing speech in his first published work (1924) but took a further decade to settle on the spoken word, the simplest act of 'psychological exchange', as the *unit of analysis* for his final work.

Using this unit of analysis, Vygotsky analysed the development of the *intellect*, that is, of verbal thinking. The unit of 'practical intellect' is a tool use, and has a distinct path of development, side by side with (verbal) intellect, whose unit is a word meaning. The word is also a 'germ cell' in the sense that it is the cell which can grow into an entire theory and practice, just like a cell can grow into an organism. Different units would give different insights, and human science demands the use of different units, each shedding light of a particular hue on to the human condition.

2.1.2 Concepts as Units of the Intellect

Although word meaning is the basic unit of the intellect, a larger, 'molar' unit is required to understand the structure and development of the intellect. This molar unit is the *concept*, which is an aggregate of many word meanings. The centre of Vygotsky's analysis in *Thinking and Speech* is the formation of concepts, which only reach a fully developed form in late adolescence. Vygotsky's task was to trace the development of the intellect from infancy to adulthood, by observing the development of speech. It is the intellect which is the real subject matter of *Thinking and Speech*, just as capital, not commodities, is the real subject matter of Marx's *Capital*.

Vygotsky summarised his study of the emergence of speech in young children as follows:

1. As we found in our analysis of the phylogenetic development of thinking and speech, we find that these two processes have different roots in ontogenesis.
2. Just as we can identify a 'pre-speech' stage in the development of the child's thinking, we can identify a 'pre-intellectual stage' in the development of his speech.
3. Up to a certain point, speech and thinking develop along different lines and independently of one another.
4. At a certain point, the two lines cross: thinking becomes verbal and speech intellectual.

    1934, p. 112

Speech *Thinking*

FIGURE 2 The codevelopment of thinking and speech

Vygotsky traced the changes in word meaning from the first emergence of speech in the form of *unconscious expressive* speech, to communicative speech (calling upon adults for assistance), to *egocentric* speech in which the child gives itself audible instructions or commentary, with the child taking the place of the adult in commanding their own behaviour, to egocentric speech which becomes more and more curtailed and predicative passing over into *inner* speech, and later, as he notes in the final chapter of *Thinking and Speech*, thinking which goes *beyond* speech with the most developed forms of thinking which are no longer tied to putting one word after another. The changing form of word-meaning allowed Vygotsky to trace the emergence and construction of the verbal intellect and thereby understand its essential nature.

The development of thinking and speech takes the form of a double helix (Figure 2).

This model of co-development is used throughout by Vygotsky in understanding the complex development of all the higher forms of activity acquired by human beings.

By use of a germ cell, which is open to observation, and by tracing its internalisation as it is gradually transformed into something private and inaccessible to observation, Vygotsky created an objective scientific basis for Cultural Psychology. This was an astounding achievement.

2.1.3 The Formation of Concepts

In his study of the early formation of concepts in the fifth chapter of *Thinking and Speech*, Vygotsky describes experiments using the method of dual stimulation with children set sorting tasks. Children were invited to sort a variety of different sized, shaped and coloured blocks into groups that were 'the same'. The problem could be solved by looking at nonsense words written on the base of the blocks. The children were only gradually introduced to these clues so that the researchers could observe the children's actions in forming better and better groups, aided by reference to the signs. Vygotsky was able to describe a number of discrete types of concepts, according to the different ways children sorted the blocks.

Vygotsky identified each of these concepts as a *form of action*, rather than as a logical structure, as Hegel might have categorised them, and nor did Vygotsky reify them as mental functions or capacities; they were just forms of action. Thus, by using sign mediated actions as his unit, Vygotsky was able to study the emergence of concepts, the units of the verbal intellect. These concepts, constructed in the laboratory on the basis of features of the objects being sorted, were not yet truly concepts, but exhibited the type of concepts which arise among children, who have not yet left the family home and entered the world of adult concerns and concepts assembled and worked out on the historical and cultural plane of human life.

True concepts, acquired through instruction in some real-world institution and actual concepts developed through participation in both everyday and professional life, are yet different forms of activity. These Vygotsky investigated in the sixth chapter with experiments involving speech. Typically, young people would be asked to complete a narrative sentence with "because ..." or "although ...," observing their efforts to verbalise causal relations with which they were well-accustomed, but now with conscious awareness. The insight behind these experiments is that a child, or even a domesticated animal, can learn to respond rationally to a situation, demonstrating an implicit understanding of the relevant causal connections between events. However, the ability to isolate this relation in a form of thought, and with conscious awareness use the thought form (concept) as a unit in verbal reasoning – intellect – is something characteristically human. True concepts are transmitted through the generations by cultural institutions, professions and so on, and are invariably carried by words which are part of a real language. So, a concept is the conscious awareness of a form of activity organised around a word or other meaningful artefact.

By characterising concepts in this way, as formations of artefact-mediated activity, Vygotsky laid the basis for an interdisciplinary science. Social formations are made up of a variety of forms of activity, each of which is apprehended as a concept, and these concepts together constitute the culture of the given community. Vygotsky has given us a down-to-earth laboratory method for studying how people acquire these concepts.

Marx did not take value as some intangible quality, but rather began with a specific type of social action – exchange. Likewise, Vygotsky did not take 'concept' to be some intangible mental entity, but rather a specific type of social action. And this is true of all Vygotsky's units of analysis – they are specific, observable forms of activity.

Note that in the above we have seen *two* units: word meaning and concept. The 'larger', or molar unit, concept, arises on the basis of the 'smaller' or molecular unit, word meaning. Words only exhibit their full meaning as part of a system of meanings constituted by the concept they evoke, and conversely, concepts exist only in and through the large number of word meanings and other artefact-mediated actions associated with them. Nonetheless, Vygotsky showed that children learn to use words long before they master conceptual thinking, at which point their speech activity is transformed.

This process whereby a molar unit of activity arises on the basis of the action of a molecular unit, is a common feature of the analysis of processes by units. It is found in Marx's critique of political economy with commodity and then capital, and in activity theory where the molecular unit is an artefact-mediated action, and the molar unit is an activity. The method of analysis by units allows the researcher to trace step by step how the more developed unit emerges out of the action of the fundamental units which can be grasped viscerally.

2.1.4 Germ Cell and Unit of Analysis

The concept which Marx referred to with the term 'cell-form' is referred to in Cultural-Historical Activity Theory (CHAT) by two different terms: *unit of analysis*, and *germ cell*. These are two different expressions for the same concept but indicate two different aspects of that concept.

'Germ cell' indicates the germ from which more complex forms develop, just as the cell grows into an organ. For example, actual exchange of commodities is rarely seen in modern capitalist society, where everything is bought and sold, not literally traded. But Marx showed how, historically, once a community starts producing for exchange, perhaps on its borders or with passing merchants, it is more or less inevitably drawn into the world market, and with that comes the need for a universal measure of value. Thus, a universal commodity, emerges – gold, paper money, credit and so forth all 'unfold' themselves from the original simple practice of exchange. This first unit, C–C, through the mediation of money, opens up into C–M–C, in which a person sells in order to buy. From this mediating element there arises a whole class of people who buy in order to sell at a profit: M–C–M', and thus arises *capital*, a new unit of value, a new social relation which arises on the basis of the 'logic' of that simple relation, *exchange*. With the emergence of capital – firms buying in order to sell at a profit – economic life is reorganised, with production of commodities now subsumed under capital (rather than under pre-existing feudal relations) and reoriented towards the accumulation of capital rather than simply the cooperative provision of human needs. The 'germ-cell' of capital, M–C–M', exhibits this course of development in embryo.

Likewise, in psychology, the simple word meaning, when developed through discourse, gives rise to more developed forms of thinking and speech, namely concepts (which is not to imply that a society of speech without true concepts ever existed). 'Germ cell' emphasises this aspect of *development*, the relation between the simple undeveloped relation, on the one hand, and on the other hand, the mature, concrete relation.

Vygotsky appropriated the term 'unit of analysis' from social science, in which it meant the 'resolution of the analytical microscope', so to speak, the smallest entity which is taken account of in a given theory. In mainstream social science, the unit of analysis is usually taken to be individuals, sometimes groups, classes or even nations. The difference with how Vygotsky used the term is that he recognised that the unit of analysis is already implicitly a *concept of the whole*. That is, he merged this analytical concept with Goethe's idea of the *Urphänomen* as a representation of a Gestalt.

I will illustrate how the idea of a unit of analysis figured in Marx's work. The young Marx was outraged by the treatment of the poor, censorship and other social issues, but realised that he knew nothing of the root causes of these phenomena. Thus, he turned to a study of political economy. Twenty five years later, when he wrote *Das Kapital*, 'bourgeois society' was now conceived of as an integral whole, a market place – just millions and millions of commodity exchanges, and nothing else. Other phenomena, such as censorship, political corruption, cruelty, now came to be seen as *inessential* and contingent. By taking commodity exchange as the unit, the whole, the *Gestalt*, was now re-defined and was not coextensive with his original conception of the whole. This is the other aspect to the concept of 'cell' – it means taking the whole process to be nothing other than millions and millions of this one simple relation, a relation which can be grasped viscerally, without the need for abstract theories and forces and so on. The 'unit of analysis' expresses the results of analysis in terms of a relation between the whole and the part. The whole is *nothing but* millions and millions of the same unit of analysis. It is possible to see the water cycle – rain, rivers, ocean, evaporation, clouds and back down again as rain – as one whole process, a *Gestalt*, because all these are nothing but billions and billions of the same unit: H_2O molecules.

Identifying the unit of a complex process is an Aha! moment, seeing that the process is nothing but such and such a simple action or relation. This becomes the *starting point* for a truly scientific understanding of the process, an understanding which allows us to grasp the phenomenon not just as a process with this or that features, but as a whole, as a *Gestalt*.

Thus the germ-cell and the unit of analysis are one and the same thing, but in one case the developmental aspect is emphasised and in the other case the analytical aspect is emphasised.

2.1.5 Five Applications of the Method of Analysis by Units

'Unit of analysis' is a relative term: analysis of *what*? A unit of analysis is always used for the analysis of some specific problem or phenomenon. Some writers only ever analyse one phenomenon and devote their lives to that issue. For example, among philosophers, Kant takes the judgment as the unit of experience, Frege takes the smallest expression to which pragmatic force can be attached, and Wittgenstein the smallest expression whose utterance makes a move in a language game, Bakhtin uses the utterance (speaking turn) as the unit for discourse analysis, and Robert Brandom takes the proposition as his unit of analysis.

Vygotsky's work covered *five different domains* of psychological research. He used the unit of *sign-mediated actions* to analyse a range of distinct psychological functions, such as will, attention, memory and so on. And he used *word meaning* to study verbal intelligence and concept formation. In addition to these, Vygotsky found a unit of analysis for three other areas of research.

2.1.5.1 *Perezhivanie*

Perezhivanie is an untranslatable Russian word meaning 'an experience' together with the 'catharsis' entailed in surviving and processing that experience. One and the same event does not have the same significance for every person, so *perezhivaniya* are 'lived experiences' which depend not only on characteristics of the event itself, but also on characteristics of the individual. Vygotsky wrote that alongside heredity, it was *perezhivaniya* which formed the personality. Understanding the personality (*lichnost*) as a process rather than a product, he claimed that *perezhivaniya* were units of the personality. *Perezhivaniya* stand out from the general background of experience, have a beginning a middle and an end and throughout the course of the experience, have a unity and a certain emotional colour. *Perezhivaniya* have a definite psychological form. Reflect on your own life, remember those seminal experiences, the daring moves you got away with, the public humiliations you suffered, the reprimands, injustices or accolades you received – your personality is the aggregate of all these *perezhivaniya* and analysis of them would give a therapist or prospective partner insight into your personality. It is these *perezhivaniya* which makes up the story you tell yourself of your own life, your identity.

Vygotsky dealt only briefly with *perezhivaniya* in a lecture called 'The Problem of the Environment' (1934a) in which he defines a *perezhivanie* as a "unity of environmental and personal features." This expression has been the source of some confusion. A personal feature might be a child's stage of intellectual development, and an environmental feature might be the school-entry age; neither of these features by themselves shape the personality of a child, but *taken together* – whether at school age the child is *ready* to attend school – is self-evidently a factor in the forming of the child's personality. Further, *perezhivanie* is often translated as 'lived experience', which in contemporary social science is taken to be entirely subjective, whereas *perezhivaniya* have objective as well as subjective sides. *Perezhivanie* does not mean 'experience' (as in an applicant's 'work experience') – for which the Russian word is *opit*. *Perezhivaniya* are discrete episodes which stand out from the background of experience and include the active contribution of the subject and its aesthetic character.

2.1.5.2 Defect-Compensation

Vygotsky devoted much of his efforts to work with children affected with a variety of disabilities. In those days, the Soviet government grouped all kinds of disabilities together under the heading of Defectology. But Vygotsky did not see the defect as being on the side of the subject. Rather, the defect lay in the relation between the subject and the cultural environment, including the failure of the community to provide for the full participation of the subject in social life.

For every defect, there is a compensation. That compensation is a combination of measures on the part of the community to facilitate the participation of the subject, and the psychological and practical adjustments made on the part of the subject to overcome the barrier to their participation. Vygotsky took the unit of analysis for defectology as the unity of the defect and the compensation – the 'defect-compensation'. Vygotsky's writing on defectology are in Volume 2 of his Collected Works. To a great extent, Vygotsky appropriated Alfred Adler's work on the 'inferiority complex'.

2.1.5.3 Social Situation of Development

In his work on child development, Vygotsky developed the concept of 'social situation of development'. Vygotsky insisted that the social situation is not just a series of factors – age of mother, salary and occupation of father, number of siblings, etc. – it is a *specific situation* or predicament. Each of these situations has a definite name in a given culture, such as 'infant' or 'elementary school child', etc. Each of these situations entails certain expectations placed on the child and their specific needs are met in a corresponding appropriate way. The child is more or less obliged to fit into this role. In the process of normal development however, at a certain point, the child develops needs and desires which cannot be met within the current social situation, and a crisis breaks out in the family group, both the child and its carers. The child may become difficult and rebellious, and if the family and carers respond, the child and the whole situation will undergo a transformation and a new social situation will be established, with the child occupying a new social position. Child development is constituted by this specific series of situations, with both family and child going through a series of culturally specific transformations through which the child eventually develops into an independent adult. The social situation of development is a unity of the child and its carers in a specific caring relationship.

In each of the areas of psychological research into which Vygotsky went, his aim was to establish a unit of analysis. He was not always successful, and for example, his study of the emotions failed to arrive at a unit of analysis before his death in 1934 (see Holodynski, 2013). But he did discover five units: artefact-mediated actions, meaningful words, *perezhivaniya*, defect-compensations, and social situations of development.

2.1.5.4   *Activities*

The Activity Theorists, who continued Vygotsky's work, particularly contributed to the notion of 'germ cell' as an agent of social and psychological change.

A.N. Leontyev also famously defined a hierarchy of three units of analysis: (1) The *operation*, a form of action which can be done without conscious awareness, adapting itself to conditions, (2) The *artefact mediated action*, and (3) The *activities* (or projects or forms of practice). Note that here 'activities' means the discrete aggregates of actions all having a common motive, each action having a distinct goal differing from the shared motive, and possibly executed by different individuals. This is distinct from the notion of 'activity', meaning the generalised substance of human life. Activities as units of analysis is a rendering in social rather than psychological terms of Vygotsky's unit of *concepts*. Indeed, it is important to remember that the motive of the activity is always a concept even though the object of the activity is an objective part of the larger social formation. Hegel used the same idea in his *Philosophy of Right*.

2.2 The Importance of Vygotsky for Social Theory

Hegel, Marx and Vygotsky each made an important development on the methodology originated by Goethe. Hegel replaced the *Urphänomen* with the abstract concept which could be a subject of reasoning, rather than merely intuition. Marx insisted that the real subject was social practice rather than thought, and critique could only reconstruct what was given in social practice. Consequently, rather than an abstract concept such as 'value', the germ-cell would be a practical action such as commodity exchange. In his critique of psychology, Vygotsky showed that this germ cell had to be a discrete, finite, observable interaction. Whereas Marx left us only two instantiations of this method, Vygotsky applied the method to the solution of five different problems and provided five different instances of a 'germ-cell', thus making the idea explicit and the method reproducible.

Vygotsky was a psychologist, in particular, a cultural psychologist, not a social theorist. He approached the cultural formation of the psyche, as mentioned above, by means of a study of the collaborative use of artefacts originating in the wider culture, in some social situation, also a product of the wider culture. But he did not investigate the processes of formation of the social environment itself. These problems were taken up by the Activity Theorists who followed on from Vygotsky's work. Although the Activity Theorists made important developments, they were not all able to consistently maintain Vygotsky's method of analysis by units.

Nonetheless, through the method of analysis by units, and in particular through the unit, artefact mediated action, Vygotsky has given social theorists an approach which can fully integrate the psychological, social and historical sciences. Rather than psychology on one side, and social theory on the other, Vygotsky has given us the opportunity for a genuinely interdisciplinary human science. Concepts are equally the unit of a culture and the unit of the intellect, and Vygotsky's research on concepts in *Thinking and Speech* shows us how we can understand concepts, not as invisible thought forms, but as forms of activity. Vygotsky's approach is a powerful alternative to the 'ideology critique' which is the usual fare in Marxist social theory and suggests an approach which can generate new insights into the complex social problems of today.

The special value of analysis by units for social theory is that units/germs can be viable vehicles for social action for those of us who wish to change entire social formations.

2.3 A Note on Reification and Units of Analysis
2.3.1 Marx's *Capital*

Marx says (1881) "What I start out from is the simplest social form in the which the product of labour is presented in contemporary society, and this is 'the commodity',"and in the opening lines of *Capital* (1867) he says: "The wealth of those societies in which the capitalist mode of production prevails, presents itself as 'an immense accumulation of commodities'." So, he clearly says that he believes that values take the form of *things* in bourgeois society and this is his starting point.

And yet we have good reason to believe that Marx wanted a 'philosophy of praxis'. In *Theses on Feuerbach* (1845), he says in a dozen different ways: "All social life is essentially practical. All mysteries which lead theory to mysticism find their rational solution in human practice and in the comprehension of this practice." So why in *Capital* does he insist on the ultimate reality being *things* rather than practices? Why does he start from the commodity rather than the practice of commodity exchange?

I see three reasons.

First, how can a social theorist observe and measure human activity en masse other than by observing the things which are the products and means of their activity?

Second, it is a feature of bourgeois society that wealth is conceived of as 'an immense accumulation of commodities', and indeed this is essential to the practice of *accumulating* wealth. Even if you grant that a service can be a commodity and therefore a form of value, the buyer can only possess the product once the service has been enjoyed, not the service as such. When a builder builds a house for you, you look to owning the house, not the builder's action of building the house, whether your object is that of a homemaker or a real estate speculator.

So, the *reification* of value into material products at some point is essential to the practice of accumulating value. In the further development of capitalism wealth comes to be rendered in the form of writing in ledgers (including electronic ledgers), but the meaning of these symbolic forms of value lies in their standing for things, and failing that, symbolic wealth evaporates, just as contrariwise possession is not property unless legally legitimised.

The third reason is that Marx put forward his theory in *opposition* to the idea of exchange of commodities being cast as an exchange of *services*. Such a conception of commerce renders the activity of the wage worker as a service to the employer, while the provision of means of production is cast as a service on the part of the employer. This has the effect of conflating the industrial worker with the domestic servant, and the exploitation of wage labour with purchase of personal services for immediate consumption. Such a conception mystifies the source of surplus value which, according to Marx, lies in the appropriation of unpaid labour arising from the difference between the socially necessary cost of production of labour power and the value of the product of labour. In Marx's conception, the capitalist *directs and uses* the 'labour power' of the worker to add value to products and thereby acquire a product worth more than the sum of the value of its components. Marx saw services, on the other hand, as objects of personal consumption. However, he does allow that "a schoolmaster who is engaged as a wage labourer in … a knowledge-mongering institution, is a productive worker" (1867, ch. 2) and *does* produce surplus value. Thus, Marx's insistence that a service provision cannot be productive of surplus value is not held consistently. It is just that he takes the production of tangible commodities as the archetypal form, the *germ cell*, of wage labour.

In the 150 years since *Capital* was published, it has become clear that services can be bought and sold on the market for the purpose of accumulation of surplus value in any branch of industry. Indeed, industries that are exclusively reliant on the production of stuff are in general less successful in appropriating surplus value than the service industries. It remains the case that wealth cannot be accumulated but only consumed in the form of services. Generally speaking, wealth is accumulated in symbolic commodities, not piles of stuff, so there is little point in insisting on the priority of production of stuff as opposed to services. Though, of course, the stuff has to be there to buy and use or the size of your bank account is useless.

On close examination, Marx's units of analysis of bourgeois society are the practices of (1) selling labour in order to buy the means of life (C–M–C') and (2) buying in order to sell at a profit (M–C–M') – both *forms of practice*. However, the actions in question are *artefact-mediated* actions, that is, essentially, the practices in question necessarily entail actions *with* artefacts. In the case of pure services, the artefacts in question are human bodies and human energy and means which are not the property of the worker.

So, my thesis is this. The reification of actions in the form of commodities which can be accumulated as wealth is a feature of any society based on the accumulation of wealth, and the use and production of things is an essential moment in labour activity. However, even though Marx does not say so, the units of analysis he uses in *Capital* are forms of *practice*, (C–M–C') and (M–C–M').

See my *Goethe, Hegel and Marx* (2016) for more on this.

2.3.2   Vygotsky's *Thinking and Speech*

It is generally agreed that Vygotsky used artefact-mediated actions as a unit of analysis across a range of studies. This claim is reiterated in significant works by A.N. Leontyev, Mike Cole and Yrjö Engeström, and is taken to be the foundation of activity theory. In the first chapter of *Thinking and Speech*, Vygotsky elaborated the idea of 'unit of analysis', but only in connection with 'word meaning', and explicitly had speech and not writing in mind. In *The Instrumental Method in Psychology* (1930) he distinguished between 'technical tools' (used for acting on nature) and 'psychological tools' (used for acting on the Mind).

So, Vygotsky identified three different kinds of artefact-mediated action:
- the spoken word (by 'word' is meant a sign for a concept),
- the psychological tool (sign, written word, map, diagram, …) and
- the technical tool (the hand-tool is the archetypal technical tool).

Three types of artefact-mediated action, corresponding to the three types of artefact, have developed in the biological and cultural evolution of the human species:
- speech evolved in close connection with labour (i.e., tool use) in the early evolution of the species, and probably evolved out of manual sign use,
- (technical) tools developed in the course of evolution of the species and continue to develop culturally, but Vygotsky believed that tool use *led* speech development in human evolution,
- signs (i.e., psychological tools) developed as an outgrowth of the development of technical tools, although expanding the communicative function formerly belonging to spoken words and gestures. (See Chapter 12, this volume.)

Formally speaking, speech is a sub-category of the use of psychological tools, the word a type of sign, but the two are markedly distinct *genetically*, in the evolution of the human species and in the development of the human individual. All children spontaneously master the form of speech which they find in their environment, but children have to be deliberately instructed in reading and writing. Although all human communities use tools of one kind or another, many communities have been illiterate. Writing is an invention of bureaucratic, class societies, although less developed forms of sign use (marking of land, cave painting, jewellery, …) are ancient.

Tool use and sign use are closely interlinked in the development of human culture. In Vygotsky's aphorism: "in the beginning was the *tool*, but … in the *beginning* was the tool." This developmental, genetic distinction between tool, word and sign is of primary significance for Vygotsky, rather than their all being categorised as artefact-mediated activity.

Words and tools play distinct, albeit interconnected, roles in human development. Vygotsky resisted the subsumption of words as a subset of artefacts, implicitly subordinate to tools, resisting the theoretical subordination of communicative action to the labour process. In this he was taking a stand against the Soviet orthodoxy in Marxist theory (see Blunden, 2014a). In the analysis of social history, technical tool development (the development of the means of production) leads the development of communicative action (the superstructure, cultural activity), but this is *relative*, not absolute, and certainly not the case in psychology. Tool use certainly leads the development of practical intelligence but not the intellect properly so called. Access to technical tools may widen the field of a person's activity and promote the development of social structures, and thereby promote learning, but it is only thanks to the use of signs, mainly words, that that wider field of experience may be productive of intellectual development. You may need a car to get to school, but you will only learn if you listen to what is said at school. My point is this: word meaning, psychological tool use and technical tool use are three *distinct* lines of artefact-mediated action.

As a unit of analysis, 'word meaning' is not itself an artefact, such as an entry in the dictionary, far less an entry in some neural look-up table. 'Word meaning' is an *action* in which the mediating artefact is a spoken word. 'Meaning' is the gerund of the transitive verb 'to mean', as in doing what you mean to do with a word. By 'word' is meant the sign for a concept, be it a phrase or a single word. No other interpretation of the term is tenable.

In Chapter 5 of *Thinking and Speech*, when Vygotsky discusses the experiments in which children constructed groups of blocks by referring to the signs written on the underside of the blocks, they were engaged in performing a concept, reified in the group of blocks gathered together by the sign-mediated actions of the child. Each action is a sign-mediated action, of the same kind as using a spoken word. All the actions taken together are an activity, a concept characterised by the criteria implicit in the mode of grouping blocks and *reified* in the blocks so grouped.

Now, 'meaning' *also* means that reified artefact, the relevant entry in a dictionary. But not only dictionaries – the entire mass of cultural artefacts in a language community constitute a reification of the meaning of the users of words (and signs) and constitutes a kind of 'living dictionary'. Words 'carry' a meaning given to the word by the entire cultural history of the community. It is well-known that misunderstandings can arise when someone hears a word and ascribes a meaning to the speech act which can *differ* from the meaning of the speaker. So, it is not the actual meaning (intent) of the action which *has effect* but the meaning implicit in the word (as spoken in its context, with the given accent, emphasis, etc.). Ultimately, it is the culturally determined meaning of the word, its use-value, so to speak, which is materially active in the action, whatever the speaker's intention. The listener in turn realises the meaning of the word in their own interpretation.

Vygotsky points out that word meaning is the unity of sound and meaning, of speech and thinking, of affective and intellectual processes, of generalisation and social interaction, of thinking and communication. And we must add also, a unity of the speaker's intention and the hearer's reception. A unit of analysis is a *concrete concept,* and as such, a concentration of diverse determinations, the contradictions between which unfold in the manifold phenomena under consideration.

CHAPTER 3

Concrete Historicism as a Research Paradigm

It has long been widely accepted among Marxists that Marx's theoretical legacy is essentially that embodied in *Capital*. Marx never got around to writing his theory of the state, which he had foreshadowed in 1844, let alone his own Logic, and his voluminous writings on political and historical subjects were never worked up into a systematic text like *Capital*. Although anticipated more than a century ago by Lenin, it has been mainly during the last 25 years that a body of literature has developed around the relationship between Marx's *Capital* and Hegel's *Logic*, and this author (Blunden, 2016a, 2018) is among those who see this relationship as key to understanding *Capital*.

However, it remains the case that for all the ink that has been expended examining the affinity between these two texts, hardly a word has been written which goes beyond describing this relationship towards applying what has been learnt to an analysis of the development of the world capitalist economy in the 180 years since Marx died, let alone to the analysis of social formations other than political economy. One exception to this is the work of this author (Blunden, 2016) devoted to the fundamental principles of political life, but the connection of the method used in this analysis to *Capital* and the *Logic* were not made explicit. It is the aim of this paper to justify the method which, following Evald Ilyenkov (1960), shall be called 'concrete historicism'. The article originated as a draft for the 'theoretical introduction' to a collaborative work analysing the socio-political situation in a specific state.

1 Structuralism and Abstract Historicism

When Ferdinand de Saussure (1911) turned from 'evolutionary linguistics' to 'synchronic linguistics', he claimed that its "general principles provide the basis for a productive approach to the details of a static state or the law of static states." Therewith, a tradition of structuralist analysis, chiefly based on logical analysis of binary distinctions, unfolded throughout the 20th century, shedding light mainly on how social formations of all kinds sustained and *reproduced* themselves. Indeed, apart from the professional work of the historian which generally focuses on analysis of a specific period or event in the past, the object of analysis for social theorists is the social formation before us, and history is useful only to the extent that it can shed light on the existing situation.

Logical analysis, i.e., structuralism, would seem to have the primary place in the analysis of any social formation. The aim of such analysis, however, is not to show how the present state of affairs reproduces itself – it does that perfectly well without our help – but to disclose *unstable* categories and relationships and *contradictions* in existing conditions, because these contradictions render the formation as something which is *in motion* and point to the possibility of changing it. Our interest in the present situation is to bring to light the potential for change.

However, the primacy of this structural interest does not rule out or diminish the significance of historical analysis, or at least, historical analysis of a specific kind, something like a *genealogy*. Meaning is, as they say, 'path dependent'.

Any existing social situation is always like the situation following the making of a peace treaty in the aftermath of a war – you can only *make sense* of certain aspects of the constitution or customs of the people by reference to prior history. For example, the Second Amendment to the US Constitution says: "... the right of the people to keep and bear Arms, shall not be infringed," but it is necessary to understand the context in which that line was written to understand what it meant at the time. In the end, however, its significance must be assessed in the light of the ubiquitous gun culture in the US today, and the impact of *that* on citizens' freedom. For example, again, the marriage ceremony *may* have originated as a form of the transfer of property, symbolised by the wedding ring and the father 'giving away' the bride, but it is not that *now*. Institutions and the broader context in which they exist change, and if they don't change, nonetheless their meaning changes. Yesterday's peace treaty can become the battleline in a different dispute today.

'Abstract historicism' is what I call 'Just So' stories. A narrative about how a given social formation came to be, whether plausible or implausible, does not tell us the nature of that new social formation. A history of the 1930s and World War Two does not tell us anything about the nature of the post-war world, even if it provides some kind of *description* of how it came to be. The structure of the Postwar Settlement, whose various elements were put into place between 1944 and 1948, *does* show us the nature of the postwar period. Although the events of the preceding decades make this Settlement intelligible, minor events could have made it otherwise. Nonetheless, the events of the 1930s and 1940s help us understand the Settlement which mediated between the pre- and post-war worlds.

So the question is: what is the proper relation between logical and historical analysis in the analysis of an existing social formation.

1.1 Logic and History in Hegel

It may come as a surprise that Hegel was, in this specific sense, a structuralist. Both in his *Philosophy of History* and in the only instance where he explicitly applied his *Logic* to social formations, the *Philosophy of Right* (1821), Hegel was clear:

> The historical origin of the judge and his court may have had the form of a patriarch's gift to his people or of force or free choice; but this makes no difference to the concept of the thing.
> 1821, §219 n.

And

> But if we ask what is or has been the historical origin of the state ... all these questions are no concern of the Idea of the State.
> 1821, §258 n.

So it is the *logical* relations between the various components of Right which determine their real relations and the sequence in which they are analysed in the *Philosophy of Right*, not their historical sequence and these are two different sequences. And Marx agrees. While arguing that the categories in *Capital* are to be presented in *logical*, not historical sequence, Marx cited Hegel's *Philosophy of Right*:

> But do not these simpler categories also have an independent historical or natural existence preceding that of the more concrete ones? *Ça dépend.* Hegel, for example, correctly takes possession, the simplest legal relation of the subject, as the point of departure of the philosophy of right. No possession exists, however, before the family or the relation of lord and servant, which are far more concrete relations. It would, on the other hand, be correct to say that families and entire tribes exist which have as yet only *possession* and no *property*.
> 1858, p. 102

Self-evidently, property cannot exist in any real sense in the absence of a state, and yet property precedes the State in the logical elaboration of the *Philosophy of Right*. The emergence of the state effects a transformation of what were really only 'premonitions' of what would become *organs* of the state. The state transforms possession (a 'premonition' of property) into a judicial relation. In Hegel's words:

> The state is an organism, i.e. the development of the Idea to the articulation of its differences. Thus these different sides of the state are its various powers with their functions and spheres of action, by means of which the universal continually engenders itself in a necessary way; in this process it maintains its identity since it is presupposed even in its own production. This organism is the constitution of the state; it is produced perpetually by the state, while it is through it that the state maintains itself.
>
> 1821, §269ad

That is, the various organs of the state are its *presuppositions*, but once in place, the State transforms them into subordinate *organs* of itself and reproduces them as such. It may well appear that with the emergence of rights, moral subjects, corporations and courts, that a State is already in existence, but this would be a mistake. Only with the specific historical acts which transform these various formations into *organs* of the state does the state truly exist, and is capable of reproducing itself.

Hegel does not see the succession of states and their constitutions as a *logical* sequence like the sequence of categories in the *Logic* is taken to be. Hegel explains this in his *Philosophy of History*:

> The Constitutions under which World-Historical peoples have reached their culmination, are peculiar to them; and therefore do not present a generally applicable political basis. ... From the comparison therefore of the political institutions of the ancient World-Historical peoples, it so happens, that for the most recent principle of a Constitution – for the principle of our own times – nothing (so to speak) can be learned.
>
> In science and art it is quite otherwise; e. g., the ancient philosophy is so decidedly the basis of the modern, that it is inevitably contained in the latter, and constitutes its basis.
>
> 1837, §§48–49

The anti-historicism which applies to the unique and concrete formations of social life does *not* completely apply to religion, science, art and philosophy, the phases of what Hegel calls 'absolute spirit'. This contrary, and probably more familiar moment in Hegel's idea, is captured in his description of the *Encyclopaedia* as a 'circle of circles':

> *Each of the parts of philosophy is a philosophical whole, a circle rounded and complete in itself.* In each of these parts, however, the philosophical

> Idea is found in a particular specificality or medium. The single circle, because it is a real totality, bursts through the limits imposed by its special medium, and gives rise to a wider circle. The whole of philosophy in this way resembles a *circle of circles*. The Idea appears in each single circle, but, at the same time, the whole Idea is constituted by the system of these peculiar phases, and each is a necessary member of the organisation.
>
> 1831, §15

It would be untenable to claim a logical progression in the unfolding of history, with its succession of states, invasions, migrations, wars, etc. But, after each discontinuity – revolution, war, invasion, etc. – the peace treaties, laws and constitutions which settle these disruptions make a starting point for further development. According to Hegel, if they are subject to critique, such principles must undergo some kind of logical progression, even if uneven and interrupted, from the more abstract to the more concrete, until ultimately breaking down, qualified by the possibility of outside intervention.

Recall Hegel's famous antimetabole in the Preface to the *Philosophy of Right*: "What is rational is real; And what is real is rational," and its converse, viz., that laws and customs, and specific institutions which are irrational ultimately fall. The various principles develop in a 'logical' way, in just the way which is captured in Hegel's *Logic*. This kind of logic is exhibited in the unfolding of principles, that is to say, of *specific forms of activity* captured in a concept, rather than in entire, concrete social formations. Nonetheless, states and other institutions (*Gestalten des Bewusstseins*) stand or fall by such principles.

Not every institution in a social formation is essential but amongst them there will be one upon which the entire nature of the social formation depends. Further, there is a limited 'normative essentialism' (see Blunden, 2016b) for Hegel, in which institutions which are untrue to their concept tend, over time, to more perfectly accord with their concept, or, failing that, perish. It is in this way that an emergent state gradually refashions its various subordinate institutions so as to make them organs of itself, according to its own logic.

Each of the 'circles' within Hegel's 'circle of circles' draws itself by means of systematic dialectical logic, but the *starting point* of each circle comes from outside that circle. Although these circles are outlined in a logical way in the *Encyclopaedia*, the perception of the principle at the root of each 'circle' depends on what Hegel calls 'natural cognition', that is to say, reflects the real unfolding of the concrete whole of human activity.

I will return to this below in outlining the concept of 'concrete historicism' but let it be noted at this point that while history is intelligible (rational), the kind of dialectical-logical critique which Hegel exhibited in the *Logic* cannot be applied to *entire, concrete social formations*, such as states. The *Logic* retains its relevance to the analysis of the *principles* and finite institutions which underpin such formations, however, and their development from abstract concepts to concrete, self-conscious, mature systems of human activity. But not every such principle is of equal significance.

1.2   Logic and History for Marx

In 1859, Marx reflected on how as a radical young graduate in philosophy, concerned with issues like censorship and the mistreatment of the peasants, he had become aware of his own 'dilettantism' and returned to his study of Hegel. He came to the conclusion that political life had its roots in the conditions of civil society, the anatomy of which was to be found in political economy, and thereafter turned his attention to the critique of political economy rather than what had appeared to be the political issues of the day.

Marx determined that the root cause of social injustice lay in economic relations. As he explained in the famous passage 'Method of Political Economy' (1858), he saw his task now as a *logical reconstruction* of the given economic formation beginning from the single abstract relation which constitutes it as an integral totality. However, this concept was by no means something known and obvious. The root concept of political economy could only be abstracted from an exhaustive study of the history of political economic theory, before the logical reconstruction could begin, finally revealing the contradictions at work in the economic foundation.

This reconstruction is comparable to the reconstruction of the various sciences which Hegel exhibited in the *Encyclopaedia* and is referred to as 'systematic dialectic' (Arthur, 2011). The only *historical* investigations which we find in Marx's research in political economy are firstly, the *schematic* outline of the genealogy of commodity relations in §3, Chapter 1 of Volume I of *Capital* and his exhaustive immanent critique of *theories* in the history of political economic theory.

Capital is distinguished among structural analyses in that it places *contradictions* at its centre. It is by this means that a social formation can be grasped as *in movement*, rather than simply in terms of its tendency to reproduce itself in a kind of dynamic equilibrium.

Chris Arthur (2011) has argued persuasively that while Marx began *Capital* with an analysis of the commodity relation, this does *not* imply that Marx believed that 'simple commodity production' is a social formation which ever existed let alone constituted an historical precursor to modern bourgeois society. The commodity relation, the practice of exchanging products of labour, is the *logical* starting point of *Capital*, but there was never a pure market society without capital. Identifying the contradictions which had been overlooked by the political economists (and Hegel) – between use-value and exchange value, and between the rate of profit and the rate of surplus value – were the central achievements of Marx's analysis. These contradictions, though belonging to a structural analysis of capital, point to the movement and change inherent in the structure of economic relations.

Marx makes clear that the beginning is made from the *present* – the real object of analysis, which can be known viscerally and in detail and in which the relevant social formation is at its most mature. But the task of making that beginning is not straight forward because the writer is confronted with an infinite mass of data.

As Marx explained in the famous passage in the *Grundrisse* (1858, p. 100) referred to above, beginning the dialectical reconstruction of the formation requires the identification of that single relation which is the product of the *history of the theory of the social formation* of which the theory is a part. The historical part of Marx's analysis is the critical examination of its self-concept along with the broad outlines of the social formation as it develops. "It is not necessary to write the *real history of the relations of production*" (1857, p. 389), he wrote. The aim is to determine the concept which is to form the starting point of analysis, the germ cell, unit or prius, which provides the key to the understanding of the present, mature formation as a whole. This concept does not however come ready-made from the history of the science or of the phenomenon itself, but has to be critically appropriated and reconstructed, and this Marx does in the first chapter of *Capital*.

It is the same with Hegel – in order to justify beginning philosophy with the Being of Parmenides rather than with the earlier naturalistic speculations of Thales, Hegel had to give rigorous meanings both to Philosophy and to the concept of Being. Many bourgeois writers believe that capital arose in the ancient world. But according to Marx:

> ... important for us is that our method indicates the points where historical investigation must enter in, or where bourgeois economy as a merely historical form of the production process points beyond itself to earlier historical modes of production. In order to develop the laws of bourgeois economy, therefore, it is not necessary to write the *real history of the relations of production*. ... Just as, on one side the pre-bourgeois phases appear as *merely historical*, i.e. suspended presuppositions, so do the contemporary conditions of production likewise appear as engaged

in *suspending themselves* and hence in positing the *historic presuppositions* for a new state of society.

1857, pp. 388–389

Marx sees that the insight into the present which indicates where the historical analysis must begin, also foreshadows the *future*. Also, Marx agrees exactly with Hegel about the logical and historical relations between the 'organs' of a complex social 'organism':

> where agriculture predominates, as in antiquity and the feudal period, even industry, its organisation and the forms of property corresponding thereto, have more or less the character of landed property. ...
>
> The reverse is the case in bourgeois society. Agriculture to an increasing extent becomes merely a branch of industry and is completely dominated by capital. ... Capital is the economic power that dominates everything in bourgeois society. It must form both the point of departure and the conclusion, and must be analysed before landed property. After each has been considered separately, their interconnection must be examined.
>
> 1857, p. 44

In fact, the logical order of the categories is the *reverse* of their sequence in history:

> It would therefore be inexpedient and wrong to present the economic categories successively in the order in which they played the determining role in history. Their order of succession is determined rather by their mutual relation in modern bourgeois society, and this is quite the *reverse* of what appears to be their natural relation or corresponds to the sequence of historical development. The point at issue is not the place the economic relations took relative to each other in the succession of various forms of society in the course of history; even less is it their sequence 'in the Idea' ..., but their position within modern bourgeois society.
>
> 1857, p. 44

Both Marx and Hegel recognised that the 'real subject' outside the head of the theorist produces the material in which the theorist aims to determine what is rational, that is to say, historically necessary. Marx differed from Hegel, however, in strictly adhering to Hegel's advice that the "Owl of Minerva takes its flight only when the shades of night are gathering," whereas Hegel frequently overestimated the capacity of dialectical logic to trace the progression of the rational in advance of the social process itself. Marx consistently maintained the empirical moment in his dialectical analysis and reconstruction.

1.3   Logic and Development for Vygotsky

Another thinker who applied these principles for the combination of logical and temporal development is Lev Vygotsky (1934). Vygotsky's best-known work is his study of the intellect. He took intellect to be the capacity for 'symbolic thinking', or typically 'thinking in word-meanings', and as a psychologist he had the benefit that, unlike the social theorist, he could study the development of the intellect repeatedly under different conditions, over a relatively short span of time, in children. Analysing the development of speech and thinking in young children:

1. As we found in our analysis of the phylogenetic development of thinking and speech, we find that these two processes have different roots in ontogenesis.
2. Just as we can identify a 'pre-speech' stage in the development of the child's thinking, we can identify a 'pre-intellectual stage' in the development of his speech.
3. Up to a certain point, speech and thinking develop along different lines and independently of one another.
4. At a certain point, the two lines cross: thinking becomes verbal and speech intellectual.

   1934, p. 112

Subsequently speech becomes self-directed, predicative, silent, transformed and internalised in the form of the mature intellect. However, for Vygotsky, the intellect properly so-called emerges embryonically only with the use of meaningful words, that is, when the verbal and cognitive lines of development intersect, not before. Consequently, Vygotsky chose as his 'unit of analysis' for the study of the intellect the *meaningful word*, despite the fact that both thinking and speech pre-dated the formation of the first meaningful word. This is the same insight that we referred to in connection with Hegel on the state and Marx on capital.

Vygotsky also advocated for the study of his subject matter 'historically', that is in the development of the person from infancy to old age:

> ... historical study simply means applying categories of development to the study of phenomena. To study something historically means to study it in motion. Precisely this is the basic requirement of the dialectical method. To encompass in research the process of development of some

thing in all its phases and changes – from the moment of its appearance to its death – means to reveal its nature, to know its essence, for only in movement does the body exhibit what it is. Thus, historical study of behaviour is not supplementary or auxiliary to theoretical study, but is a basis of the latter.

1932, pp. 42–43

Development and not personality as such is to be the subject matter at hand. But 'historical study', 'applying categories of development', studying individuals 'in motion' and 'in movement', meant identifying the movement and the motor forces driving development at a given *moment*, not normative patterns of development over time. This obviously presupposes the study of episodes of development in order to identify their dynamics. The 'laws of development' Vygotsky derived were all directed at shedding light on moments of development, not idealised life cycles or patterns of development. He gave us a series of units of analysis (social situation of development, *perezhivanie*, defect/compensation) each of which captures a 'moment' of contradictory unities of the person with their social situation. None of these include a dimension of time or are 'covering laws' ('after this always comes that') but rather express a contradiction in the relationship of the person to their social environment.

The formation of that contradiction and its later playing out will mark a entire period of development, a history, but the aim is not to predict that path of development, which is after all determined in large measure by the social and cultural environment, but to identify the contradiction which is the motivation, the meaning of the whole development.

1.4 Logic and History for Foucault

Outside of the Marxist and Hegelian tradition there are other critics of structuralism who aim to combine logical and historical critique in the analysis of social formations. One such is Michel Foucault. Specifically, I have in mind Foucault's concept of 'genealogy' as exhibited in his well-known works such as *Discipline and Punish* (1975). Foucault viewed the world he found around him as an impersonal omnipresent apparatus of social control, seeing every aspect of society as oriented to the monitoring and control of individuals.

To theorise this claim, Foucault looked back to the mid-18th century founding of the prison system and professional soldiering as a systematic enterprise of social control and set out to demonstrate that this system had engulfed the entirety of social life. Self-evidently, this analysis led Foucault to radically different conclusions than those of Marx. Where Marx saw a society whose wealth "presents itself as 'an immense accumulation of commodities'," Foucault saw a immense apparatus of social control. On what basis could it be argued that Marx was right and Foucault was wrong? Is it merely a question of different analytical lenses? In what sense have Marx or Foucault *proved* their claim?

Each writer had an insight into the essential nature of the present reality and identified the starting point in history of this essential relation. Marx found that capital had its beginning from primitive accumulation – basically large-scale theft – but found that capital reproduces itself *not* by theft but by exchanging commodities at their value – a fair day's pay for a fair day's work. The real meaning of capital belied its historical beginnings. But I believe that Foucault's starting point was selected subjectively and arbitrarily, as a kind of original sin, a 'Just So' story, intended to 'explain' the existing state of affairs. It is implausible that modern society grew out of the prison system and is typified by it. Marx on the other had correctly implemented the approach of 'concrete historicism' which I shall now outline.

2   Concrete Historicism

'Concrete historicism' is a term coined by the Soviet Marxist-Hegelian, Evald Ilyenkov, for a paradigm of social analysis which uses a particular combination of logical and historical analysis. It involves a movement back and forth between a detailed analysis of the existing social formation which is the object of study and an historical search conducted in the light of what is evident in the present situation, on the hypothesis that relations can be found in the past which may be embryonic forms of what is manifested in mature form in the current formation. But not every form of practice found in past formations is the germ of something in the present, far less the germ of the dominant relation in the present. Where this does prove to be the case, however, a great deal of light is shed upon the existing formation by tracing the evolution of a specific form of practice, having particular regard to the *conditions under which it emerged*, and its place in the wider, changing social formation. That is, to make a *logical-historical reconstruction* of the specific practice.

In analysing the present situation, one has the advantage of personal experience of both events and sources. However, knowledge of the state of the world at some moment in the past is possible only through the critical assimilation of information from sources, information which is not simply 'data' but is saturated with theory, theory which itself reflects the forms of practice dominant at the time, theory through which data has been processed and conceptualised. Given that the object is a form of human practice rather than simply a natural phenomenon, the lens is as much part of the object as the data itself.

The object of interest is forms of human practice and such forms are implicated in the concepts by means of which the practices are both organised and described. This is crucial for historical investigations in which the object itself is accessible only through the reports of contemporary participants and their theoretical reflections. One must study the records of the past not only critically in their capacity as reports, but particularly as a *part of the object itself*. The theoretical lenses through which the data of the past are transmitted are not a *barrier* standing between subject and object, but rather the *form of appearance* of the data itself.

The object of this historical research is to determine the historically earliest realisation of the logically simplest form of a social practice. This embryo and the conditions under which it was conceived may prove to be key to understanding the present configuration and its inner contradictions. The recognition of this prius is complicated by the fact that it must be distinguished from any precursors by its key place within the whole social formation of the time.

I will briefly cite four examples: the commodity exchange, the capitalist firm, the meaningful word and the collective decision. Each practice is grasped as a 'concrete individuality', that is, as a simple act which is the unity of two distinct concepts.

1. *Value*: Marx (1867, ch. 1, §3) traced the concept of value schematically from ancient times up his own time, and in MECW vols. 31–33, examined the political economists as the theoretical voice of bourgeois society. He identified (1881, p. 544) the exchange of commodities as the simplest social form of value and schematically (1867, pp. 57–80) traced the evolution of the form of value from ancient times, predating money, up to modern capitalism, showing that it was only with modern capitalism that commodity production became the predominant and characteristic form of social interaction. Through conceptual analysis of the exchange of commodities he showed that the commodity was the unity of exchange value and use-value, two contradictory concepts of value.

2. *The capitalist firm*: Marx went on to trace the history of *capital* in the same way, its simplest social form being a *firm* which purchases products of labour to sell for a profit (M–C–M'), but again showed that this form of social practice was marginal until modern times when it became the dominant form of association. His analysis of capital accumulation showed that the rate of profit enjoyed by an individual firm was in contradiction with the rate of surplus value on which the expansion of social capital was based.

3. *Intellect*: Vygotsky (1934) traced the origin of meaningful speech in ontogenesis and found that speech predated intelligent speech and

intelligence predated speech, but intellect properly so-called had its beginning only when the two lines of development intersected in the use of word meanings. Word meanings were a unity of speech and thinking, of sound and meaning, of generalisation and social interaction, of thinking and communicating. These contradictions, rooted in the relation between the individual and the community, all drive the development of the intellect.

4. *Political life*: This author's (see Chapter 18, this volume) study of origins of collective decision making was based on the thesis that the simplest unit of politics is a group of people making a binding collective decision. It was found that the earliest forms of collective decision making, Counsel, predated voting and was a specific form of decision making still found within families, firms and other hierarchical institutions. Majority voting only emerged with the formation of voluntary associations with an ethos of equality and mutual aid. Consensus voting in its modern form originated in the 1960s when an ethos of inclusion and individual autonomy arose alongside the notions of equality and solidarity which had underpinned decision-making by majority voting. A collective decision is constituted by the unity of the individual will and the universal (collective) will, and is therefore primarily an ethical, not a cognitive or psychological problem. This contradiction generates the development of political life and the changing position of the individual in political life.

2.1 Units of Analysis

It was Lev Vygotsky (1934) who introduced the concept of 'unit of analysis' for this germ cell which is the embryonic form of a social practice. The unit is the same as the germ cell, but the concept of 'unit' indicates that the whole social formation which is characterised by the germ cell or unit is an aggregate of many such units. Bourgeois society is just a mass of commodity exchanges, a market in other words; the intellect is thinking in words and symbols; politics is people making collective decisions which are binding on one another.

The value of identifying the unit, as the simplest social form of practice of which a whole formation is composed, is three-fold. Firstly, it allows both writer and reader to understand the concept *viscerally*, connecting it with their personal experience and grasping the concept as something concrete and meaningful. Secondly, it marks the point in the history of the social formation at which it truly exists, marking it off from its precursors. Thirdly, it allows the thinker to distinguish what is essential in the social formation which constitutes it as an integral whole from what is transitory and contingent.

A conception which cannot be linked to a unit or germ cell is 'just an abstraction', grouping together diverse entities arbitrarily or subjectively.

I will now look more closely at what Hegel, Marx and Vygotsky have told us about how to identify this germ cell or unit of analysis.

2.2 The Germ Cell

Marx (1867) referred to the prius of his analysis of capital as the "economic germ-cell" of bourgeois society, Vygotsky identified "units of analysis" in five different fields of psychology (see Chapter 2, this volume), and in my work (2016) on politics I determined the germ cell or unit as a collective decision. It is not immediately obvious how this prius is determined, but it is the key to the dialectical reconstruction of the whole, the key to the comprehension of the whole phenomenon.

Students of Vygotsky's psychology have struggled to more clearly describe *how* the germ cell or unit of a process is determined and lacking the depth of Ilyenkov's Hegel scholarship there has been a lot of confusion. Nonetheless, in this current the idea of unit of analysis has been creatively applied in the determination of a 'germ cell' as the starting point of an *intervention*, a *practical* reconstruction of the whole formation.

I have outlined elsewhere (2018) the origins of the idea of 'germ cell' in Goethe's idea of *Urphänomen* and its reflection in Hegel's idea of the abstract concept. I will confine myself here to what Hegel has to tell us about *das Erste* or 'prius', the 'germ cell' which is the beginning point for the dialectical reconstruction of a whole. This is found in a rather little-known passage in the *Science of Logic*:

> ... the beginning [must] be made with the subject matter in the form of a universal (*Allgemeinen*). ... it is the concrete individuality (*die konkrete Einzelheit*) that is given to subjective, natural cognition as the prius (*das Erste*); but in cognition that is a comprehension, at least to the extent that it has the form of the Concept for basis, the prius must be on the contrary something simple (*das Einfache*), something abstracted from the concrete, because in this form alone has the subject-matter the form of the self-related universal or of an immediate based on the Concept.
>
> HEGEL, 1816/1969, p. 801, S. 779

See Chapter 2, this volume for a more detailed explanation of the concept of germ cell and unit. A few points can be mentioned here, however.

Hegel illustrated the method of dialectical reconstruction throughout the *Encyclopaedia*, but offered little clue about how the prius which makes the beginning of each 'circle' is to be identified other than that it arises *outside* of the specific science of which it is the beginning and "is given to subjective, natural cognition," and that it is a "concrete" "simple something" which is "universal." When Hegel says 'concrete' as in "concrete individuality," he means the identity of two distinct (contradictory) concepts, which thereby carry within them the potential for the development of contradiction.

The *Encyclopaedia* gives the *impression* of a logical derivation of the entire circle of circles, but in fact Hegel has to agree with Marx that the source of these *aperçus* (to use Goethe's word) lies outside the head:

> The totality as a conceptual totality seen by the mind is a product of a thinking mind, which assimilates the world in the only way open to it ... The real subject remains outside the mind and independent of it ... Hence the subject, society, must always be envisaged as the premise of conception.
>
> MARX, 1858, pp. 38–39

That is, the starting point for each circle of dialectical reconstruction comes not from subjective reflection but from the social process itself and is acquired by the theorist by means of critical examination of, and insight into the conceptual material produced by the social process itself, a 'thinking over' (*Nachdenken*) of the thought of the times.

According to Ilyenkov:

> The difficulty lies in singling out from the empirically given picture of the total historical process the cardinal points of the development of this particular concrete object, of the given, concrete system of interaction. Logical development coinciding with the historical process of the formation of a concrete whole should rigorously establish its historical beginning, its birth, and later trace its evolution as a sequence of necessary and law-governed moments. That is the whole difficulty.
>
> 1960, p. 216

There is no formula for determining this 'something simple', that discrete social act which is at the same time *universal*. What is clear though is that the researcher sees in the prius a simple expression of what is universal in the mature formation with which they are acquainted firsthand. So this cognitive act requires a movement *back and forth* between analysis of the present situation, attempting to characterise the formation as a whole, and searching the historical record to discover the circumstances of the emergence of this simple relation which expresses the universal in a nutshell, and tracing it forward as it changes in interaction with the larger social formation.

What is the basis for the practice? What were the conditions which first made it possible for the practice to appear and then *reproduce* the conditions for its own existence? Until you find these conditions, you have to keep looking deeper.

Primary accumulation (as in the Enclosures, or in the plunder of state property after the fall of the USSR) was *not*, as such, a practice which could reproduce itself. It was a by-product of this robbery – the denial of a whole class of people to access to means of production, freeing them from their traditional ties and forcing them to sell their labour power on the market – which made capital possible as a self-sustaining practice. Historically speaking, capitalism originated in aristocratic robbery, but the Enclosures merely set up conditions for exploitation of a class of people denied access to the means of production. This really existing contradiction emerged slightly *after* the Enclosures but did not rely on the Enclosures for its successive reproduction.

It was not aristocratic violence which made it possible for a state to take root in a nation, but rather its introduction of enforceable law into the day-to-day life of the community. Law without the means of enforcement is not a state, but aristocratic violence was not enough in itself to create a true state, which also presupposes the moral development of the citizenry.

Neither intelligence nor speech are sufficient conditions for the emergence of the intellect properly so called; the embryo was formed by the *intersection* of the emergent intellect with the pervading form of speech.

It was not the coincidence of individual and collective will which made political life possible, but rather the normalisation of practices in which strangers with diverse wills make binding collective decisions.

3   Conclusion

I have outlined above an approach to the analysis of social formations, such as specific states, institutions or movements, which entails investigating both the inner *structure* or logic of the social formation, and the *history* from which it inherits its customs and laws. It entails a movement *back and forth* between reflection on the existing state or affairs and analysis of the past history of the situation.

The aim is to be able to characterise the social formation as a whole by means of a simple praxis or relation such that the 'organism' can be understood as the *proliferation* and *concretisation* of its germ cell and its development into an entire *self-sustaining* social formation. Discovery of this cell involves an historical investigation, especially the history of the self-expression of the social formation itself which expresses not just facts, but the concepts through which these facts were grasped, the same concepts by means of which the participants had explained to themselves why they did what they did.

If carried out successfully, such an analysis should be able to identify the contradiction which lies at the heart of the germ cell or unit, the contradiction which has driven the development of the practice and which, if correctly identified, may bring about the rise and fall of the regime in question, thus providing guidance for intervention.

CHAPTER 4

Perezhivanie as Human Self-Creation

1   Introduction

Perezhivanie is a complex concept and its translation from Russian into English as 'experience' fails to capture the core content of the concept, let alone the range of connotations entailed in it for the native Russian speaker. Hitherto, only one English translation of Vygotsky's works contained any indication at all of the meaning of the word. *The Problem of the Environment* (1934a) is the text of a lecture on pedology, the previous lecture being *The Problem of Heredity*. The point of the article was to set out a foundation for analysing the role of a child's social environment in the formation of the person's personality, as opposed to the part played by their genetic inheritance.

Although *perezhivanie* also figures in other works, such as the early *Psychology of Art*, the English translations make Vygotsky's use of *perezhivanie* invisible. Vygotsky was not inventing an entirely new concept, however. The concept of *perezhivanie* had a firm place in Russian literature and culture generally, but its place in a scientific theory of psychology is another matter. However, over and above its origins in Russian culture and history, its meaning within Vygotsky's theory is by no means easily grasped *whatever* your native tongue, as the concept is inevitably modified by its being subject to a Marxist interpretation and incorporated into a scientific theory.

2   No Mystery

Perezhivanie is not a complete mystery to English-speakers, however. To the extent that the relevant phenomena are manifest within the British and American cultures, they are known to English speakers, and the psychological implications have been examined by English and German-speaking psychologists with whom English speakers will be familiar, and many of the relevant concepts have entered popular consciousness. The recognition of points of commonality between the English-speaking and Russian traditions have been obscured, however, by the difficulties encountered, not just by English speakers in reading Russian, but also by Russians in trying to explain the concept in English, and the difficulty in grasping Marxist/Hegelian concepts, especially the concept of 'unity'.

The first thing to know about *perezhivanie* is that it is a *countable* noun (like 'tool' or 'cup') not a mass noun (like 'equipment' or 'water'). So, when we use *perezhivanie* as a word in the English language it must carry an article (i.e., 'the' or 'a') or be used in the plural, *perezhivaniya*, or with an appropriate pronoun like 'every'.

The countable/mass distinction is available in all languages, but it is indicated in different ways. In English it is the use or absence of articles, but Russian does not use articles, and it is difficult for speakers of languages, such as Russian or Farsi, which do not have articles, to figure out how to use them when speaking English. So, it is quite common for a Russian speaker to explain *perezhivanie* by saying something like: "*Perezhivanie* is unit of personality." The English-speaking listener knows that 'unit' is a countable noun, and if they were to repeat this expression they would probably say: "*Perezhivanie* is a unit of the personality." Being unfamiliar with Russian, they do not realise that '*perezhivanie*' is, like 'unit', also a countable noun. Yet only countable nouns can be units of anything! So, an English speaker who says "*Perezhivanie* is a unit of personality," and goes on to discuss *perezhivaniya* without ever using the plural or an article, is suggesting that they do not understand the meaning of the word 'unit'. For example: "Tool is unit of equipment" is broken English, but "Equipment is a unit of property" is an oxymoron. Even though few native English speakers are aware of the countable/mass distinction, we all use it without conscious awareness. 'Tool' and 'cup' are countable, so we say something like: "Tools are units of equipment," and "The unit of water is a cup," but "Equipment is an *element* of property," not a unit.

We have the same situation with 'activity'. 'Activity' (without the article) is a mass noun, but we use the same word as a countable noun for the units of activity. So: "Activity is made up of many activities" is a grammatical and coherent sentence. But for a Russian speaker: "Activity is the unit of activity," and alas English speakers have often been content to emulate this incoherent oxymoronic English.

So it has come to pass that English speakers have both accepted '*perezhivanie*' as a mass noun (never having heard anyone use it in the plural or with an article), *and* deprived the word 'unit' of its meaning. This suggests that when people read Vygotsky on 'unit of analysis' they interpret 'unit' to be something other than what they know it to mean, perhaps just the 'subject matter'. Consequently, the claim that "*perezhivaniya* are units of the personality" is still completely mystified. Since *perezhivanie* is a scientific concept by virtue of its inclusion in a scientific theory, this mistake obscures Vygotsky's scientific concept of *perezhivanie* as well as his concept of unit.

Perezhivaniya have a beginning, a middle and an end. They are events, episodes, activities, tragedies or experiences, chapters in a person's life in which the subject is an active participant.

The typical English translation of *'perezhivanie'* is 'experience', sometimes carrying the qualifiers: 'emotional experience' or 'lived experience', or the neolog 'experiencing'. The word 'experience', whether or not qualified as 'emotional' or 'lived', when used without an article, is a mass noun. 'Experience' is that passive background of activity which is the fundamental concept of *Empiricism* – the historically dominant current in Anglo-American analytical science, referring to an accumulated mass of knowledge and ability. When *perezhivanie* is interpreted as 'experience' and taken to be the fundamental factor in the formation of personality and knowledge for Vygotsky, then this is in effect to assimilate Vygotsky's Marxist Psychology into Anglo-American Empiricism and Behaviourism. On the contrary, Vygotsky takes personality and knowledge to be something *actively constructed* by the subject.

In Russian, there is a word for 'experience' in the sense it is used in Empiricism – 'experience' as in the opening words of Kant's (1787) *Critique of Pure Reason*: "There can be no doubt that all our knowledge begins with experience" – and the sense in which 'experience' is used, for example, when an employer asks for your 'work experience'. That word is *opit*. *Perezhivanie* is different from *opit* – Russian has two different words for the two concepts. It was only with Vygotsky, however, that the distinction was given a clear, scientific basis.

3   An Experience

The idea of 'an experience' was outlined by John Dewey in his article "Having an Experience" (1939) in perfectly clear English prose which any English-speaker could understand.

Dewey explained the 'double-barrelled' nature of the concept of 'an experience' in that "it includes *what* men do and suffer, *what* they strive for, love, believe and endure, and *how* men act and are acted upon, the ways in which they do and suffer, desire and enjoy, see, believe, imagine" (1929, p. 256). That is, experiences are not just things that happen to you, but how you *respond* to them. Experiences are countable: "each with its own plot, its own inception and movement toward its close, each having its own particular rhythmic movement" (1939, p. 555). He explained that 'an experience' was an 'original unity', not a combination: "The existence of this unity is constituted by a single *quality* that pervades the entire experience in spite of the variation of its constituent parts. This unity is neither emotional, practical, nor intellectual, for these terms name distinctions that reflection can make within it" (1939, p. 556), demonstrating that the American Pragmatist understood Marxism better than many a self-proclaimed Marxist. We do not get *perezhivanie* by adding intellect and emotion together – intellect and emotion are abstractions we make from experiences. And he understood that experiences have their origin in the resolution of problems or crises, or what I have called 'predicaments': "The unsettled or indeterminate situation might have been called a *problematic* situation. ... Without a problem, there is blind groping in the dark" (1938, p. 229). All these are facets of *perezhivaniya*.

Dewey's concept of 'an experience' goes only halfway to covering the concept Russians have of *perezhivanie*, however but it is the best approximation we have in *a single word*, within the English language and Anglo-American culture.

Freud (1914) was familiar with *perezhivanie*, too, and his psychoanalysis aimed to assist patients in "remembering, repeating and working through" past experiences, supposedly concerned with childhood sexuality. The British child psychoanalyst, Donald Winnicott's (1971) work on weaning, that is, the successful parting of mother and child, was also concerned with *perezhivanie*. Swiss psychiatrist Elisabeth Kübler-Ross, whose work (1969) on dying is well known in the Anglosphere, was also dealing with how *perezhivaniya* play out in time.

4 Etymology

A look at the etymology of *perezhivanie* gives us a glimpse of why 'an experience' fails to capture the concept of *perezhivanie* (see Robbins, 2007).

Perezhivanie comes from the verb *perezhivat*. *Zhivat* means 'to live' and *pere* means carrying something over something, letting something pass beneath and overleaping it. So *pere-zhivat* means to be able to sur-vive after some disaster, i.e., to 'live over' something. To illustrate the force of *pere*: *terpet* means to endure some pain, so *pere-terpet* means to outlive some pain; *pereprignut* means to overcome some obstacle, to jump or fly over it.

In the same way, *perezhivat* means that you have passed as if above something that had made you feel pain; and in the base of each 'again living' lies a pain and you know that. There, inside of a recollection that we call an 'again living' – lives your pain, not letting you forget what has happened, and you keep living through it over and over again, working through it, repeating it until you have passed through it, and have survived. Most of the above words are quoted from an email message from Dot Robbins (2007), who goes on to remark that *perezhivanie* "really captures the 'Russian soul'."

But it is also important that there can be positive as well as painful *perezhivaniya* (Kotik-Friedgut, 2007), that *perezhivanie* is not only surviving a life-changing disaster, but also achieving and consolidating on a dramatic leap forward in your life, a daring move, a risk that paid off and opened a new phase of your life.

Fully developed *perezhivaniya* are tied up with the discovery and fate of one's life-projects and are life-changing episodes in your life, and they begin in a moment of especial clarity, as depicted in the movies *An Education* (2009) and *Brief Encounter* (1945), when confronted with the danger of the moment and the formation of the resolution to overcome it.

5 Catharsis

Having had an experience and surviving it is no guarantee that there will be any impact on your psychology, or any personal development made from it. The experience has to be '*processed*' in some way. *Perezhivaniya* differ from experiences in that a *perezhivanie includes* the processing of an experience, working over and assimilating it into your personality and your relationship to the rest of the world. As such, a *perezhivanie* may continue for years after a catastrophic experience, such as the death of a loved one. *Perezhivaniya* may also constitute experiences which extend over many years, such as a period in prison or exile or a childhood with an alcoholic parent, provided only that the experience and the working over has a certain unifying quality, that it comprises a coherent and memorable episode in your life.

So it is evident why we cannot find a single word in the English language to translate *perezhivanie*: a *perezhivanie* is *both* an experience (in the sense in which Dewey explained) *and* the 'working over' of it.

This process of working over is known as 'catharsis'. In its original meaning in ancient Greece, catharsis was the experience of an audience who, while watching a tragedy at the theatre, externalised their emotions by empathising with the performers who were acting it out for them on stage. This was deemed to have a healthy effect, 'purging' oneself of the emotion. Later, the early medical profession used 'catharsis' to refer to the use of a purgative which would induce catharsis, namely a vomiting out of the material causing the illness. Freud (1914) gave catharsis a psychoanalytic meaning, referring to a patient remembering and repeating an emotional experience through a therapist (playing the role of the actor on the ancient Greek stage), and working through the experience aloud, overcoming and 'surviving' (to use the Russian idea), 'transcending' it or 'sublating' it to use the Hegelian term. So this process of working through is well known to English speakers, but we do not have a single word which encompasses *both* the traumatic experience *and* the catharsis as a unity. It appears to be an integral part of 'processing' an experience, to be able to 'externalise' it and reflect on it, as if observing it from outside. This is why the assistance of another person is often necessary, sometimes just someone telling you what you have just done.

So we should not attempt to translate *perezhivanie* – *perezhivanie* is a uniquely Russian concept, though one which is accessible to English speakers provided that it is explained. We need to assimilate *perezhivanie* as a word in the English language, using it in our research and writing and thereby building up a concept of *perezhivanie* within English language scientific literature – not identical with the word as it is within *Russian* culture and literature. We need *our* concept of *perezhivanie* – based on the understanding that *perezhivanie* means the *whole process* of a potentially life-changing experience *inclusive of* the working over of that experience in a 'catharsis'.

As an activity which is drawn out in time, a *perezhivanie* typically passes through stages. In a chapter on grief in his *Psychology of Experiencing* (1984, pp. 221–234), Fedor Vasilyuk has outlined a series of stages of *perezhivanie* (which for Vasilyuk meant 'impossible situations' and not the potentially positive experiences): (1) shock and stupefaction, fury; (2) searching; (3) despair and suffering; (3) residual shocks and re-organisation; (5) completion. In each of these phases, a different activity leads the development and transformation into a new situation.

Elisabeth Kübler-Ross (1969) studied the stages through which a person passes when undergoing an uncontrollable change in their life circumstances, particularly the death of a loved one or one's own terminal illness: (1) denial, (2) anger, (3) bargaining, (4) depression and (5) acceptance. Kübler-Ross's work is essentially a study of one particular type of *perezhivanie*: grieving. For Kübler-Ross, grieving is not simply an emotion, but an *activity* one carries out, together with others, in response to a crisis coming from the world outside your control – *work*ing through the meaning of this loss and reorienting your life projects now without the active presence of the loved one. Some contemporary psychologists extend Kübler-Ross's work to understand other life-changing experiences, though in my view usually unsuccessfully, because it is wrongly taken for granted that the relevant circumstances are always beyond the subject's control. This makes sense when it is used by managers to implement organisational change, for example – the subject is not expected to play an active role in determining the course of the change.

Vasilyuk (1988, see Chapter 10, this volume) used the word '*perezhivanie*' specifically to mean the process of *working over* an 'impossible situation'. In his opinion, to successfully complete a *perezhivanie* requires the aid of another person, be that a therapist, a parent or an actor. Freud also believed that everyone needed a psychoanalyst. Whether Freud and Vasilyuk are right or not, it seems that the aid of another person who is capable of objectifying and reflecting back the feelings of the person going through a *perezhivanie*, guiding them and making use of the resources of the culture to assist them in finding an accommodation with their new situation, is normally needed. What is definitely required is that others around the subject *respond* to the change which has taken place in the subject and reorient themselves accordingly.

It has been rightly pointed out (Clarà, 2016) that Vasilyuk was probably unaware of Vygotsky's use of the term when he used it in 1984, and this accounts for the differences in their meaning. Nonetheless, both Russians drew from the same well of Russian culture and psychology. And Veresov and Fleer (2016) were also right in pointing out that Vygotsky used the term in his early work in a sense which was conventional within Russian psychology and which was much more consistent with the everyday usage which fails to emphasise what Dewey called the 'double-barrelled' nature of an experience.

6   Personality

What does this expansive concept of *perezhivanie* mean for the development of the personality (*lichnost*), which is the subject Vygotsky is addressing in "The Problem of the Environment"? How does it help a person answer the question: who am I?

If you were to write a biography of a person, you would have to connect together the *perezhivaniya* of their life and demonstrate to the reader how the person came to be who they are through the experiences they had and how they overcame them. And as a biographer you would be unlikely to view the series of life-crises, the experiencing and overcoming of which made the person who they were, to be simply events that *happened to* the person. As John Dewey notes, these experiences arise in the course of a person's active effort to overcome some problem.

Perezhivaniya are tied up with one's orientation or commitment to various life-projects, and it is in the fate of these projects that psychological challenges arise. As Vasilyuk outlines, they could be value conflicts (like family/work commitments, or the betrayal of your values by respected leaders), or real clashes between two valued projects (like when your parents go through an acrimonious divorce), blockages (like being disgraced in your career or losing your job), or simply the inability to formulate a life project.

These considerations could be summed up by saying that *perezhivaniya* are units of the personality or units of the formation of the personality, *which is the same thing*. The personality is both the product and the producer of life's *perezhivaniya*.

According to I.A. Meshcheryakova (n.d.), A.N. Leontyev remarked that *perezhivaniya* are "manifested as internal signals, by means of which are realised the personal sense of an event" and S.L. Rubenstein claimed: "*Perezhivaniya* become for the person that which proves to be personally significant for them." *Perezhivaniya* are the units of life, the chapters of one's autobiography, the episodes which stand out in the memory from the background of one's life, and, having been worked over by you and told and retold (to yourself or others), and 'coded' in language and images, become meaningful indicators of your character. Together, *perezhivaniya* form the basis of who you are: not just what *happened* to you, but what you *did*, what you *made of* your life, in the context of the life-projects to which you were committed and which made the event life-changing and emotion-charged, how you worked over them and gave them meaning.

This is the sense in which Vygotsky said that *perezhivaniya* are units of a consciousness, or more correctly, units of the personality as a whole.

7 Continuity and Discontinuity

It can be seen that from this standpoint that personal development is made up of an alternation between periods of gradual development and periods of crisis. This could be characterised as an alternation between continuity and discontinuity. During the period of continuity, personal development is constituted by gradual adaptation of the personality to its life situation – the enhancement of skills and knowledge, expansion and improvements of relationships, etc. This continues until some crisis arises in the relation of the person to their environment. If development is to continue, then rather than simply adapting themselves to the new situation, the person must change the situation, and overthrow the existing relations in which they have hitherto lived.

Thus the process is better expressed as an alternation between periods of adaption of the person to an existing situation and (generally briefer, more traumatic) periods during which the situation itself is overthrown.

At the same time, the question is raised: how is 'gradual development' possible? Does this idea imply that the person is developing 24/7, even while asleep?

If such were the case, the very meaning of 'development' would be called into question. In fact, even 'gradual development' is constituted by steps or tiny leaps, but they are steps in which aspects of the environment are appropriated, small steps of adaptation of the person to the environment. Conversely, as we have seen, the discontinuities in development are not instantaneous, but essentially entail a more or less rapid change in (relation to) the environment followed by a period of reorientation in which both the person and their social environment adapt to the new situation.

In this sense, *perezhivanie* can be seen as a unity of both phases of development, both continuous and discontinuous.

8   Unity

Misunderstanding may arise not from only translation, but from unfamiliarity with Marxist and Hegelian ideas, and in particular, the concept of *unity*. The issue of the meaning of unity arises in two aspects of the concept of *perezhivanie*. The first is in the part of *The Problem of the Environment* where Vygotsky says (in a passage which Vygotsky italicised):

> So, in a *perezhivanie* we are always dealing with an indivisible unity of personal characteristics and situational characteristics, which are represented in the *perezhivanie*.
>
> 1934a, p. 342

By "unity of personal characteristics and situational characteristics," Vygotsky obviously meant the situation, the *relation between* the personal and the circumstantial, not the person *plus* the circumstances, the person *plus* the entire world political economy which might impact on a person's life. In Set Theoretical terms, the unity more is like the intersection, not the union, those aspects or features which are both personal *and* environmental. For example, depending on the place of a job in a person's life project, the loss of a job has a different significance. If a young backpacker loses their job, it is not the same as it is for someone's whose job is their career. Vygotsky meant that the *perezhivanie* is both subjective and objective; it is 'double-barrelled', a very specific *correlation* between the development of the personality and affairs in the wider world which could *in themselves* be irrelevant to the subject's psychology and unknown to them. A person could lose their job because of a tyrannical boss or because of changes in technology making their skill redundant, and each has a different implication for how they respond. The oldest son in Vygotsky's well-known case study, overcomes the problem of an alcoholic mother by *transforming the objective situation* by stepping into the role of being the 'senior man' of the house, and then adapting to the new role he had created for himself.

Vygotsky saw *perezhivaniya* as *units* of the changing relation between the person and their environment, the series of situations, brought about through the subject's own activity as opposed to what the subject inherited in their genes. Vygotsky puts this view forward in opposition to the idea of a series of environmental *factors* – social status of parents, locality, number of siblings, etc. – as determining development. The environment presents the child with a whole *situation*, and their development depends on how the child responds to that situation.

There is a second respect in which *perezhivaniya* are said to be a unity; many writers note that *perezhivaniya* are "a unity of affect and intellect." As Dewey explained above, a person's activity, that is, their experiences, are each a *whole*, an *original* unity. Perezhivanie is not a *combination* of intellect and affect. On the contrary, it is only by reflection that we, as observers, can *abstract from* experiences the various psychological functions for the purpose of our analysis. We need not stop at intellect and affect. We could also list attention, will, memory, and any other psychological function we care to name. In the first place (except perhaps in infancy when some psychological functions still subsist in a specific biological substrate), there is just the activity of the person as whole, not emotion and intellect, but a whole person. Experiences are a *whole*. From this, we can abstract the separate functions. Further, it is through the traumatic processes entailed in *perezhivanie* that the various aspects of a subject – the various psychological functions, the different relationships in a person's life, their various commitments – are re-ordered and reconstituted in a new whole.

I can illustrate the idea of 'unity' in the following example. Dough is made by adding water and flour, dough is a *mixture* of flour and water, but not a *unity* of flour and water. Milk is a unity of curds and whey however, because curds and whey exist only as products extracted from milk, which comes whole from the cow. No one adds curds and whey without first having separated them.

So when we say that *perezhivaniya* are a 'unity' of emotion and intellect and ..., we mean that *perezhivaniya* are *wholes* from which various psychological functions can be abstracted. So a person's intellect develops, along with their emotions and their will, etc., as aspects of their whole personality, through the *perezhivaniya* of their life.

9 Lived Experiences

'Lived experience' differs from 'experience' in that rather than insisting on the correlation between situational features and personal features, it focuses exclusively on the subjective meaning or interpretation by the subject themself. The concept of 'lived experience' has gained prominence in the professions of social work and counselling, emphasising the *perception of the subject*, irrespective of what may have happened objectively, or at least in the eyes of the rest of the world. So for example, for a person who thought they were doing their job well and was devastated when they were sacked, 'lived experience' has a strong sense of how it feels *to that person*, what the sacking meant for them. That is what the therapist has to deal with. But is this solely a problem for a therapist, rather than a union delegate, employment agency or training college? Perhaps the subject really *was* inadequate in the role and recovery entails acceptance of that fact, but perhaps on the contrary, the boss is a tyrant who needs to be brought before a court for his actions. Or perhaps the subject needs to reskill for a profession in a service industry? The eldest boy in Vygotsky's scenario did not seek a therapist, he transformed his situation. *Perezhivaniya* are *both* objective *and* subjective, and success entails changing the social situation, either transforming the object, transforming the subject, or transforming the relation between the subject and the object.

Perezhivanie is probably the most important concept in general psychology because it is a unit of development of the person *as a whole*, and all the other aspects of their personality must be grasped as arising from these *perezhivaniya* which have contributed to the self-formation of the whole person. But also, it is precisely through *perezhivaniya* that the subject matter of psychology joins up with the great societal forces active in the world beyond the immediate circle of the person's social situation. This world is made and remade through people's life projects, the projects to which people commit themselves, invariably along with many others, and whose fate is to fashion their personality and the world they live in. *Perezhivanie* is a 'hinge' joining the social and psychological sciences.

10 Units

The idea of a unit of analysis characterised Vygotsky's whole contribution to science, and yet its only extended elaboration is in Chapter One of *Thinking and Speech*. However, the roots of *perezhivanie* as a unit of analysis may be found in Vygotsky's early interest in the theatre and in particular in the ideas of Constantin Stanislavskii (1936). Stanislavskii says that every performance must be broken down into units, each of which must have its own unique emotional content and motivation within the artistic objectives of the plot. Stanislavskii's elaboration of these 'units' reminds us of the 'living-through' and 'repeating' which we associate with *perezhivanie*. The actor must draw on their own life experiences to be able to reproduce the outward forms of *perezhivaniya* on stage and allow the audience to share them and enjoy the catharsis. Stanislavskii insists that each unit has to make sense in terms of the dramatic objective of the play as a whole. This surely suggests the idea of *perezhivaniya* as units of analysis of a really lived life.

Each *perezhivanie* can be understood in itself, in the light of the objective circumstances contributing to the situation, and the relevant life project of the person as they had become in the wake of previous *perezhivaniya*. They are units of analysis, the understanding of which provides the key to how specific changes in their personality and social position were achieved and constitute a person's *Bildungsroman* – to use Goethe's term – the story of their development as a person.

This brings us to the fact that not only the person, but their *capacity* for *perezhivanie* also develops from infancy through childhood and up to adulthood – their capacity to not only survive and accommodate to a changing world but to change the world around them and their place in it.

11 Development

In *The Problem of the Environment*, Vygotsky illustrates the idea of *perezhivanie* by the case of three siblings coping or not with their single mother who is a drunk. The infant is "overwhelmed by the horror of what is happening to him" and develops neuroses; the middle child is traumatised; and the oldest child, a teenage boy, understands that he must become 'the senior man' in the family, makes an accelerated development and takes responsibility for looking after his siblings *and* his mother. That is, it is only the adolescent who is able to master the *perezhivanie*, and even in his case, without outside assistance, his development may be damaged by the loss of childhood. In this way, Vygotsky showed how *not just* the social environment, but the significance of features of the environment *for the subject*, the subject's *capacity* to process them, the subject's action in responding to the situation and the capacity of the environment to respond to the child, make up the essential elements for understanding the development of the child.

Given that in the Anglosphere Vygotsky is mostly read by educators and child development people, rather than psychotherapists, social workers, anthropologists or social theorists, it is not surprising that *perezhivanie* has been taken up within the discipline of child development. In Russia, on the other hand, thanks to the work of Fedor Vasilyuk in psychotherapy, the concept of *perezhivanie* is widely used, but mainly in connection with adults. In fact, only adults can successfully complete the full range of psychological phenomena associated with *perezhivanie*. But as I.A. Meshcheryakova remarks (n.d.):

> According to the theory of Vygotsky, *perezhivanie* can be approached as any other mental function, which in ontogenesis is developed from the involuntary and direct forms to the highest forms, which have status of actions or activities. This approach offers possibilities for distinguishing the different genetic forms of *perezhivanie*, and also for the search for the cultural-historical means of mastery of *perezhivaniya*.

Ferholt, Nilsson and their colleagues (2016) have been able to observe *perezhivaniya* in very young children, a moment of calm in the midst of mayhem when the subject glimpses something new. In the light of the remarks above, to the effect that development is always both discreet and continuous, it is not entirely surprising that 'little *perezhivaniya*' are observed in children. Mike Cole has noted that in each case, the attention and intervention of experienced adult carers was necessary to achieve the 'reflection' required for the child to make this leap. This confirms that it is instruction which leads development, and that social interaction is always involved in the development of the higher mental functions, or as Vygotsky expressed it in the 'general genetic law of cultural development':

> every function in the cultural development of the child appears on the stage twice, in two planes, first, the social, then the psychological, first between people as an intermental category, then within the child as a intramental category.
> VYGOTSKY, 1931

A child does not have a life-project. Having a life-project is part of the very meaning of being an adult. Development during childhood is characterised by a series of 'leading activities' which are arranged for the child by responsible adults as appropriate to their degree of maturity in the given culture. It is in relation to their leading activity that *perezhivaniya* occur, not life-projects. For a child it is in the critical periods of transition between developmental stages within an appropriate social situation of development that the most fully developed *perezhivaniya* occur.

This leaves us, however, with an imposing research problem: how does *perezhivanie* develop in the course of development from childhood through adolescence to adulthood? How frequently the advice of respected adults figures in our development during our teenage years! And yet as adults, unless severe trauma is involved, we are usually able to 'process' experiences ourselves, or with the support of family, and we consult professionals only in the event of our failure to overcome a crisis.

So *perezhivaniya* figure in our development at all stages of our life, but they change in form and develop like all the higher mental functions. *Perezhivanie* develops in line with and in connection with the leading activities in a person's life situation.

12   Reflection

It seems to be a general rule that *perezhivanie* is an activity which cannot be successfully completed without the support of others, be that a parent who listens to the child's schoolyard story and helps them interpret the experience, friends who enclose the bereaved person in loving support or work colleagues who reorient their relations to a colleague who has been promoted and give them the respect due to a more senior colleague, or the psychotherapist who talks it through with their patient, helping them to re-interpret a catastrophe and find meaning and/or solutions in an impossible situation.

Freud insisted on the importance of the therapist assisting the patient to be able to confront their childhood traumas and repeat them as adults, reworking them and giving them new meaning as mature adults, fully cognisant of what was done to them.

Donald Winnicott was concerned with mothers and children who had become so dependent on one another that when the child finally detaches from physical reliance on the mother, either the mother becomes depressed and anxious or the child does, or both; or on the other hand, the mother-and-child actually fail to make that critical transition and remain codependent or experience a range of pathologies. According to Winnicott, successful weaning is essential to future development of the child's personality, as well as that of the parent.

Like Kübler-Ross's (1969) study of dying, Winnicott's study of weaning is a special case of *perezhivanie*: difficulties arising in the completion of a life-project and one's relation to others entailed in the fate of life-projects. But in fact, these crises are manifested throughout life as one passes through critical phases in the working-out of one's life projects. *Perezhivaniya* is what we call these transitions. Invariably, the resources for making such critical transitions are to be found in the culture, and often it is necessary to have the assistance of more experienced others to successfully navigate life transitions and utilise the possibilities for semiotic mediation, leading to *mastery* of the transition.

The concept of *perezhivanie* allows us to understand experiences which are not so dramatic, and what has been said above applies to those relatively minor joys and embarrassments which 'stick in our minds', still evoke an emotional response and are connected with our motivation, without becoming life-changing traumas. Following Marx's aphorism that "the anatomy of man is the key to the anatomy of the ape" (1857, p. 105), Vygotsky remarked: "I proceeded from the idea that the well-developed forms ... provide the key to the underdeveloped ones" (1928, p. 319). Understanding *perezhivaniya* as life crises allows us to better understand those less dramatic, but memorable moments in our life and to learn how to successfully navigate them.

13 Examples

To make matters clear I offer now two examples of *perezhivaniya* which I have gleaned from autobiographies. The first is that of James Lawson, the architect of Martin Luther King's non-violence strategy and founder of the SNCC (Student Nonviolent Coordinating Committee) in April 1960.

Unlike his father, Lawson's mother was decidedly nonviolent. Lawson's challenge, which was to form his character, was to reconcile his father's militancy with his mother's nonviolence. One day, at the age of ten, Lawson was asked by his mother to run an errand:

> A little white child in an automobile yelled 'nigger' out the opened window. I walked over ... and, since I was in a hurry running my mother's errand, I smacked the child and went on my way. When the Lawson kids got called 'nigger' on the streets or at school, we usually fought. I don't know where we got that from, except that we figured that it was something to fight over.
> LAWSON, cited in KING, 1999

On the return trip home, aware of possible repercussions, Lawson tried to find the parents of the offending child, to talk to them, but the car was gone. Once home, he told his mother of the incident. Lawson's mother replied, "Jimmy, what good did that do?"

> She talked about who I was, the fact of God's love, that we were a family of love and that such an incident could not hurt me, because of who I was. I don't remember anyone else being around, but a stillness took over my being at that moment. It was, as I realised much later on, a mystical experience. In a very real way, my life stood still. I realised in that stillness that I had changed forever. One of the phrases my mother used in her conversation with me was that 'there must be a better way'. I determined, from then on, that I would find the better way.
> LAWSON, cited in KING, 1999, pp. 187–188

My second example comes from Sally Rugg, the activist who led the Marriage Equality campaign on behalf of GetUp! in Australia in 2017. Sally (2019, p. 16) tells of how she was fundamentally shaped as a determined activist when she was about four years old. Her sister was pestering her for a toy and after her throwing a tantrum she gave in and let her have the toy. Her mother then swooped in and told her: "If you were going to give it to her all along, you should have given it to her at the start. If you're not going to give her the toy, you need to stick to that, Don't make your sister cry, if you're going to change her mind." Rugg tells another story (p. 15) of how her opinion about gay marriage was transformed by attending a spectacular gay wedding ceremony. Any of us who have lived through great social movements of past decades know that these experiences changed us forever, and fashion who we are.

14   Critiques

There have been critiques of Vygotsky's concept of *perezhivanie* by Soviet colleagues. Lydia Bozhovich (2009) claimed that *perezhivanie* is a unit of the social situation of development – "the child's 'affective relationship' to the environment." But the social situation of development is itself a unit of analysis for the study of child development, which Vygotsky expresses in relational terms but abstracts from the response of the child. On the other hand, the response is taken as integral to *perezhivaniya*. Secondly, Bozhovich claimed that "[Vygotsky] felt that the nature of experience in the final analysis is determined by how children understand the circumstances affecting them, that is, by *how developed their ability to generalise is*." Here Bozhovich mixes up the *actual* relation between the child and their social environment (grasped psychologically at whatever level of development the child has) with an *intellectual conception* of that relationship formed by the child. In the same article, Bozhovich makes the correct point that *perezhivanie* being a unit does not mean that it is 'indivisible' and not amenable to analysis. On the contrary, a *perezhivanie* can be analysed into its elements and its phases, just as the water molecule can be analysed into its elements. Broadly, I think, '*perezhivanie*' and 'social situation of development' are concepts which describe phases of development in the self-determined life of adults on the one hand, and in the managed life of children on the other. In that sense, they are closely related concepts, but one cannot be reduced to or subsumed under the other.

In an undated article entitled "Study of the environment in the works of L.S. Vygotsky" (2005), A.N. Leontyev quoted Vygotsky: "The situation will influence the child in different ways depending on how well the child understands its sense and meaning," which he glosses as "*perezhivanie* itself is determined by understanding, that is, by consciousness. ... the effect of the environment depends on the child's degree of comprehension of the environment." Leontyev thus interprets Vygotsky as viewing *perezhivanie* as primarily an *intellectual* process, one of a subject *comprehending* their social situation. But this turns Vygotsky's idea upside down: first of all the subject has a *perezhivanie*, and this determines their whole relationship to the world, their development and response to the situation, including whether or not and how they 'comprehend' it, that is to say, respond successfully to it. In the case of the most developed *perezhivaniya*, an adult *will* gain an understanding of their experience, but generally only thanks to later analysis of the *perezhivanie*. But in the first place it is a *whole*.

15 *Perezhivaniya* on the Social-Historical Plane

Having established that *perezhivanie* is a well-established concept in psychology, I will now address the question of its applicability to social and historical science. I asked a Russian friend, Misha, whether he thought that the movie *Destiny of a Man* (1959) represented the *perezhivanie* of the Soviet Union's experience of the Great Patriotic War, and he responded:

> This movie is not an *illustration* of *perezhivanie* but it *is* really the *perezhivanie*.
>
> I re-watched the movie. Had a wonderful, unforgettable experience. Andrey, being a simple Soviet carpenter before the War, fell into the millstone of hard, bloody war by fate. He miraculously managed to survive,

losing his son on the front, his beloved wife and two daughters in his native village near Voronezh. The war has warped him, forced to endure emotional anguish, physical pain and spiritual suffering. The war has truly wounded his soul, humiliated him as a man, but he remained a man of great kindness, taking care of the orphan boy, treating him like his own son. The film shows massive heroism of the Soviet people. ... Pain and anxiety for homeland and personal tragedy of the individual and the specific family were organically fused in the fate of Andrey Sokolov.

Andrey's suffering is simultaneously private and public. But the hero of the film found the strength in himself not to fall down, and continue to work for the use and benefit of the country in the post-war period, and, staying alone, to raise the kid, ...

The film triggers a strong, intense *perezhivanie* from the audience, where an experience of art even gives priority way to *perezhivanie* of life itself, without losing at the same time tonality of high art.

email message on XMCA listserv, 18 January 2017

The trauma of the Great Patriotic War in which at least 21 million Soviet citizens were killed was experienced not only by each soviet citizen – each of whom had, like Andrey, to repair their lives and find a way to keep on living – but also transformed the country and its relation to the rest of the world, and the movie *Destiny of a Man* was one of the means by which people "remembered, repeated and worked through" the experience.

Let me give another example. To mark the 50th anniversary of the 1968 Uprising in France, Mitchell Abidor (2018) spoke to 35 people who had been participants in one way or another in the events of May 1968. Every one of them affirmed that "May made me," the title of the book – and 50 years later almost all were still activists or organisers of one kind or another.

The aims of the protesters were far-reaching to say the least ("Demand the Impossible! Down with Work!"). A technical school student in Lyons recalled thinking to himself when his school went on strike: "*Merde! Nous existons!*" Although the protests are widely portrayed as having been disappointed in their outcome, the reality is that France was changed, irrevocably. Unlike other European countries and the US, France was still a hidebound Catholic country and according to *La Monde* of March 15 1968: "What currently characterises our public life is boredom. [The French] don't participate in any way in the great convulsions shaking the world. [The Vietnam War] moves them, but doesn't really touch them" (cited in Abidor, 2018). Two weeks later, Paris was universally recognised as the radical centre of the world and soon caught up with the social changes which had been at work in the US and the rest of

Europe since the end of the War. May *made* modern France as well, and this despite the fact that in the wake of the uprising, De Gaulle was returned in a landslide election.

I have already emphasised that even in its psychological meaning, *perezhivanie* is not the accomplishment of an individual alone; their personality is changed to the extent that those around them change the concept they have of the subject and act differently towards them. In that sense, every *perezhivanie* is a collective experience which changes everyone.

When a person undergoes a *perezhivanie*, all the people around them now see them in a different light, they act differently towards them. That is, they have a different *concept* of them. Now in large measure that concept will be a concept supplied by the surrounding culture together with the particularities of the situation and individualities of the person involved. It may be a combination or modification of available concepts – troublemaker, good manager, leader, spokesperson for …, etc. Or it may be (and strictly speaking always is in fact) a brand-new concept. A concept is, after all, nothing but a normative system of actions directed at a common object on which the concept is reified. So *perezhivanie* is a process of human self-creation, even at the most humdrum level. Teachers have reported (March and Fleer, 2016) collective *perezhivaniya* in classroom exercises in which all the pupils underwent a profound change, creating and acquiring a new concept with their own interaction.

When we talk of an entire country going through an experience like a war or a revolution or a pandemic, there is in the first place the change in every individual, and in the second place the change by means of which every person acts differently towards those around them, but also *thirdly*, change in the way the whole way the country works – its institutions, customs, laws, its national culture and its relation to other countries. This must be the case insofar as the country is itself a 'project', and not just an arbitrary group of people holding the same passport. Any institution – that is to say, any group of people working together towards some common aim, according to shared laws and customs and using shared resources (be that land, property or means of communication) – if its aims are thwarted or it is thrown into a conflict of values, … the same kind of conditions that Vasilyuk cited as an 'impossible situation' – it will be thrown into a crisis, and being human, it will manifest all the phenomena of *perezhivanie*. It will descend sometimes into periods of introspection, emotions will run high, its most fundamental aims and methods will be called into question, leaders sacked, new leaders and new concepts created, and it undergoes a kind of self-transformation which we can call a *perezhivanie*.

16   Conclusion

Once our attention has been drawn to the meaning of *perezhivanie* and the idea that *perezhivaniya* are the units of the active self-creation of a person or collective project, and we embrace the idea of thinking of crises together with their catharsis as completed phases of development, then two things follow.

Firstly, the idea of a unit implies that a subject (person, institution, ...) can be understood through the study of its *perezhivaniya*, and that its essential character is both exhibited and produced in these episodes, each of which is to be understood as an *activity* rather than simply something which *happened* to the subject.

Secondly, we should revisit the literature, philosophy and psychology available to us as English speakers where we can now recognise that these same issues are being dealt with. This literature should be used to deepen our understanding of *perezhivaniya*.

Thirdly, Vygotsky's Psychology – with its view of the human being as the ongoing product of phylogenesis, cultural-historical development and ontogenesis, the method of analysis by units and the experimental-genetic methodology of his psychological research, the conception of the sign mediation of all human interactions – can be mobilised for a critical re-appropriation of a wide range of contemporary psychological and social theory and practice.

Fourthly, the problem of the development of *perezhivanie* from infancy to adulthood is posed for us, presently as an unsolved, indeed unasked question. And how important this question is for the understanding the development of our young people! What *are* the conditions for the successful completion of *perezhivaniya*; under what conditions is a person able to achieve 'closure', as they say nowadays? Does the concept of *perezhivanie* suggest how Vygotsky scholars could intervene in contemporary discussions about Post Traumatic Stress Disorder and problems such as domestic violence and youth suicide? How much of the response to these questions can be found in the scientific literature of our Russian colleagues?

CHAPTER 5

Agency

'Agency' is a term which has recently become ubiquitous in academic writing. But I have never heard an explanation of what this term actually means, far less a unit of analysis which could bring discussion of agency down from clouds and allow us to understand what it is and how it develops. Closer inspection shows that 'agency' covers a range of distinct phenomena, and different units are required for an analysis of the whole field.

1 The Domains of Self-Determination

Hegel wrote on the concept of the will. He said that the will is free according to its concept, that is, an unfree will is a contradiction in terms. But abstracted from their culture and upbringing, a human being has a 'natural will', shared in common with the entire animal kingdom, which is not free at all. We become free only in the course of the lifetime of an individual and centuries of social and cultural development of the states in which we live. Hegel's examination of the development of the will is found in the *Philosophy of Right* (1821), but there is little in Hegel's psychology to explain how the will of the adult human being differs from that of a new-born child. Indeed, the psychological research did not exist in Hegel's day to solve this problem.

The concept of the will unites both *what* a subject desires and the *resources* it mobilises in pursuit of that motive. In this light, it is clear that the freedom of the will cannot be seen just as an attribute of the person's psychology, but is equally a feature of the subject's social situation. The conceptual conundrums entailed in the idea of a will which *becomes free* can be untangled by looking to Hegel's essay on free will in the Introduction to the *Philosophy of Right*.

It was Vygotsky (1934b) who explained to us how the will, which in the new-born is like that of a lower animal, is shaped through a series of stages in interaction with its supporting environment, to grow up to become the will of an adult citizen. Vygotsky (1931) further explained how *self-control* is developed throughout life by the appropriation of cultural artefacts and (1934a) pointed to further development of the will through *perezhivaniya*. The will is an abstraction from the entire personality. Nonetheless, the will is a central theme of the development of the personality, and Vygotsky's theory allows us to trace its development throughout the course of an individual's life.

On the other hand, Hegel's exposition of the development of Freedom in the *Philosophy of Right* is at a high level of generality, and for an analysis to be useful it is necessary to move to a finer grain of analysis, particularly in relation to voluntary association, which is the essence of modern life. This is possible only by a logical-historical analysis of collective decision making, which is applicable to the wide variety of settings in which people develop their will by collaborating with others in the projects to which they are committed. For this we must turn to my own work in *The Origins of Collective Decision Making* (2016).

There are important psychological aspects to the process of forming and pursuing commitments and dealing with crises which arise in the world with the projects to which one is committed. It is Fedor Vasilyuk's *Psychology of Perezhivanie* (1984) and A.N. Leontyev's (1978) theory of personality which are most useful here.

The psychology entailed in participating in collective decision making has been widely studied by contemporary writers in activity theory, psychology and other related disciplines. However, there is already a vast literature on collective decision making which is addressed to the real world participants as subjects, without the need for a teacher, facilitator or change consultant to manage their activity. Psychological studies of collective decision making invariably miss the point that collective decisions are morally binding on participants and the formation of a collective will is irreversibly tied up with moral convictions with a long cultural history. The development of collective will is missed if we only study it in either managed or artificial forums.

I think that at an abstract level all these processes could be theorised as the development of something called 'agency', but a glance at the above field makes it clear that a single unit of analysis cannot grasp the whole development. The objection to lumping all these distinct phenomena together as 'agency', can be compared to Vygotsky's objection to the lumping together of tools and signs under the concept of 'artefact':

> The basis for this identification is ignoring the essence of both forms of activity and the differences in their historical role and nature. Tools as devices of work, devices for mastering the processes of nature, and language as a device for social contact and communication, dissolve in the general concept of artefacts or artificial devices.
> 1931b, p. 61

Vygotsky objected to this conflation because it obscured the qualitative differences between tool and sign and in particular "the real connection of their development in phylo- and ontogenesis" (*op. cit.*). For the same reasons, I conclude that 'agency' is a bad concept, an abstraction, and the word suffices only as a general heading. What we have is a number of distinct, qualitatively different but developmentally interconnected processes which together can take us from the helpless new-born babe to the adult citizen of a democratic socialist society.

Consequently, to use the concept of double stimulation, which Vygotsky used to theorise culturally acquired self-control, to theorise the formation of life-commitments, collective decision making and the constitution of a democratic republic, is nonsense. We need to identify a number of distinct units/germ cells to anchor our understanding of the distinct processes at work in each domain, and how they interact with one another. Although there are many theories relevant to this broad field of research, I will look only to writers within the same tradition from Hegel to Marx to Vygotsky and the Activity Theorists to review the variety of phenomena entailed in the conception of 'agency'.

2 Free Will

Hegel draws our attention to the fact that the will is free by definition, so that a will which is not free is a contradiction in terms. Nonetheless, it makes sense to see that the blind striving of a simple organism to find food and avoid threats expresses an *embryonic* will, while more developed forms of life have successively overcome the limitations on the will, and become more and more free.

The first limitation on the will is external nature, but human communities more and more transcend the limitations of nature by appropriating the laws of nature for their own ends, ultimately able to fly (in aeroplanes), produce food from mineral products and painlessly cure illnesses. In the process of overcoming (*aufheben*) nature, human beings have created a 'second nature', that is, an artificial environment. But this proves to be as much a threat to the welfare of human beings as nature itself.

The greatest threat to the flourishing of any person, however, can be other people. Consequently, the creation of *rights* meant that an individual did not live in constant fear of attack from another person and could pursue their own ends however they wished, while respecting the rights of others. The establishment of rights and a settled system of law and custom allows for the development of a collective will in which people can pursue their own ends through collaboration with others.

However – and this is the real crunch! – any organism, from the single cell up to the modern state, pursues its own end; this is after all what was meant by a free will, but precisely in this they are prisoners of their own desires, their *internal* nature. We can be free of hunger, but we cannot be free of the need for food. Further, the person who knows no desire beyond having enough to eat, cannot be said to be free just because they have plenty of food. The consumer who wants just what the advertisers tell them is not free just because they can shop. Hegel concludes that in order to be free, the will must be turned on itself, so that a subject decides what they want to do with their lives, rather than being a slave to their given needs and those who would manipulate them.

However, the will of every person is now tied up with that of every other person in the state in which they live. To achieve anything, you need to mobilise others to pursue the same goal. It is not enough to devote yourself to the good life, we must also see to it that everyone else does so as well. Consequently, the pursuit of freedom of the will entails the continuous struggle to raise the level of the whole political culture so that everyone is collaborating towards the good life for all. Free will thus turns out to be a problem of the democratic perfection of the state.

For the moment, the point is to see that the contradiction in the very concept of 'free will' does not invalidate the concept, but rather, extends the problem out from one of personality to one of the formation of a good state, in which human flourishing is possible.

3   The Natural Will

When we are talking about human beings, 'natural will' means the will abstracted from all cultural development. This is obviously an abstraction because the human will develops in the medium of culture from birth till death. Nonetheless, a human animal raised outside of human culture is a plausible analytical abstraction which allows us to distinguish the role of culture in the formation of the human will when a person is raised within the 'second nature' provided by human activity.

This issue bears only tangentially on our topic so I will sketch an outline of the formation of the human will by supplementing Hegel's speculative genesis of the will in the Subjective Spirit (1830) with A.N. Leontyev's (1978) systematic, experimental investigation of the evolution of consciousness.

At the very base of what could be called the psyche we have just *feelings*. Feelings do not have any object, they are just feelings. A living organism will respond in some stereotyped fashion to this feeling, maybe shouting if angry or withdrawing into itself if ashamed, and so on.

Next, certain feelings are associated with certain situations and so the organism will take the feeling as caused by some object in the environment. Such a feeling is called a *sensation* which orients the organism's activity at the object so as to restore equanimity. This is an important, though extremely primitive, step forward in the formation of the will.

At the next level, the organism recognises the sensation as a sign pointing to something else, as *meaning*, which allows for the development of practical intellect and planned activity. This is as far as the 'natural will' can go.

This is a line of development of the relation of the subject to its environment as outlined by Hegel. It creates the conditions of possibility for the development of the free will. At the same time, the organism must develop control over its own organs in order to act on the object. Here I draw on Leontyev's three-step development of the will.

When an organism does something, it uses one element of its environment to act on another. Hegel, Marx, Vygotsky and Leontyev all agreed on this. That element could be a tool, their own hand or, if they are acting on a mind, a sign of some kind. This unit is the *artefact-mediated action*, or simply 'action', the basic unit of activity. As the only means by which the will can manifest itself, it is the basic unit of the will. The action is oriented by the subject's goal, and actions like this can be done by all the higher animals up to and including human beings. Human beings differ from animals in their propensity to use artificial rather than natural means.

More complex actions aimed at achieving relatively remote goals, such as walking to the letter box, can be achieved like this: the organism masters some simple action, such as taking a step, so that it can be done without conscious awareness, adapting to conditions. For example, once having mastered taking a step, the organism learns to angle the foot and shift the weight slightly forward and so on, all without conscious control. This elementary action is called an *operation* and is controlled by conditions. If something goes wrong, if the person slips or momentarily loses balance, the operation springs back into conscious awareness and is consciously controlled.

Once complex actions can be accomplished without paying attention to the component operations, it is possible to achieve more remote aims by a series of actions, each with their own goal, ultimately achieving some motive. With this level of self-control, it becomes possible to share the actions out to be completed by different individuals in a collaborative division of labour. Having walked to the letter box, the actions of a hundred other people are then mobilised to deliver the letter to some far away destination according to the address written on the envelope.

In this way, we can see how the free will can achieve quite marvellous objects when the self-control which the human organism is able to exercise on its own organs is supplemented by a social division of labour. With material culture adapted to the achievement of human motives, an individual's control of their own mind and that of others by means of signs, and a readymade division of labour which an individual can mobilise, a person can attain otherwise remote goals.

This shows us all the elements needed for the fulfilment of free will, beginning with the organism gaining control of its own organs, so long as it can count on the collaboration of the rest of the community. The units of analysis are artefact-mediated actions and activities (a.k.a. practices or projects).

Actions are not a suitable unit for the analysis of social processes. It is this 'molar unit' – activities or practices or projects – which are the units that can be used for analysis of social formations, the arena on which free will is ultimately realised. But none of the activity theorists were able to develop an adequate theory in this domain. They stopped short at the point of a bureaucratically planned economy. On the other hand, Hegel's theory took for granted the complex evolution of the will as the new-born child develops under the umbrella of the family and other social institutions to the point where they can take their place in adult society. For this we must turn to Vygotsky's theory of child development.

4   The Development of the Will in Childhood

Vygotsky (1934b, see Chapter 6, this volume) built his theory of child development on a unit of analysis called the *social situation of development*. This refers to the situation of a child in its relation to its parents or other system of support, which is conceived of as a 'predicament': the child has certain needs and is subject to certain expectations represented as a concept – new-born, toddler, primary school kid, teenager and young adult (or some cultural variation of these concepts) – and their will more or less matches the expectations and benefits of the conception those around them have of them. However, as the child develops it becomes aware of other forms of activity which had hitherto been 'over the horizon' for them. They develop *new* needs and rebel against their situation, ultimately overthrow it in a crisis phase, and establish a new situation, a new place in the household, with new expectations and possibilities open to them as they enter a new period of development. It is during these crisis phases in their development that their will is fashioned. These are often *difficult* periods in the relation between adult and child as the child engages in disruptive behaviour. This disruptive activity is transient and passes away once the development of the will has been accomplished. It may return, however, in the event of a breakdown in the new situation.

The human will thus develops through a definite series of stages which will be different in different communities where expectations on a child may be different. Also, depending on how the child's disruptive activity is handled by those around them, the will develops differently, and the child learns to handle the world around them differently according to these experiences.

The stages of development of the will are as follows.

The act of birth, escaping from the safety of the mother's body, is of course the child's dramatic first step to self-determination, freeing itself from total physical dependence on the mother.

Around the age of 12 months, the child becomes a 'toddler' and begins to exert its own will for the first time in interaction with adults, marking itself out as a distinct personality rather than simply reacting to stimuli provided by others. They are no longer satisfied with having food put into their mouth and might push it away, and try to actively control their eating, establishing their biological independence from their mother.

The child is still controlled by the mother *psychologically* however, easily manipulated by rewards, punishments and distraction. Around the age of 36 months the toddler learns to separate their behaviour from their immediate desires, and so to be able to resist their mother's attempts to control them, willing to do things they positively dislike rather than give in to commands. This kind of defiant behaviour fades away once the child has established psychological independence.

Developing within the bosom of the family the preschooler does not differentiate their internal life from their behaviour. They are an open book. If they are to develop their own relations to people outside the immediate circle of the home, they must learn to act strategically. This is a new development in their self-determination and is also an intellectual achievement as it means that the child can now solve problems by the self-conscious use of mental technique.

The next crisis comes as the child becomes a teenager and begins to feel the need to enter the adult world. They cannot, however, because they have become aware that they are governed by the opinions, values and skills of the social position into which they have been born, and they need to establish their own opinions, tastes, values, etc., but they do not yet have the social experience to do so. This is the period of teenage rebellion, when the youth belittle everything they have been raised to revere. Once they have established their social independence, usually with the aid of peers, they will return to the parents, but now on an equal footing.

Thus, the journey from the womb to young adulthood is marked by a series of periods of gradual step-by-step adjustment, separated by phases of crisis in which the personality makes not a step but a leap. These leaps are marked by qualitative transformations of the *will*, manifesting itself on successively wider planes.

But the mastery of one's own activity is not merely the passage through stereotyped stages, and nor is it completed when the child reaches young adulthood. Vygotsky gave us two units to understand respectively the minutiae of development of self-control and the dramatic transformations of agency achieved in key episodes in a person's life.

5   Self-Control

Vygotsky showed (1931) how a person learns to control their own activity by appropriating signs, technical tools and psychological tools from the surrounding culture and using these artefacts to control their attention, perception and sensorimotor activity. This idea was first formulated by Hegel and expressed in his maxim: "There is nothing in heaven, earth or anywhere else which is not both immediate and mediated" (1831). The elementary form of self-control achieved by means of *sign-mediation actions* is *selection*, focusing attention on one aspect of the field of perception and selecting it from its background.

Signs are material objects, products of social labour, and present in the cultural environment, which people incorporate into actions, through their collaboration with others. Vygotsky showed that words, which are initially used by adults to control the child's activity, can be appropriated by the child to control their own behaviour. This is part of the development of the will in childhood. Initially, the child actually commands themselves aloud, but this private speech is gradually abbreviated, internalised in the form of inner speech, and ultimately integrated into the psyche, allowing the child to carry out complex procedures, without even conscious awareness. But this self-control has its genesis in the appropriation of cultural tools, including spoken words and gestures.

This capacity to appropriate cultural signs and psychological tools in the course of mastering one's own activity is not something confined to childhood but continues throughout life. Here the development of the will is generally limited, however, to mastery of the existing culture.

6   Acquisition of Ideals

There is more to the appropriation of signs than the incorporation of signs and tools in actions. In the course of acquiring the *meaning* of the various words and artefacts while participating in the broader circle of social life – work, politics, social life generally – a person grasps the various *concepts* which are orienting the practices or activities (referred to above in the synopsis of Leontyev's work) in which they participate or with which they interact. A concept is not merely a neutral representation of a form of activity but represents some motive. In acquiring the concept, through participation at some level in the relevant practice, the person makes a commitment. To acquire a concept is to determine the will. That commitment may be marginal, or it may be life-defining. Leontyev (1978, see Chapter 9, this volume) shows how the personality includes a hierarchy or structure of such commitments.

This idea is central to the conception of free will and self-determination. It is in the course of making these commitments that a person *shapes their own motivation* and at the same time, by engaging with others who share that commitment at one level or another, the person is able to *realise* that motive.

Further, in the course of pursuing its aim, the project to which a person is committed comes up against difficulties and conflicts. In the course of the resulting crises two things can happen: (1) the project enters into relations with other projects, be they supportive or opposing, deepening and broadening the conception of its motive, and (2) the individual is faced with personal crises (impossible situations) which have to be overcome. The units of analysis for these aspects of the development of the will is the *collaborative project* and the commitment of the person to a project.

Number (1) is dealt with in my introduction to *Collaborative Projects: An Interdisciplinary Study* (2014, see Chapter 13, this volume) and I will defer discussion of this till later. Number (2) was dealt with by Leontyev in his theory of the personality, but more satisfactorily in my view by Fedor Vasilyuk (1984, see Chapter 10, this volume), and I will now turn to his contribution.

7   *Perezhivaniya*

The appropriation of cultural artefacts characterises how a person acquires ends and means from material provided by the wider culture. Broadly, this is what it means to get an education. However, in the course of life, people do more than absorb the culture into which they are born. People have *perezhivaniya* (experiences) – tragedies, unexpected and traumatic experiences, affairs, daring career moves, and so on. And things don't just *happen* to people. People meet challenges and overcome them, or at least survive. It is in the course of these crises that the will of the adult human being is shaped, just as it is in those periods of critical development that the child's will is shaped.

In general, these experiences are possible only because people had already formed commitments as described above. But things may unfold which place them in 'impossible situations', and Fedor Vasilyuk (1984, see Chapter 10, this volume) elaborated four types of crisis:

1. The *infantile* crisis, in the 'easy-simple' world. Here the subject's will meets no resistance and faces no conflicts, as the subject is ruled by the pleasure principle; the smallest difficulty creates stress, and is usually met with denial of reality. This seeming non-crisis is widespread in the modern world.
2. The *fanatic's* crisis, in the 'difficult-simple' world. The subject's project is blocked; they do not deny reality and believe the problem can be resolved. Going on demands realism, and the subject either overcomes the crisis with patient determination or abandons the project and adopts an alternative pursuit.
3. The *moral* crisis, in the 'easy-complex' world. Although none of their projects face significant resistance, the subject finds that two of their commitments have come into conflict with one another. The subject either discredits one of their projects or finds some way of reconciling them in their mind, restructuring their value-system.
4. The *creative* crisis, in the 'difficult-complex' world. The subject must reconstruct their entire personality to process this crisis. They might transfer the threatened value to a different object, decide that their former life was based on false commitments, or creatively abandon egoism and pursue a higher goal which is proof against disappointment and validates sacrifice.

This broad classificatory scheme represents the range of crises which a person confronts when they develop their personality by participating in the pursuit of collaborative projects. It takes as given that life is never smooth, and the realisation of the subject's ideals requires the development of the personality, ultimately moving to the plane that Aristotle recommended to us when he said that "the good life for a human being is the pursuit of the good life for humanity". A.N. Leontyev (1978) came to similar conclusions in his analysis of personality development.

This is as far as I will go in terms of the development of the personality as an element of 'agency'. The remaining problems take us to the problems of the legal and political structures of the state and the structure of voluntary association.

8 Freedom and the State

In his *Philosophy of Right* (1821), Hegel set out his social theory in the form of a theory of ethics. The subject is taken to be a nation state. As is the case in all Hegel's systematic works, the philosophy of right is expounded through a series of interconnected units, the 'concrete simple somethings' which make a beginning for understanding each domain. The subject matter of the book is variously described as the unfolding of the will, or the realisation of freedom, the expressions being synonymous in that it outlines how the will becomes truly free.

The first phase of Right Hegel calls 'abstract right' and its germ cell is private property. A person can only be free to the extent that they can put their will into some external object, be that their own body, a plot of land to call home or the tools of their trade. Without these it is nonsense to call someone free or to say that they have 'agency'. Private property, the right to own something, is the *sine qua non* of freedom. (Need I say that there is nothing inconsistent with Socialism in this principle. Hegel did not envisage the tools of your trade being *someone else's* private property.)

On the basis of a community of households, each of which enjoys the right to private property, the next necessary phase of Right is morality. The 'germ cell' of morality is a purpose, and Hegel outlines a theory of *morality* which has a startling parallel to A.N. Leontyev's theory of *activity*. Hegel traces the forms of consciousness necessary for the achievement of an individual's purposes. He shows that in order to realise their own purpose each person must have regard to the customs and laws of their community, using only such intermediate goals as are consistent with law, and ultimately merge their conception of their own welfare with the general good. Remarkably, this is the same conclusion that Leontyev and Vasilyuk arrived at by means of a psychology of the personality. (See Chapters 9 and 10, this volume.) This suggests that morality, in Hegel's view, corresponds to the psychology of a person who rationally pursues their own welfare in a good state.

The third phase of Right is *Sittlichkeit*, usually translated as 'ethical life'. Ethical life goes from the (nuclear, patriarchal) family to the (monarchical) state. Initially, the state and family are more or less identical as land is held entirely through familial relations. But as family and state differentiate, they are mediated by *bürgerliche Gesellschaft* (usually translated as 'civil society').

Altogether, ethical life encompasses all the norms and laws of a society, inclusive of the means of their determination and enforcement. Hegel claims that although the state is *born* of violence, its *concept* is freedom, and freedom can only be realised by living in a good state. Hegel believed in a constitutional monarchy, in which civil society is more or less self-governing, under the supervision of an altruistic, meritocratic civil service and protected by the monarch as chief of the armed forces in the event of war. Aspects of this view are obviously outdated today.

The philosophy of ethical life is expounded from a variety of units – Family, Market, Public Authorities, Corporations (i.e., voluntary associations) – each of which is essential for the development of a modern society, in Hegel's view. Each of these units is a quite distinct concept, and I think the argument is fairly made that a theory of the free will cannot dispense with these relatively concrete units, even though Hegel's theory is 200 years old and inevitably antiquated. No theory of 'agency' can dispense with dealing with the relation between the market and the public authorities, between voluntary associations and the state, etc.

Nonetheless, while problems with the family, the state, the market and regulatory authorities remain, it is my view that the path to the solution of the problems of self-determination today, at this critical moment in modern history, lies in the development of voluntary association.

9 Voluntary Association

Political life, or voluntary association, is essentially collective decision making (see Chapter 18, this volume), and the unit for political life is therefore a group of people *making a decision* which will be binding upon them all. This unit is indeed commonly studied by CHAT writers, but it is invariably assumed that the collective is bound together by nothing more than the situation given to them by the researcher and makes its decision in isolation from any tradition of collective decision making. Indeed, researchers aim to isolate subjects from such traditions for the purpose of psychological research. Centuries of the culture of voluntary association are dispensed with and the problem is approached as if the subjects were human atoms. The central principle of Cultural Psychology however is to 'put culture in the middle'. Psychological research carried out in isolation from culture is meaningless.

My historical investigation found that there are essentially three paradigms of collective decision making: Counsel, Majority and Consensus (leaving aside the process of making decisions by throwing dice). Collective decision making is distinct from projects making agreements with each other without sacrificing their autonomy. Such external relations may be Colonisation (or philanthropy), Negotiation (or bargaining), Solidarity and Collaboration, and are dealt with below under the heading of Alliance Politics. But let us focus first of all on how voluntary associations make decisions.

(1) The most ubiquitous and ancient paradigm of collective decision-making is what I call Counsel – the participants are not social atoms, but have a social structure in which there is one person who bears moral responsibility for the decision – the Chief, the paterfamilias, the CEO or whatever, but before announcing the decision, the Chief must listen to the views of all members of the group. This paradigm was codified by St. Benedict in the fourth century AD, is used in traditional societies in Africa, for example, and in modern businesses and public service departments. Counsel relies chiefly on the moral qualities of the Chief.

(2) With the emergence of commerce and the first towns, merchants and tradespeople created voluntary associations which were based on the principles of equality, tolerance and solidarity, and since the tenth century, used the principle of Majority voting. Combinations of Counsel and Majority were practiced inside the early Christian Church.

(3) Beginning in the US in 1960, voluntary associations began to use Consensus, though this paradigm had been used by the Quakers since 1666. Consensus is based on the principles of inclusion and respect for difference reflected in a preference for the *status quo ante* over making a decision which does not enjoy near-unanimous support; failing the achievement of consensus, participants prefer to go their own way and the group breaks up.

It is by participating in making collective decisions that individuals and groups achieve their ends and acquire the relevant virtues – recognition, equality, respect for difference, tolerance, solidarity, inclusion – necessary for the pursuit of personal and collective purposes.

10   Alliance Politics

The first fact of fulfilling a purpose is that you can only succeed with the collaboration of others, that is, by means of a collaborative project. The second fact, which is most important in our times, is that only a minority of people will join you in your project and that achievement of your purpose will entail overcoming or forming alliances with other projects. The anatomy of relations between projects depends on the way in which one project *assists* another project, and there are four paradigms for this as follows.

(1) *Colonisation* is the first relation in which one project assists another. This may take the form of philanthropy in which the other is discounted and extinguished by the first, even while its participants are 'rescued'. Colonisation means 'taking over' and invading another project's territory, extinguishing it, and this is usually done with the best of intentions. This was the dominant mode in ancient times.

(2) *Exchange*, or bargaining or negotiation, is where (perhaps through delegates) two projects each retain their distinct identity and continue to pursue their own motives but make some exchange for mutual benefit. This is the norm in the marketplace. It demands honesty, mutual respect and equality in mutual relations, but builds no lasting bonds, using others merely instrumentally. Alliance politics, which is dominant in the current period, is chiefly based on this mode of cooperation where alliances and 'treaties' are for a given purpose, pro tem, agreeing where and when to meet for what end, thereafter each going their own way.

(3) *Solidarity* (see Chapter 16, this volume) is where one project comes to the aid of another by placing itself under the direction of the other, while retaining its own identity and goals. This relation builds new ties and fosters trust and mutual understanding. This is the mode of collaboration which best promotes Socialism.

(4) *Collaboration as such* means that the two projects merge their separate identities altogether in making common cause, ceasing to deal with each other through delegates, entering fully into joint decision making.

11 Conclusion

In the above I have outlined the development of 'agency' across eight domains. An entire book at least would be needed to elaborate the analysis of Cultural Psychology in each of these domains, and I have dealt with each in about 600 words. But what is more important is that *a different unit of analysis is needed in each domain* because each phenomenon is a different subject matter grasped with a different concept.

Doubtless all represent components in the development of human freedom. However, the lumping together of distinct processes under a heading like 'agency' merely serves to obscure the differences and genetic connections between them, preventing the establishment of clear concepts each with their own unit of analysis. The ability of the toddler to feed themselves cannot usefully be theorised in the same way as an adult learning a second language or a feminist getting a sexist law changed or a nation protecting itself from a pandemic.

A general conception of 'agency' or 'freedom' of which all these are but examples can form the subject matter of a fascinating after-dinner talk, but even when Hegel wrote the *Encyclopaedia of the Philosophical Sciences*, although he brought a single unifying method to bear on the encyclopaedic subject matter, he used numerous units of analysis for numerous distinct concepts.

Rather than using the term 'agency' it would be preferable to use a term specific to a relevant domain of phenomena and a unit of analysis appropriate to that domain.

CHAPTER 6

Tool and Sign in Vygotsky's Development

There is a tension within Vygotsky's writing and in its interpretation, hinging around the relation of sign and tool, sometimes taken up under the heading of word and deed (or action). This contradiction turns out to be a microcosm of the tension between language and labour in the wider field of Marxist theory, which in turn evokes the class antagonisms underlying the original work of Marx and Engels, antagonisms which have continued to be reflected in the development of theory and of social and political conflict up to the present time, as a result of changes in the labour process.

Vygotsky's final position was expressed clearly enough on the last page of *Thinking and Speech* (1934), where he speaks about word and deed:

> The connection between thought and word is not a primal connection that is given once and forever. It arises in development and itself develops. "In the beginning was the word." Goethe answered this Biblical phrase through Faust: "In the beginning was the deed." Through this statement, Goethe wished to counteract the word's over-valuation. … we can agree with Goethe that the word as such should not be overvalued and can concur in his transformation of the Biblical line to, "In the beginning was the *deed*." Nonetheless, if we consider the history of development, we can still read this line with a different emphasis: "In the *beginning* was the deed."
>
> 1934, pp. 284–285

Although Vygotsky does not here explicitly touch on the question of tool and sign, this is, as will be seen, a clear and succinct statement of the relation, leaving to the reader the work of unfolding from that relation the richness and complexity of the history of intertwined development alluded to. However, there are other statements of Vygotsky, at other times and in other terms, and interpretations of his writing by other writers which oblige us to look more deeply into this problem.

I shall first review what Vygotsky himself said on the topic, which is variously framed in terms of tool vs. sign/symbol or action/deed vs. word, as well as technical tool vs. psychological tool.

1   Ape, Primitive Man[1] and Child

The story begins with *Ape, Primitive Man, and Child: Essays in the History of Behaviour* (1930), a book which Vygotsky wrote in collaboration with Alexander Luria. Vygotsky wrote the first two chapters of the book, mainly drawing on the reports of contemporary zoologists, anthropologists and ethnologists. In Chapter 2, "Primitive Man and his Behaviour," Vygotsky clarified what he meant by "primitive man" as follows:

> This term is commonly used, admittedly as a conventional label, to designate certain peoples of the uncivilised world, situated at the lower levels of cultural development. It is not entirely right to call these peoples primitive, as a greater or lesser degree of civilisation can unquestionably be observed in all of them. All of them have already emerged from the prehistoric phase of human existence. Some of them have very ancient traditions. Some of them have been influenced by remote and powerful cultures, while the cultural development of others has become degraded.
>
> *Primitive man, in the true sense of the term, does not exist anywhere at the present time,* and the human type, as represented among these primeval peoples, can only be called 'relatively primitive'. Primitiveness in this sense is a lower level, and the starting point for the historical development of human behaviour. Material for the psychology of primitive man is provided by data concerning prehistoric man, the peoples situated at the lower levels of cultural development and the comparative psychology of peoples of different cultures.
>
> 1930, pp. 41–42, italics in the original

By 'relatively primitive', Vygotsky meant people living in *non-literate societies*. Vygotsky's ideas were tested out by Luria in an expedition to Uzbekistan in 1930. There Luria studied the peasants who were undergoing a transition from feudal village life into the modern, collectivised Soviet economy. The background which frames *Ape, Primitive Man, and Child* is the conception that

---

1   Vygotsky uses the term "primitive man." This expression is unmentionable in the light of postcolonial and feminist sensibilities. However, it would be dishonest to excise this and similar terms from Vygotsky's writing, written at a time before these terms were problematised. But to make it clear that they are not *my* terms, I have everywhere placed inverted commas around "primitive man." This is not the only issue with this work, which has been omitted from Vygotsky's Collected Works. However, in amongst the problems there are some important insights which need to be excavated and preserved.

human behaviour is the product of three processes of development: (1) biological development, or phylogenesis, i.e., the biological evolution of the human genome, (2) cultural development, i.e., the history of the tools and signs used and produced by people, and (3) ontogenesis i.e., the development of the individual person over their life time (see Blunden, 2020).

In tracing the development from apes to "primitive man" to modern human beings, Vygotsky aimed to identify just one feature of behaviour which could be taken to be the essential component of development which "served as a link connecting a given stage in the development of behaviour with the very next stage of development," (p. xi), that is, that behaviour in the earlier type of being which generated a qualitative change and transition to a new type of being.

Vygotsky had drawn on the work of Wolfgang Köhler (1887–1967) to show that apes used tools in the normal course of their activity, in particular that they would use sticks as multi-purpose tools for digging, eating, fighting, poking, etc., and were on occasion capable of using other objects which they found to solve problems, chiefly gaining access to food. According to Köhler, the apes' problem solving was characterised by their perception of a problem situation as a Gestalt, so the discovery of a tool-mediated solution to a task depended on being able to fit the tool into the visual-spatial structure of the problem.

Although frequently taken as the archetypical characteristic of Homo sapiens, Vygotsky took tool production as that aspect of *animal behaviour* which brought about the transition from ape to human. Originating among apes, the production and use of tools reached a high level of development in "primitive man." This activity constitutes cultural development. Implicit in this conception is a protracted epoch of evolution during which cultural development operates *in tandem with* biological development in the formation of the human biological type with the emergence of hominids about 6 million years ago.

However, according to Vygotsky, it is *not* the production and use of tools which brings about the transition from "primitive" to *modern* human beings.

On the basis of evidence available at the time, Vygotsky correctly concluded that all human societies currently in existence were of the *same biological type*, biological differences being insignificant. Biologically, literate and non-literate human communities would be the same. Yet culturally, there would be profound differences. They would be at a different point in their cultural history. If literacy was posited to be the marker of modern, as compared to "primitive" humans, then non-literate communities could be said to approximate the condition of human communities prior to the historical emergence of writing. Writing, after all, emerged independently in Mesopotamia c. 3200 BCE, in China c. 1200 BCE, in Phoenicia c. 1000 BCE and in Mesoamerica c. 700

BCE, and spread from there to other societies. There were in 1930 in the Soviet Union many communities that remained non-literate. In order to study what marks or enables the transition from "primitive" to 'modern' human beings, therefore, it made sense to search for the first, rudimentary use of writing in non-literate communities, and observe its impact on their behaviour.

1.1 History and Evolution

According to Vygotsky, it is not that at a certain point biological evolution ended and cultural history began. Rather, there are *two distinct principles of development*, biological-evolutionary and cultural-historical. Up to a certain point, cultural change, that is, the development of tools and signs and their use, was *subordinate* to and constrained by biological change – in particular, the gradual change in the genotypical form of the hand and the organs of speech. But then, from some point in the past, "biological change of the human organism now became subordinate to and dependent upon the historical development of human society" (Vygotsky, 1930, p. 50). Far from holding that evolutionary change ceases when history begins, he actually suggests that "the hand and the brain, as natural organs, probably never developed so rapidly, and at such a gigantic pace, as during the period of historical development," (*op. cit.*, p. 36) and in 'The Socialist Alteration of Man' (1930b), written about the same time, he says of Socialism: "this change in human behaviour, this change of the human personality, must inevitably lead to further evolution of man and to the alteration of the *biological type of man*" (p. 182). Nowhere does he suggest that capitalism has generated any development in the biological type of human being.

The epoch of "primitive man" intervening between the formation of the biological type of modern human beings and the creation of the first literate communities in China, the Middle East, North Africa and South America, is characterised by a highly developed *practical intelligence*, associated with the development of 'technique', i.e., tool production and use. According to Vygotsky, far from lacking logical thinking, "primitive man" had to be logical in their interactions with nature or they would not survive. There was no room for fools in their world. But Vygotsky differentiates between *practical intelligence* and *verbal intelligence*.

A contrary view has been repeated in different forms, however, across 'ethnic psychology' research: a subject from a non-literate society is presented with a formal logical problem to solve verbally. But the so-called 'logical' solution *flatly contradicts what the subject knows very well* from their practical intelligence and experience. The result is that the subject is unwilling or unable to solve the puzzle 'correctly', according to the dictates of formal logic applied to the hypothetical counter-factual scenario. It is concluded that the subject is incapable of logical, syllogistic thinking. As we shall see, Luria fell into this fallacy in his research in Uzbekistan.

1.2 Periodisation of the Intellect

Vygotsky periodised the development of the intellect of "primitive man" as follows: (1) practical intelligence, by which human beings well understand nature, but cannot be said to have anything like a 'theory of nature', (2) verbal intelligence, differentiated from practical intelligence but still inadequate and including 'magical thinking' and (3) verbal intelligence, which is stabilised in a rational understanding of nature, distinct from practical intelligence. "More advanced technical development eventually separates the laws of nature from the laws of thinking, and magical action begins to fade away" (Vygotsky, 1930, p. 85) with the development of natural science.

Vygotsky says that the historical period of development is not marked by any significant development in the biological type of human being (there are changes, but these are relatively superficial and reversible). The point is that *a different principle of development is dominant* during this epoch. Development during the period prior to the emergence of literate societies is essentially grounded in the *tools* we use to mediate our action upon nature, and in the forms of social organisation corresponding to these tools. It is during this epoch that rudimentary signs first emerge from tools.

To be clear, at this time, Vygotsky used the term 'sign' or 'symbol' to mean an *artefact* which is used to regulate our behaviour by controlling our mind. *He did not count spoken words as signs*. In the study in question, Vygotsky was only concerned with 'material culture' in the sense in which the term is used by archaeologists, referring to enduring objects which, unlike the spoken word, are available for direct observation: jewellery, tattoos, marks on trees, message sticks, etc., and eventually writing.

Just as the turning point in biological evolution was the emergence of tool use, which is found in apes in rudimentary form, it is the emergence of *sign* use which brings about the *cultural-historical* transition to 'civilised man'. So Vygotsky expected to find sign use amongst "primitive man," but in rudimentary form. Once the use of signs to control our *own* behaviour (and subsequently that of others) emerges, a *new principle of development* becomes dominant and thus begins the transition from "primitive man" to modern literate societies. The crucial thing in the transition from "primitive man" to civilisation, according to Vygotsky, is the emergence of rudimentary forms of *writing*. This is the *cultural-historical* principle of development. It is no longer tool use, but sign use which is the dominant force in human development.

Vygotsky always carried out his psychological investigations in relation to *specific psychological functions*, so he never conceptualised cultural development as a single totalising, linear narrative. Instead, he allowed that each psychological function had its own path of development, including regression of some functions. This is important, because despite the totalising categories – 'animal', 'primitive man', 'civilised man' – which imply a single narrative, his approach actually relied on the intermingling of multiple narratives. One of the sections of his chapter on "primitive man" concerns the function of memory. In respect to memory, the problem is that without signs such as the written word, the *accumulation* of knowledge relies exclusively on oral memory and the natural surroundings.

> Everything that civilised humanity remembers and knows at present, all the accumulated experience in books, monuments and manuscripts – all this colossal expansion of the human memory, without which there could be no historical and cultural development, is due precisely to external human memorisation based on symbols.
> 1930, p. 62

'Symbols' in this sense encompasses everything that Vygotsky would call 'psychological tools' – maps, plans, books, movies, up to computers, all of which have developed out of and in close connection with the development of industry and technology in general. Although it was a novel idea in Vygotsky's day, it is uncontroversial today that such psychological tools have a profound effect on our thinking, not only as mediated through their impact on social relations, but *immediately*, in the hands of an individual user.

Again, to be clear: for Vygotsky at this point in his development, prior to the writing of *History* (1931), a spoken word is *not* a sign. The spoken word does not, like the written word, have the same irreversible 'ratchet' effect which fosters technological escalation. More importantly, however, the developmental path of the spoken word is different from that of the written word. Language arose in close connection with the first use of tools millions of years ago, whilst writing arose as an outgrowth of technical tool use in bureaucratic class societies a couple of thousand years ago.

1.3   *Periodisation of Tools*

To track the transition from "primitive man" to "civilised man," Vygotsky periodised the emergence of sign production out of tool production, into three phases in line with the above periodisation of the intellect of "primitive man."

(1) At first, the tools used to control nature also necessarily regulate and mediate human behaviour in the labour process. Tools control the mind mediately through their use in acting upon nature.

(2) Then rituals, music, symbols, incantations, icons and so on are used which function to regulate human behaviour, but the people using them are unclear as to whether the rituals, etc., are controlling nature or controlling their own actions in nature. Thus, technique and magic (i.e., incipient verbal intelligence) develop side by side without fully penetrating one another.

(3) Verbal intelligence, that is, the ability to represent nature and human activity symbolically, matures sufficiently to be able to provide adequate theories of nature which are capable of informing the effective regulation of technique. Psychological tools are adequately differentiated from technical tools, and with that, verbal intelligence fully differentiated from practical intelligence.

Vygotsky did not use the word 'tool' in the metaphorical sense in which people nowadays use 'tool' to refer indifferently to words, concepts, mental images and methods. *A tool is a useful material artefact*. The appropriate word to use for a metaphorical tool is a 'means'. 'Psychological tools' emerge from technical tools as a *special type of tool*, a tool which, unlike the 'technical tool', is directed inwards, rather than outwards at nature. A 'sign' is a type of psychological tool, but so are "algebraic symbolism, works of art, writing, schemes, diagrams, maps, blueprints, etc." (Vygotsky, 1930a).

According to Vygotsky:

> the basic components of the psychological development of primitive man are to be found in the development of technique and in the corresponding development of social structure.
>
> 1930, p. 84

Note the inclusion of 'social structure' here. Marx (1847) had said: "The hand-mill gives you society with the feudal lord; the steam-mill society with the industrial capitalist," and in his exposition of the development of human behaviour, Engels (1876) sees homo sapiens developing from the stone axe to the steam engine through a series of *social formations* corresponding to the development of technique. But Vygotsky's purpose was different. Vygotsky's concern went beyond the characterisation of entire social formations to the psychology of individuals. Engels' concern, on the other hand, was not psychology as such but social formations, which do in turn condition the psychology of a people.

The rudiments of the regulation of behaviour with psychological tools are to be found in "primitive man," even during an epoch in which, by and large, psychological tools did not figure. In turning to the development of civilised humanity, technical tools not only continue to develop and develop at a gigantic pace, but they develop in close connection with the development of psychological tools.

Using a term from a later time, once the transition from "primitive man" to modern societies is set in motion, the development of psychological tools could be said to be the 'leading activity'.

1.4   Tools and the Mind: Technical Tools and Psychological Tools

It is widely accepted nowadays that technology and its use plays a large part in the formation of the mind. Vygotsky was one of the first to recognise this. It is obvious that the use of psychological tools like mobile phones and personal computers have a big impact on the psychology of this generation. Also, the use of such tools as the motor car effects a change in mentality by how it expands the scope of a person's activity, and by the vast changes it has wrought in social structures which in turn bring about changes in mentality. But the motor car does not affect people's thinking *in the same way as the smart phone*. The smart phone operates on the mind; the car operates on nature. You can't be run over by a smart phone.

Books, computers, search engines, WiFi, video cameras and other tools for thinking not only transform the production and use of tools (technique), and with technique, social structures – they do so by operating on the mind. This is what makes them psychological tools. Invariably, they are also either directly or indirectly vehicles for communication, so psychological tools are directly and intimately connected with the development of social structures as well as the mind as such.

Psychological tools and technical tools do not form a dichotomy or dualism. As a status symbol, the automobile is also a psychological tool, and a mobile phone can also control other devices such as the air conditioning. But the respective *objects* being acted upon – mental or material – are clearly distinguished in each specific practice.

According to Vygotsky at this point in the development of his thinking, the study of technical tool use as *the essential factor* in the formation of the psyche, is applicable *only* to the epoch of "primitive man." This is not the case for modern people, people already familiar with modern means of communication and part of a worldwide system of production and distribution. For our time, it is psychological tools which are the essential factors in the formation of the psyche.

Nonetheless, historically speaking, psychological tools arose *as a special kind of tool* for the regulation of behaviour in contradistinction to technical tools, for the regulation of nature, which first arose in the early evolution of homo sapiens. 'Signs' first arose as a type of tool, as an application of the technology of the time.

There are two aspects of *Ape, Primitive Man and Child* which do not directly bear on our topic, but which have to be dealt with so that the above reflections are properly contextualised. The first is Vygotsky's periodisation of word use in the transition from "primitive man" to literate societies; the second is which feature Vygotsky would take as the essential feature of the ontogenetic development of behaviour and distinctive for the third line of development mentioned in the title of the book: the development from child to adult.

1.5 *Vygotsky's Periodisation of Word Use in "Primitive Man"*

Vygotsky later claimed that the development of the 'verbal intelligence' of non-literate peoples is manifested in the passage of word use through three stages:

> [from] the first method of using words as *proper names* to a second method, whereby words serve as symbols for *sets* of things having some common attribute, and lastly to a third, involving the use of words as tools or means for the elaboration of *concepts*.
>
> 1930, p. 71

To use words only as proper nouns would imply that all individual objects, situations and actions in the life of "primitive man" each bore a unique name, thus a "proper noun" in the sense that proper nouns generally indicate a unique individual. However, this is not what he describes. What he meant is that, for example, 'young, male crow' may have a unique name, distinct from an older crow, or the female young of a different species of bird, etc.; however, each word designates a *relatively* concrete kind. This is just as 'MG' or 'Corvette' each denote a particular concept to us, but *not* an individual vehicle, such as 'the Batmobile' or 'Air Force One', nor a noun qualified by its features, as in 'expensive sports car'.

"Primitive man," said Vygotsky, "thinks not in concepts but in sets" (1930, p. 70). He explained the difference between the second and third stages, between a set and a concept, by taking a family name such as "Petrov" as an example of a word designating a set:

> A set differs from a concept by virtue of the relationship between the individual object and the group name. By looking at an object I can say with full objectivity whether it is a tree or a dog, because 'tree' and 'dog' serve as the designations of *concepts* – in other words, generic groups to

which, by virtue of substantive features various individual objects belong. I cannot, by looking at a man, tell whether or not he is a Petrov, because in order to do so it is simply necessary to know, as a matter of fact, whether he goes by such a name.[2]

1930, p. 70

But from the point of view of this writer (Blunden, 2012), and of the Vygotsky who later wrote *Thinking and Speech*, and of Hegel, this is not only *plain wrong*, it is *upside down*. The definition Vygotsky gives of a 'concept', as a collection of objects sharing a "substantial" – evidently meaning visible or at least observable – attribute, and a 'set' designating objects the connection between which requires knowledge of the inner connection between the objects, not given to immediate perception, are the wrong way around. It is the elements of a *concept* which are held together by inner, hidden relations. Vygotsky's second level of word use (picking out a common feature) is an associative complex and the third level what he would later call a pseudoconcept.

Lizards and pangolins are both four-legged, scaly little land animals, but lizards are reptiles and pangolins are mammals. Dolphins and sharks are both large sea-bound predators, but dolphins are mammals and sharks are not. Emus and kangaroos are both two-legged Australian animals, but one is a bird the other a mammal. 'Family resemblance' whether in Wittgenstein's or Vygotsky's sense, is a feature of true concepts like 'mammal'. Dolphins and pangolins and kangaroos are mammals because of an evolutionary connection which is not immediately apparent but depends on their 'family connection' in the *system* of concepts given by Darwin's scientific theory of phylogenesis. *True* concepts unite things according to some theory of the world lying *behind* appearances. Modern dialectical thinking is shared by ancient and indigenous societies as well as by genuine science. Modern bureaucratic consciousness, on the other hand, like children, forms concepts according to superficial attributes, using tick boxes, survey forms and pigeonholes.

Luria took Vygotsky's erroneous distinction between a set and a concept with him on his expedition to Uzbekistan in 1930 (Luria, 1979). In one of his experiments to reveal the method of thinking of the Uzbek peasant, he showed a man, Rakmat, drawings of three wheels and a pair of pliers and asked Rakmat

---

2 Note that Vygotsky's example of a family name for a group of individuals differs from the way Wittgenstein used the idea of 'family likeness', in which all members of the family can be grouped at least pair-wise through a common observable feature, while there is no one feature which is common to all. In Vygotsky's later sense, Wittgenstein's 'family likeness' is a 'diverse set'. An interesting idea, but nothing to do with the issue here.

to say which did not belong because it was unlike the others. Rakmat refused to single out the pliers because "I know the pliers don't look like the wheels, but you'll need them if you have to tighten something in the wheels" (Luria, 1979, p. 70).

This verified that Rakmat could only tackle the test of verbal intelligence by calling upon his practical intelligence (even though he knew full well that pliers did not look like wheels). Likewise, he would not separate log from the group (hammer, saw, log, and hatchet) because he would "need the tools for working on the log." Rakmat refused to approach the artificial group of objects from a taxonomic point of view. In the terminology of Chapter 5 of *Thinking and Speech*, he was given a test to reveal what kind of concept he would form in a test of the formation of artificial concepts. He was judged as forming a collection complex, which in 1928 Luria and Vygotsky ranked as a 'set' – a lower grade of complex than an associative complex or a pseudoconcept, while what they would later call a pseudoconcept, they were then ranking as a 'concept'.

Luria demonstrated that some subjects who had attended school had learnt to categorise objects taxonomically according to shared visible attributes. Others however "saw no need to compare and group all the objects and to assign them to specific categories" or "tended to deal with the task as a practical one of grouping objects according to their role in a particular situation rather than as a theoretical operation of categorising them according to a common attribute" (1979, p. 69). It appears that Rakmat responded to Luria's experiment much the way we would respond if a man in a white coat showed us three white kids and a black kid and asked us which was the odd one out. We would simply refuse to answer.

By the time of writing up Sakharov's 1928 experiments on concepts for *Thinking and Speech* Vygotsky put it this way:

> The adult's thinking is often carried out at the level of complexes, and sometimes sinks to even more primitive levels. When applied in the domain of life experience, even the concepts of the adult and adolescent frequently fail to rise higher than the level of the pseudoconcept. They may possess all the features of the concept from the perspective of formal logic, but from the perspective of dialectical logic they are nothing more than general representations, nothing more than complexes. ...
>
> ... traditional psychology acted like a slave in following the description of the process of concept formation assumed by formal logic, ... representations ... can be decomposed into their constituents, into their form, colour, and size. The constituents of these representations that remain are those that correspond to one another. A process of

assimilation occurs for each of these constituents, the result of which is a general representation of each feature. Following a synthesis of these representations, we obtain one general representation or concept ...

1934, pp. 160, 162

The *pseudo*concept which Vygotsky is describing in 1931 (when this chapter was written) is exactly what Vygotsky was calling a *concept* in 1930!

Nonetheless, it seems that Luria may have correctly identified a problem with Rakmat's verbal intelligence in that Rakmat simply didn't get what Luria was asking him even though he very well knew everything about the objects in question. If Rakmat was going to live in a modern society dominated by bureaucratic thinking, he would have to learn to understand this inhuman way of thinking. It was the same in Dickens' *Hard Times*, when Cissy, who had an intimate practical knowledge of horses, was demanded by Mr. Gradgrind to give the definition of a horse, proving to her great embarrassment that she does not know that the answer is "four legs, forty teeth, etc., etc."

The importance of this mistake is that Vygotsky appears to have established that "primitive," that is, non-literate peoples *do not have true concepts* while 'civilised' peoples do. This mistake had, of course, political implications at the time and caused grave difficulty for his project. But the claim is based on what Vygotsky himself came to see as a *grave misunderstanding*. In fact, what was shown is that many *schools*, like Mr. Gradgrind's, especially elementary schools, teach only pseudoconcepts, and in populations where practical intelligence outstrips verbal intelligence, such instruction could, in the relevant contexts, supplant true concepts with pseudoconcepts. This might be a benefit for people in their dealings with the bureaucracy, but is a step backwards in their cultural development, insofar as it relates to their own lives.

Contra the Vygotsky of 1930, 'non-literate' peoples, *must have* had true concepts, otherwise they could never have survived as a people, not only because they could not otherwise regulate their relation to nature, but even more so because they could not have maintained and regulated their social structures. Nonetheless, the most uneducated and despised sections of a people *could be excluded* from access to the professions by being educated into pseudoconcepts at school, surviving only thanks to the knowledge indigenous to their own ethnic community.

The people of Uzbekistan did not think in pseudoconcepts. Archaeological findings tell us that the earliest human communities used religious rituals and seemed to believe in a life after death, which implies that they did *not* organise their understanding of the world on a sensory-taxonomic basis, but had *concepts, true* concepts. Such concepts must have rested on some conception, though certainly not a scientific one, of the place of people in the cosmos. Such concepts allowed them to organise their activity so as to successfully reproduce their communities and care for their land for millennia, whether that was rain forest, desert or tundra.

Further, the forced substitution of taxonomic categories for true concepts is a *degradation* of conceptual thought, flowing from inhuman, *bureaucratic*, administrative methods of social organisation. Doubtless, these bureaucratic means, adapted to the impersonal management of large numbers of people and things, is also associated with the use of writing in preference to speech. Both written speech and bureaucracy are inventions of civilisation, but they are not both conditions which foster true concepts. There is little romance in the discovery that the first writings were not poems, stories or epitaphs but accounts of property. Bureaucracy, in fact, militates *against* true concepts, while literacy on the whole supports and promotes true concepts.

Thus, we have to conclude that Vygotsky's periodisation of word use in terms of sets and concepts was mistaken.

Modern positivist philosophers create sophisticated concepts. But when it is concepts which are the object of study, they invariably grasp concepts as what Vygotsky called pseudoconcepts. This expresses a general law: that when we are required to do an operation which we can do effortlessly without conscious awareness, under conscious control, our performance falls to a lower level.

1.6 Lines of Development Differentiate and Interact

Each critical point in the development of behaviour was considered by Vygotsky from the standpoint of the new function or relation it brings to the process of development. That is, each critical point provides a starting point for the higher process of development.

> We will consider as such turning points in the behaviour of the apes the use of implements, or tools; in the behaviour of primitive man, work and the use of psychological symbols; and in the behaviour of the child, the splitting of its line of development into psycho-physiological and psycho-cultural development.
>
> 1930, p. xii

Tool use fostered the development of the hand and speech in our immediate evolutionary predecessors, and their further development characterised the whole epoch up to the formation of literate civilisations, and continues its involvement in development, but now interconnected with the development of psychological tools, whose rudimentary forms appeared in the period of "primitive man." But in the formation of the human species, tool use occurred in conjunction with the spoken word. Tool use stimulates speech and speech participates in the development of technique. Language and technique develop hand in hand.

According to Vygotsky, it is the *separating out* of verbal intelligence from practical intelligence which marked the cultural transition from "primitive man" to civilisation. Vygotsky believed that it is only with the adoption of writing that this separation becomes possible. This explains Vygotsky's idiosyncratic interest in the exotic and antique mnemotechnical artefacts, as precursors to writing.

What child development brings to the question is the separation of the *cultural* development of the personality from its *physiological,* inherited basis – unlimited cultural formation of the personality. That inherited basis includes the capacity to pay attention to signs from other people and find meaning in them, and an interest and facility in handling artefacts. Each of these lines of development *interacts with* the other in ontogenesis, allowing each line of development to far surpass the limits which would be possible along one line alone.

This last paragraph alludes to material which constitutes the field of cultural psychology but this is not the place to elaborate any of it. What is of interest here is only problems with the concept of tool and tool use and its relation to the concepts of sign and sign-mediated action. How can the material on tool use reported in *Ape, Primitive Man and Child* be taken forward? Where did this report leave Vygotsky's research project in 1930?

In this context it is noteworthy that speech, which appears together with labour at the very beginning of human phylogenesis (see Chapter 12, this volume), played no part in Vygotsky's schema in *Ape, Primitive Man and Child,* other than to manifest the stages of word use which marked the distinction between practical and verbal intelligence during the epoch of "primitive man," and in this case, Vygotsky had the relation back to front, mixing up true concepts and pseudoconcepts!

1.7   *Instrumental Psychology: History or Method?*

The kind of scientific activity which Vygotsky is advocating in *Ape, Primitive Man and Child* is an ethno-psychology or social history based on a history of artefacts. Is there any reason to think that this is a fruitful approach to the building of a general psychology, which was Vygotsky's explicit aim? Very little, I think.

I believe this is the activity to which Vygotsky was referring when he agreed with A.N. Leontyev, in a letter of 29 July 1929, that 'instrumental psychology' was an unprofitable pursuit. I take this to be something quite distinct from "The Instrumental Method in Psychology," which remains among his most important contributions to Psychology, and on which I will touch shortly.

That the cultural and historical development of human society and psychology is tied up with the production and use of both tools and signs, is an insight by no means unique to Vygotsky. What is unique to Vygotsky is the *experimental technique* – "the instrumental method in psychology" or "functional method of dual stimulation" – which made it possible to take the philosophical insights of Marxism, cultural analysis and classical German philosophy *into the psychological laboratory* as an effective method for the practical investigation of the human mind. (See Blunden, 2012, Chapter 12)

So when Vygotsky (2007) writes to his younger colleague, A.N. Leontyev on 29 July 1929:

> Dear Aleksei Nikolaevich, thank you for the letter. I wholeheartedly share your sentiments. There is some benefit to a situation in which I[nstrumental] P[sychology] winds up in the category of unprofitable pursuits. In particular, I cannot say strongly enough how highly I value (in ethical terms as well) the thought that the idea must be as pure and rigorous as possible. This is our principal task – to fight against muddled ideas and 'making ourselves comfortable'.

It is this historical/archaeological study of instruments which seemed to be 'unprofitable'. In other letters collected in the same journal Vygotsky makes references to the instrumental method in psychology: "everyone should work in his field according to the instrumental method. I am investing all the rest of my life and all my energy in this" and "Most important, I want to convene a 'conference' in spring or summer of people working with the instrumental method." In his later work, especially in *Thinking and Speech* (1934) he realised his commitment to this experimental-genetic method which in 1930 had been dubbed the "instrumental method" (see 1930a) as an approach to cultural-psychological research. This was possible however only because he had completely revised his conception of the place of *speech*.

There are two reasons to believe that Vygotsky wanted to abandon a 'history of tools' and *not* the 'instrumental method': (1) Much later, Leontyev used the word 'instruments' exclusively to refer to tools for working on nature and not psychological tools while *in fact* including the 'instrumental method in psychology' in his theory, and crediting Vygotsky's 'early work' for the idea; (2) Vygotsky did not in fact abandon the 'instrumental method'.

This proposition throws up four possible sharp objections which cannot be dealt with summarily. (1) isn't it the production of tools which distinguishes mankind from the animals? (2) didn't Engels himself suggest that the history of development of the means of production was the essential narrative of human psychology? and (3) isn't it a basic premise of Marxism that it is the labour process (i.e., tool use and tool production) which is the determining factor in social life? And (4) is not every tool also a sign for the means of its use, through which human beings understand the natural world in the process of changing it with tools?

These are four serious objections which will be dealt with in due course. But first I want to briefly consider some of Vygotsky's post-1930 works as to what he had to say about the relation of tool and sign. Up to this point we have only considered one pre-1930 work of Vygotsky which has a number of serious defects.

2   Tool and Sign in Vygotsky after 1930

2.1   *The Instrumental Method in Psychology*

It was at a talk given in 1930 entitled 'The Instrumental Method in Psychology', that Vygotsky introduced the term 'psychological tools or instruments' by analogy with 'technical tools', characterising symbolic devices such as books and maps as a type of tool – "artificial devices for mastering one's own mental processes" as opposed to devices for controlling nature – 'labour tools'. All "instrumental acts" can "without remainder" be reduced to natural (i.e. unmediated) ones, just like a machine all parts of which obey the laws of physics, but combine to serve human purposes. Vygotsky introduced with this talk the triangular diagram of 'instrumental processes' which can represent actions mediated by psychological tools or actions mediated by technical tools.

Vygotsky goes on to explain how with the instrumental method:

> We can also look at the behaviour of man from the viewpoint of his use of his natural mental processes and the methods of this use and try to comprehend how man utilises the natural processes of his brain tissue and masters the processes that take place in it.
>
> VYGOTSKY, 1930a, p. 86

So far then, the 'instrumental method' *in fact* concerns only the use of tools to act on nature, provided we accept the proposition that the human body in general and the brain in particular are natural, material things which can be shaped for human purposes, just like other artefacts. Admittedly, the inclusion of one's own brain as a part of nature on which a person acts when they use a tool, seems somewhat idiosyncratic, but it makes for the continuity of tools, from technical tools to a special type of tool called a 'psychological tool'. This is not just a metaphor.

He goes on to describe how a mental task is solved by introducing the use of a psychological tool. "Any behavioural act then becomes an intellectual operation." The 'instrumental act' (the act that involves mediation through the use of some instrument) is described as "an elementary unit of behaviour"[3] for the purposes of research. He again stresses the continuity with technical tools, from which the psychological tool is differentiated because it is used to act on the *mind* ("the natural processes that take place in the brain"), not external material processes.

Then: "By its very essence the instrumental method is a historical-genetic method" (p. 88), and he points to three areas where this method can be used: (a) social-history and ethnic psychology, (b) investigating the higher mental functions in the laboratory, and (c) child and educational psychology. "The instrumental method studies the child not only as a developing, but also as an educable being" (*op. cit.*, p. 85). The instrumental method provides a method for both research into the development of an individual and for education, by the introduction of a psychological tool into the activity of a child who is engaged in some task with which they are experiencing difficulty.

This is an *epoch-making discovery*, unique to Vygotsky and arguably his most important legacy. By showing how internal mental processes could be studied objectively, in the laboratory, Vygotsky unified the 19th century currents of 'brass instrument' psychology and 'cultural' psychology into a single science, able to produce useful results applicable to the full range of human behaviour. It also created the unit of analysis which would be later elaborated in *Thinking and Speech* (1934), introducing a key Hegelian insight into the methodology of modern science.

But Vygotsky also included under the heading of 'the instrumental method' an approach to social history and ethnic psychology which I believe he judged to be 'unprofitable'. Vygotsky was now using the term 'instrumental method', for a method which proved to be immensely 'profitable', also referred to as 'the functional method of dual stimulation'.

---

3 This is the first time that Vygotsky uses the idea of a unit, here a unit of artefact-mediated behaviour.

It is in 'Tool and Sign in the Development of the Child', evidently written in 1930, that Vygotsky first used the reference to Goethe to explain the relation of tool and sign in a short section entitled 'Word and Action'. Vygotsky here uses the word 'action' to mean only 'tool-mediated action', in contrast to 'word' which would *henceforth* be taken as the archetypal 'sign-mediated action'.

> To certain psychologists the ancient biblical 'In the beginning was the Word' retains all its fascination. New investigations, however, do not leave any doubt as to the fact that the word does not stand at the beginning of the development of the child's mind. ...
>
> Practical intellect is genetically more ancient than verbal; action precedes the word, even intelligent action precedes the intelligent word. Now, however, while repeating this thought, very true in itself, there is a tendency to overestimate action at the word's expense.
>
> ... we have tried to show how the *word,* becoming intellectualised and developing on the basis of *action,* lifts this action to a supreme level, subjects the child to its power, stamps it with the seal of will. But since we wanted to express all this in one short formula, in one sentence, we might put it thus: if *at the beginning* of development there stands the act, independent of the word, then at the end of it there stands *the word which becomes the act,* the word which makes man's action free.
>
> 1930c, pp. 166–170

In the course of this section he says: "To consider speech as a more particular case of action means to depend upon an incorrect definition of the concept of action" (*op. cit.*, p. 66). I interpret this to mean that *speech is not a type of tool-mediated action, arising from labour activity as if it were a type of tool,* something which *could* be said of writing. Speech has to be considered as a qualitatively distinct function *alongside labour*. He specifically negates any idea of the spoken word arising from, as an extension of, tool use in the sense he had held with respect to the written word.

2.2 History of Development of Higher Mental Functions

In 1931, Vygotsky wrote a manuscript which has been published in Volume 4 of LSV CW under the title *History of the Development of the Higher Mental Functions*, and Chapter 2 on 'Research Method' has a short treatment of tool and sign. He says:

> ... the basis for the analogy between the sign and the tool is the mediating function of the one and the other. From the psychological aspect, they

may, for this reason, be classified in the same category. ... from the logical aspect, both may be considered as coordinative concepts included in a more general concept – mediating activity.

1931b, p. 62

He then refers to Hegel's use (cited by Marx in *Capital*) of the concept of mediation as "the most characteristic property of the mind," and cites the chapter in Marx's *Capital* where Marx is discussing the instruments of production and refers to Hegel's concept of the "cunning of reason" to the effect that in using material objects and material processes acting according to their own natural law, they yet serve human purposes. Vygotsky then quotes Marx again in connection with the tools of labour:

> [Man] makes use of mechanical, physical, chemical properties of things in order to change them into tools to act on other things according to his purpose.
>
> MARX, 1867, pp. 189–190

Vygotsky then justifies the idea of signs mediating actions, just as tools mediate actions. He also notes that the mediating role is not restricted to tools and signs "since the activity of the mind is not exhausted by the use of tools and signs." (Referring perhaps to thinking which is 'beyond words' and aesthetic judgment.) He reiterates the functional distinction: the tool is directed at changing nature, while the sign is directed at changing a mind, and points to their interconnection in both phylogenesis and ontogenesis.

> the first use of a sign signifies going beyond the limits of the organic system of activity which exists for each mental function. The use of auxiliary devices, the transition to mediated activity radically reconstructs the whole mental operation just as the use of a tool modifies the natural activity of the organs, and it broadens immeasurably the system of activity of mental functions. We designate both taken together by the term *higher mental function*, or higher behaviour.
>
> loc. cit.

So, both technical tools and psychological tools are implicated in the construction of the 'higher mental functions', but the contribution to this change is *different* in the case of tools on the one hand, and signs on the other.

Vygotsky has by now developed an *antipathy* to the metaphorical use of the word 'tool' to indicate a sign:

> The indeterminate, vague meaning that is usually connected with figurative use of the word *tool* actually does not lighten the task of the researcher interested in the real and not the picturesque aspect that exists between behaviour and its auxiliary devices. Moreover, such designations obscure the road for research. Not a single researcher has yet deciphered the real meaning of such metaphors.
>
> loc. cit.

The discussion continues in Chapter 4, where Vygotsky describes how sign-mediation is used as an *experimental technique* to investigate the development of various psychological functions in children – "the instrumental method in psychology," a.k.a. the "functional method of dual stimulation." He makes the point that "a tool directed outward and a sign directed inward fulfil technically different mental functions" (Vygotsky, 1931c, p. 89), and makes it clear that it is *signs*, not *technical tools*, which are to be used in this research. Vygotsky defends, against criticism from various sides, the idea of the construction of an 'intellectual reaction' through the incorporation of signs into behaviour. It is clear that Vygotsky has identified the use of psychological tools, including signs and words, in ontogenesis as an extraordinarily fruitful area of experimental research.

Once taken for granted, *spoken words* were now recognised as the primary *signs*:

> In order to trace how the natural formation of the sign, which is not at all an intellectual discovery, develops in the child, we must deal with how speech in general is formed.
>
> 1931d, p. 126

This is a departure. Previously, 'signs' had referred to outgrowths of labour tools, archetypically, the written word, and Vygotsky had taken no account of the spoken word as a sign mediating speech action. But now, in 1931, for the first time he talks about spoken words *as signs mediating actions* as a means of mastering one's own behaviour.

Now, with labour and speech (action and word), developing in intimate connection with one another, even merging, they each develop at each step beyond what either line of development could have achieved separately.

2.3   *Thinking and Speech*

Produced in Vygotsky's last days, *Thinking and Speech* (1934) is Vygotsky's masterpiece. Here the key mediating element is for the first time, the *spoken word*.

The genetic relation between thinking and speech as two interconnected lines of development is expressed succinctly in the chapter on 'The Genetic Roots and Thinking and Speech':

1. In their ontogenetic development, thought and speech have different roots.
2. In the speech development of the child, we can with certainty establish a pre-intellectual stage, and in his thought development, a pre-linguistic stage.
3. Up to a certain point in time, the two follow different lines, independently of each other.
4. At a certain point these lines meet, whereupon thought becomes verbal and speech rational.

   1934, p. 112

This general schema applies equally well to language and labour, or word and deed, and other instances of interconnected processes of development. Each has independent roots and an independent line of development, but at a certain point they intersect and transform one another.

Thinking and Speech opens declaring its aim to be the analysis of thinking and speech, in which the *word is taken to be a sign*. The essential process is not the written word, but the *spoken word*, a unity of sound and meaning – the spoken word that has been there, together with and intimately connected to labour, from the very beginning of humankind.

In Chapter 5, reporting Sakharov's experiments on concept-formation, Vygotsky no longer refers to complexes as concepts, but simply as stages in the process of concept formation. Chapter 6 deals with true concepts (i.e., what are *truly* concepts). But further, Vygotsky now includes in the chapter on concept formation the 'potential concept'. This is a pre-intellectual form of activity which children share in common with many animals. A potential concept registers the practical significance of a situation, as a signal for some action which has become a *habitual* response to a given perceptual Gestalt. In this way, Vygotsky gives recognition to the co-existence of 'practical intelligence' along with the development of verbal intelligence, which is the subject matter of *Thinking and Speech*, and the role of tools in ontogenesis.

None of this detracts, however, from the significance in social history of the invention of writing and other psychological tools, nor of the impact of literacy in ontogenesis. It does emphasise, however, the importance of restricting our use of the word 'tool' to *material artefacts being used to act upon material*, and to not mix up the specific meaning of the word 'tool' as Vygotsky used it, with the metaphorical use of the word 'tool' as the means, and applicable to concepts, methods, theories, techniques of activity, etc.

3   Marx, Engels, Vygotsky and the Marxist Tradition

I shall now deal with some issues which arise from the Marxist tradition of which Vygotsky is a part.

3.1   *Marx and Engels on 'Just So Stories'*

The idea that the production and use of tools was not just an essential characteristic of the human species, but was the essential process which, through Darwinian natural selection, *created* the human species, originated with Engels' article *The Part Played by Labour in the Transition from Ape to Man* (1876). This claim was Engels's original idea, published only 17 years after the publication of Darwin's *The Origin of Species* (though prefigured by Benjamin Franklin and Samuel Johnson in the 18th century).

It is hardly possible that a leading ideologist of the communist movement of the 19th century, based on the *industrial working class*, was unaware of the ideological implications of the claim that industrial labour created the human species – not the Christian God, or competition and survival of the fittest, but industrial labour.

As Engels had written in 1875:

> The whole Darwinian theory of the struggle for existence is simply the transference from society to animate nature of Hobbes' theory of the war of every man against every man and the bourgeois economic theory of competition, along with the Malthusian theory of population. This feat having been accomplished – (… I dispute its unqualified justification, especially where the Malthusian theory is concerned) – the same theories are next transferred back again from organic nature to history and their validity as eternal laws of human society declared to have been proved.
> ENGELS, 1875, pp. 107–108

The ideological bourgeois interpretation of natural selection has since been challenged, with the anarchist Pyotr Kropotkin, for example, emphasising the role of *cooperation* in natural selection. These kind of 'Just So Stories' (Kipling, 1902) were not the invention of the 19th century. Marx wrote in 1867, alluding to a comment by Benjamin Franklin published in 1780:

> The use and fabrication of instruments of labour, although existing in the germ among certain species of animals, is specifically characteristic of the human labour process, and [Benjamin] Franklin therefore defines man as a tool-making animal. ... It is not the articles made, but how they are made, and by what instruments, that enables us to distinguish different economic epochs.
>
> MARX, 1867, p. 189

Later, he noted wryly:

> Aristotle's definition is that man is by nature a *town-citizen*. This is quite as characteristic of ancient classical society as Franklin's definition of man, as a *tool making* animal, is characteristic of Yankeedom.
>
> MARX, 1867, p. 331

So, Marx well understood how social classes and movements legitimise themselves by elevating their particular mode of existence and social position to be the essentially human one. The Marxist Evelyn Reed, for example, continued the defence of the origins of the human species in tool making in the 1960s against claims for the brain, speech and aggression being the essence of humanity responsible for the origin of our species. In 1970, she participated in the furious debate amongst feminists to establish that early human society was *matriarchal*, and that the patriarchy was instituted as part of the transition to feudalism, in which the women were robbed of their inheritance.

So, let us be clear. Origins stories are always interesting, but they are also invariably *ideological*, discovering in ancient history and nature conceptions which in reality have their origin in the problems of today. I believe that this was how come Vygotsky and Luria found themselves pursuing an avenue they eventually realised was 'unprofitable' – "Instrumental Psychology" – in pursuit of their aim, Cultural Psychology. In the end, Vygotsky discovered what was before his eyes in the first place: *speech*, which originated at the same time as labour and in close connection with it. It was the production and use of tools in labour, *in combination with speech* which created mankind.

3.2 *Labour and Language*

The 'linguistic turn', beginning in the 1960s, could not but impinge on the ideological differences over the essential features of Cultural Psychology. In his day, Marx had said:

> One of the most difficult tasks confronting philosophers is to descend from the world of thought to the actual world. *Language* is the immediate actuality of thought. Just as philosophers have given thought an independent existence, so they were bound to make language into an independent realm.
>
> 1845a, p. 446

The problem of the priority of language versus labour has long been the arena for a struggle for supremacy between the professional, upper layers of the working class and the industrial working class. The linguistic turn came at a time when the industrial working class itself was losing its hegemonic position in progressive politics, at the same time as the most advanced sections of the working class were increasingly becoming a class of 'symbolic analysts' more likely to be wielding a keyboard than a hammer. One should not be too quick to judge the ideological content of the tension in Cultural Psychology between Activity Theorists and Semioticians or Discourse Analysts. *Science needs to follow its own logic*. It is inevitable that social tensions arising from the development of the productive forces will intrude into science and determine its directions. But the scientist must *try* to remain above that, and follow the logic of their subject matter, not partisan imperatives, and thereby *anticipate* social movements, rather than be driven blindly along by them.

The same is true of choosing whether to use the term 'labour' or 'activity'. Insofar as these terms are correctly used in Cultural Psychology, they are co-extensive. The labour process is the determining factor in *historical* development, that is true. Nonetheless, 'activity' means purposive activity, activity aimed at changing the world – both the world of nature and the social world and is inclusive of all activity in the labour process. All that the word 'labour' brings to cultural psychology is *connotations* which emphasise (wrongly) industrial labour in contrast to other kinds of activity, such as personal services, child rearing, political activity, supervision of labour, child's play, writing poetry and scientific treatises. Ideological prejudices do no favour to science or to the social movements they serve.

Vygotsky began his social history and ethnic psychology project on the assumption, shared by most of the Marxists of his time, that it was the development of the *means of production*, i.e., tools, which was the decisive factor in history. But this is not the case. According to Marx, the first steps in the accumulation of capital are (1) primitive accumulation, which means outright robbery, driving the peasantry off their land thereby creating a class of labourers who do not own their own means of production (*Capital*, vol. 1, part viii); (2) the subsumption of the *existing* labour process under capital as wage labour (1861–63, p. 424ff.); (3) the transformation of the labour process into capitalist production and the concomitant revolutionising of the forces of production (Marx, 1864, p. 424ff.) – 'forces of production' being a category which includes the skills, organisation and energies of the workers. So in fact, it is not the means of production themselves but the social relations in which these means are utilised which are decisive. Were this not the case, capitalism would have emerged centuries earlier in China, not in 18th century Europe.

Vygotsky got there in the end, with the inclusion of the spoken word as a sign, and his formulation of the relation between word and deed as independent lines of development each with their own roots, while mutually interpenetrating and transforming one another – but in the *beginning* was the deed. This captures the relation free of the distorting lens of ideology. The relation is *not fixed once for all*, but changes in the course of development.

•••

Vygotsky underwent at least two major reversals at the time of writing *History* (1931): he reversed his idea of set *vs.* concept, and abandoned his pursuit of the history of tools, putting the spoken word rather than the tool in centre stage. What brought about this reversal? It seems to this author that Hegel lies behind it. A study of references to Hegel in Vygotsky's *Collected Works* (Blunden, 2009) suggests that it was only from the time of writing *History* in 1931 that Vygotsky had more than a superficial familiarity with Hegel. But it seems unlikely that even by this time, he had read more than a paragraph or two of Hegel. Vygotsky did collaborate in a project with some supporters of the Hegelian-Marxist Abram Deborin in 1930, so this may be where the Hegelian influence came from. This is a problem for further research.

3.3   A.N. Leontyev on Labour and Tools

The mediation of actions by tools was taken up by Vygotsky's younger colleague, A.N. Leontyev, as part of activity theory and it continues to play a role in activity theory, including that of Yjrö Engeström. So Vygotsky's work on tool-mediation did not go to waste. Before outlining the use to which tool-mediation has been put by Activity Theorists, I should mention a rather unpleasant manifestation of the ideological use of the word/deed relation by Leontyev in the toxic political atmosphere which prevailed in the decades of the Soviet Union after Vygotsky's death.

In 2005, the *Journal of Russian and East European Psychology* published a formerly unpublished and undated article by Leontyev entitled 'Study of the environment in the pedological works of L.S. Vygotsky'. This work was a rather scurrilous attack on Vygotsky, labelling him as an idealist (see Blunden, 2014a). The charge of idealism is based on Vygotsky's 'linguistic turn' in 1930:

> What, indeed, is communication as the term is used by Vygotsky? We are aware of two usages of the term: first, its usage to signify the general fact of people's interrelations, which encompasses their 'material dealings', and second, its usage in the ordinary, more narrow sense, in the sense of 'spiritual' relationships, that is, in the sense of communication using language. Obviously, for Vygotsky, it has only the second, narrower meaning. So, the process of verbal communication is defining for the child's psychological development; and consequently, the child appears in Vygotsky's work as *social*, and first and foremost as *a socialised* being. But, behind the superficial similarities of these two words lies a gulf separating their sense – the same gulf that separates materialism and idealism.
> 2005, p. 19

This is an empty criticism because language *is* a material interaction, and it is ultimately *material* relations which are communicated and psychologically appropriated by means of words. Conversely, the central weakness of Leontyev's own theory is that he overlooks that it is the *concept* a person forms of their situation that frames their psychological response to it, and that a true concept is generally formed only through the mediation of words. But Leontyev "sets aside [Vygotsky's] complicated idea of the different course of development of the 'spontaneous' and 'scientific' concepts" (p. 18), made possible by his analysis of word meaning.

3.4 Tools and Operations in Activity Theory

Origins play a very significant role in Leontyev's approach to psychology. He spent the major part of his scientific life tracing the emergence of life from its simplest manifestations through the lower animals to primates to human adults, and his highly structured theory reflects its genetic derivation.

In Leontyev's view, the most primitive forms of activity are *operations*. These are movements which may originate as a simple reflex response to a situation, whether conditioned or innate, and cannot be said to have any aim distinct from the operation itself, as the organism has no conscious awareness of the operation. More complex activities necessitate the concatenation of multiple such operations to achieve a goal (or 'object'). Thus, these operations now share an object which differs from the immediate goal of each. The operation adapts to its conditions rather than being controlled by the organism and its motive and can be executed without conscious awareness.

The aggregate of these operations is an *action*, which the organism consciously controls towards its object. More complex objects may be achieved by an aggregate of actions, *an activity*, with the aim of each action being distinct from the object or motive of the aggregate. Thus, *activities* constituted by a series of actions, each controlled by its own subordinate goal, can be carried out either by successive actions by the same organism, or actions distributed between different members of a community, via a division of labour. Only humans and the higher animals are able to carry out activities.

Conversely, when an action is carried out *habitually*, so that it can be executed and adapted to conditions without conscious awareness, each such action reverts to the status of an operation, until something upsets the operation, and it springs back into conscious awareness. It is then subjected to conscious control as an action. What can be done habitually, controlled by conditions, can be done by an algorithm or by a machine.

Tools can be incorporated in the labour process if a routine operation carried out by a person is *objectified* and given material form in an artefact. In the earliest phase of cultural development, the natural means of production were common property, like the language.

> The need for awareness of operations already arose in the transition to the fashioning of differentiated tools, and especially of composite ones. The earliest tools, as archaeological finds have shown, could still have been the result of simple 'adaptation' of natural objects to the conditions of labour activity (for example, the 'natural retouching' of universal stone implements in the course of using them).
> 1981, p. 14

Leontyev argued that in apprehending a tool, and knowing how to use it, a person forms a concept of the human labour operation objectified in the tool. The invention and fashioning of tools is the process whereby human communities form concepts of nature, in the form of all the operations by which human beings interacted with and changed nature, and the material means used to do so.

A tool is an objectified operation. Every action, once it has become habitual, is ripe for objectification as a tool.

The consciousness of early humans was composed of 'potential concepts' (to use Vygotsky's term) based on tools, objects which exist outside of consciousness and can be sensuously apprehended like other objects and processes. Language developed in the labour process and as each operation was mastered, so far as possible the operation was objectified in a tool and named in the language. In this way, the practical intellect of human beings was constructed from the tools we use to interact with the world around us. Practical intelligence, at first, led the development of verbal intelligence.

Leontyev credited Vygotsky's early work, i.e., that reflected in *Ape, Primitive Man and Child*, for the ideas behind this theory:

> The idea of analysing activity as a method of scientific human psychology was proposed, as I have already said, in the early works of L.S. Vygotsky. The concept of tooled ('instrumental') operations, the concept of purposes, and later the concept of motive ('motivational sphere of consciousness') were introduced.
>
> 1978, p. 98

This approach also underlay Davydov's (1990) idea in which a tool which objectifies an operation forms the 'germ cell' from which a more concrete concept can develop. Yjrö Engeström (1999; 2015) has further developed this idea. For James Wertsch (1985), on the other hand, "It is Vygotsky's later interpretation of signs and their mediational capacities that will be the primary focus." These writers *all* acknowledge that their work is based on Vygotsky's concept of the *artefact-mediated action*.

3.5   Postscript: Engels and Vygotsky

It is clear from Vygotsky's writing that he was an avid reader of Engels' popularisations of dialectics. *The Part Played by Labour in the Transition from Ape to Man* (1876) and its more developed version as the Introduction to *Dialectics of Nature*, must have had an influence on him. A couple of observations on this essay are in order.

Engels was the first to say that it was labour which brought about the transition from not-yet-human apes to human beings. "Labour begins with the making of tools." Freeing the hands by the adoption of an erect gait led to the making of tools, that is, labour, and this led to the expansion of the brain, language and sundry other changes, and eventually to the emergence of human beings as a species. So

> ... the development of labour necessarily helped to bring the members of society closer together by increasing cases of mutual support and joint activity, and by making clear the advantage of this joint activity to each individual. In short, men in the making arrived at the point where *they had something to say* to each other ... and the organs of the mouth gradually learned to pronounce one articulate sound after another...
>
> 1876, p. 455

and summing up

> First labour, after it and then with it speech – these were the two most essential stimuli under the influence of which the brain of the ape gradually changed into that of man.
> *loc. cit.*

Vygotsky seems to have paid attention to that. In the introduction to *Dialectics of Nature*, published in Russia in 1925, Engels says:

> With humans we enter *history*.
> 1875a, p. 330

That is, once the human species has arisen, thanks to the biological transformation of the ape effected by labour, a new principle of development takes the lead. Engels then presents a short history of human activity from the stone axe to the socialist revolution:

> the more that human beings become removed from animals in the narrower sense of the word, the more they make their own history consciously.
> *op. cit.*

Engels placed the history of the human race in the context of the eventual extinction of life on Earth and the death of the solar system itself, but he makes no particular distinction between the cultural-historical, psychological and biological development of human beings or the principles governing these processes of development. He also told this story as if it were a single undifferentiated line of development encompassing all of human history in a single 'grand narrative'. Engels' concern was with the possibilities for the transformation of social relations, not psychology. So in terms of constructing the foundations of cultural psychology, Engels left all the work still to be done.

Nonetheless, it is remarkable that Engels' speculations, made only 17 years after the publication of Darwin's *Origin of Species*, are now, 140 years later, widely accepted, namely, that tool making and language developed side by side in the predecessor species before the emergence of homo sapiens, and it was at this earliest point in evolutionary development that the brain underwent its most rapid expansion. The eons over which homo sapiens then evolved were marked by cultural evolution and relatively modest anatomical change, and brain size has actually *decreased* during the last 15,000 years – perhaps because we have been able to rely more on our 'extended mind'.

Tool and sign have each had independent roots in the development of Marxism and Cultural Psychology. These two lines of development continue to interact and transform one another in the work of Cultural Psychologists and Activity Theorists, an interaction which can surpass what either line of development could achieve separately. As Hegel (1802) said: "The word is the tool of Reason."

4   Conclusion

We have traced the development of Vygotsky's thinking from his early *Ape, Primitive Man and Child* up to his mature work embodied in *Thinking and Speech*. Vygotsky changed his mind 180 degrees on more than one major issue in the course of this development. The conclusions he arrived at are too subtle and complex to summarise in a few lines, so I will not attempt to do so.

The prejudices with which he approached his study of prehistoric human society were largely those of his time. Much of what he later considered to be mistakes remain conventional wisdom elsewhere, but even in this early work omitted from his *Collected Works* there are outstanding insights which remain generally unknown to analytical science.

I think one of the key insights that he developed in the course of his scientific career was how any concrete feature of human beings originates through more than one line of development when those separate lines of development intersect and become intertwined with one another. It is never just this feature or that feature, but the mutual imbrication of two unfolding lines of development.

This is in contrast to the tendency to counterpose one feature of human beings to another as the essential feature, the abstract, either-or mentality which always fails to grasp the concrete. The way in which Leontyev wilfully misunderstood Vygotsky, denouncing him as an idealist, rejecting his ideas about concepts as 'complicated' and conflating the subject matter of psychology with orthodox 'historical materialism' may have been made under Stalinist compulsion, but it is something which has been seen throughout the history of Marxism. Doubtless these struggles between opposing lines of development have been necessary and not without fruit. We see in the history just outlined how Vygotsky himself passed through these struggles. The issue however is how to understand the human being *concretely*, and Vygotsky has shown us how.

CHAPTER 7

Vygotsky's Theory of Child Development

1   The Concepts of Vygotsky's Periodisation

Vygotsky saw child development as consisting of passing through a series of periods of stable development, namely, infancy, early childhood, pre-school age, (primary) school age and puberty. These periods of stable development are punctuated by periods of crisis: at birth, and at the ages of one, three, seven and thirteen years.

Vygotsky named these stages in terms that evidently made sense in the USSR of the 1920s and 1930s, but his periodisation essentially depended on the occurrence of specific structural transformations in the child's relation to their social environment and correspondingly in their mental life. The timing of these crises is in large measure set by custom and social practice. He claimed that under different social conditions these transformations will still take place, but will happen 'differently', and up to a point, at different ages. For example, when referring to the crisis at age seven, Vygotsky notes:

> Facts show that in other conditions of rearing, the crisis occurs differently. In children who go from nursery school to kindergarten, the crisis occurs differently than it does in children who go into kindergarten from the family. However, this crisis occurs in all normally proceeding child development.
> VYGOTSKY, 1934b, p. 295

What is important in every case however, is the *concept* Vygotsky proposes for each of the structures and transformations. Child development takes place differently in different cultural circumstances. This is not just a matter of empirical fact, but rather points to the need for concepts which allow us to understand the route by which cultural factors, which can be determined empirically, are active in shaping the development of the child. This allows us to understand the mechanism whereby the culture and institutions of a society are reproduced from generation to generation. The fundamental character of the structures with which Vygotsky is concerned forces us to consider that the same series of transformations may be experienced by children developing in *any* society, though in every case, they will be experienced differently, at different ages, and the outcomes will be different.

There are several unique concepts which Vygotsky introduced, and understanding them is the main thing we have to look at.

2 Social Situation of Development

The first and most important concept is the *social situation of development*.

> ... at the beginning of each age period, there develops a completely original, exclusive, single, and unique relation, specific to the given age, between the child and reality, mainly the social reality that surrounds him. We call this relation the *social situation of development* at the given age. The social situation of development represents the initial moment for all dynamic changes that occur in development during the given period. It determines wholly and completely the forms and the path along which the child will acquire ever newer personality characteristics, drawing them from the social reality as from the basic source of development, the path along which the social becomes the individual.
> *op. cit.*, p. 198

Vygotsky conceived of the social environment in which the child finds itself and the relationship of the child to other people not just as a collection of factors, as influence or resource or context or community, but concretely, as a *predicament*.

The child begins life more or less helpless. Even the cortex of the brain does not yet function sufficiently well to perceive the figure of objects or people, or even distinguish the child's own body from its background. Aside from some reflexes, the child is unable to contribute to meeting or even determining any of its own needs. At the end of the process when the child enters the world of work, if each of the periods of stable development and crises have been successfully negotiated, the child has become a fully mature member of the wider society, able to determine and meet their own needs in a manner consonant with their social position, aware of other possible social positions, taking moral responsibility for their actions, and participating in the reproduction of the culture and institutions of the society.

At each successive stage in the child's development the child becomes able to perceive that the very situation through which their vital needs are being met, has *ensnared* them in a trap from which the child can emancipate themself only by *striving* in a way that *stretches* the capacities that they have at the given stage of development. In the case of a stable period of development, this striving helps bring one central function to maturity and eventually makes the social situation of development redundant, bringing into being a new predicament. In the case of the periods of crisis, with their striving, the child forcibly breaks from the predicament and opens the way directly to a new period of stable development in a new mode of behaviour and interaction.

The predicament is therefore contained in the way the child's needs are being met through the adults related to the child, which lock the child into certain modes of activity that they are capable of sensing, at one point as a mark of respect or degree of freedom, but at another, as a limitation, and even come to see as a kind of insult, the transcendence of which becomes a need and a drive in its own right. But they are not yet capable of transcending that limitation, and their efforts to do so are frustrated. The mode of activity through which the child's needs are being met is created in response, on one hand, to the adults' expectations of the child, and the resources acquired from their culture, and on the other hand, to the child's behaviour and age, according to the child's capacities. Numerical age may be a factor, simply because institutional norms impose age level expectations on the child irrespective of the child's actual level of functioning.

As the child develops within the social situation of development a contradiction develops. Whereas the child's needs have been satisfied up till now through the existing situation, due to the child's development, the child becomes aware of new needs, new needs which presuppose the child occupying a new role, and a corresponding change in the social situation. An infant may be quite happy having its mouth stuffed with food ... up to a point, but they soon feel the need to have control over what is put in their mouth. They need to disrupt the situation in which absolutely everything is done for them.

This ability to sense new needs does not yet mean that the child is able to satisfy them. This is both because they do not yet have the ability to do so and because the adult carers do not treat them as a child who has that ability. The child is stuck in this situation and has begun to see it as a restriction, even though it is the situation in which their needs are being met. For example, a child might be angry and want to defy their mother, but at that moment they simply can't overcome their own inclinations. Their mother finds it easy to manipulate them with rewards or distractions and in this circumstance the child may become defiant and refuse to do anything, so as to free themselves from the mother's manipulation by developing their own will and letting their mother know they have a mind of their own.

It is this striving to take on a new role and change the situation which actualises development. The development however can only be actualised if the adult carers respond by entering into the new mode of interaction with the child. The child perceives the situation as a constraint and strives to overcome it. To overcome those constraints which fall within the child's capacity to perceive, is also a key *need* of the child, a drive which is not facilitated, but *frustrated* by the social situation which created it. If the child does not feel a need to overcome these constraints on the determination and satisfaction of their newly perceived needs, or does not strive to overcome these constraints and emancipate themself, then a pathological situation exists and the child will not develop. For example, a young teenager who *never* feels any need to criticise the views and ways of their own family and their teachers will never fully develop as an adult and take their own position in society.

Notice that the child must become aware (at *whatever level* it is sensible to speak of a child of the given age being aware) of the limitations of their present position. That is, they must in some way be able to imagine a different role for themselves. The conditions for becoming aware of such a role are created by the current social situation of development, but there are always limitations on the ability of a child to see what could be, but is not yet the case.

Thus we have an abstract definition of the social situation of development which tells us how to understand the multiplicity of relationships around the child so as to grasp concretely, and as a whole, how the social environment both determines and affords development of the child. A culture only offers a finite number of distinct roles for people according to their life course. These will be different in each culture, but every society has such roles each with appropriate rights and expectations for everyone from the maternity ward to the retirement home. Each of these life stages constitutes a viable form of life in the form of specific relationships between the person and those around them.

As a general concept, the driving force of the development is the predicament created by a gap between the child's manifest needs and *the current social means of their satisfaction*. This conception of the social situation of development is *universal*, but in every single case the situation is different because the adults providing for the child's needs do so differently in different cultural circumstances. They have different expectations of the child and will react differently to the child's behaviour, not to mention the indeterminate impact of differences in diet and physical conditions of existence that the adults provide for the child. For example, the infant may grasp for their mother's breast, but the mother may or may not respond; the child's predicament is the same, but the outcome is different. Actualisation of the social situation of development is different in every different social and historical situation, and the course of development is therefore different in each case. In this sense, development is culturally determined. But in each case, to understand the factors that determine the course of development, we should look to the contradiction between the level of the child's development which more or less corresponds to the manner in which the child's needs are being met, and the constraints that this mode of interaction imposes on the child's ability (at their relevant stage of development) to intuit those constraints and overcome them. For example, the child who proudly turns up at school, ready to take on their new role outside the immediate care of their own family, but, unable to distance their consciousness from their behaviour and adopt an intellectual disposition, will not only fail at their schoolwork but may also suffer in the playground. The child will thereby feel an intense need to master strategic behaviour and adapt to the demands of school life. This can be traumatic for any child, but it is only by being thrown out of the nest, so to speak, that this development is made.

Vygotsky gives an example (1934a) of a social situation which demonstrates how one and the same circumstance may bring about different development outcomes according to the child's age. A single mother had three children, but had become dysfunctional due to becoming a drunkard. The oldest child made a development, acting well above his age, taking over the role of head of household and looking after his mother as well; the middle child had been close to her mother and could not adjust to her wild behaviour and her development suffered; the youngest child is "overwhelmed by the horror of what is happening to him" and develops neuroses. This shows clearly how the *social situation of development* is about the *relationship between* a child's felt needs and their circumstances insofar as they are able to perceive them.

3   Central Neoformation

Neoformation. This rather strange word is used by Vygotsky to mean a psychological function, or more precisely a mode of the child's interaction with their social environment, including the specific mode of mental activity implied in the given type of social interaction. A neoformation is so-called because it newly appears at a specific stage of the child's development, differentiating itself from other functions (or combining them) and enabling a new mode of social interaction.

Each age level of development of the child is characterised by a social situation, with its specific predicament, and one neoformation above all others, plays the leading role in restructuring the mental life of the child – the one that Vygotsky calls the *central neoformation.*

In the case of stable periods of development, the central neoformation gradually differentiates itself in the first phase of the period, and then in the latter phase, it drives the restructuring of the child's behaviour and eventually makes the social situation of development redundant by overcoming the former constraints, generating new modes of interaction and setting up a new predicament. The central neoformation does not disappear, but continues to develop and play its part in the child's activity, but no longer plays the central driving role in development. Later it will develop along a peripheral line of development.

> These neoformations that characterise the reconstruction of the conscious personality of the child in the first place are not a prerequisite but a result or product of development of the age level. The change in the child's consciousness arises on a certain base specific to the given age, the forms of his social existence. This is why maturation of neoformations never pertains to the beginning, but always to the end of the given age level.
> 1934b, p. 198

In the case of the *critical* periods of development which mark the transition from one period of stable development to the next, the central neoformation forces a break from the old relationships and lays the foundation for a new social situation of development, but it is *transient*. In the normal course of development it *fades away* and will reappear later only under extreme conditions. These are called *transitional neoformations*.

> The most essential content of development at the critical ages consists of the appearance of neoformations which ... are unique and specific to a high degree. Their main difference from neoformations of stable ages is that they have a transitional character. This means that in the future, they will not be preserved in the form in which they appear at the critical period and will not enter as a requisite component into the integral structure of the future personality. They die off, ...
> *op. cit.*, pp. 194–195

This means that the kind of negativity which children resort to during critical periods in order to break into the new relationship will fade away and generally only reappear in the event of a breakdown in the new situation. Also, during the earliest phases of life, infants and their parents often manifest very advanced modes of interaction, not based on cortical functions of the brain and which will not go on to be the foundations of mature psychological functions, as they fade away in the following critical phase.

4 Lines of Development

In its development from a helpless newborn to a mature and responsible young adult, the child must pass through a series of age levels, each of which constitutes a viable form of social practice, a *Gestalt*. At each point in this development, the child is able to utilise only those neoformations which have been developed so far, pulling themselves up by their own bootstraps, so to speak. Each chapter in this story involves transformation of the mental life and mode of interaction of the child from one whole, viable form of life to another. At each age-level there is a *central line of development* which is the story of how the central neoformation of the age level differentiates itself from the psychic structure. This brings about a new constellation of psychological functions, transforms the relationship between functions, and stimulates the development of others, while suppressing still others, transforming cause into effect and effect into cause and turning means into ends and ends into means. The central line of development in each age level is driven by the requirements of development of the central neoformation. But, at the same time, *peripheral lines of development*, or 'subplots' so to speak, continue. Sometimes these are in support of the central lines of development and at other times they continue the work begun in previous age levels, by refining and strengthening functions which are, however, no longer the driving force of development. The central line of development is the story of how the child overcomes the predicament contained in the social situation of development and leads into a new predicament, and how the central neoformation restructures the mental life of the child and their relationship to the social environment.

> ... at each given age level, we always find a central neoformation seemingly leading the whole process of development and characterising the reconstruction of the whole personality of the child on a new base. Around the basic or central neoformation of the given age are grouped all the other *partial neoformations* pertaining to separate aspects of the child's personality and the processes of development connected with the neoformations of preceding age levels. The processes of development that are more or less directly connected with the basic neoformation we shall call *central lines of development* at the given age and all other partial processes and changes occurring at the given age, we shall call *peripheral lines of development*. It is understood that processes that are central lines of development at one age become peripheral lines of development at the following age, ...
>
> *op. cit.*, p. 197

5   Age Levels

Thus, the *age levels* are characterised by the specific mode of interaction which arises on the basis of the social situation thanks to the central neoformation that moves to the fore and matures in the given age period along the central line of development. Each of the phases of development entails biological changes in the organism as well as changes in institutional expectations based on the historical experience and practices of the given society. Consequently, although the age levels entail regular years of age, they are defined not by age, but by the central neoformation of development in the age level.

Stable age levels are periods during which the growth of a central neoformation takes up a central role in development, through its becoming a mature and continuing part of the child's psyche. In *critical age periods*, the child forcibly breaks away from the former social situation of development by the premature exercise of more developed forms of wilfulness, manifested in forms of *negativism*. It is in traversing these critical periods that the child's will is developed, and they are therefore crucial in shaping the child's personality.

These forms of negativism that rest on the child's striving despite every effort to overcome the frustration of their drive to do that which they cannot do, disrupt their former relations and open up conditions for a new period of stable development. Once new conditions are established, the negativism of the critical period fades away.

Vygotsky says that during the periods of stable development, it is the change in a single neoformation which drives the development of the whole, but during the critical periods of development, it is the change in the *entire structure* of the psyche which determines the changes in the separate neoformations and the *relations* between them.

> At each given age period, development occurs in such a way that separate aspects of the child's personality change and as a result of this, there is a reconstruction of the personality as a whole – in development [i.e., during the critical periods] there is just exactly a reverse dependence: the child's personality changes as a whole in its internal structure and the movement of each of its parts is determined by the laws of change of this whole.
>
> *op. cit.*, p. 196

Thus, during the stable periods of development, the child's personality undergoes gradual change along the central line of development. The process is *gradual* because it has the form of maturation of the central neoformation, without disruption to the child's relation to its environment. The central neoformation gradually matures and reorients the entire personality, but as it matures, the personality gradually comes into conflict with the situation, and the child is unable to find satisfactory resolution for this conflict. During the critical periods, the whole personality undergoes a structural transformation and all the psychological functions are rearranged according to the success of this transformation towards a new relationship between the child and their environment. In each stable phase of its development, the child acts out a role defined by a concept specific to the given cultural formation, such as 'toddler' or 'primary school child'.

At the beginning of the critical period, the child exhibits *negativity* in relation to its current role, and then in the latter phase of the critical period, the child exhibits *instability* in adoption of its new role.

6 Self-Relation and the Crisis Periods

From birth through to the crisis of puberty, the child develops a more and more developed relation-to-self, that is, grades of consciousness or self-consciousness and self-determination. According to Vygotsky, the periods of critical development are marked by transformations in the development of the *will* or capacity for self-determination. We can summarise the changes Vygotsky saw in self-relation through the periods of crisis as shown in the table below.

The child begins life totally undifferentiated from their mother, physically, biologically, psychologically and socially, and their psychological functions are also undifferentiated. So long as behaviour is not differentiated from affect, the child is a slave to their own feelings. For example, so long as a youth does not differentiate themself from their social position they are unable to take moral responsibility for their own actions. It is only by the complete differentiation of the various psychological functions that the young person gains control over their own behaviour and participation in society, and differentiates themself as an individual from those around them. It is only through this complete process of *differentiation* that the individual can actually become a *real part* of their society, and actually contribute to the production, reproduction and transformation of the culture and society.

Thus the process is contradictory in the sense that integration into a truly human society presupposes a process of differentiation of the individual. The whole process of becoming human is driven, from beginning to end, by the striving of the child to overcome the limitations to their self-determination and emancipate themself from imprisonment by their own drives. This drive

TABLE 1 Periods of crisis in child development

Crisis period	Self-relation
Birth	The child physically separates themself from the mother and creates the conditions for the 'front brain' to begin work, through which alone social interaction is possible.
Crisis at 12 months	Still unaware of themself as a person distinct from those around them (*Ur-wir*), the child manifests their own will and their own personality for the first time through interaction with adults.
Crisis at age 3	Having gradually developed a consciousness of themself as a distinct person, the child separates themself from the mother psychologically, and by differentiation of behaviour from affect, brings their behaviour under control of their own will.
Crisis at age 7	Having gradually expanded their radius of activity beyond the family, the child gains control over their relations with others by the differentiation of their internal and external life, manifested in an ability to act strategically.
Crisis at age 13	Having acquired knowledge appropriate to their social position, the child distances themself from their birthright by taking a critical stance toward it. This entails dissociating all conceptions, formerly taken as parts of a single whole, now to be grasped each in itself.

for emancipation then proves to be the only genuinely human drive, the drive which knows no end and transcends all barriers.

7 'Leading Activity' and Zone of Proximal Development

The Zone of Proximal Development (ZPD) is the most widely known and used of Vygotsky's concepts. There are many things that a child may see others around them performing, which no amount of coaching or trying will allow them to even *imitate*. There are a range of psychological functions, however, between those which, on the one hand, the child is able to master even without assistance, but on the other hand, the child cannot manage even if given assistance. The range in between these two limits is called the ZPD, within which he child can manage the activity if given assistance. According to Vygotsky these are the functions which lie within the child's reach and the child can be taught. Trying to teach the child something which lies beyond their ability to achieve even with assistance is a waste of time, and will have to wait until the child has further matured in their current situation. If two children are judged to be at the same level according to what they are able to do unaided, but one child is able to achieve more than the other when given assistance, this indicates to the teacher the additional potential of the child in terms of their as yet untapped development.

If we know the central line of development at a given stage in the child's development and the identity of the central neoformation, then we may consider what conditions or modes of interaction the child will need in order to promote that line of development and ensure its successful completion. At each level, the child's personality undergoes a reconstruction, and one function above all others is destined to play the leading role in *that* reconstruction. If instruction can bring about development of that function then development of other functions will follow *as a matter of course*. On the other hand, there are always peripheral lines of development which play only a secondary role in the child's overall development, that is, the reconstruction of their personality in preparation for the adoption of a new mode of interaction with their environment.

In such critical phases, the identification of this central neoformation in the ZPD is crucial to the teacher interested in assisting the child in making a critical development, rather than in simply learning to do more things. However, during the long stable periods of development, that is precisely what the child needs. The central line of development then is the maturing and consolidation of the central neoformation which characterises the whole stage of development, and during the early phase of that stage, a child is still stabilising the neoformation of that stage and operating at the higher level is still somewhat beyond the child's imagination and ability. This stability only comes when the child's central neoformation has matured.

Hence, during the stable periods of development, the social situation of development obliges the child to strive to master the psychological functions that lie within limits imposed by their social situation of development, and as a result of this striving, the central neoformation develops and leads the whole process of development. Vygotsky assumes that carers and teachers will be aware of those psychological functions which lie within the ZPD, and which neoformations are central and which are peripheral. Appropriate instruction that promotes the striving of the child and the differentiation and growth of their central neoformation will assist development, whereas efforts to interest the child in other activity, which involves peripheral lines of development or lie beyond the child's age level of ability, will not be expected to bring any significant developmental benefit.

During the latter stages of the stable phase of development the child begins to perceive new possibilities, and by assisting the child, the teacher or carer may be able to see that qualitatively new functions are within the child's reach, and at this time instruction should be directed at encouraging these new forms of activity.

It is here that Vygotsky's concept of the 'Zone of Proximal Development' is relevant. *Instruction may lead development*, if and only if instruction assists the child in promoting the differentiation of the *leading* neoformation. Vygotsky proposed that what the child can do *today with assistance* (for example by asking leading questions, offering suggestions) or *in play* (which allows the child to strive to do what they actually cannot yet do), they will be able to do *tomorrow without assistance*. The desired 'flow over' to different functions that result from success in performing the given activity, will occur *only if the intervention has promoted the central or leading neoformation*. Otherwise, teaching by assisting the child with a task may help them learn that task, but there will be no *flow over* to development. In that sense, we could introduce into the concepts Vygotsky uses in this work the idea of 'leading activity'. The leading activity and the corresponding social interaction is that which promotes the striving of the child in the exercise of central neoformation of the age-period.

For example, a three-year-old showing the first signs of being able to carry out tasks without supervision would be carefully encouraged and supported because the development of this capacity for independent, unsupervised activity is the central line of development, in Vygotsky's view, for the period of middle childhood.

During the periods of critical development, however, the situation is different. The child is trying to rupture the social situation of development and create a social position for themself in a new social situation. The child's behaviour in these periods of crisis is disruptive of the existing relationships. Here again, instruction can lead development, but in this case, development will entail a 'leap' in the child's activity into a new relationship to their social environment. The child's carers need to understand what lies behind the child's behaviour and assist the child through to the new social situation. Again, this is a question which will exercise the *skill and art* of the educator and carer, and Vygotsky did not live to offer advice on this matter beyond helping to give us an understanding of the dynamics that underlie the child's behaviour and development.

CHAPTER 8

The Concept of Object

The aim of this paper is to determine a concept of 'object' which can be used in the sense of 'the object of an activity (or project)' so that the full range of the concept of 'project' can be elaborated consistently and without ambiguity. Such a concept must be helpful in understanding the motivation of individuals participating in a project, the perception of a project from both inside and outside, how a project undergoes qualitative change as a result of experience, and how a project finally integrates itself into the community having changed the way that the community thinks and acts through realisation of its object.

1   The Various Concepts of Object

The Latin *objectum* (Inwood, 1992, p. 203ff.), literally 'something thrown before or against', was first used by Duns Scotus in the 13th century as something ascribed to the 'subject'. At this time, 'subject' had the meaning of the 'subject matter of discourse', so the 'object' was what was thrown against it, i.e., what was said of the subject, the predicate.

In the 17th century, the meanings of subject and object underwent an inversion. René Descartes made *subjectum* the mind rather than what was before the mind, and Christian Wolff gave *objectum* the meaning of something thrown before the *mind*, i.e., the object of knowledge but also of striving, of desire and of action by the subject. This inversion reflected the first efforts to focus on what was in the mind as something distinct from what the mind was thinking of.

The German *Das Objekt* is derived from the Latin *objectum* in the later sense. *Das Objekt* does not have to be a real or material thing, though Kant also used it in that narrower sense, and in common speech it means just that. But *Objekt* is taken to be an 'objective' situation, though imagined or perceived and given meaning by the mind. In English, the issue has been somewhat confused by 'subject' retaining its earlier meaning of the passive subject matter of discussion or work, subject of a murder plot or of a king, alongside the usage more common in philosophy as the active agent or mind.

The native German word *Gegenwurf* – 'what is thrown against' – was synonymous with *Objekt*. From the 17th century, however, *Gegenstand* – 'what stands against' – displaced *Gegenwurf* in everyday speech and in philosophical writing, including that of Kant, while remaining synonymous with *Objekt*.

It was Hegel who introduced differences in meaning between *Gegenstand* and *Objekt*, and all the various meanings of the word 'object' were anticipated by Hegel and all point to one or another aspect of Hegel's concepts, so let's start with Hegel.

2   Hegel's *Objekt* and *Gegenstand*

Whilst in ordinary German speech, *Objekt* and *Gegenstand* remained synonymous, meaning something existing independently of the subject, Hegel made *Gegenstand* an object ('subject matter') of knowledge, of consciousness and intention, and in this meaning, *Gegenstand* played a key role in his *psychology*. The logical-genetic derivation of Hegel's psychology begins with an organism that simply *feels*, without any sense of an other. Through sensation, the organism becomes aware of an independent source of sensations and this is the *Gegenstand*. Later, the organism comes to know itself mediately through the *Gegenstand* and the way is opened to understanding the *Gegenstand* as a product of its own activity bearing meaning. *Gegenstand* does not have a role in his logic or social theory, however.

The *Objekt*, on the other hand, had a central place in Hegel's Logic and social theory. The *Objekt* was a real object, independent of the subject, but nevertheless the object *of* a subject, and like the subject, the *Objekt* is taken to be a system of activities and relations, somewhat consonant with the modern concept of 'The System'. *Das Objekt* is not a psychological concept as such for Hegel, but in his *Logic*, the *Subjekt-Objekt* relation is central to the formation of a concept in the phase of ascent from abstract to concrete. Concept formation for Hegel is first of all a cultural-historical, rather than a psychological process. The *Objekt* is not taken to be an individual person or thing. Both the subject and the *Objekt* of the subject are independent cognising, practical subjects, i.e., formations of consciousness, and the development of each involves a mutual interpenetration and transformation. It is in this sense that a social formation is a 'subject-object' – an active subject which produces and reproduces its own conditions of life.

For Hegel, the *Objekt* refers to the *other* subject, especially the dominant, universal subject in the community and its construal of the world, with its language, activities and artefacts. In this context, the *Subjekt* is some individual, social movement or new concept which likewise construes the world in its own way and consequently strives to transform the *Objekt* so as to conform to itself. Here the *Objekt* is both the object acted upon and the means used. Contrariwise, the *Objekt* obliges the *Subjekt* to act according to its norms. The rest is history.

This leaves *Gegenstand* as the object of attention, desire, striving, etc., some problem or issue confronting a subject, rather than the entire social formation from within which both the subject (individual or collective) and object (*Gegenstand*) are constructed. For example, in the relation between the Women's Liberation Movement and the patriarchal society it seeks to transform, the Women's Liberation Movement is the *Subjekt* and patriarchal society is the *Objekt*, but the gender bias in appointments to some institution might be the *Gegenstand* a woman confronts in her career. Likewise, in the relation between Sociology and a social formation a sociologist is studying – Sociology is the *Subjekt* and the social formation (including those who study sociology) is the *Objekt*. This is not a psychological problem, but a problem which belongs to Social Theory and Logic in the expanded sense given to Logic by Hegel. If a sociologist were to study the Women's Liberation Movement, the relation is clearly a two-sided one as the 'object' has its own point of view, namely, the feminist critique of sociology.

3   Objective and Universal

There are at least two quite distinct senses for the word 'objective'. 'Objective' has a psychological meaning indicating that state of affairs, one's objective, which the subject is striving to bring into existence, either directly or indirectly, which therefore provides an explanation for their action. The word 'object' can be used synonymously with 'objective' in this sense. It is best to avoid this usage of 'objective' as its ambiguity is unnecessary. We can say 'aim', 'goal' or 'object'.

Another sense of 'objective' describes a state of affairs whose existence is not dependent on or relative to one's point of view, in contrast to 'subjective' which describes those states of affairs whose existence or not depends on one's point of view, inclusive of states of mind. The difference between subjective and objective is relative because the boundaries of human knowledge and the scope of human activity is always subject to historical change, and what was objective at one time may turn out to be a mere appearance, or subjective, at a later time. The judge is meant to be 'objective' precisely because they do *not* have any 'objective' in the matter under discussion. Knowledge can be said to be 'objective' because it is based on widespread experience, not just imaginings or the experiences of a few. Science is always striving for knowledge which is objective.

'Objective' is not the same as 'universal'. 'Universal' means a state of affairs applicable across an entire community, but more as way of resolving or transcending disputes than as something which is really beyond question. For example, the law of the land and the foreign policies of a nation are applicable to everyone, even those who don't agree with them, and are thereby *universal*. Whereas objective truth stands firm against subjective opinion, the universal does not abolish particular truths, but rather transcends and includes them. 'Universal' contrasts with 'particular' and 'individual'. The particular is what applies to some group of individuals, so 'particular' lies somewhere *between* the individual and the universal, and mediates between them. But there is no 'third point' between subjective and objective. Something can be *both* objective and subjective, such as a material object which has meaning for a subject: its material form is objective, but its meaning is subjective. On the other hand, an exemplar can be said to be both universal and individual.

4   Marx's Critique of Hegel and Feuerbach

Hegel, says Marx, "does not know real, sensuous activity as such" (1845, §1), because Hegel saw cultural and historical development as arising from the production of ideas by theorists, artists, priests, generals and so on, whose ideas are in turn translated into activity and generate social progress and history. According to Marx (1857, p. 38), on the other hand, "the real subject remains outside the mind and independent of it" – social practice developing according to its own logic, the evolving social practice which provides an object for the theorist to reflect upon. So it's not the idea as such which is significant, but the social practice which gives rise to the idea.

For materialist philosophers on the other hand, Marx says, "the Object (*der Gegenstand*), actuality, sensuousness, are conceived only in the form of the object (*Objekts*), or of contemplation, but not as human sensuous activity, practice, not subjectively" (1845, §1). In this excerpt, *Gegenstand* is used in the sense of the object of attention, desire, activity, etc. and *Objekt* is used in the sense of an independently existing entity which the subject perceives. Marx's criticism was that the materialist philosophers had followed the natural scientists of the time in regarding knowledge as that of an independently existing world, be it natural or historical. On the contrary, as Hegel said, the world and our knowledge of it are products of human practical activity. So we have to treat our *Gegenstand* as something constructed by social practice, as a *Subjekt-Objekt*. This goes to show that the ambiguity is no worse in English than it is in the original German!

The two chief tasks to which Marx devoted himself were his political economic studies culminating in *Capital* and his political work in the workers' movement. In his work on *Capital*, Marx regarded capital as subject as well as object. Capital is a social relation not simply a quantity of money. In short, capital is the capitalist class, not as a group of people, but as a subject constituted by economic activity. Its units are companies, each commanding a share of social labour according to its capital value. Each company is a project with its own means of decision-making constituting it as an individual within the larger 'runaway' project of global capital. Decisions are made in the economy, always by human beings, but usually via aggregates of independent subjective decisions, rather than by design or consensus. The resulting movement of capital looks from one side like a force of nature but from the other side like a broad social movement. Capital is a Subject in its own right.

At the same time capital has the distinction of also being an object, in the sense that it creates the conditions of its own existence. As such, it is a 'self-contained' social formation, like the various forms of social life which have gone before it and will come after it. Marx's work in writing *Capital* entailed studying this subject-object, exhaustively studying all the 'objective thinking' of capitalists in the form of their theoretical productions, political economy, and the actual movement of capital, available through the economic data. Capital as Marx saw it was not an *identical* subject-object (cf. Postone, 1993) because thinking and behaviour, needs and their means of satisfaction, were always at odds with one another.

In the case of his political work, his starting point was an historical subject which was only just beginning to become self-conscious – the working class. In this context, the Hegelian *Subjekt-Objekt* has the *Subjekt* as the emergent workers' movement and the *Objekt* as the modern, capitalist world which had given birth to the proletariat and which the workers' movement was destined to overturn.

Marx patiently studied the actual strivings of the workers' movement, contributed to them on the occasions when this was possible, and gave voice to the most far-reaching aspirations of the movement, astutely noted every new form of resistance, every new development in the labour processes, and particularly new forms of revolutionary activity, and only rarely went beyond what was already emerging within the movement itself.

In both his political and his economic studies, Marx took Hegel at his word and conceptualised subject and object at the broadest possible historical level.

Mostly we tackle more modest tasks, and our concepts of subject and object have been tailored accordingly.

5   *Arbeitsgegenstand* – The Object to Be Worked Upon

In his discussion of the labour process in *Capital*, Marx says:

> The elementary factors of the labour-process are 1, the personal activity of man, *i.e.*, work itself, 2, the subject of that work, and 3, its instruments.
> 1867, §7.1

In German, these three factors are: "*die zweckmäßige Tätigkeit, ... ihr Gegenstand und ihr Mittel*," or literally purposive activity, its object and its means. Later, Marx introduces the term *Arbeitsgegenstand*, or work-object to unambiguously indicate what in English is translated as "subject (*sic*) of labour", and I will use *Arbeitsgegenstand* in the same sense. Marx goes on to demonstrate that there is no essential difference between the material worked upon and transformed by the labour process and the instruments (means), which are also consumed in the same labour process (an observation with which Hegel agrees). He remarks:

> He makes use of the mechanical, physical, and chemical properties of some substances in order to make other substances subservient to his aims.
> 1867, p. 189

and in a footnote quotes Hegel:

> Reason is just as cunning as she is powerful. Her cunning consists principally in her mediating activity, which, by causing objects to act and re-act on each other in accordance with their own nature, in this way, without any direct interference in the process, carries out Reason's intentions.
> HEGEL, 1831, §209 n.

Hegel and Marx remind us that while we focus on our own *Arbeitsgegenstand*, our intentions and our instruments are 'borrowed' from the world we live in and more often than not we find ourselves merely acting as agents of great social forces, and the changes we make will survive or not according to circumstances beyond our control.

'Object' is often used in the sense of *Arbeitsgegenstand*. For example, in this outline of Engeström's approach:

> The object refers to the 'raw material' or 'problem space' at which the activity is directed and which is molded and transformed into outcomes with the help of physical and symbolic, external and internal mediating instruments, including both tools and signs.
> CAT&DWR, 2003

Here 'object' is defined as the *Arbeitsgegenstand*, but further qualified as not only the 'raw material' but also the 'problem space', meaning that the ideal form into which the *Arbeitsgegenstand* is to be transformed is *implicit in the object*, as for example a patient with an illness or a child who has not learnt what was on the curriculum. This conception takes it that it is given that there is a problem, but does not presuppose any image of how the problem is to be resolved. It is a very 'objective' approach in this sense. However, the activity itself is surely not to be characterised by the problem it addresses but *the solution it seeks*. Otherwise, we would have the Conservative Party and the Labour Party as engaged in the *same project* because they share the same *Arbeitsgegenstand*.

In the reduction of the object to a problem space much is lost because the problem space is the entire social formation, the *Objekt* – the social conditions which have produced the problem and are the source of solutions. Restricting the conception of the object to an *Arbeitsgegenstand* understood as a 'problem space' is sufficient only on the condition that the conception of the ideal to which the object must conform is unproblematic. But for example, if a patient presents to a doctor complaining of pain, then solving the problem, i.e., administering the right painkiller, is not necessarily what should be done. Perhaps how the patient sustained the injuries needs to be looked at, or perhaps the child's dislike of school is the issue, or perhaps the girl needs to be taught about menstruation, or why did a minor scratch warrant a visit to the doctor? In any case, the situation needs to be solved in collaboration with the 'patient' which presupposes not treating *them* as a 'problem'.

5.1 The Imagined and Desired State of the World

Let us expand the scope and consider the normal situation of work activity in which the worker has before them some material which is just as it should be: a well-equipped industrial chemistry lab, the usual contents of a commercial kitchen, or a classroom full of lively, interested children. What to do? Even though the subject may be aware of social norms, there is nothing emanating either from the object itself or from elsewhere which tells the subject what is to be done. The *Arbeitsgegenstand* itself does not contain the motivation or explanation for the subject's actions – it is not in itself a 'problem space'. Not every patient is really ill and the curriculum is not always as it should be.

Most work activity takes place within a social and economic formation in which every activity makes sense only within a vast network of interconnected activities, each pursuing its own aims. Some other process organises affairs so that the whole somehow reproduces itself. In capitalist countries – almost any country today – this process is capital accumulation in a regulated market, including a labour market.

In reality, the objects of the various activities are multifarious. They could be expansion of the capital value of a company or other types of profiteering, the performance of some public good, the pursuit of sectional interest, raising a family or the furthering of some social practice for its own sake. Whichever the case, the only meaningful answer to the question: "What is the object of this activity?" is whatever change in social conditions the activity 'aims' to bring about. 'Aims' is in inverted commas because prima facie activities are not beings which can have aims. Formally, 'aims' and 'motives' are psychological categories and 'activities' is a social category.

5.2 *The Problem of 'Objective Motives'*

Having clarified the difference between the work-object and its desired state, the problem of giving meaning to the concept of the 'object of activity' reduces to the problem of imputing motives and intentions to activities on the understanding that activities are objectively existing social entities not the subjective projects of individuals.

In A.N. Leontyev's genetic derivation of the concept of 'activity', activities originate as chains of actions which are executed by a single individual, achieving intermediate goals towards gaining an object which is the motive for all the actions along the way, rather than the intermediate goals in themselves. Here, the concepts of 'motive' and 'goal' are unproblematically psychological. The activity, in which all the composite actions are those of the same individual, is the *germ cell* of a collaborative project, containing in embryo the essential characteristics of the mature form of activity which entails a social division of labour. A collaborative activity is formed by dividing up the actions among a number of participants each of whom takes responsibility for an intermediate goal, while sharing in the consumption of the object by means of some system of distribution and exchange. In this specific sense then a project is an extension of a natural person.

As a first approximation, it is not difficult to discern the object of a collaborative project, as activities are not purely objective processes (such as an increase in unemployment, a road accident or a pandemic), they are *organised*, and so usually have documented aims, leaders and spokespeople, and in general everyone knows what those involved in a social practice are trying to achieve. As I said, a first approximation.

A deeper analysis, however, always reveals a gap between intentions voiced by rank-and-file members and leaders or written in statutes and rulebooks, on one hand, and objective tendencies on the other hand. Even objective tendencies which superficially confirm stated aims can mask the real fate of an activity as it evolves, and which generally cannot be foreseen.

The determination of the *immanent tendency* of an activity or project begins from a study of the evolution of the component actions. Actions are purposive, so a study of actions implies an indirect study of the consciousness behind each action. Hegel's *Logic*, what Hegel calls 'speculative logic', aims to determine the direction of movement and immanent tendency of an activity, by disclosing immanent contradictions within a formation. *The immanent tendency* or apparent motive or aim of a project is scientifically determinable and may be set alongside the stated aims of the project, disclosing internal contradictions at work within the project.

So, we can talk about the object of an activity as its motive or aim in this sense. This does *not* mean taking the consciousness of actors at face value, however. The manager of a business says he is there to provide a service, but if he doesn't make a profit, he will go out of business. Schools educate children to give them a better future, but find themselves helping to rank young people for their place in a hierarchical social system. Determination of the immanent tendency of an activity is a process of critical interpretation, of practical hermeneutics, so to speak.

5.3 The Object Is Consumed and Reproduced

Instead of approaching activities, as above, in terms of the "change in social conditions the activity 'aims' to bring about," let us make the opposite assumption. Let us presume that we have a world in dynamic equilibrium, and consequently a world in which all its inhabitants are perfectly adapted to the world in which they live and whose aim is simply to participate in reproduction of this or that component of the social formation in the course of reproducing their own life and that of their family. As A.N. Leontyev put it:

> In reality, however, we have to deal with *concrete, specific activities*, each of which satisfies a definite need of the subject, is oriented towards the object of this need, disappears as a result of its satisfaction and is reproduced perhaps in different conditions and in relation to a changed object.
>
> LEONTYEV, 1977, p. 399

In this view, the difference between the two limited definitions of 'object' we considered above disappears – the *Arbeitsgegenstand* becomes identical with the *motive* – the object is a kind of flux. The way an activity changes the world is incorporated within a conception of the world in which a subject has a need and this need finds its object in the objective world, and this object consequently functions as the motive for the activity, and the need is satisfied by the production and consumption of the object. The cycle is then repeated under formally changed conditions. This conception allows room for the conception of the object as an *already-existing object* which meets an *already-existing need* of the subject. The object therefore constitutes a problem space (how to acquire and get hold of it), the *motive* for the activity (the subject needs to consume the object), *and* the *Arbeitsgegenstand* (the object must be worked upon in order to satisfy the subject's need). This made perfect sense in the Soviet Union at the time.

This approach provides a satisfactorily objective framework that absolves us of the troublesome idea of activities having subjective and possibly misguided intentions. Here the motive is objective. It allows for social change only as an unintended by-product of human activity, because of the constant need for reproduction, reminding us of Hegel's maxim cited by Marx above, leaving individuals and states "all the time the unconscious tools of the world spirit at work within them" (Hegel, 1821).

6   Object-Concept

Objects don't 'attract' human activities. Activities are driven by purposive, motivated actions, actions that are done 'for a reason', so to speak. The object does not in itself motivate actions, although the object *mediates* the formation of motivations directed at the object.

Conceiving the *Arbeitsgegenstand* as a 'problem space' presumed that it was obvious what the problem was, and only the solution was problematic. But we have not yet touched upon the problem of how and when the subject determines what the problem is. It is only by reference to the wider social formation that we can understand the ideal to which the object is expected to conform. The subject will act on the object according to their concept of the ideal object, an ideal formulated in the broader culture.

Vygotsky showed that concepts are formed by identifying a problem and finding a solution to it. If the same need is to be constantly reproduced, this leaves us with an impoverished view of social life. Further, different solutions may be formed for one and the same problem, depending on how the problem is conceived, and different solutions are constituted by different activities and represented by different concepts of the object:

> Concepts are always formed during a process of finding a solution to some problem facing the adolescent's thinking process. The creation of the concept is dependent on a solution to this problem being found.
> VYGOTSKY, 1931, pp. 257–258; see also VYGOTSKY, 1934, pp. 123–124

When we talk of the object being an "imagined and desired state of the world," it is not suggested that we need to read minds. There will be *objective* indications of what a person's actions are working towards, their immanent tendency, but we do not thereby know whether this activity, the activity implicit in the collaboration being observed, is the *really effective motivation* for the action, or some other activity (what the individual plans to do with their wages) or what the individual's concept is of the project(s) their action is furthering.

In general, to understand a person's motivation we need to know the concept the person has of the object of activity. This is the *object-concept*. It is possible to surmise the object-concept behind a person's actions in the same way that it is possible to surmise the object of an activity by observation of the component actions. This is a problem of hermeneutics. This is what Vygotsky was doing in the experiments described in Chapter 5 of *Thinking and Speech*. Materialistically speaking, an object-concept is *nothing other than* the aggregate of all the actions serving to realise that activity, expressed in ideal form.

In fact, *only* the object-concept can elucidate human action. In ideologically homogeneous conditions this requirement is null because to all concerned there is no meaningful distinction between the object and the object-concept (recalling the situation prior to the inversion of the meaning of 'subject' in the 17th century). But under conditions of cultural and ideological diversity and change, the difference is by no means null. What the object-concept implicates is the *Subjekt-Objekt* relation implicit in the interactions between individuals. Differences in object-concept are not arbitrary, individual differences, but differences arising from differences in social position.

To say that it is only the object-concept which motivates human action is not to *intellectualise* human motivation, unless you were to take concepts to be mere psychic formations. Concepts are a mode of human action.

7 Boundary Objects

The fact that objects (here we have in mind institutions and artefacts) are not unproblematic but are carriers of social and cultural difference is highlighted in the idea of 'boundary objects'. This term was originally coined by Susan Leigh Star in 1989 as an "arrangement that allow[s] different groups to work together without consensus" (Star, 2010, p. 602). Star had in mind shared instruments rather than shared *Arbeitsgegenstände*, but she has explicitly consented to the range of uses the term has been subsequently given and two such usages are significant here.

In social theory, a 'boundary object' would mean the judicial, political, administrative, educational and welfare infrastructure and systems in a country. The concept of boundary object expresses the social theorist's conviction that such infrastructure is never 'neutral'. They are social arrangements put in place to settle past struggles, and like all peace treaties they tend to reflect the interests of the victorious party. Having the same issue in mind, researchers in 'socio-technical theory' ascribe agency to artefacts.

But just as we found in considering the concept of 'object', the research questions which Star had in mind are of a narrower scope. It is easy to overlook apparently neutral and peripheral objects in the research environment which carry the hidden signs of dominant social subjects sedimented in routines, institutional practices, design of databases, styles of writing, norms of work, etc., even furniture design. It is these apparently neutral elements of infrastructure which facilitate collaboration between different social and cultural groups, and which have built into them presuppositions about how they will be used which are not at all neutral. Here the question is always to recognise that any activity takes place within a cultural and historical environment in the aftermath of past and continuing struggles on a wider arena.

The concept of 'boundary object' is also used when the concept of object in play is the *Arbeitsgegenstand* rather than apparently neutral instruments. The scenario here is an institution or social situation in which more than one project is at work. This is a more or less universal scenario. For example, it could be a community suffering from social disadvantage with half a dozen NGOs trying to ameliorate the situation according to their own lights. The issue of the problematic character of the *Arbeitsgegenstand* is highlighted, not so much because the *Arbeitsgegenstand* harbours undisclosed presuppositions but because each of the collaborating subjects have different presuppositions. The supposedly unproblematic nature of the ideal to which the *Arbeitsgegenstand* needs to be brought harbours potential conflicts between the subjects.

It is important to note that it is *only* through a shared *Arbeitsgegenstand* that collaboration (including both conflict and cooperation) takes place at all. At the same time, the very idea of collaboration is meaningful only to the extent that the various collaborating parties (I am referring to NGOs, for example, not individuals) find some different ideal implicit in the *Arbeitsgegenstand*. Collaboration is ubiquitous wherever an 'intervention' is under consideration, because in such cases there are always at least two parties collaborating – the *Arbeitsgegenstand* itself and the intervening party.

Consequently, to define the object as the *Arbeitsgegenstand* is always naïve – it is always the *concept* of the object drawn from cognition of the *Arbeitsgegenstand* which motivates the activity and gives meaning to all the actions composing it. This raises a further difficulty. Just as imputing motives and intentions to an activity is problematic (because 'activity' is a *social* category), we now have to justify imputing cognition, that is, learning, concept formation and ethical qualities, to an activity. From the point of view of both psychology and sociology social formations which have motives and ideas is outlandish. However, I put it that such a view is essential for an interdisciplinary theory of activity. Projects (activities) are learning processes. They also have what could be called 'personalities' and exhibit all the characteristics of personalities, including ethical characteristics.

8 The Object of a Project

Given the spectrum of meanings of the word 'object' in connection with activity theory, an interdisciplinary theory of activity requires a concept of 'object' which is unambiguous and clear, and from which the more specialised meanings can be made transparent.

One of the upshots of this will be that an activity to some extent appears as a quasi-personality, and I will henceforth refer to an activity as a *project*. As in Leontyev's original implementation of activity theory, a project is defined by its object, but more particularly, by the concept it forms of its object, that is, what it is 'trying' to do, its object-concept, the ideal of the *Arbeitsgegenstand*, which it is realising. *A project is defined by its object-concept, not its Arbeitsgegenstand*.

A project is just like a project carried out by a single person, guided by their conception of the object throughout, except that the actions are carried out by many people who self-evidently share a concept of what the project is about.

A project has an object-concept, i.e., the concept of an imagined and desired (ideal) state of the world, and therefore a *motive*. This concept is explicable in terms of the intermediate goals towards which individual actors strive, just as the object-concept functions as a source and explanation for the motives of individual actors. That is, the determination of the object-concept entails a *hermeneutic circle*. This is not a novel concept, but is well established in literary theory (see Gadamer, 1960).

This means that at any given moment, any individual actor in a project may ascribe a different *meaning* to the object of the project, manifested in the individual actions and their place in realising the object. The meaning the object has for them is realised in the goal of their actions. This appears to create a quandary in that if there is an object-concept, surely this concept must be apprehended in *someone's* mind, presumably identically the minds of *all* the participants in a project. But this is not the case. It is normal that each participant in a project has their own distinct conception of it, realised in the meaning of their actions in pursuit of the object. But does that make it meaningless to speak of the concept of the project altogether? Surely not.

The problem before us is this: how can we determine a universal concept given a number of diverse individual meanings for one and the same entity? This entity is the "imagined and desired outcome" of collaborative actions. So, it is always provisional, and only ever has an implicit existence. But a project is distinct from an arbitrary collection of actions in two respects: (1) All actions bear on the same *Arbeitsgegenstand* and (2), all the actions form part of a *coherent form of collaboration* through the achievement of intermediate goals. The object-concept is constituted in the system of meanings of individual actors, manifested in the coherence of their collaboration.

On this basis, a universal concept of a project is formed by its object-concept. Such a universal concept is expressed symbolically by a word or name or some icon or symbol, behind which a coherent combination of collaborative actions is deliberatively organised.

Among the factors which are involved in considering the concept an individual actor has of a project in which they are participating is that people are commonly participating in more than one project and any individual action may be motivated by one or another or a combination of motives (i.e., projects). People 'have their own reasons', as it is said.

9 Conclusion

The suggestion is that the *Arbeitsgegenstand* be clearly distinguished by whatever word you like from the object-concept, or the ideal *Arbeitsgegenstand*. Further, it is this ideal, the *object-concept*, by which a project is recognised both by participants and others by identifying the project as a coherent social practice. That is what is meant by the object of a project. This ideal has a different meaning for every individual, but the ideal itself remains also objective, constituted by the immanent tendency of the activity. The project *produces* this concept and by realising it, forms a concrete and realistic concept of its ideal, and changes the way that community thinks and acts.

CHAPTER 9

Leontyev's Activity Theory and Social Theory

A.N. Leontyev, the younger of L.S. Vygotsky's closest colleagues, is widely recognised as the founder of activity theory. In the following review of Leontyev's activity theory, I have called upon the insights of his most well-known successors – his son A.A. Leontyev and grandson Dmitry, Fedor Vasilyuk, and Victor Kaptelinin – lest it be thought that the criticisms that follow are mine alone. I still count myself as an activity theorist.

A.N. Leontyev's creative work was conducted in the Soviet Union under Stalin, Khrushchev and Brezhnev, a period during in which every aspect of life was controlled by the Leader and in which normal conditions of human social life were absent and open scientific debate was impossible. In 1966, he became the first ever (!) Dean of Psychology at Moscow State University, where he worked until his death in 1979. He was the most influential of the distinctive current of Soviet Psychology. It is impossible to overestimate the crushing effect of this environment on scientific creativity in the human sciences. It is therefore a matter of great significance that Leontyev made a number of unique discoveries in both the form and the content of psychological science.

Vygotsky had approached the cultural formation of the mind in terms of how artefacts, including language, which originate in a wider culture, are used by individuals to resolve situations, which are also the product of the wider culture. He did not, however, investigate how these situations and a person's motivation, a key element in constituting situations, originate in the social environment itself. This issue was taken up A.N. Leontyev.

Vygotsky had recognised 'activity' (i.e., social practice) as the *substance* of psychology, its most fundamental, irreducible category. Vygotsky had identified the ('molecular') *units* of activity – the smallest units of social life: *artefact-mediated actions*. But an artefact-mediated action cannot be understood in isolation. Actions make sense only in the context of a whole series of actions by an individual and the interrelated actions of other individuals. To extend the theory so as to understand the individual's situation as part of a wider community and its motivation, it was necessary to determine a 'molar' unit of activity – a meaningful aggregate of artefact-mediated actions, whose internal unity would reveal the motivation for individual actions. The psychological investigation of *activities* was Leontyev's project.

Leontyev's psychology led directly to an approach to social theory, and he did not shy away from taking activity theory into that domain, but Leontyev always remained a psychologist and despite the great potential of the framework he provided, his contributions to social theory were fatuous.

1   Objects and Activities in Leontyev's Activity Theory

Leontyev genetically reconstructed Vygotsky's concept of an action as follows. He began his analysis by considering an organism whose behaviour is directly controlled and motivated by the object (see 'On the Concept of Object' in this volume) of its activity, the organism's perception of the object being internally linked by nervous reflexes to the processes driving its activity. In the course of evolution, forms of behaviour develop so as to be 'portable' and adapt to conditions, and these he calls 'operations'. Although not completely stereotyped, operations are not consciously controlled by the organism. Operations are controlled by the conditions. Through evolution, more elaborate forms of behaviour develop which entail a chain of operations to achieve an object and these 'chains of operations' are called 'actions'. At this stage, the goal of an action is identical to its motive (its object). So, an action is controlled by its object, which meets some need of the organism. All the operations making up the action are motivated by the same object which is achieved only by the complete action. So long as everything goes smoothly, the component operations are regulated by the conditions without conscious control. If an operation goes awry, then it springs back into awareness and is consciously controlled until equanimity is recovered. An operation is not 'unconscious' like the heart-beat, but once mastered, it is done without conscious awareness.

More elaborate forms of behaviour entail a whole series of actions, each achieved by accomplishing an intermediate *goal*, and motivated to attain the same object. Thus the immediate goal of each action is no longer identical to its motive. And this is the definition of a fully developed action – *a form of behaviour the motive for which is not identical to its goal*. An action is done for a reason, so to speak. This is a profound and important insight.

Once behaviour has evolved to this point, social creatures utilise a division of labour to achieve their objects by dividing actions between different members of the group. These aggregates of actions are called 'activities'. An individual can execute a chain of actions each achieving an intermediate goal while constantly having the motive of the activity in mind. But when these intermediate goals are divided up according to a social division of labour, then 'motive', being a *psychological* category, is not an appropriate term for the object of an activity, because it does not act as the really effective motive of each individual's actions, even though the object of the activity is *understood*. The 'motive' of the activity is achievement of its *object* and object is now a social category, and only indirectly a psychological category. The object is achieved by *social regulation* of the actions of the various participants. The object of an activity is implicit in the activity, and is represented in the psyche of an individual in the *personal sense* of the activity, in general quite different from the object which analysis can show is driving the activity as a whole.

Thus Leontyev defined a three-level 'macrostructure' of activity – operations, actions and activities – each representing activity at a different level of analytical abstraction.

1.1 *Problems in Leontyev's Conception of 'Activity'*

Leontyev defined the molar unit of activity, 'an activity' as follows:

> Thus, the principal 'unit' of a vital process is an organism's activity; the different activities that realise its diverse vital relations with the surrounding reality are essentially determined by their object (*predmet*); we shall therefore differentiate between separate types of activity according to the difference in their objects.
>
> 1978, p. 29

(1) Within this English translation of Leontyev's Russian there are two points of confusion.[1] The Russian language does not use articles such as 'an' or 'the'. English, on the other hand, uses articles, and moreover nouns may be used with or without articles, and have different meanings accordingly. In general, when an English noun is used with an article or in the plural, it is a *countable* noun; when an English noun is used in the singular without an article, it is a *mass* noun. So 'an activity' and 'activities' are countable nouns and 'activity' is a mass noun. A unit is *essentially* a countable noun, so "an organism's activity" in the above excerpt must mean "the activities of the organism," but the excerpt, like so much written about activity in translation from the Russian, seems to be saying: "Activity is the unit of activity," which is a senseless statement. All living organisms engage in activity, but only humans, and maybe some higher mammals, are capable of 'activities'.

---

1 There are, as the reader will see, a host of points of terminological confusion in this area. I have tried so far as possible to retain the terminology found in English translations of the Soviet writers. Where appropriate, I have noted points of confusion. Only in the last instance have I replaced the original terms with my own, because it is part of the purpose of writing this article to facilitate the reader in reading the classics of activity theory for themself.

(2) *An activity* is an aggregate of actions which combine to achieve a shared object. In the quote, Leontyev tell us that "we shall therefore differentiate between separate types of activity according to the difference in their objects." But the leap from activities to *types* of activity masks a further elision, and this time the confusion lies with Leontyev himself. As is confirmed by Kaptelinin (2005), when Leontyev says 'an activity' he often means 'a type of activity'. If I say "He was motivated by his work," that seems to be a clear explanation of the person's actions. But not so. To understand the content of an action one must know what the person's work is and what their role is at work. So to make sense of a person's actions and its motivation, we must take 'an activity' to be the *specific* activity, not a general *type* of activity.

According to his son, A.A. Leontyev (2006), Leontyev remained vague about the concept of 'unit':

> Throughout, even within the framework of activity theory itself, an ambiguous understanding of the units and levels of activity organisation can be seen. ... As is well known, A.N. Leontyev does not provide an explicit definition of it; as a rule, he puts the term 'unit' within quotation marks, and in so doing, 'determines' it. And this is justified: after all, as it applies to his point of view, the concept of unit has little applicability to activity, action, or operation, since it presumes their *discrete* nature. ... In A.N. Leontyev's conception, the only thing that can be called a 'unit' in the strict sense is [an] activity (an activity act).
>
> LEONTYEV, 2006, pp. 30, 32; [an] inserted by AB

According to Fedor Vasilyuk (1984, pp. 84–85), a Soviet continuator of Leontyev's work, Leontyev used in fact two distinct concepts of activity: "when life is viewed in a non-individualised manner, as abstract 'human life in general' ... the word 'unit' has to be understood simply as 'a part'," but as his focus moved from life in general to analysis of the motivation of individual persons, 'activity' moved from the 'mass' to the 'countable' meaning of specific activities.

1.2 *Motivation*

But further than this, to make sense of a person's actions, in a workplace for example, you have to know what *concept* the person *themself* has of their job: "that actual need is always a need of something, that at the psychological level needs are mediated by psychic reflection" (1978, p. 161).[2] If a worker

---

[2] I find it concerning that this prestigious Soviet psychologist relegated to the general category of 'psychic reflection' all those aspects of the personality which makes us the kind of person

carried out their task incorrectly this could be because they only cared about collecting their wage and so did a sloppy job, or they may have taken too long over the task because they wanted to deliver a good service rather than do it quickly, as required by the profit motive. People have different concepts of the activity in which they are engaged. Leontyev deals with this under the concept of the 'personal sense' of the object of the activity. It seems that for Leontyev the object is implicit in the social arrangements made for the activity, which are objective. The object has a 'personal sense' though, according to what the object means for the individual. This *reification* of the object of activity is a problem with Leontyev's elaboration of activity theory.

Vasilyuk argues, and I agree, that a person's actions cannot be motivated by the object itself, as Leontyev says, but only by the concept the subject has of the object. Leontyev's method of genetic derivation of his concepts meant that he began from the activity of primitive organisms as part of their 'lived-world'. Tracing this forward he has in mind at all times individuals whose species has co-evolved with their environment. Moving on to human life, Leontyev relies on the fact that the environment, individuals' needs and the objects of their activity have all *historically evolved* together, but now as products of human activity. But in human societies, the subject's relation to the objects of their activity is not innate. It is socially constructed and *learned* by individuals, and internalised in the form of concepts. These concepts originate as objects of activities in the past, and are provided to the individual by the given culture and the specific social layer in which the subject is raised, by means of language and technical systems. Psychologically, according to Vasilyuk, the subject's environment is not a world of things but of culturally produced concepts, a 'lifeworld'. This is consistent with the Hegelian concept of a 'formation of consciousness' as an integral subject-object.

So Vasilyuk corrects Leontyev by pointing out that it is these culturally and historically produced concepts which, once acquired by a person, motivate their actions. However, Leontyev retained the ontology where he began with single-cell organisms. Vasilyuk argues that for Leontyev:

> An object [*predmet*] is thus not simply a thing lying outside the life circuit of the subject, but a thing already absorbed into the subject's being, which has become an essential feature of that being, has been subjectivised by

---

we are. There is no concern as to whether a person is an introvert or extravert, optimist or pessimist, a thinker or a 'people person', courageous or cautious. However, these are issues for psychologists, and are incidental to my project.

> the life process even before any special appropriation (cognitive, exploratory, informational, etc.) takes place.
>
> VASILYUK, p. 89

But Vasilyuk argued *against* the claim that it is the concept of the object that a person forms by 'psychic reflection' and not the object itself which motivates a person's actions by claiming that such a view is based on "the model of … the goal-directed, voluntary, conscious activity of a human adult" (p. 88) but:

> … the everyday 'obvious fact' of a living creature existing separately from the world cannot serve as an ontological base-point, because nowhere do we find a living creature before and outside of its interconnections with the world. It is from the first 'implanted into' the world, linked with it by the material navel cord of its own life. This world, while still an objective, material entity, is not the 'physical world' in the sense which that carries for the science of physics, which studies the interactions of things: this is the lived world. It is the lived world, in fact, which is the sole stimulator and source of content for the creature living in it. That is our primary ontological picture.
>
> VASILYUK, p. 89

And Vasilyuk continues, arguing that as activities are units of life, so their main constituent cause – the object of the activity – is a *unit of the lived world* (p. 89).

> When we start from that and begin to construct a psychological theory, and pick out (abstract) a particular activity as the 'unit of life' for the subject, then the object of that activity appears, in this abstracted form, not in its own self-sufficiency and self-identity, not as a thing representing itself, but as 'a unit' representing the lived world, and it is by virtue of this representative character that the object acquires the status of a motive. To base a psychological theory on the statement that the object is the motive of activity is to start from the conviction that life is ultimately determined by the world.
>
> p. 90

Vasilyuk has corrected Leontyev's ontology by replacing what was effectively a *natural* world with a *culturally figured lifeworld* (cf. Holland et al., 1998; Bourdieu, 1984). The object of the activity, meaningful only within the context of the activity, a unit of the lifeworld, objective to the individual, remains the object of the individual's activity and consequently the external *cause* of their activity. For Vasilyuk, individuals have 'their own' commitments, whereas for Leontyev individuals join or are assigned to established activities already found in the world, as part of the social division of labour. As a result, Vasilyuk does not confront the difference between the object of the activity and its personal sense for the individual actor. His theory is more narrowly psychological.

1.3 *Objectivism*

For Leontyev, objects in the lifeworld *stimulate* and *determine* activities. This "primary ontological picture" places activities in the subordinate role in a lifeworld in which objects are primary. My response to this is to advocate with Vasilyuk, for a more *thoroughgoing* activity theory, one in which *activities* rather than objects are what is primary, what is given to subject and researcher alike. It is *activities* which create objects, are the source of a person's concepts of objects, and orient the person's activity, as opposed to a theory of objective needs 'stimulating' activities.

So we come back again to Leontyev's dualism.[3] According to Vasilyuk:

> An object is not simply a thing lying outside the life-circuit of the subject, but a thing already absorbed into the subject's being, which has become an essential feature of that being, has been subjectivised by life process even before any special ideal appropriation (cognitive, exploratory, informational, etc.) takes place.
>
> p. 89

So according to Vasilyuk, what Leontyev would call the 'personal sense' of the object does not derive from psychic reflection, but arises unreflectively in the subject's upbringing and life-experience. If a crisis arises in pursuit of this object, then that might be an occasion for reflection on the part of the individual.

But a person forms a concept of the object of an activity through participation in activities. It is activities which are the units of life and both the subjects

---

[3] In 2014, I attended a lecture at the ISCAR (International Society of Cultural-historical Activity Research) Congress in which the grandson, Dmitry Leontyev, explained ANL's theory. At the start of the lecture Dmitry drew a line down the centre of the whiteboard, and the subjective went on the left and the objective went on the right. By 'objective' he meant basically, what everyone thinks, as opposed to what one individual thinks. It seemed to me that ANL's dualism rests on his experience in a society in which there was only one valid point of view, and any divergence from that one view was taken simply as an individual idiosyncrasy, not a view having *some social basis*.

and the objects of activities are products of those activities. I believe that we should not have a dualism of units, one unit for life and another unit for the world, but just one unit, activities, for the lifeworld.

1.4   *The Object*

'Objective' indicates the properties of processes and situations, etc., which are not relative to one's point of view. 'Subjective' indicates those features which are dependent on one's point of view, including but not limited to inner processes of the mind.

Being an 'object' is something different from the concept of 'objective'. The concept of 'object' is always a point of confusion. Whatever language you are using, the word for 'object' is ambiguous. For Leontyev, the object is a condition in the world which is objective for any individual, and is implicit in social arrangements. In general, Leontyev's assumption is that an activity is reproducing 'its' object within a social formation which is consuming its object and needs to continuously reproduce the same object. Objects are thus part of a process of self-reproduction of the whole social formation, which in turn is sustaining the life of each subject and raising and educating them in preparation for participating in social activities, and providing appropriate motivation for that participation. The object is both the material on which the subject acts and that which constitutes their aim and motivation. In this picture we can see the echo of the organism in its natural habitat.

In human society, activities are also generated by the needs for inputs to other activities. So if the object is automobiles, there will also be a host of subordinate objects, such as steel, carburettors, tyres, etc. There are consequently, a host of distinct activities such as 'making steel' or 'assembling carburettors', etc. Thus, each activity is defined, or characterised by its object. So this is a conception of human life driven by *needs*. Activity is driven by human needs and the demands generated by those needs. It is needs which generate and motivate the activities, and human consciousness is formed by these activities and the human needs they are providing for.

Leontyev puts it this way:

> In reality, however, we have to deal with *concrete, specific activities,* each of which satisfies a definite need of the subject, is oriented towards the object of this need, disappears as a result of its satisfaction and is reproduced perhaps in different conditions and in relation to a changed object.
> 1978, p. 5

Here, Leontyev recognises the fact that one and the same activity reproduces itself despite changes in its object. However, because Leontyev has blurred the distinction between an activity and a type of activity, the significance of this important nuance is lost, I believe. Likewise, any distinction between the *needs* of the acting subject and the object of the activity are elided. Every individual is taken to be an integral part of a homogeneous, self-reproducing unit with no divergence in interest.

The distinction between the motivations behind an activity and an action is illustrated by a well-known scenario involving a primeval group of hunters:

> When a member of a group performs his labour activity he also does it to satisfy one of his needs. A beater, for example, taking part in a primeval collective hunt, was stimulated by a need for food or, perhaps, a need for clothing, which the skin of the dead animal would meet for him. At what, however, was his activity directly aimed? It may have been directed, for example, at frightening a herd of animals and sending them toward other hunters, hiding in ambush. That, properly speaking, is what should be the result of the activity of this man. And the activity of this individual member of the hunt ends with that. The rest is completed by the other members. This result, i.e. the frightening of game, etc., understandably does not in itself, and may not, lead to satisfaction of the beater's need for food, or the skin of the animal. What the processes of his activity were directed to did not, consequently, coincide with what stimulated them, i.e., did not coincide with the motive of his activity; the two were divided from one another in this instance. Processes, the object and motive of which do not coincide with one another, we shall call 'actions'. We can say, for example, that the beater's activity is the hunt, and the frightening of game his action.
>
> 1981, p. 187

In a modern economy, however, a person's needs are always met by a highly mediated process of distribution and exchange, so this may turn out to be more complex than it appears at first sight – it cannot be taken for granted that a person knows what tribe they belong to, so to speak, nor that they will in fact receive a fair share of the object. Nor is it guaranteed that the subject has any need at all for what is produced, even indirectly.

1.5   *Personal Sense*

For Leontyev, 'meaning' is something objective for the individual:

> Meaning is the generalisation of reality that is crystallised and fixed in its sensuous vehicle, i.e. normally in a word or a word combination. ... Meaning thus belongs primarily to the world of objective, historical phenomena.
>
> 1978, p. 202

He derived this concept of 'meaning' using his historical-genetic method. In the first stage of development of human society, the use of tools and language – each a material objectification of human modes of action – facilitate a division of labour, but there are not yet class divisions or differences in social position. Consequently, he says, the psyche develops through two sources – the immediacy of an individual's own sense-interactions with the world and their interactions with the system of signs used in communication. By means of sense-images constructed through participation in social practices people get to know about their own world, and by means of the meanings carried by language (and other cultural artefacts) they get to know about the world beyond their immediate horizons. Neither the 'image' (in Soviet writing, the word 'image' does not imply a visual image like it does in English) of the world presented to the individual by the senses nor the 'image' of the world presented by signs are psychological; that is, they do not form parts of the individual's psyche. Both, however, figure together in the *formative processes* of an individual's consciousness. In this way the abstract meanings contained in words, for example, are filled with sensual content by means of their association with the individual's concrete experiences, and socially developed modes of action are introduced into the individual's interactions with nature. The constellation of meanings encoded in words Leontyev calls 'social consciousness', and these meanings he characterised as '*objective*'. Social consciousness is a *social* and *not* a psychological category, and alongside the practical activity of individuals is one of the formative components of their psyche.

This analytical conjuncture can be expressed by saying there is *not yet* an *opposition* between the objective meanings of things and their personal sense. Personal sense and therefore consciousness differs from one person to another simply because of incidental differences from one individual to another. With the introduction of *class divisions*, people's experiences are conditioned by their social position so personal senses express social positions. Social consciousness enters into the formation of the consciousness of every individual, but systematic differences in consciousness arise because of the divergence in people's class position. With the growth of inequality and in particular the emergence of wage labour and capital, alienation arises and personal sense may find itself not merely divergent from but in *opposition* to social consciousness.

For example, the worker knows intimately how a commodity is made, but relates to it only as work. On the other hand, the capitalist owner knows nothing of the production process, but sees in the product a thing which can be sold for a profit. As Leontyev saw it, at both ends of this scale the personal sense of the activity is divorced from its objective meaning, that is, from the social process in its entirety. This rupture is manifested as *alienation*. The social formation has to reproduce itself, and consequently, arrangements are formed which motivate capitalists to hire workers to produce what is needed for the social formation to reproduce itself. These arrangements include the profit motive and wages. The functionalist fallacy (see Chapter 23, this volume) must be noted here: one can deduce from the fact of the continued reproduction of the social formation, that there must be some reason for these various institutions, but this does not in itself constitute an *explanation* for how this comes into being and sustains itself, unless one postulates the entire social formation as a self-conscious agent.

People cannot resolve the problem of this alienation by producing a 'personal language' of their own, having access only to the ready-made 'objective meanings' encoded in social consciousness. If social consciousness is unable to express personal senses a fundamental contradiction is created in the person's consciousness.

1.6   *Ideology*

Leontyev says that people acquire words and concepts via interaction with their circle of associates, and these may include 'ideological' notions which are at odds with social consciousness and enter into the conflict between personal senses and social consciousness. He talks of the ideological struggle in society in which people strive to acquire concepts and words to interpret and express their personal senses.

Leontyev formulates this problem as follows: on the one hand, personal senses arising from a person's unique experiences in their world, which are concrete, personal and *subjective*, and on the other hand, *objective* abstract meanings, encoded in words, but which, as we have seen, can be *more or less adequate* to a person's life experiences. As opposed to differences in consciousness arising from incidental differences in experience or personal development, differences in meaning borne by ideology express systematic differences in social position. In seeking to resolve conflicts in their comprehension of the world, people effectively choose not between meanings, but between social positions, expressed and comprehended through concepts and the associated meanings. Leontyev said that ideologies obey socio-historical laws and at the same time obey the inner logic of their own development. He says that all the meanings expressed by ideologies are *objective*, but are *more or less adequate* to the lives of individuals.

This approach to handling the problem of the objectivity of systems of concepts or ideologies has some virtues. It is never useful to claim that such-and-such a theory is objectively simply true or false. It is always a question of *how adequate* a theory is for someone faced with certain tasks and problems, or to put it somewhat differently, *how much of a basis* does the theory have in the reality of a particular life: a substantial basis or a very slight one?

So although some meanings are more adequate than others, whether those of 'social consciousness' or those of 'ideologies', all meanings are *objective*, he says. They have *some* social basis. Objective meanings interact with personal senses (tied up with a person's individual life experiences) in the formation of a person's consciousness, which is *psychological*, subjective and personal. Perception is *both* immediate and mediated.

The relation between the individual and the universal is thus rendered by Leontyev on to the axis of the subjective and the objective, and in the deployment of Leontyev's theory in psychology, the idea of an objective meaning being *more or less adequate* is rarely utilised. Invariably, writers in this tradition, pose problems of learning and behaviour in terms of personal, subjective meaning versus objective, 'societally agreed' meaning. Even in the capitalist West, the difference in power between, for example, teacher and pupil, easily leads to meanings being cast as simply objective or subjective.

Consider the following illustration offered by Leontyev himself:

> For example, all older schoolchildren know the meaning of an examination mark and the consequences it will have. Nonetheless, a mark may appear in the consciousness of each individual pupil in essentially different ways; it may, for example, appear as a step forward (or obstacle) on the path to his chosen profession, or as a means of asserting himself in the eyes of the people around him, or perhaps in some other way. This is what compels psychology to distinguish between the conscious objective meaning and its meaning *for the subject*, or what I prefer to call the 'personal sense'. In other words, an examination mark may acquire different personal senses in the consciousness of different pupils.
>
> 1977, p. 19

It corresponds to the consciousness of some teachers and psychologists to neglect the fact that what Leontyev calls 'objective meaning' is also determined by ideologies corresponding to social positions and may be *more or less* adequate to the needs of someone according to their social position. Differences in 'personal sense' are taken to be just that: personal. Conflicts between the individual and the universal are rendered along the axis of subjective-objective, and the teacher or psychologist takes themself to be guardians of the objective.

This is a false dichotomy, and in fact throughout Leontyev's theory, we find many distinctions wrongly rendered into dichotomies rather than relations of mediation, and this is the case here. Rather than introducing 'degrees of adequacy' to the concept of objectivity, the relation between the *individual* and the *universal* must be seen as mediated by the *particular* and not confused with the subjective/objective relation. We could think of this as a scale: on the one end is the universal – what is true for everyone; in the middle is the particular – what is true for this or that social group or class only; and on the other end, the individual – what is true for this person alone. The relation of individual, particular and universal is both simpler and more rational than subjective and more-or-less objective. What is more, it is activity theory which is best placed of all to represent this mediated relationship.

Leontyev's conception of a homogeneous subject-object belongs to another world, a world in which there were apparently no class or ethnic differences, but certainly not the world we live in today.

1.7   *Particularity*

As Leontyev has already outlined, concepts (I prefer to speak of concepts rather than meanings) do not exist in isolation but rather belong to what Leontyev calls 'ideologies' (systems of concepts) which in turn express the needs of certain social positions. But this is just as true of concepts which claim the mantle of 'social consciousness' except that by 'social consciousness' Leontyev meant the concepts of the hegemonic ideology. A better word for this hegemonic subject position is 'universal'. 'Universal' does not mean 'general' – what every single one of us believes, and nor does it mean the standpoint of the boss or the Prime Minister, but rather that of the community *as a whole*. The universal is represented in law and institutionalised knowledge shared by the entire community, rather than any sectional interest, including the dominant one. The universal is akin to the concept of 'public reason' or the terms of a peace treaty, conventional knowledge, even if doesn't always stand up well under critique. The difference between the universal and the particular is relative as is the difference between the individual and the particular. In our times, in many parts of the school curriculum, it must be difficult for teacher to know what to teach without attracting accusations of partisanship – nothing is proof from critique.

Leontyev has explained that 'ideologies' express different social positions, but everyone in a social formation occupies *some* social position and what is more, shares to one degree or another in the viewpoint of *numerous* social positions. It is inescapable that the various groupings of concepts found in social life express one or another social position. But looking at it more closely, and in the spirit of Leontyev's own approach, we can be more specific. Each ideology found in a community represents the system of concepts associated with a specific *activity* directed at resolving some social problem or task generally characteristic of some social position. A scientific concept flows from the pursuit of science, a religious concept flows from the pursuit of religious observance, the concepts of the wage worker flow from struggling to improve wages and working conditions, and so on. Although there are also developmental differences and contingent, individual differences, systematic differences in meaning are associated with *particular* interests and particular activities.

Individual ideas reflect contingent individual differences *as well as* particular differences and what is universal in the culture. What is distinctive in an individual's consciousness arises from individual experiences, but contingencies aside, these experiences reflect in large measure the particular activities in which an individual participates as well as their relation to other social positions and their exposure to ideologies. In short, the particular (i.e., various activities) mediate between the individual and the universal. The universal exists only thanks to those activities in which all individuals participate in *some* way.

This means that in dealing with a child's learning, it is not just the child's personal interests and proclivities on one side and objective truth on the other. Rather, the child comes to the universal and the dominant culture as a participant in a certain cultural and social position, in addition to the various developmental and incidental issues they face. For example, teachers may become frustrated that students find classical literature uninteresting and impenetrable. Teachers overcome this by finding some need, some interest that the child has which provides a motive for struggling with a text which can lead them to an appreciation of literature which is otherwise foreign to them. The key to finding that bridge is sometimes, but usually not, the personal attributes of the child, but the child's *cultural and social position*. Unless we understand this, activity theory occupies a position of dogmatism: "your opinion is subjective but my opinion is objective."

The universal is something objective in the sense that every individual has to deal with it, like it or not, but in its content the universal is far from objective, and may express the point of view of one (dominant) class and not another. The difference between the subjective and the objective is relative, and with the development of social practice, the limits of human knowledge

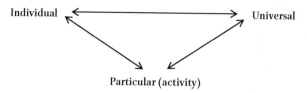

FIGURE 3   Mediation in Activity Theory

are continuously changing: what was objective may turn out to be a mere appearance or partisan.

In relation to the example of the examination mark, the mark itself is something objective, but it would be wrong to insist that the marking of the student's exam paper was objective (disinterested) or that its significance for the student was objective (invariant), even though, being the results of institutionalised practices, both have universal implications. It may be the case that within the student's cultural community the topic under examination was viewed differently, and its teaching held in such contempt that a poor mark would have been worn as a badge of honour, or, the examination result may have been meaningless for progress in the student's chosen trade. These are not *individual* factors, but *social* factors, representing *particular* social activities, which rank on the same level as the factors which motivate particular other students to strive for a good examination result. Leontyev was right (despite falsely equating 'ideal' and 'mental') when he said:

> Being, the life of each individual is made up of the sum-total or, to be more exact, a system, a hierarchy of successive activities. It is in activity that the transition or 'translation' of the reflected object into the subjective image, into the ideal, takes place; at the same time it is also in activity that the transition is achieved from the ideal into activity's objective results, its products, into the material.
>
> 1977, p. 396

My point may be summed up by saying that Leontyev did not fully work out these relations in terms of an *activity theory*. His treatment of ideology in terms of objective meanings which are more or less adequate, that is to say, particular rather than general, suggests that the relation between the individual and the universal is mediated by activity, in logical terms (see Figure 3 above).

There is in fact a pervasive dualism in Leontyev's writing. The rendering of the relation of the individual to the universal as subjective vs. objective is the most serious but there are others. For example:

> Moreover, the object of activity appears in two forms: first, in its independent existence, commanding the activity of the subject, and second, as the mental image of the object, as the product of the subject's 'detection' of its properties, which is effected by the activity of the subject and cannot be effected otherwise
>
> 1977, p. 397

What Leontyev means by the object "commanding the activity of the subject" is the 'hard necessity' of life, that one must work to live, and that collectively a community must produce a certain range of goods, and by one or another social arrangement individuals find themselves obliged to participate in activities which regularly produce the given object. The 'mental image' refers to the socially constructed consciousness a person has of their participation in the activity. But it is not as clear cut as that for there may be (more or less organised) *social differences* of motivation and interpretation of the object in play, and it is the sum total of these particular social relations which determines both the 'independent' existence of the object and the subject's 'image' of it.

For example, quite aside from the remuneration a worker gets from employment at the Post Office, or the service a resident gets from the deliveries, some postal workers see the Post Office as a public service and some residents see the Post Office as a profit-making enterprise of which they are customers, while private courier companies see the Post Office as either a competitor or a collaborator. Employees of a capitalist firm might see the firm solely as a means of earning a wage, but others will not 'merely understand' the role of the company but have a genuine commitment to it, the more so given that most public services are delivered by for-profit private companies these days. And these are *social, not personal*, differences, *differences mediated by participation in activities* and constituting an individual's social position. So between individuals' actions and the outcome of the activity there are a number of particular, socially constructed concepts of what it is all for, not just one.

Consider this dichotomy:

> ... mental reflection occurs owing to the bifurcation of the subject's vital processes into the processes that realise his direct biotic relations, and the 'signal' processes that mediate them.
>
> 1977, p. 410

I would say that mental reflection is not just 'caused' by the introduction of sign use in the self-regulation of the organism. Rather, as Vygotsky said: mental reflection facilitates self-regulation by *mediating between* the physiology of the organism and its behaviour.

Later, he refers to:

> This is the problem of the specific nature of the functioning of knowledge, concepts, conceptual models, etc., in the system of social relations, in the social consciousness, on the one hand, and, on the other, in the individual's activity that realises his social relations, in the individual consciousness.
>
> 1977, p. 410

Here Leontyev mystifies this relation, reducing it to a dichotomy of the individual versus 'society', neglecting an important distinction in the constitution of social consciousness, i.e., on one hand the *material conditions* including the technical means of production, land, built environment and the literature, language and human material, and on the other the *activities* by means of which these material conditions (artefacts) are put into motion and penetrate individual consciousness. In other words this is actually a *three*-sided relation: material conditions, activities and actions.

And this is an important observation. Leontyev takes 'social consciousness' to be an objective, material category, and in doing so he is consistent with orthodox Marxist approaches. On the other hand, individual consciousness is a subjective, psychological category. The process which 'bridges' or mediates between these two is activity, and activity is both material and psychological. This observation is important for social theory because if activities are to be units for social theory there must be no ambiguity as to whether activities are psychological or material entities. They are *both,* and this is given concrete content by the fact that activities mediate between the material conditions, including the ideal (i.e., social) properties of artefacts, and human consciousness, just as consciousness mediates between material conditions and human behaviour and material conditions mediate between consciousness and behaviour. 'Activity' is a union of both behaviour and consciousness, as is 'experience', one placing emphasis on the behaviour, the other placing emphasis on the consciousness.

As a result of Leontyev's failure to grasp these mediated relationships and his persistent rendering these dialectical relations as dichotomies, a number of weaknesses have developed in his theory.

1.7.1   Dogmatism

It is generally recognised that there may be a number of legitimate opinions on any given question arising in social life and if our interlocutor has a different opinion, we do not normally recommend they visit a psychologist or go back to school. We understand that one's life experience, social position, commitments and the activities in which one is engaged will give a person a different angle on things and sometimes it is quite impossible to find an answer to some question which is genuinely satisfactory to everyone regardless of their social position. To deny this, and on the contrary suggest that there is only one 'objective' meaning to something and cast other views as biased and partial, as Leontyev does, is dogmatism. Science always seeks after objective truth, but this is never final.

Within the context of a specific activity or institution, such as a certain branch of science, such an insistence may be justified to an extent, and with qualifications, in the context of education and child development. Nevertheless, to equate the universal and the objective is a category mistake.

Further, an activity may be oriented to a certain object at one moment, but contradictions and problems will emerge, and the concept of the object will change. The concept which participants have of the object of an activity (which will differ from person to person) develops over time. Activities are learning processes. To insist at the outset on a certain definition of the object, which is continuously consumed and produced, would be misplaced dogmatism.

1.7.2   Functionalism

The social theory which flows from Leontyev's theory is a variety of functionalism. Functionalism is a trend of social theory associated with the name of the American sociologist, Talcott Parsons, which was ascendant in the period after World War Two. Functionalism sees the society as an *organism* in which all the constituent parts have 'functions', i.e., answer to the question "What is this *for*? What is its *role*?" and like biological organisms, social organisms have an inherent tendency towards stability; disturbances to its functioning stimulate new processes which restore the status quo. It is descriptive to an extent but it is not explanatory. Anthony Giddens' (1984) critique of Functionalism is decisive.

Leontyev sees social activity in terms of various objects each of which answer to a certain social need and every social formation has evolved social arrangements such that these objects "command the activity of the subject," and determine the actions of everyone in the community.

But who determines the *needs* of society? And is 'the needs of society' even a coherent notion? One gets the impression that in Leontyev's world, which had supposedly surpassed the class differences, 'anarchy of production' and alienation of capitalism, it was the Politburo which determined all the needs of the society and set goals and objects for the various industries in Five Year

Plans. But it is widely accepted now that such a view was a fantasy. The real object, though rarely realised, was always whatever a stratum of administrators determined.

In the case of a liberal capitalist society, the situation is even worse: rarely does the government or anyone else give consideration to the needs of the whole community. Anarchy of production reigns.

Since every existing activity is by Leontyev's *definition* directed at a social need, we evidently have among those needs: war, drug smuggling, advertising, cigarettes and obesity-producing foods. The theory simply fails as an explanatory tool. The market is not a process for determining and balancing the needs of the community, any more than nature is 'for' human enjoyment. Certainly, *demand* regulates the economy, but 'demand' is conceptually quite distant from 'need'. Need places limits on human behaviour, but these are very elastic limits. Further, the object of every capitalist firm is accumulation of capital. Any collateral social benefit is purely accidental.

1.7.3 'Productivism'

In common with all social theory in the Soviet era, human 'activity' is rendered as 'labour' with the strong implication that a certain kind of labour, industrial labour, is the archetype and has a determining function. The genetic derivation of the theory, beginning from micro-organisms and working its way up through early humans to class society, justifies a productivist explanation. As useful as this Marxist approach might be for historical analysis this by no means justifies its place in psychology. Language co-evolved with the production of tools so there is no reason to privilege labour over communication in the foundations of psychology. Developing a foundation for social theory from a psychology which has surreptitiously introduced a productivist theory of history into its foundations risks misleading social theory as well as psychology.

Further, although signs do figure throughout as mediating communication, and artefacts in general remain the mediators of all actions, Leontyev seems to have put a distance between himself and Vygotsky by emphasising labour, i.e., *tool*-mediated activity, rather than *sign*-mediation. Leontyev's productivism is an upshot of this marginalisation of sign mediation. In today's world it is difficult to draw a line between communication and production, especially in the most dominant economies. This problem can be corrected by removing the bias inherent in the word 'labour' and sticking with 'activity'. The more so as Leontyev never had anything to say about the *actual* labour process in the USSR where he lived.

2   Leontyev's Theory of the Personality

'Personality' (личность) is a complex and chameleon concept: which attributes of an individual are to be counted under the heading of 'personality' and which not? Leontyev relegates to the category of 'substructures' of the personality "such various traits as, for example, moral qualities, knowledge, habits and customs, forms of psychological reflection, and temperament" (1978, p. 154). What he sees as composing the structure of a personality are units that I will call 'motives' for the moment, and it is these motives which both express and give meaning to a person's life, or more generally form the *structure of meaning* for the person. What is more usually understood as 'personality' nowadays more closely approximates what Leontyev calls 'forms of psychological reflection', but as I hope to show it is precisely the structure of meaning as understood by Leontyev which is of importance in connection with framing a social theory, even if it is only partially explanatory in the domain of psychology.

During the first phase of development of a personality, the child or youth is just an expression of the class fraction and cultural group in which they have been raised.

> The subject's belonging to a class conditions even at the outset the development of his connections with the surrounding world, a greater or smaller segment of his practical activity, his contacts, his knowledge, and his acquiring norms of behaviour. All of these are acquisitions from which personality is made up at the stage of its initial formation.
>
>   1978, pp. 178–179

Leontyev says that at this stage it cannot properly be said that there is a personality because the person is merely an instance of their social group:

> later this situation is turned around, and they become a *subject* of their social group, unconsciously and then consciously, … decisive or vacillating … at every turn of his life's way he must free himself of something, confirm something in himself, and he must do all this and not simply 'submit to the effect of the environment'.
>
>   1978, p. 179

What were formerly the traits of a person of their kind become later merely the *conditions* for the formation of a personality properly so called. The subject gradually frees themself from their biography, discarding some aspects of their 'parochial' personality while consciously developing others.

Personality thus no longer seems to be the result of a direct layering of external influences; it appears as something that man makes of himself, confirming his human life. He confirms it in everyday affairs and contacts, as well as in people to whom he gives some part of himself on the barricades of class struggles, as well as on the fields of battle for his country, and at times he consciously confirms it even at the price of his physical life.

1978, p. 185

A person's motivation is represented to the person in the shape of the activities to which they are committed, so to the extent that the subject actively commits themselves to an activity, acquiring in the meantime the knowledge and skills, the norms and all the attributes associated with the activity, these motives, represented by the object of the activity, become a stable part of the person's personality. The activities themselves wax and wane, prove successful or fail – their fate depending on factors in the wider social world. The personality however constitutes a relatively stable base in the inner world of the subject. Development of the personality is tied up with the development of the subject's will and the subject's emotional life is linked to the fate of these activities, but the personality remains a relatively stable psychic formation.

In the next phase of development, the subject arranges the units of their personality into a *structure*. The units of this structure are the 'motives', so this lifeworld could also be called a 'motivational structure'. Some motives make their way to the top of a hierarchy, dominating and leading others which become conditional upon it. Sometimes, the personality becomes split with some motivations dominant in some situations while others predominate in other situations. There will also be conflict between motives, and development of the personality entailing resolution of these internal conflicts, either sublating a motivational conflict into more profound motives which transcend the conflict, or by relegating or discarding one motivation.

The final phase of the development of a personality is entailed in the raising of motivations above the material needs tied up in maintaining their life in their social group up to more abstract motivations. Ultimately, following Aristotle, "the good life for humanity" becomes the leading motive, conditioning and leading other motivations in the subject's life and personality.

In the earliest stages of personality development, development is driven by *need*. Needs develop of course and never remain at the animal level, but in conditions where motivations are driven by needs the person is simply a product of their environment. "Personality cannot develop within the framework of need; its development necessarily presupposes a displacement of needs by creation, which alone does not know limits" (1978, p. 186). Once the subject begins to free themselves from subordination to the needs and norms of their social group, and their personality composes itself of ideal social motives, Leontyev now increasingly refers to the motives as *otnosheniya* (отношение, *pl.* отношения) rather than motives (мотивов). 'отношения' is usually translated as 'relations', but it is also used to mean 'priorities' or 'attitudes' or 'orientations'. (On *Otnosheniya*, see Chapter 10, this volume.)

> ... the personality of man also 'is produced' – it is created by the *otnosheniya*, into which the individual enters in his activity.
> 1978, p. 152

These priorities or relations are the *commitments* the person makes to activities, and which take up more or less leading positions in the structure of their motives. What is indicated is an ideal motive, which I would prefer to call a 'life-project' inasmuch as in the fully developed personality it does not represent a 'need' so much as a commitment to an ideal of some kind.

Leontyev notes a pathology of the personality found in "superprosperous consumer society" when the intrinsic value of objects as means of satisfaction of needs has been been lost and commodities perform only the function of confirming a person's prestige. In such a situation the personality may take on a "configuration of flatness devoid of real summits when what is small in life man takes for something large, and the large things he does not see at all" (1978, p. 183).

Although Leontyev correctly emphasises the subjective side in the formation of personality, his theory lacks a satisfactory explanation of how the subject adopts some motives and discards others in the early formation of the personality or how and why a person might change their lifeworld. It seems to me that the concept used by Vygotsky and later by Fedor Vasilyuk, *perezhivaniya* (переживания) – deeply-felt or life-changing events in a person's life and the person's response to them – has more explanatory power.

Leontyev's activity theory remains a powerful and complex approach to psychology, especially if it is used in conjunction with Vygotsky's Cultural Psychology. It has been subject to at least two generations of development since Leontyev's day, and most of its shortcomings may be overcome.

Finally, I am going to review an alternative conception of an activity which I believe could render Leontyev's activity theory suitable to be part of a foundation for social theory.

3   A 'Project' as an Activity

A project is an activity, that is, a unit of activity characterised by a shared object-concept, but whereas Leontyev saw activities as aimed at reproducing ongoing objects, I take it that the object, archetypically, is an ideal form of the object acted upon, generally a *change* in reality. But projects are unambiguously *discrete* entities, and I shall call the unit of activity a 'project' both because the word has connotations which are helpful in clarifying the concept of a unit of activity, and so that I can outline a version of activity theory without conveying the impression that I have merely misunderstood Leontyev. At the same time, I do not monotonously refer to every institution, movement, life-commitment, social practice or whatever as a 'project'. But whatever word is used, it is as a *project* that I conceive them.

'Project' denotes a future-oriented, collaborative endeavour in which people work together towards some goal, despite the fact that not every participant holds exactly the same notion of what the project is about. In addition, the object keeps changing as the project unfolds, like a design project. ('Design' and 'project' are the same word in Russian). Projects often end up producing something which is quite unexpected for *all* of the participants.

That is, rather than *first* defining an object or motive and *then* defining the project as that aggregate of actions directed towards that object, I say that projects exist, and they are constituted by *collaboration* towards a shared object, but what this object is *has to be determined by analysis of the project*; it might be an utter fiction. Equally, it is quite feasible that more than one distinct project could be working on one and the same object with differing goals, just as many different motives could coexist within the same project. The *relations of collaboration* between the actions mark out the extent of a project.

A project is launched to solve some social problem, a problem that has arisen for some category of individuals. Some members of this group form a concept of what has to be done and begin to act together to realise that concept. Usually, this is past history. Once the project is launched it takes on an identity and a life of its own, so to speak. The project becomes a kind of social movement (in the broadest sense); it adopts an identity representing the concept it aims to realise, but this object-concept is subject to ongoing revision, according to both its inner logic and the events engendered by the project activity. Individuals can participate in the project, but the terms on which they participate are quite diverse, taking into account their other commitments. To the extent that the project makes headway in realising its object, it eventually becomes institutionalised and progresses from an institution in which people work on a more or less instrumental basis to become an indistinguishable component of everyone's daily life. So the concepts people use to orient their individual actions, all are the products of projects, which begin life as contradictions within the existing social formation.

A project progresses through a number of distinctly different phases, a *lifecycle*, and people's relation to participation in the project is diverse. Through all the changes in the forms of activity and object-concepts, we can distinguish between phases of one and the same project and what are distinct projects. The inner logic of the object-concept is what is decisive, but the collaborative coherence and continuity of the component actions and overlapping continuity of the participants allows us to trace the logic of that development.

Everything that Leontyev says about the role of activities in the shaping of consciousness remains true for projects, with the qualifications which have already been outlined. Our conception of activities as projects has to give a higher profile to social critique, rather than accepting the dominant social consciousness as 'objective' and only mentioning other ideologies as alternatives to the dominant social consciousness or an afterthought. The formation of a project is not a passive response to need, but a creative process of problem solving which also involves the construction of identities and meaning in life and testifies not to the subordination of human being to need, but rather to human freedom and the capacity of human beings to change the world they live in. More than one project can arise in response to one and the same problem, and distinct projects may cooperate or conflict with one another.

I believe that Leontyev's theory of personality as a structure of meanings each related to a collaborative project captures how projects enter into the formation of the personality. However, an investigation of *perezhivanie* is needed to clarify how people come to be committed to projects.

CHAPTER 10

Fedor Vasilyuk's Psychology of Life-Projects

In 1984, Fyodor Vasilyuk published a seminal book on psychotherapy, *The Psychology of Experiencing* (1984), and according to Alex Kozulin (1991) it was "the first important contribution to the field of psychodynamic theory made by a Soviet author in the last 50 years" (p. 14). The aim of Vasilyuk's book was to provide a foundation for psychotherapists to assist patients dealing with life crises.

The key concepts of the work are переживание (*perezhivanie*), translated somewhat inadequately as 'experiencing' and understood by Vasilyuk as an active process of 'working over' and overcoming a crisis which has arisen in what he calls an отношение (*Otnosheniye*), translated as 'life relation'. 'Life-relations' collectively make up what Vasilyuk calls the subject's жизненный мир (*zhiznniyi mir*), literally 'lifeworld'.

Crisis situations arise in a person's lifeworld from failures in life-relations, or conflicts between them. He says:

> During the period of acute pain [such as following the death of a loved one, or failure to win a desired career move] *perezhivanie* becomes the person's leading activity ... which occupies a dominating position in the life of a person and through which his personal development is carried out.
>
> VASILYUK, 1984, p. 231

In his review of Vasilyuk's book, Alex Kozulin (1991) interpreted this as follows:

> The individual must bring about the unity of the self, and not only as an internal conscious project, but as an actual existence in a difficult world. The ... unity of the self first appears as life-intent or life-project. This intent as related to the system of values is felt by a person as a 'calling', and in its relation to the spatio-temporal actuality of existence it becomes 'life work'.
>
> p. 15

1 *Otnosheniye* (отношение)

Otnosheniye is the same concept found in Leontyev's description of the structure of personality, and translated as 'life-relation', but I agree somewhat with Alex Kozulin's view just quoted. 'Life-relation' has the advantage that as a relation it is neither internal nor external but both. And yet this term fails to convey what it is which is related internally and externally and fails to convey the drama with which it is to be associated. For Leontyev and Vasilyuk, the specific life relation at issue is a subject's commitment to a project.

An action is defined as a behaviour with a motive which differs from its goal and is therefore both subjective and objective; otherwise it is not an action. Thus there is a sense in which every composite of actions is also necessarily both subjective and objective.

Activities are both subjective and objective, but an activity gains its objective unity from the objectively synthetic tendency of the composite actions, each being carried out by a different person, each of whom may have a subjectively divergent intent. Activities are units of a social formation and exist independently of any participant's consciousness. It is the collaboration of the participants, with the aid of shared artefacts, which creates an objective unity, not the common goal as such.

The subjective unity of an activity, derived from unifying symbols and sensuous experiences, represents the activity to an individual subject. A subject's commitments form a structure, which, in Leontyev and Vasilyuk's terms, constitutes the subject's personality. These two structures, that of a subject's commitments and that of the projects making up a social formation – are not correlates of one another, but *the units of each are* correlates. The subject's external world is a part of the external world in itself, subjectively compiled from the subject's commitments.

The unity of the subject's external and internal world is the subject's 'lifeworld'. Units of this lifeworld are *otnosheniya*. *Otnosheniya* are both objective and subjective, but to properly convey what is entailed in an *otnosheniya* we must use different words to denote their internal or mental aspects and their external, worldly aspects.

Otnosheniye expresses both a subject's commitment (to a project) and the project itself, as something that exists independently of the subject (like 'my wife'). In the case of that project which comes to express the subject's lifeintent, the words 'vocation' and 'life-project' are appropriate. It is this lifeintent or life-project which integrates the subject's personality and during 'normal times', is the leading activity in the subject's personal development. The life-intent is built, generally over many years, with the development of the subject's will as the leading function in the creative formation of their personality.

The meaning of *otnosheniye* for Vasilyuk is further clarified when he explains that the absence of resistant forces makes action meaningless, so an activity, and therefore an *otnosheniye*, can exist only so long as there is resistance which must be overcome. Imaginary commitments, which in principle never see the light of the external world, don't count, and nor does pursuit of readily satiable desires. As Vygotsky (1928) wrote in the context of the development of character in disabled children: "The existence of obstacles creates a 'goal' for mental acts, that is, it introduces into development a future-directed mentality" (LSV CW, vol. 2, p. 158), and "compensation is a battle, and every battle can result in two completely opposite outcomes: victory or defeat" (p. 159).

2 The Lifeworld (жизненный мир)

The lifeworld is not merely an aggregate of a person's commitments, but is inclusive of the objective reality of these life-projects; so it is both subjective and objective in the same sense that an action is both subjective and objective, though we lack a word to adequately express this in English. Nor is the lifeworld simply an additive sum of these projects and commitments. It is a *structure* which includes the interconnections between the *otnosheniya* both in the subject's belief and in reality, and hierarchical relations between them in the subject's life-work. The kind of interconnections and structures which are applicable to the internal world of the subject's commitments differ from the interconnections and structures of the material world where projects are played out. So for this reason, different characterisations must be made of the internal and the external aspects of the lifeworld.

Vasilyuk's theory is based on a four-part typology of lifeworlds:

> This typology is structured as follows: the object of analysis is the 'lifeworld'. This has external and internal aspects, denoted … as 'external world' and 'internal world'. The external world can be either easy or difficult. The internal world can be either simple or complex. The intersections of these categories give us four possible states, or types of lifeworld.
> p. 92

The lifeworld is meant to be considered in the context of a specific crisis arising in a specific commitment, not necessarily the subject's life-intent, and not necessarily descriptive of a person's entire life and personality. Only the commitments and projects relevant to a specific life-crisis figure in the characterisation of the lifeworld.

The ease or difficulty of the external world describes the status of projects to which the subject is committed, that is, whether or not the subject is able to make progress towards their goal. An easy world is one in which no effort at all is required to attain the goal. A difficult world is one in which attainment of the goal has become impossible. Both are critical conditions. Normal life takes place between these two extremes.

The simplicity or complexity of the internal world describes the interconnections between a subject's commitments and their relative value or theoretical incompatibility, irrespective of their fate in the external world.

Each of the four types of crisis is characterised by a single word: stress, frustration, conflict and crisis.

1. *Stress* is the crisis of the *easy-simple* lifeworld. Here the subject has no goals and pursues no project because they demand and receive immediate gratification. Having no direction in which to strive, their diffuse anxiety is manifested as stress. A person may have many commitments, but pursues each commitment one at a time and encounters no resistance, so the subject's world is simple and easy. Vasilyuk calls this a hedonistic crisis and it is widespread in modern, prosperous, democratic states.

2. *Frustration* is the crisis of the *difficult-simple* lifeworld. The subject is focused on their life-defining project, but achievement of their goal is blocked and nothing can be done about it. The typical example of this crisis is a disaster in a treasured career which has hitherto defined a subject's whole life, and the subject may be unable to go on in a life which has now become pointless.

3. *Conflict* is the crisis of the *easy-complex* lifeworld. The subject is committed to more than one project, both of which are immediately attainable, but the options have nothing in common by means of which to compare them, except that the subject has a commitment to both and must choose which to pursue: "should I have a child or should I continue my career?"

4. The crisis of the *difficult-complex* lifeworld is a *life crisis*, combining features of the other three sectors. The subject's chosen life-project is blocked and there is a temptation to abandon former strong commitments to overcome blockages in others, and only a creative response offers the possibility of recovering a meaningful life.

On the basis of these four types of crisis, Vasilyuk defines a typology of four kinds of *perezhivanie*, respectively hedonistic *perezhivanie*, realistic *perezhivanie*, value *perezhivanie* and creative *perezhivanie*. The four types of *perezhivanie* are not restricted to the critical situation which constitutes the archetypal crisis generating the *perezhivanie*, but affect the entire life and personality.

3   *Perezhivanie* (переживание)

Vasilyuk clearly states that he is not using the term '*perezhivanie*' ...

> in the sense most familiar in psychological literature – that of a direct, usually emotional form in which the content of his consciousness is given to the subject – but to denote *a special inner activity or inner work* by means of which an individual succeeds in withstanding various (usually painful) events and situations in life, succeeds in regaining the mental equilibrium which has been temporarily lost – succeeds, in short, in coping with a crisis.
>
> p. 15

Interestingly, while acknowledging himself as a student of A.N. Leontyev's activity theory, Vasilyuk says that "there is no appropriate category or term available within this body of work" (p. 15). *Perezhivanie* had long existed as a category within mainstream psychology in the sense in which Vasilyuk mentions above. The more specific sense Vasilyuk uses is generally associated with the work of L.S. Vygotsky.

Perezhivanie is an *activity*, a particular type of work which produces "mental equilibrium, comprehension, tranquillity, a new sense of values, etc. ... reconstructing a psychological world and directed towards the establishment of correlation between consciousness and existence in terms of meaning, the overall aim of the world of experiencing being to give greater meaningfulness to life" (pp. 16, 31).

Like any other activity, the capacity for *perezhivanie* develops from rudimentary to mature as the subject grows from infancy to adulthood, and utilises all the psychological functions and culturally available resources.

4   Types of *perezhivanie*

1. The prototype of the *easy-simple* lifeworld is that of the *infantile* personality. *Perezhivanie* is impossible in the purely easy-simple lifeworld, because everything is provided and the pleasure principle faces no resistance. With immediate satisfaction there can be no contradiction or any situation creating

psychological challenges to be 'worked over'. However, as soon as some small difficulty arises in this infantile lifeworld, the only psychological resources available are those already acquired in the easy-simple world of hedonistic, here-and-now satisfaction. Whatever the nature of the difficulty or complication which has arisen, the infantile response will be manifested in diffuse, senseless activity. *Perezhivanie* entails a denial of reality, a delusion that the need has in fact been met or that it was never felt. The world of the actual infant, which passes through severe crises in its social situation of development, is not in reality such an easy-simple lifeworld. Rather, Vasilyuk has in mind the caricature of an adult who retains the traits of infancy.

2. The prototype of the *difficult-simple* lifeworld is the *fanatic*. The *perezhivanie* of the difficult-simple lifeworld is realism, but *perezhivanie* in this world begins with *patience*. Patience differs from denial in that although it believes in a good which is not present, it does not deny the problem and believes it can be solved. But when patience runs out, and frustration sets in and it is faced with the impossible situation, the reality principle offers two alternative ways out. The first way is to postpone satisfaction, or lower one's sights and make do with a substitute for what is impossible according to the reality principle. In the second way, the subject abandons the former pursuit (the meaning of their former life) and takes up another which cannot be a substitute for the loss of the first or a continuation of it by other means. This may be what is called 'coping behaviour'.

3. The *easy-complex* lifeworld is an aesthetic and moral world. The *perezhivanie* of the easy-complex world is *value-perezhivanie*. The critical situation may arise when an activity attractive to the subject comes into conflict with the subject's life-project. Either the offending activity is morally discredited and postponed or abandoned, or the subject finds a way of mentally reconciling it as not really in contradiction to the life-project. Alternatively, value-*perezhivanie* is required in the wake of a wrecked life-project, searching amongst other projects for that which is most valued and could restore meaning to their life, such as 'in memory of' the lost life-project. Alternatively, the crisis may be resolved by a radical restructuring of the subject's entire value system, maintaining continuity through forgiveness and redemption. The principle of value-experiencing is *phronesis* or wisdom, rather than intelligence. Vasilyuk describes this re-evaluation as theoretical not practical work.

4. The *perezhivanie* of the *difficult-complex* lifeworld is *creative perezhivanie* and entails an entire reconstruction of the self.

– The first alternative is to continue the pursuit of the values which had hitherto defined one's life but were identified with a particular person or project which is no longer available. However, the identification of the

life-intent with this particular form of realising it can be overcome by reformulating these values in more general, abstract terms, so they can be realised in some other particular form (or person), making the fixation on that former particular embodiment unnecessary.
- The second path is to discover that life has hitherto been based on false values and to formulate a new value system, but in such a way as to preserve the meaning of the past life, showing how it conquered error and finally won through to life's true intent.
- The third type of creative *perezhivanie* is connected with the highest stages of personality development as the life-intent moves away from egoistic projects and places the self in the service of higher motives, secure against any misfortune and for which the person is ultimately prepared for any sacrifice including life itself.

In a *perezhivanie*, the leading psychological formation in the lifeworld is the *will*. The integrity of the person as presented in self-consciousness is not something present and achieved, but has to be *actualised* in life-activity and the will is the only faculty which can achieve that actualisation. The will is the central psychological function in the formation of the personality. The will is first developed in childhood, according to Vygotsky, in the passage through the series of childhood life crises which separate the successive phases of childhood. These crises arise when the social situation of development which defines the social position of the child must be transformed for child to 'grow up' and the child break through to the next station in life. It is in these childhood crises that the will is formed as a concrete, higher mental function, and the various forms of psychic reflection which characterise a person are formed.

Likewise in adulthood, the personality develops precisely in the passage through life crises by means of creative *perezhivaniya*, which reconstruct the self while not discarding the former self, but allowing the past to be rationally understood from a new, higher standpoint.

5 Social Theory

Vasilyuk is exclusively focused on psychotherapy and there is no element of social theory in his work, beyond the use of *otnosheniye* as a unit of a subject's lifeworld, both in its internal and its external aspect. He provides a concrete basis for understanding how individuals relate to the wider world specifically through their participation in and commitment to collaborative projects. Vasilyuk's focus is on how new, generally more profound, commitments are made in the passage through crises that arise when projects fail or reach an impasse or when they come into conflict with other valued projects.

Social theorists would also be interested in how young people first begin to participate in projects and make their first commitments. In general, the formation of a commitment to a project is the mark of adulthood and the formation of a life-project the mark of maturity. Some young people enter adulthood directly, so to speak, already committed to a struggle for personal survival and the hope that the family will do better. Once crises arising in this simple-difficult lifeworld have exhausted the subject's patience, then the subject works over the situation in a realistic *perezhivanie*, and the subject can develop from fanaticism to the creative search for other means.

But in general, children do not enter adulthood with strong commitments to difficult projects. Vasilyuk tells us that when this simple-easy world is disrupted, the reaction is stress, generally manifested in meaningless activity. "Any failure or situational mishap is likely to be perceived as a general life-crisis" (p. 148). So in fact, Vasilyuk's ideas are applicable in the case of young people, once their carefree life has been disrupted by some life-changing experience.

CHAPTER 11

The Invention of Nicaraguan Sign Language

1   Introduction

In the 1980s, Nicaragua was a poor country, emerging from civil war, lacking in specialist resources and with low levels of literacy even amongst the hearing population, and was a country in which the deaf had no sign language. If a new sign language were to be created from scratch, it was hardly likely that children with no language capacity to begin with were going to be the ones to do it.

So linguists and psychologists were stunned when it was reported[1] that in the 1980s, in Nicaragua, without even the awareness, let alone assistance of adults, deaf children themselves had *invented* a brand new sign language, Nicaraguan Sign Language (NSL), linguistically distinct both from spoken Spanish and other sign languages – a fully-fledged mature language with syntax, recursion and the capacity to reference abstract concepts and hypothetical or distant events. Since the children had no access to *any* language – spoken Spanish or sign language, and mostly not even written Spanish – it seemed impossible that children should have been able to acquire a language, let alone collectively *invent* one, unaided, from scratch. It was the only recorded case of the creation of an entirely new language, as opposed to a dialect or a creole of existing languages, like the Pidgin English spoken in Hawaii or New Guinea, or AUSLAN, which is derivative from British, New Zealand, US and Irish sign languages.

"[Normal speech] development is achieved," said Lev Vygotsky (1934a), "under particular conditions of interaction with the environment, where the final or ideal form [of speech] … is not only already there in the environment and from the very start in contact with the child, but actually interacts and exerts a real influence on the primary form, on the first steps of the child's development." It follows from this that a deaf child will not develop either spoken language or sign language if he or she is denied the possibility of interacting with others using such a language. Denied the possibility of acquiring the knowledge and wisdom of their community, their entire psychological development will be stunted. In a minority of cases, deaf children *can* master

---

1   See the Wikipedia entry: https://en.wikipedia.org/wiki/Nicaraguan_Sign_Language for the conventional wisdom on this event.

speech without the aid of sign language, through lip reading and intensive professional training, and with the aid of the written word (where that is the norm) go on to achieve a normal cognitive development or better. But for the vast majority, in the absence of sign language, development of language is entirely blocked and consequently, the normal psychological development associated with language use is also blocked.

So Vygotsky's claim – that ontogenetic development was unique and distinct from any other kind of development (historical, cultural or biological evolution) in that the final point of development must be present throughout to act as the *model* and *source* of development – must be wrong. It appeared that language could develop among a limited group of children hitherto lacking any language beyond 'home sign' (see below) without interaction with the final form functioning as the source of development, and achieve the complexity of a mature language in a couple of decades.

•••

The solution to the puzzle is simple. This *did not in fact happen*. Nonetheless, it is true that in 1980 there was no sign language in Nicaragua and only a handful of the thousands of deaf Nicaraguans could speak intelligibly and lip read and the vast majority were illiterate. But by 1990, there was a self-conscious Deaf community with its own sign language distinct from that of other countries, whilst the education system, far from having taught children to sign, continued to actively *suppress* the use of gesture and signing by their deaf pupils.

So somehow, during the 1980s, a new sign language developed in Nicaragua simultaneously with young deaf people acquiring it and beginning to use it. So the puzzle remains as intriguing as ever and the answer should tell us about the minimal conditions for the development of a new language and the minimal conditions of interaction with an ideal for the normal cognitive and linguistic development of individuals.

The problem of language development posed by NSL is particularly sharp because we depend on speech for our socialisation which is in turn the source of the development of virtually *all* of our personality. But Vygotsky's point cited above was not made exclusively in relation to language. He made the point about child development in general and made the same point explicitly in connection with arithmetic. A language is in a strong sense a concrete concept or 'science' of the world, and every one of our higher psychological functions also is a kind of 'science', expressing the world in its own unique way, so in a strong sense this problem of the ontogenesis of language is an archetype for the development of all forms of human activity, that is, of all our psychological functions and activities and of all our institutions. Children *cannot* learn a new concept or subject matter by talking amongst themselves, unless amongst their number at least one has already acquired a facility in the relevant subject matter and can teach the others.

2   Vygotsky on the Ideal Form

Before turning to the case of Nicaraguan Sign Language, I would like to briefly review what Vygotsky said in *The Problem of the Environment* which makes the claims in relation to NSL challenging for Vygotsky's theory. Vygotsky wrote:

> … environment is a factor in the realm of personality development and its specific human traits, and its role is to act as the *source* of this development, i.e. environment is the *source* of development and not simply its setting.
>
> What does this mean? First of all it indicates a very simple thing, namely that if no appropriate *ideal* form can be found in the environment, and the development of the child, for whatever reasons, has to take place outside these specific conditions (described earlier), i.e. without any interaction with the final form, then this proper form will fail to develop properly in the child.
>
> Try to imagine a [hearing] child who is growing up among deaf people and is surrounded by deaf and dumb parents and children his own age. Will he be able to develop speech? No …
>
> 1934a

The ideal form is that which sets the expectations for "a member of a certain social group, … a certain historical unit living at a certain historical period and in certain historical circumstances" (Vygotsky, 1934a). In the overwhelming majority of communities, this includes a particular spoken, grammatical language, capable of referencing hypothetical or remote events and situations, and abstract ideas and characterised by recursiveness. 'Ideal' means the *norm* for the given community, not any individual instance. The norm finds its expression, however, only through ontogenesis – many individuals, each of them being different *realisations* of the ideal. The ideal is implicit in each and every individual, even if not a single individual in the community perfectly matches that ideal. The ideal differs from any individual in that while individuals live and die, cultural history continues, consisting in the evolution of this norm, this ideal, and it is in this sense that the norm of a given society is said to be 'ideal'. The ideal is an expression and product of *cultural history*, which in turn provides the model for each individual at the same time as generating the social interactions which promote the development of each individual. Normal development does not mean 'matching' the norm, for implicit within a norm is also an understanding of which differences constitute the normal range of diversity, and which differences represent some kind of pathology or deviance.

Vygotsky goes on:

> Secondly, try to imagine that this ideal form is not to be found in the child's environment, ... the child develops among other children, i.e. that his environment is made up of children of his own age who are all at the lower, rudimentary form stage. In such a situation, will the proper activity and traits develop in this child? Research shows that it will, but in an extremely peculiar way. They will always develop very slowly and in an unusual manner, and will never attain the level which they reach when the suitable ideal form is present in the environment.
>
> *op. cit.*

So, children working amongst themselves might find a solution to some arithmetical problem, a solution which differs from that which the teacher expected of them but neglected to teach them. The children have solved the given problem, but what they have missed out on, and which was the teacher's responsibility to provide for them, is that method of solution which contains the germ of further development leading to the acquisition of higher mathematics or other more advanced forms, solutions to problems only implicit in the problem before them, something which the children will *never* acquire by themselves, without the aid of text books and/or instruction. A true concept, the ideal, does not inhere in the *problem* as such, but in the culturally evolved *solution* to a socially evolved problem.

'Ideal' does *not* mean 'perfect'. 'Ideal' has these three interconnected meanings: it is what is *expected of* the child in the given community, that is, the norm; it is the ideological formation which exerts pressure on the child to *draw them* towards itself, and which alone gives meaning to the child's actions; and it is a cultural and historical formation which evolves over many generations in and through the birth, life and death of every individual in the community.

According to Vygotsky, not only the presence, but adequate *interaction* with the ideal, is a precondition for the attainment of the norm, or ideal, by a child of the given community.

3   Deaf Children in Nicaragua

I rely for the history of NSL on Laura Polich (2005), an audiologist who conducted exhaustive historical research into the deaf community in Nicaragua, interviewing every deaf person she could find in the country in a ten-year-long research project, as well as all those who had been involved in deaf education over the decades. Polich's testimony differs from that of all others who have written on NSL in that she investigated, on the ground, the *actual history* of NSL, rather than drawing conclusions based solely on the final product and hearsay about its genesis.

Until 1946, deaf children in Nicaragua were considered a punishment visited upon a family for past wrongs, a point of shame, to be kept out of sight and isolated from the rest of the world. Deafness was taken as a variety of mental retardation (and this remained largely the case into the 1990s). It is of course hardly surprising that deaf children exhibited mental retardation, given the conditions under which they were kept – isolated from any interaction with other human beings. Deaf children were either cared for with kindness or chained up like animals, but in no case did they have a chance to develop beyond childhood. Even today, despite the developments of the past 25 years, an unknown number of deaf people in Nicaragua are kept by their families in this condition, and though there were by 2005 ten qualified NSL-Spanish translators in Nicaragua, there was hardly a single deaf child who could communicate by sign language with their hearing parents.

It is obvious that under the conditions pertaining in 1946 there was no possibility for the development of a sign language in Nicaragua. But in 1946 the government made a decision that deaf children had a right to education, albeit in special schools together with mentally retarded children, and with no real prospect of becoming useful members of the community. So, something went on prior to 1946 which led the government to begin treating deaf children as human beings with rights like other human beings. I have no knowledge of exactly what prompted this change in the expectations which the country had for its deaf citizens, but whatever it was, it was one of the necessary precursors to the formation of NSL.

From 1946 until the Revolution in 1979, a minority of deaf children in the capital, Managua, were given an elementary education up to the age of 15. This meant that ten or 20 or on occasion up to 30 deaf children would be brought together at school, rather than being isolated in their own homes. However, the children would be taken directly to and from school in a school bus, ensuring that outside school they had no interaction with each other or ever had the need to make their own way through the city by public transport, interacting with the general public. The Nicaraguan education system right up until 1992 aimed solely at the integration of deaf children into the general community by means of speech and lip reading – the 'oral method'. However, although sign language was unknown, until 1979 teachers did use gesture, writing, mime, pointing, or whatever means worked in the process of trying to teach deaf children to speak and lip read. Sign language was regarded as a *negative* in the 'oral method' because it was presumed that only Deaf people used it, and therefore to learn sign language would be to ensure isolation from the general community.

In reality, very few of these deaf children ever learnt to speak, and those few who did, who are alive today, generally prefer to sign. The children did have a chance to meet each other in the playground during breaks and used their 'home signs' to talk to each other, a process which led to a pooling of home signs and a consequent expansion of the vocabulary of home signs. *This did not, however, lead to a development of a sign language.*

'Home sign' is a limited form of communication which uses the stock of natural gestures of the general community, together with pointing at objects, parts of the body, etc., and the iconic representation of actions (see Goldin-Meadow, 1977). Home sign can only reference real entities and feelings and is extremely limited in the range of ideas it can represent outside of the home environment. A genuine language on the other hand, can represent an open-ended and infinite variety of ideas. Illiteracy and limitation to home signing bars the way to the formation of true concepts and entry into adult life in the wider community, leaving the deaf person in a condition of dependency akin to childhood, able to execute commands and express feelings, but unable to discuss ideas and remote, complex or hypothetical events.

So, although deaf children were able to meet each other in groups of 20 or 30 over a period of decades, this was *not in itself enough* for a sign language to emerge from a collection of home signs.

4   The Effect of the 1979 Revolution

The Sandinista Revolution of 1979 had an impact on the formation of the Deaf community in Nicaragua and its language, NSL, but as it happens, despite itself. The Sandinista government appointed a Russian expert, Natalia Popova, to be in charge of education of the deaf, and whereas the teaching of spoken Spanish to deaf children had hitherto proceeded somewhat eclectically under the Somoza dictatorship, under Popova's regime the 'oral method' was enforced as an absolute dogma. Teachers were barred from using gestures or mime or anything other than the spoken word to get their meaning across, even outside the classroom, and pupils likewise were forbidden to use gestures insofar as it was in the power of the teachers to prevent it. Manual communication was *denigrated*, not only blocking the way to the education of deaf children in school, but also undermining the children's *own* efforts to communicate with their hands. This dogmatic enforcement of the oral method and active suppression of manual communication continued until 1992 despite its manifest failure to give any but a tiny minority of deaf children the gift of intelligible speech.

On the eve of the Revolution, a vocational training school for deaf and mentally retarded children, Centro Ocupacional para los Discapacitados (COD) had been set up, and it was restarted in 1980, once the chaos of the Revolution had passed. Also, the new political regime provided an opening which I will come to shortly.

Teachers at COD, being charged exclusively with making the children 'employable', were freed of the ban on gesture and could again use whatever means of communicating with their students worked, and as a consequence, the youngsters did learn. But more important than the meagre job skills they acquired in the workshops, was that they were treated as *adults*. Instead of attending for the limited hours of elementary school, they were expected to arrive on time at 8am, work till 5pm, five days a week, and rather than being picked up and dropped home by the school bus, they were expected to make their own way to and from the school on the public bus system, paying their fares and navigating the city. On completion, the COD actively sought job placements for them.

In other words, they *were treated as adults* and were expected to behave accordingly and many of them did in fact go on to find jobs, albeit unskilled work at exploitatively low wages. Also, their education together was continued into their mid-20s, and having been drawn out of the family home into the public transport system, they had freedom of movement and were now no longer confined indoors. So now we had a situation where *young adults*, rather than children, were gathering together in their own spaces, and *freely communicating as aspiring citizens* of the nation. As a result of this, the young people began to socialise and build friendship networks outside of working hours and visit each other's homes. This led to young Deaf people in Nicaragua developing *a sense of shared community* of their own, in their common situation in life. They sought each other out, and insofar as they could, talked to each other about their shared situation. Before 1986 there was only one instance of a deaf couple marrying, but now they were increasingly finding jobs and making friends in the Deaf community, and would go on to marry, set up households and raise children. In other words, despite still being without a true language, by the fact that they were being *treated as* adults, more and more they *became* adults and entered into the range of tasks and problems of the wider community, albeit invariably in extreme poverty.

Those who are familiar with Vygotsky's (1934) writing on concept formation will recognise that this is one of the preconditions to the formation of true concepts. The extension of deaf education into young adulthood and the expectation that the deaf adolescents would behave as adults and enter to some degree into the life of the community was the next essential step towards the formation of NSL. *Nothing* they had experienced during their elementary oral education had contributed significantly, however.

Nicaragua was a country of six million people. By 1984, enrolment of deaf children at school had reached 200 and remained at that level until 1997. Laura Polich shows by an analysis of the numbers of deaf children gathered together at various stages in the growth of deaf education that the hypothesis that a 'critical mass' of deaf children in communication with one another can explain the emergence of Nicaraguan Sign Language does not stack up. No number of children interacting in the playground or on the school bus would ever develop a new sign language. When NSL did emerge, only a *small number* of Deaf people were involved, whereas when much larger numbers were gathered together at school, sign language did not emerge.

However, the opening of the world of work to a cohort of Deaf *young adults* under conditions where they were treated as adults and gained sufficient independence to get about and seek out their own friends among other young deaf people did create the conditions for the emergence of sign language.

There are some individuals whose role in this story is such that they deserve to be known by name. In 1983, Gloria Minero was appointed to supervise the vocational workshops at COD. Her daughter, Morena, had been born deaf and Gloria had been training her to lip read and speak since she was a baby, and Morena attended a mainstream school. Through her job it was Gloria who first made contact with the Royal Swedish Association of the Deaf (SDR) which immediately took an interest in the position of deaf people in Nicaragua. SDR advocated a *cultural* approach to deafness, that is, that Deaf people should cherish their sign language and the Deaf culture which may be built upon it (see Padden, 2005). A touching incident between mother and daughter is not only a key turning point in the history of the Deaf community in Nicaragua, but encapsulates the necessity for Deaf people to build their own culture based on sign language. Gloria heard Morena talking in her room, and went in to find Morena talking to herself in the mirror. Asked what she was doing, Morena replied that since no one else would talk to her, she would speak to herself. It appeared that although Morena's speech was intelligible, the other children ridiculed her deaf accent and would not talk to her. Gloria determined that since Morena could not make friends among the hearing community, then she would see that Morena could make friends among young deaf people. In 1983, Gloria invited a number of her vocational students from COD to meet at her home to socialise. Morena was considerably younger than the students from COD, all products of the 1962 rubella epidemic, but was included. It was this group of young deaf adults who met regularly at Gloria Minero's house who invented Nicaraguan Sign Language. It took a number of years to form, but the linguist Judy Kegl first identified the existence of NSL in 1986. Laura Polich has determined with certainty that there was no sign language in use prior to the beginning of these meetings, and the evidence points to it being the members of this small group of friends who created NSL, achieving the level of a true language within three years.

Among the young people meeting at Gloria Minero's house, there is another individual whose importance in this story warrants his being named; that is Javier López Gómez. Javier López's interest in sign language began when he was given a sign language dictionary in 1978 or 1979, possibly during an athletics visit to Costa Rica by students at COD. He also met the American deaf educator Thomas Gibson in 1979. From this time onwards Javier practised signing and is reported to have taught other students at COD to sign in 1981, although it was abbreviated and apparently hard to understand. He actively sought out all the information he could find about signing. He also taught the other young people meeting at Gloria's to sign, though it has not been possible to reconstruct *how* he went about that. Previous to what they learnt from Javier, they had used only home signs and finger spelling to communicate with each other. At the time of the meetings at Gloria's, Javier was regarded as having good oral skills.

5   APRIAS (Association to Help and Integrate the Deaf)

In 1984 or 1985, Gloria Minero suggested that if the young Deaf adults wanted to do anything to improve their future, they would need to organise themselves formally into a self-help group to act on behalf of Deaf people. The main benefit of the Sandinista Revolution is that it legitimated the formation of an organisation to represent the interests of such a disadvantaged section of the population. The group who had been meeting at Gloria's home took the initiative, worked their way through the considerable mountain of paperwork required to register an association in Nicaragua and made up the core of founding members. The name was suggested by Gloria – Association to Help and Integrate the Deaf – but was decided upon by a vote on 22 April 1986, the date which is recognised as its founding date by what now calls itself the National Nicaraguan Association of the Deaf (ANSNIC). In 1989, Gloria secured a grant of $50,000 from the SDR to purchase a permanent building to house ANSNIC in Managua, located at the junction of the main bus routes to ensure that Deaf people could get to it.

APRIAS defined itself as a national association, that is, for *all* deaf people in Nicaragua, a qualitative leap in self-consciousness from the group of friends who had been meeting in Gloria's home. Polich points out that the purchase of a permanent building, now a landmark in Managua, meant that any deaf person who wanted to get in touch could always find their way to APRIAS without needing an introduction through the friendship network, making APRIAS a genuine national body, not just in name only. Gloria's contact with the Swedish Society, already at that time advocates for a cultural conception of the Deaf, might suggest that this moment also represented an embrace of the cultural concept of deafness and an embrace of sign language. But this is not quite the case. The name implied the object of *integrating* the deaf into the wider society, that is, learning to speak and lip read. Its slogan was "breaking down the wall of silence" and its constitution made it clear that its aim was that deaf people should gain a voice, not just figuratively but literally. As a result, all the members elected to the founding National Committee were young Deaf people who were regarded as successful in oral communication. Javier López drew the logo which illustrates a speaking voice and a hearing ear breaking down the 'wall of silence'. So even Javier, at this point the Nicaraguan most proficient in sign language, was an advocate of integration.

However, the critical point had been reached with the formation of APRIAS, what was formerly just a group of people sharing a common problem, had transformed itself into a *collaborative project* with the aim of achieving the emancipation of their class. At first they did not (as the Swedes had) clearly conceptualise what that emancipation entailed, but they had formed a concept of a voice for the Deaf, and organised themselves to realise that object.

An election of officers for APRIAS held in October 1990 was the occasion for a small group to form a slate and overturn the former Committee. The new Committee, with Javier López as their President, set a new course. No longer was their ambition the *integration* of deaf people into society by means of each individual mastering speech, but the Deaf would form *their own* community in which the language of choice would be Nicaraguan Sign Language. There were enough Deaf people able to speak and enough hearing people could be trained in NSL to communicate between the Deaf community and the wider community to ensure that integration of a Deaf individual into a Deaf community would mediate their socialisation and acceptance into the society as a whole.

In 1996, APRIAS changed its name to the National Nicaraguan Association for the Deaf and more recently changed that to the National Nicaraguan Association *of* the Deaf.

By the late 1980s, the great majority of deaf people involved with ANSNIC were married and raising a family. They were still extremely poor, many working at exploitative wages in the Free Trade Zone, mostly in unskilled jobs, but nonetheless, they were part of the community, and through their organisation, they are now able to influence the government, intervene in the country's education policies and overturn the oral method and work to bring their younger Deaf brothers and sisters out into the world. Alas, older deaf people, with few exceptions, have not been touched by this project, and in the main remain on the margins of society and lack a voice of any kind.

NSL is still undergoing development, and it still has not reached the majority of deaf people in what remains one of the most underdeveloped countries in the Americas. But there is every reason to believe that ANSNIC will achieve its goal of emancipating the Deaf of Nicaragua.

The Deaf community, and its language, NSL, was created by a small group of people, between 1984 and 1986, who continued to develop it and propagate it between 1984 and 1992. And this was *not a spontaneous process*. Javier López was recognised as the arbiter of disputes over signing standards and chaired Sign Standardisation Workshops during the 1980s which voted on its decisions. Javier visited Sweden for ten months, as a guest of Royal Swedish Deaf Society, returning in the summer of 1992, giving increased impetus to the development of NSL. His two hearing sisters have also been employed by ANSNIC as interpreter and secretary/receptionist, intensifying Javier's influence on the development of ANSNIC. ANSNIC members are noted for their vigilance in defending the standardisation of their sign language while many are also skilled in interpreting and translating other sign languages.

6   Was ANSNIC Acting Alone?

Judging by Google results, almost everyone believes that Nicaraguan children created NSL by themselves. So, it is worth reviewing the range of contacts which contributed to the formation of NSL during this period. Linguists say that NSL exhibits the influence of Costa Rican, Spanish, Swedish and American Sign Language, and this is not surprising.

By 1975, neighbouring Cost Rica had their own sign language, LESCO. Young deaf people had founded their own self-help and advocacy group, ANASCOR, on 8 June 1974 and had used sign language from the beginning. A number of them had been educated in Spain where they learnt Spanish Sign Language. Also, Deaf adolescents from Costa Rica had attended the Deaf university in the US, Gallaudet College, where they would have learnt ASL. A teaching approach known as 'Total Communication' was established in 1976, probably thanks to a Costa Rican Deaf educator who had studied in New York and returned to Costa Rica in 1974. In this approach, teachers used sign language simultaneously with speech to communicate with students. Word about this method reached Managua and special education teachers from Managua attended a workshop on Total Communication in the late 1970s shortly before the Revolution and were impressed with what they saw. But thanks to the Revolution, they never had the chance to implement this new-found insight.

Javier López was among Deaf students who participated in a sporting visit to Costa Rica by COD students in May 1978, where they contested against Deaf Costa Rican students and would have witnessed Costa Rican Sign Language in action. A Deaf youngster, Adrián Pérez, left Nicaragua in 1974 to receive an oral education in Spain, and was an accomplished speaker and lip reader by the time he returned from Spain in 1982 and was also able to use Spanish Sign Language. He was one of the founding members of APRIAS, and a major contributor in the formulation of NSL. He was not as enthusiastic an activist for APRIAS as Javier, however.

Thomas Gibson visited Nicaragua in April–May 1979 as a Peace Corps volunteer, assigned to teach sign language to special education teachers for two years, but his visit was cut short by the Revolution before it had hardly begun, and he was sent to Costa Rica instead. All the people he met were impressed with his sign language and during the three weeks he spent at the special school, he gave an ASL sign language dictionary to Douglas Vega, a friend of Javier López and later another founding member of APRIAS, and the two friends closely studied the dictionary, and were observed conversing using sign language. Vega later left Nicaragua.

Between 1988 and 1993 a number of volunteer Deaf educators visited Nicaragua. An American couple worked as volunteers from 1988 to 1992 running a kindergarten using Total Communication approach in the provincial town of Léon. A Swedish volunteer made multiple visits to Nicaragua over a ten-year period around the late-1980s and early 1990s encouraging the use of sign language in the classroom and helped set up a regional branch of ANSNIC. In 1990, officials from the Swedish Association for the Deaf visited Managua and may have been a factor prompting the change of leadership in ANSNIC.

A Deaf educator from Finland worked at the head office of the Education Department 1992–93 and advocated for the use of sign language and participated in activities with ANSNIC. In addition to the early sporting trips by students at COD, officers of ANSNIC went on fact-finding and fraternal journeys to other Central American countries where they met with Deaf organisations in their region.

So it is not the case that Javier and his friends invented and proliferated Nicaraguan Sign Language all on their own and unaided by adults and other young people who had acquired a fluency and understanding of sign language from Costa Rica, the United States, Finland, Sweden and Spain. NSL was a link in the cultural-historical chain of Deaf people across the world, not a unique and isolated creation. Nonetheless, everything that has been said about the preconditions for the formation of a *self-conscious, autonomous Deaf community* within the larger community remains the case. No number of Peace Corps volunteers and individual deaf children could have accomplished what APRIAS achieved. And no number of illiterate, speechless children could have done it on their own either.

7 Minimal Conditions for Acquisition of a Sign Language

The precise extent of exposure to a spoken or manual language, and opportunity to interact with it, which is needed for deaf children to learn it, are a matter for professionals in that discipline. The experience of Nicaragua has shown that young deaf people are drawn as if by a magnet to sign language in the event that they come across it. It can be taught with no more skill than every mother and father exercises in teaching their own children to talk, provided they take the trouble to become fluent in sign language themselves. If, however, deaf children are not surrounded by sign language, but on the contrary are growing up in a hearing community, then even the sight of other children communicating with signs seems to have been enough to stimulate the interest of a minimally socialised child. Just as the hearing children of Deaf parents have no difficult in acquiring speech from friends and neighbours, given exposure of at least five to ten hours per week, the Deaf children of hearing parents can acquire the beginnings of sign language if given the opportunity to learn from their Deaf peers or second-language signing parents.

However, the experience of ANSNIC has been that deaf people who grow to maturity without the gift of communicating with others, having been raised as 'eternal children' (Polich's phrase) or kept in childlike dependence on their families, generally do *not* develop an interest in sign language when exposed to it in later life. And without an interest in learning a language it is impossible to do so.

7.1   *Minimal Conditions for the Formation of a New Sign Language*
We now know that NSL did not develop out of nothing, but in fact drew on Spanish, Swedish, American and Finnish Sign Language which was introduced to the creators of NSL by professional Deaf educators. Several of the main creators of NSL were also proficient in spoken Spanish, and the group which met at Gloria's in 1984 created the beginnings of a sign language in a couple of years, refining it over the several years following, so that it subsequently continued to develop into one of the world's fully-fledged languages.

This was an impressive achievement but now that the facts are known, having been thoroughly documented by Linda Pollich (2005), it is not something which will cause us to rewrite the textbooks. The real achievement lay in taking that precious creation from Gloria's living room and turning it into a national language, in *institutionalising* NSL. What we have learnt from the Nicaraguan experience is that this is not a spontaneous process, a kind of 'contagion' or 'emergent process'. The formation of the Deaf community in Nicaragua is the product and result of creating their own language, Nicaraguan Sign Language. NSL is an 'ideal' prized by the Deaf community. It acts as both the model and source for the development of Deaf children in Nicaragua, and was the achievement of a *self-conscious project* on the part of the Deaf community, a project which constituted the Deaf community itself. It was carried through by *Deaf young adults*, not by children.

This one case is not a sufficient basis on its own to formulate an idea of the minimum conditions for the formation of a new language. Deaf children in Nicaragua faced special difficulties in the prejudice that led to their isolation from one another and the particularly dogmatic enforcement of the 'oral method', which was fashionable for much of the post-World War Two period across the world. But what has been the experience elsewhere?

8   In What Sense May the Case of NSL Be Generalised?

For a review of the case of NSL in relation to the history of sign languages generally, I will rely mainly on the paper by Meir, Sandler, Padden and Aronoff (2010).

According to Meir et al., sign languages are of two kinds, distinguished by their genesis: village sign languages and Deaf community sign languages.

8.1 Village Sign Languages

Most existing village sign languages (VSL) are quite ancient, having developed a long time ago in an isolated community in which genetics had raised the incidence of babies born deaf to a relatively high level, say 3%, and provided stable conditions for linguistic development free of the impact of migration and outside influences. In these cases, the number of hearing users of the sign language is commonly greater than the number of deaf members of the community – in one case 35 adults used a sign language to communicate with one Deaf child! This situation is the opposite in every way from the situation of Nicaraguan deaf children. Although the VSL is normally a distinct creation, not bearing the marks of the influence of sign languages from elsewhere, members of the hearing community, speaking a dialect of one of the world's languages, are active participants in the formation and maintenance of the language, which is nonetheless frequently quite distinct in its grammar and ontology from the spoken language, not a code for it. According to Padden (2005), to the extent that the members of the general hearing community treat their Deaf neighbours as adults and equals and make an effort to communicate with them, then a fully-fledged, albeit parochial, sign language will result.

However, Padden et al. mention that PSL – the sign language of Providence Island – did not develop into a 'fully structured' language because of the 'paternalistic attitudes' of the community towards deaf people. In the isolated conditions under which VSLs are created, deaf people are generally speaking subjected to the attitudes of the majority community, and the development of their language will reflect the place of the Deaf in the wider community.

8.2 Deaf Community Sign Languages

Deaf Community Sign Languages (DCSLs) on the other hand have grown up in modern societies, where deaf people from differing backgrounds have been brought together, or brought themselves together, most often for specialist education, and form themselves into a Deaf community. They may have been taught sign language by the institution which brought them together, or having been gathered together, they may have taken the opportunity to create a project and formed an association even without any assistance from the majority community. In either case, to the extent that the Deaf community is successful in constructing and defending its own culture, their language will, in time, become fully structured and be subject to the influences of all the world's languages with which it interacts, like any other language, and any other culture. Invariably, a mixture of home signs and VSLs provide the initial material by means of which a Deaf community first forms and creates a DCSL in the form of some kind of creole. But once having formed as a self-conscious project in a modern society, the way is open for the DCSL to become a fully-fledged, structured language.

The following examples of DCSLs exhibit the range of histories of these languages.

French Sign Language (LSF). Charles Michel de l'Épée accidentally stumbled upon an existing sign language (Old French Sign Language) used by a Deaf Community in Paris of about 200 deaf adults. In about 1771, de l'Épée learnt the language and established a free school for the Deaf. De l'Épée codified and systematised LSF but his creation was too complex and impracticable. Nevertheless, by a large number of Deaf people having been brought together and it having been made known to the general community that Deaf people could be educated, the Deaf community in France was able to take charge of LSF and it entered into a normal process of standardisation and development. LSF was instrumental in the formation of the Sign Languages in Dutch, German, Flemish, Irish, American and Russian societies. LSF has 50–100,000 native signers.

American Sign Language (ASL) originated in the American School for the Deaf established in 1817 in Hartford Connecticut, by Thomas Hopkins Gallaudet, who travelled to Europe to learn about education for the deaf. The British refused to share their methods, and he chose LSF as the sign language of choice, and appointed Laurent Clerc as director for his knowledge of LSF. Clerc taught in LSF. 58% of signs in ASL are cognate with Old LSF, but ASL evidently both drew from the LSF taught by Clerc and incorporated the various VSLS and home sign languages which deaf people first brought with them and more expressions added in the 200 years since. Even as Clerc taught in LSF, he was obliged to acquire signs from his pupils and adapt to the sign language his pupils were constructing.

ASL was developed and propagated by Deaf associations such as the National Association of the Deaf. Meanwhile, the education system did not regard ASL as a genuine language and used the 'oral method' for deaf education. ASL was maintained by the Deaf alone, through their own organisations. The linguist William Stokoe challenged the claim that ASL was not a true language, and side-by-side with the Civil Rights Movement and the other social movements of the 1960s, the Deaf Community fought, as described by Carol Padden (2005), to promote their right to be educated in their own language and for various social rights, such as interpreter services, facilitating the maintenance of Deaf culture. ASL has between 250,000 and 500,000 users, hearing and Deaf, across Anglophone North America.

British Sign Language (BSL) and ASL are not mutually comprehensible, but BSL has dialects such as AUSLAN and NZSL. Sign language was in use by the Deaf in the UK at least as far back as 1570. Thomas Braidwood set up an Academy for the Deaf and Dumb in 1760 for the deaf sons of the middle and upper classes. Braidwood's codification of sign language was the first effort to standardise what was to become BSL, but until the 1940s, BSL was maintained and passed on solely thanks to the Deaf, whilst signing was actively discouraged in schools, and the 'oral method' enforced, backed up by punishment of offenders. Only from the 1970s has BSL begun to be used in some schools, thanks to organised agitation by Deaf organisations. There are about 150,000 users of BSL in the UK.

Israeli Sign Language (ISL). ISL dates from Germany in 1873 when Marcus Reich, a German Jew, opened a special school for deaf Jewish children. In 1932, several of his teachers set up a school in Jerusalem. The sign language used here was based on German Sign Language, but absorbed sign systems brought in by Jewish immigrants from all over the world. ISL became well established during the 1940s and is used by the Deaf from all the religious communities in Israel today.

There are many other DCSLs which are also of long standing. Meir et al. separate out sign languages of the DCSL type which are still developing, such as *Nicaraguan Sign Language* (NSL) and *Costa Rican Sign Language* (LESCO), which we have already dealt with above.

9 The Development of Language Communities

Historically, in modern societies, the sign languages of the Deaf have been suppressed, though in all cases, the initiative of individuals from the hearing community has aided in the formation and ultimate acceptance of Sign Language. The story is somewhat parallel to the story of indigenous and ethnic minority languages, which were routinely suppressed until the changes in social attitudes which were wrought by social movements in the 1960s and 1970s, among which the Deaf Communities themselves were active players.

Languages obviously do evolve as well as merge, absorb and borrow from one another and so on in *spontaneous* processes reflecting the movement of peoples and changes in social relations and activities in the communities affected. But other things being equal, the Deaf are only ever going to have a true language, appropriate to a community which is fully participating in the affairs of the world, insofar as they can organise and fight for it, together, as independent citizens. Conversely, a Deaf community exists only insofar as it has a sign language of its own.

A fully structured Sign Language – capable of discussing the reasons for the election of the latest President, the danger posed by Ebola, whether computers are an aid to learning and whether Andy Warhol's work is art – is always therefore the mark of a *self-conscious project* expressing the shared needs and aspirations of the Deaf, because for the overwhelming majority of the Deaf, it is only by means of such a Sign Language that they can *fully participate* as equals in such activities.

There is one powerfully argued body of work, supported by extensive observation, indicating that it is in fact possible for deaf children to develop their own language in isolation from Sign Language, as was erroneously claimed to have happened in Nicaragua, without the aid of hearing adults or practitioners of an established Sign Language, that is the work of Susan Goldin-Meadow and her colleagues.

10   Goldin-Meadow on the Structure of Personal Sign

Susan Goldin-Meadow has conducted a comprehensive study of the gestures of a number of deaf children raised in isolation from sign language by hearing parents, in order to establish that:

> Despite their lack of linguistic input, the children use gesture to communicate. ... these gestures assume the form of a rudimentary linguistic system, a system that displays structure at both word and sentence levels.
> 2005, p. 50

and that:

> A conventional language model is *not* necessary for children to use their communications for basic and not-so-basic functions of language.
> 2005, p. 150

The chief subjects of the study were ten children aged from 16 months to four years and ten months. The children were all born deaf to hearing, middle-class American parents who were raising them in isolation from sign language with the aim of them learning lip reading and speech, but despite on-going efforts by the parents, these were children who had not made any progress in mastery of the spoken word. Their parents continued to converse with them, accompanying their speech with conventional gestures and interpreting the children's gestures in the same spirit.

So in contrast to Nicaraguan children of the pre-1946 period, these deaf children were not treated as objects of shame and isolated from human contact, and in contrast to most Nicaraguan deaf children pre-1992, they were not treated as mentally retarded with no prospect of leading a useful life, but were, on the contrary, addressed by their parents as intelligent, free agents. This would be expected to open the opportunity for the children to become full participants in the life of their own family and to acquire its norms, customs, and values.

However, being among that majority of children raised under such conditions who fail to acquire speech, their life prospects would remain extremely limited as they would lack a language by means of which they could communicate with strangers, read, and access the ideas, customs and concerns of the wider world, and could expect to remain dependent on their families with limited opportunities for work and social life.

The unique and startling contribution of Goldin-Meadow is that by bringing a team of skilled linguists armed with video recorders into the homes of these children, she was able to discover a linguistic structure within the children's developing gesture systems. Only one of the ten subjects exhibited all of the structures described, but the others exhibited significant steps towards such a structure. According to Goldin-Meadow's somewhat generous analysis, this structure included segmentation of gestures into stable units (words) and the concatenation of these units into sentences according to stable structural rules; a consistent morphology governing the composition of signs into words; the structural differentiation of noun-like, verb-like and adjective-like gestures; some basic syntactical rules governing word order, omission of subject and branching. Although no representation of tense was found in the children's gesturing (they could however indicate the immediate future and immediate past), utilising the resources of their immediate environment, they were able to use their gesture system to make requests, comments and questions about the here-and-now, communicate about the non-present, future and hypothetical, and make generic statements, talk to themselves and talk about their own and others' gestures. Although the children did appropriate their parents' emblematic gestures, there is no evidence that the structure of spoken English was the source of any of their structure, and even the appropriated gestures are transformed by their inclusion in the child's system. A truly remarkable achievement.

The tragedy is that *their parents were quite unaware* of this structure which was revealed by the linguistic investigation, simply interpreting their children's iconic gestures and pointing in the context of the household activity as more or less conventional, if somewhat idiosyncratic gestures. So, this linguistic structure added nothing to the communicative power of the children's gestures, of which the child alone was an aficionado. It took the video cameras and the expertise of linguists to bring this linguistic structure to light.

The need to communicate with their families whilst lacking a grammar or vocabulary of conventional signs beyond the limited stock of gestures provided by the family, meant that the children made full use of the resources of their environment. 'Chair' could be indicated by pointing to a particular chair, but pointing to the chair could also be used as a sign for the person who usually sits in that chair but is not present, or even chairs in general – the difference in meaning emerging from context. Thus the geography of their own home enters into the substance of their signing, and the child's vocabulary is expanded, but in a way which is tied to the home environment and is useless for communicating in the outside world. Also, a small minority of Deaf children (Javier López and Morena Minero for example), do master speech under the conditions in which Goldin-Meadow's subjects were being raised, and even many hearing children do not actually speak until after the age of 16 months. So, while Goldin-Meadow has established that nothing of the grammar of English entered into the grammar of the children's gestures, one must suppose a considerable cultural impact from this kind of parenting.

The extent to which the adult culture penetrates the child's language is brought out in a comparative study (Goldin-Meadow et al., 2006) with a group of deaf Chinese children. The relatively frequent use of evaluative gestures by Chinese parents in talking to their children shows up in a corresponding use of the same evaluative gestures in the children's signing. And quite apart from what is conveyed by explicit gesturing by family members, the totality of the movements and use of artefacts and physical interactions with the child must surely communicate a great deal. But not grammar. The grammar created by the child, which remains *unknown to all those around them* barring the trained linguists with video cameras, is a spontaneous creation, free of the influence of the local culture. Chinese or American deaf children will certainly grow up to be culturally Chinese or American, though they will not speak the Chinese or American languages. That children spontaneously create language-like structures, structures which will provide the foundation for any fully-fledged language which the child may go on to learn, is obviously of great interest, and forces us to ask where this comes from? It may help us to better understand how children learn language, but it does not help the child communicate even with their own family, let alone strangers or work associates. A certain minimum of mutual comprehensibility and expression is needed before interaction in the general community can bring about language development appropriate to a sovereign member of the broader community.

Vygotsky's claim was that successful ontogenesis presupposes the presence of and participation in the ideal or final form, that is, in order to grow up to be a competent English-speaking adult one must be exposed to English speaking (for at least five–ten hours per week according to Goldin-Meadow). Goldin-Meadow seems to have taken the claim to be rather that to develop *language competence* in general one must be exposed to *a language* while growing up. This interpretation seems to be negated by Goldin-Meadow's own work. Children not exposed to any language do develop a system of gestures which has the properties of language except that *no one except the child themself understands it*, beyond the crude interpretation of pointing and iconic gestures commonly referred to as home signs. No one previously would have guessed that the home sign of deaf children isolated from both a conventional sign language and a spoken language would have a grammatical structure, and Vygotsky would doubtless have been just as surprised as we all are. However, what is at question is a normative standard of activity, including a *particular* language required for taking up a recognised social position, and acquiring the use of true concepts, in which knowledge beyond the horizons of everyday life is contained – not language *in general*.

The fact that the deaf children evidently comment on their own and others' use of their signs (their vocabulary, but not their grammar) means that they are consciously aware of their signs, though probably not their grammar. The fact that they can use their signs to talk to themselves and command their own actions means that their signing can contribute to the early development of their intellect.

However, not "having a community of speakers or signers or, at least, a willing communication partner" (Goldin-Meadow, 2005, p. 222) bars the child's way to the achievement of mature adult citizenship. And this is the question to which we addressed ourselves. If the child's personal signing system has the capacity to reference distant and hypothetical events, tell stories and evaluate, and allows the child to talk to themself and talk-about-talk, what elements of language are missing (other than the existence of a community of users) which is required for a person to achieve sovereign independence as an adult citizen of their community? The *content*: the true concepts of the society into which the child is growing up.

I would contend that it is not any linguistic *form* as such which is missing, but the *content*. The form must be adequate to the content, and the content interacts with and modifies the form, but the content can only be acquired with the aid of appropriately well-developed language skills through participation in the world, mediated through a substantial, self-sufficient community of like-speakers, such as a Deaf community. Mastery of the true concepts which have marked every human culture since humans became humans is achieved only by means of participation in social life. Though not the end itself, language is a means to that participation. A Deaf community opens this door for the Deaf.

Aside from this, Goldin-Meadow's work obliges us to reflect on where this propensity for creation or acquisition of language comes from, if it can be manifested even in the absence of a linguistic environment. The first steps – single-sign comments, questions and commands – comes easily enough thanks to pointing and the appropriation of emblematic gestures, expressing good and bad, yes, no and maybe, stop, come and so on. Goldin-Meadow speculates that lacking linguistic input from others, the child builds on *their own* gestures as input. It seems to me that an Hegelian rather than a Kantian schema for this process makes perfect sense. Having one's needs met by other people poses communicative problems which must find their solution within the figures *already developed* in the system. The child works through the *immanent logic* of language-creation implicit in each stage of their constructive work. The same process works out differently if linguistic input from communicative others outweighs their own productions, but without such input, it is the immanent logic of the stock of gestures available to any deaf child which is exhibited in language learning. All that is presupposed are some basic human propensities – such as looking to others to meet one's needs, and the propensity to perceive objects as symbols – but not a neo-Kantian universal grammar.

What participation in the wider community gives a person, however, is the logic of problems which have arisen on a much wider horizon, the solutions to which are carried by language. But solutions to these problems simply do not arise within the home.

The information which Goldin-Meadow has received about Nicaragua, in the *absence of first-hand research or any knowledge of the history of* NSL, has led her to believe that the same process which she observed in young deaf children, at home in a hearing family, can be extended if children are brought together to share their home sign, up to the point of creating a fully-fledged language, without any input from the spoken language or a developed Sign Language. However, in the case of Nicaragua, *historical* investigation, rather than linguistic investigation of the final product, has shown that this did *not* happen, and indeed *could not* have happened.

The myth that NSL was the spontaneous creation of illiterate school children is cited as proof of the existence of Chomsky's innate Language Acquisition Device (LAD), but the reality is the opposite. People who already believed in the LAD seized upon NSL to prove their point, without bothering to look into the actual history of NSL. This is not to deny that human beings alone are *able* to learn language without instruction, but simply that this ability is not located in a specific neural structure embodying a universal grammar. (See Chapter 12, this volume.)

11 Conclusion

Deaf children participating in home life can develop home sign, and given sympathetic parents can manage quite well within the confines of home life, without exposure to a DCSL. Deaf children participating in village life, to whatever extent the expectations placed upon them by villagers permit, can learn a village sign language shared with other villagers, hearing and deaf. To be members of a modern community requires a Deaf Community Sign Language. Home signs cannot form the basis of such a community. Only an institution and/or a social movement can create the necessary basis for a shared true sign language and the capacity to participate in the wider society. Broadly speaking, the scope of a 'true language', is the same as what Vygotsky called 'true concepts'.

In order to grasp and express a true concept, a certain minimal level of language development is a prerequisite, a level which young adolescents have normally already thoroughly acquired whether speaking or using an established sign language. Content and form interact. Discourse concerning true concepts – through participation in work and social life generally, and through reading and writing – stimulates the development of language, expanding the vocabulary and complicating the structure of relations expressed. From the standpoint of the linguist there is no qualitative shift from the structure of adolescent language to that of the mature adult, but the content of adult life is reflected in the content of adult language, rather than its structure.

It is a credit to Meir et al. (2010) that they classified VSLs and DCSLs according to their *genesis* and *not* according to their linguistic features. So for example, NSL was categorically the same as ASL, even if at a given moment it were barely capable of expressing more than home sign. I would contend that home sign can *never* make the transition to a true sign language, without an institution and/or social movement intervening in children's development into adult life, offering Deaf children recognition as equals through their own sign language. Susan Goldin-Meadow's (1977, 2005, 2007) interesting studies tell us nothing about how the transition to adult life with a true *shared* language is achieved.

A new language can develop only thanks to a project having as its object the interests of the relevant community.

CHAPTER 12

Language in Human Evolution

The problem of human origins has been a central theme in philosophy and science since ancient times, and is intimately connected to the question of the human essence and the meaning of life. As a result, the problem has always been highly contested and attracts interest from the public and specialists alike. The aim of this article is to formulate some principles which can be argued simply on the basis of common knowledge and rational reflection, in contrast to questions which can only be resolved by empirical investigation, and which consequently lie outside my area of expertise.

Although information from palaeontology, archaeology, anthropology, zoology, genetic microbiology, linguistics and neurology continues to advance at an impressive rate, we still do not have clear answers to most of the important questions about the origins of human language in general and speech in particular. Books on the topic seem sometimes designed to reinforce philosophical prejudices rather than to bring incontrovertible premises to bear on the evidence. Here I shall mention some principles which can be substantiated on the basis of widely agreed science which may shed some light on what evidence exists and what evidence is lacking.

1 The Co-evolution of Animal Behaviour and Biology

Behaviour mediates between an animal's biology and its environment. Behaviour can be more or less stereotyped, controlled by reflexes without passing through consciousness (such as when a human being withdraws their hand from fire), but all the higher animals have a greater or lesser degree of voluntary control over aspects of their behaviour. By 'voluntary' I mean simply a natural will, not free will – minimally, the tendency of an animal to modify its behaviour if an habitual action fails, rather than endlessly repeating the same reaction. All higher animals, at least, will change their behaviour in response to failure.

An animal's biology and behaviour co-evolve with its environment, but at *differing rates of change*. The time-scale within which voluntary behaviour can adapt, whether in the life of an individual animal or in cultural development, is qualitatively shorter than the time-scale within which the anatomy of a species can evolve to facilitate that behaviour. The anatomy generally adapts to changes in the demands of behaviour rather than directly to demands of the environment. So behaviour leads biology.

Catastrophically rapid changes in the environment do occur, bringing about extinctions and near-extinctions and thereby 'punctuated evolution'. But since behaviour mediates between environment and biology, biological adaptation still cannot happen faster than the behaviour changes even when responding to rapid environmental pressures, and even if voluntary behavioural change fails to be adaptive. Sudden environmental change does not contradict the fact that behavioural adaptation is faster than biological adaptation. Still, behaviour leads biology.

For instance, okapis, the surviving predecessors of giraffes, eat leaves from trees and bushes, but giraffes gained an advantage by evolving a taller neck. It is hardly likely that this neck grew to enormous length and then one day a giraffe discovered it could nibble from tops of trees and changed its behaviour accordingly. Clearly it was its behaviour in nibbling whatever it could reach which created the selection pressure which after many generations led to the giraffe's enormously long neck. Animals are always pushing the boundaries of their biology and their environment.

The biology of the species evolves under selection pressures determined by the relationship between the organism's behaviour and its environment. The behaviour of the species co-evolves with its environment, within the constraints of its biological make-up – constraints which evolve very gradually. Natural selection determines that the biology of the species will evolve so as to enhance the fitness of the species for a relevant *existing behaviour* in the given environment. Behaviour is the relation of the species to its environment. In other words:

> Behaviour leads biology.

One qualified exception to this rule is *exaptation*, in which biological changes which have developed under selection pressure arising from one behaviour incidentally enhance another behaviour. So long as we take behaviour as a whole (rather than taking specific behaviours separately) this is consistent with the general rule.

2   Bipedalism

It is widely agreed that the hominin group emerged about six million years ago, with about 20 different species having been identified by palaeontologists, all but one of which, homo sapiens sapiens, are now extinct. What uniquely characterised this entire group was *bipedalism*. Based on the principle that behaviour leads biology, we can conclude that it was the adoption of the bipedal gait which set off the train of evolutionary changes which led to modern human beings.

So, in line with the principle just elaborated, we can conclude that:

> Hominin anatomy evolved to accommodate bipedal behaviour.

According to Corballis (2002), the dropping of the larynx, one of the anatomical preconditions for articulate speech, may have also arisen by exaptation from bipedalism. But while being necessary for articulate speech, the descended larynx was far from being a *sufficient* precondition for speech. Other anatomical changes are required around the tongue and lips as well as *voluntary control* of the larynx, which is *absent* in our evolutionary predecessors. So bipedalism might have given us upright hominids with a descended larynx, but not an upright hominid biologically capable of speech.

We don't know for sure what rudimentary bipedal behaviours and environmental pressures led to this departure. Was it standing up to see over the long grass, like meerkats, or the better to run away from lions? No one knows, but we have one important principle to guide us, namely that:

> The behaviour which distinguishes a species from its precursor is found in rudimentary form in the precursor species.

As Vygotsky (1930) pointed out, a behaviour which provides the motive force for the formation of a new species, must be present in rudimentary form in the predecessor species. Were the relevant behaviour to be completely absent, there could be no means for a selection pressure to act on the species to *enhance* the behaviour. If the given behaviour is entirely absent in a species, its improvement cannot be what drives the transition to a new species. Either the relevant behaviour existed in rudimentary form or the capacity for the relevant behaviour arises by exaptation from whatever behaviour is actually driving the transition. That is, the relevant behaviour emerges later as a side benefit of a behaviour which, as we have said, existed in rudimentary form in the precursor species.

At this point, I am going to speculate. Throughout, I have stuck so far as possible to what is already widely agreed or is simply inescapable. However, no one has yet provided a satisfactory hypothesis as to what it was that drove the move to bipedalism, far less empirical evidence, so I am making the following suggestion:

> Bipedalism enhanced the pre-existing behaviour of carrying things.

If we were to look for the essential characteristic of being human in some attribute which humans possessed but our evolutionary predecessors did not, then we might conclude that human beings are primates with ear lobes. This is obviously unsatisfactory. We must look not for the behaviour which *distinguishes* us from chimps (such as voluntary control over our vocalisation), but what we have *in common* with chimps, but which *they* have only in *rudimentary* form but which we humans have mastered.

We can learn a lot by observing the surviving representatives of the species who were the immediate predecessors of the hominin line. The evidence shows that we can gain a good picture of how these primates, who had *not* adopted the upright gait, were built and how they behaved by observing our present-day cousins, the chimpanzee. What we will be looking out for is 'rudimentary forms' of bipedalism, and in particular what behaviours are being facilitated by that rudimentary bipedalism which would tell us how, if at all, there could be selection pressure for the improvement of bipedalism.

What situations cause present-day chimps to adopt a bipedal stance or gait? They can be seen 'scurrying' when they are in a hurry, but this behaviour still entails steadying themselves with their knuckles, not full bipedalism, and in any case they scurry just as fast as a fully bipedal human runs. They do stand up to look sometimes, but their anatomy is already quite adequate for that behaviour, not rudimentary. But when you see a chimp carrying things, something that requires full bipedalism as their hands are fully engaged with holding whatever they are carrying, it is obvious that they are ill-equipped for this task. They look clumsy, ill at ease, and can manage only short distances, sometimes dropping their load.

Consequently, it is reasonable to explore the hypothesis that carrying things was the behaviour which drove the move to bipedalism. And everything flowed from carrying things.

On the other hand, it has been widely suggested that the behaviour which drove the transition to our species was *speech*. But all our surviving evolutionary cousins lack voluntary control over their vocalisation. Primates do not have rudimentary speech, they lack it altogether. If the predecessors to homo sapiens lacked voluntary control over their vocalisation, then it cannot be said that speech existed in even rudimentary form among earlier hominids. Primate vocalisations are immediate, *involuntary* emotional responses to situations and are not uttered with an intention to communicate, even if they do generate appropriate responses in other creatures. But unlike voluntary vocalisation, carrying things is a behaviour which *does* exist in rudimentary form in our primate cousins, so presumably in our ancestor species.

Tool-making also exists in rudimentary form in our surviving predecessor species, so tool-making cannot be not ruled out from playing a role in the evolutionary origins of human beings. There is no reason, however, to suppose it played a part in the formation of *bipedalism* and it is bipedalism which *marks out* our whole evolutionary line from our nearest cousins and forebears. To say that bipedalism evolved to 'free up the hands' for tool making is, in my view, unconvincing. It is more likely is that improved tool-making was an exaptation from the evolution of bipedalism and carrying things, something that was enhanced by bipedalism, and would only have become a subject for evolutionary pressure *after* bipedalism had evolved. The hands, having been freed for carrying things were also free for tool-making. Indeed, it could be said that the free hand was the first tool.

Thanks to Youtube and the ubiquity of the mobile phone camera, we are all familiar with the astonishing intelligence of birds, especially crows, who are able to solve complex problems and make and use tools, and are extremely vocal as well, not to mention that they like to play, and all this with a tiny 'bird brain'. But as it happened, the species which produced Einstein and Mozart did not evolve from crows, it evolved from primates. Self-evidently, there must be things about us primates which are necessary conditions for human evolution. But that is another question.

2.1 *Carrying Things*

An efficient facility for carrying things brings considerable survival benefit for hunter-gatherers. It is a precondition for the establishment of fixed camps which can be supported by extended foraging and hunting, supporting intensive care for children, and extended for a longer period, and the accumulation of stocks of food and artefacts. Ursula Le Guin's (2017) speculation that the carrier bag was the first tool has a lot going for it. The Han, a hunter-gatherer people in Namibia, don't have much, but they do have carrier bags, which they use when they are moving camp. Carrying things promotes cooperative living, and several behaviours associated with the emergence of Homo sapiens, namely, extended childhood, division of labour, the sharing of food, production and use of artefacts, and the formation of relatively large stable communities. The fact that carrying things is found in rudimentary form in our predecessor species, and that when carrying things, primates commonly adopt a bipedal gait, is empirical evidence in support of this hypothesis.

To suppose that carrying things was the practice which drove the adoption of bipedalism, and therefore the development of the entire hominin evolutionary line, does not presuppose any dramatic anatomical leaps. All that is required is gradual improvement of bipedal locomotion and facility in carrying things continuously enhancing the effective formation of large, stable communities with stocks of goods for hard times, conditions for raising children and using their hands to modify an environment which they can now call 'home', and so on. And carrying things home opens lots of opportunities for learning.

Carrying things implies important *psychological* adaptations which can develop in response to innovations in behaviour. There is another general rule here:

> Behaviour leads conscious control.

In much the same way as we learn by doing, we can begin to consciously control a given behaviour only *after doing it* and experiencing failure and success in relatively uncontrolled behaviour. A gymnast learns a particularly difficult manoeuvre only after repeatedly trying with inadequate control, and gradually improving that control. Collecting food and bringing it back to camp confers survival value on the individual and groups practising it. Being able to carry things even makes *moving camp* (including stocks of food and tools) easier and more efficient. So it is easy to see that the development of bipedalism frees up the hands for carrying things while walking long distances, and that the settled conditions it makes possible also provide for prolonged childrearing, improved tool making, cultural inheritance of tools, expansion of range, deliberate modification of the environment, and cooperation.

But a number of *psychological* adaptations can also result, which are significant for the evolution of language and the intellect.

3   Delayed Gratification

The first psychological implication of carrying things is *delayed gratification* – the opening up of a gap between stimulus and response, so that behaviour is no longer governed by the immediate stimulus → response relation. Any creature can consume what is immediately found in nature, with no gap between the sight or smell of the food and its consumption. But to pluck the food from its environment and save it for later, is the privilege of foragers and species which build nests and feed their young.

We upright primates are far from being the only creatures who forage or hunt and bring food or building material back home. But this is not a behaviour found amongst our primate cousins, who may be relatively clever creatures, but they overwhelming prefer to eat what they find or kill on the spot. The bees, birds and beavers who collect material and take it home all do so with highly stereotyped behaviours. These complex behaviours are generally achieved by means of independent stimuli that have evolved for carrying as a behaviour in its own right, much like the cat which hunts and pounces even when there is no prey and it is not hungry, gaining independent gratification from the acts of hunting and pouncing in themselves. But this is not the case for humans or our cousins. Our collecting behaviour has been culturally evolved from the beginning, because we are universal creatures, capable of adapting to almost any environment on Earth.

Delayed gratification is crucial to the emergence of intellect. As Leonard Cohen said: "There is a crack in everything, that's how the light gets in" (*Anthem*, 1992).

Delayed gratification must be present to a rudimentary degree before carrying things is possible at all. Further, improved capacity for delayed gratification enhances the survival benefits derived from carrying things. A capacity for delayed gratification is both a precondition for and a result of carrying things. Consequently, given that it seems that both exist in rudimentary form in the predecessor species, they will *co-evolve* once the behaviour of collecting food, etc., and bringing it back to camp develops as a part of the species' way of life.

Delayed gratification is a psychological precondition for cooperative living. Indeed, without delayed gratification only immediate individual consumption of nature is possible.

> Delayed gratification is the gap through which conscious awareness enters.

Voluntary delayed gratification entails psychic representation of the consumption of the item extracted from its natural setting and carried home with a view to sharing its consumption. These abstract representations are retained and shared in the shared use of the objects themselves in the *absence of the situation in which the object is found* in nature. If an object is consumed immediately in its natural setting, then no conscious representation of the object is needed. To find and recognise the object and its use but withhold from consuming it, and carry it back to camp for self or others to consume, requires a representation of the object to be formed. Indeed, the object itself, torn from its location in nature, *is* a representation of the thing, something which is now well-established in the world of modern art.

Production and carrying creates a *surplus* which supports the whole community and strengthens social bonds. If nature is consumed immediately, then there can be no surplus. Carrying mediates the formation of community.

Chimps and other primates live in bands, but beyond the mother-and-child, their social structure hinges almost exclusively on sex – immediate gratification again. This is unsurprising given that they consume their food on the spot and do not build permanent shelters or otherwise change their environment. Once individuals can and do carry food and material back to camp a whole new driver for social structure – sharing, giving, hoarding, exchanging – opens up. As is well known, beyond the immediate human family, the structure of our very large communities is driven by distribution of surplus product, with all the vast communicative superstructure that entails.

In the absence of independent stimuli, the only psychological precondition for extraction and carrying home is the awareness of the subject's own remote object in foraging, that is to say, a motive for taking it home. *Practical* abstraction and 'recursion' (that is, the inclusion of one behaviour as an element of another behaviour) lay the basis for *psychological* abstraction and recursion, which can later be embodied in language which exhibits both abstraction and recursion. Without delayed gratification, which is made possible by bipedalism, this abstraction and recursion, and therefore language, would have been impossible. The language of food would be nothing more than grunts expressing disgust or satisfaction.

3.1   *Abstraction*
We have introduced another general rule here:

> Practical abstraction leads communicative and mental abstraction.

For instance, buying and selling things makes us consciously aware of the value of things. Collecting butterflies makes us aware of their beauty and variety. Likewise, extracting an object from its natural situation for later consumption allows us to form a psychological representation of the object in our hands – to make an abstraction of it, in other words. Practical abstraction can arise from within the logic of a system of behaviour without prior conscious awareness of that system. You do not need any understanding of economic theory to be aware of the value of commodities. But once established, the abstracting behaviour can be mirrored in psychological abstraction, initially simply in the form of conscious awareness of the act of abstracting. The subject of course knows nothing of 'abstractions' as such, merely *ex*-tractions. The psychological representation remains immediate and sensual, but it is psychologically removed from its natural location and surroundings, and that is a gigantic act of abstraction as compared to immediate hand-to-mouth consumption.

The implications of these observations for the psychological impact of tool making and tool use are obvious. The anatomical and psychological adaptations entailed in bipedalism and carrying incidentally enable better use of the hands in tool making and gesturing, both of which behaviours exist in rudimentary form in the present day representative of our evolutionary predecessors. Tool making could be said to be an exaptation from carrying things, both practically and psychologically, both culturally and biologically.

The tool is already both a useful artefact and a symbol. It comes about by isolating a human action and embodying it in an object which can be incorporated in individual and collective activity. Later on, tools and other objects singled out from their natural context will be given names and become motors for language and cognitive development. But we are getting ahead of ourselves. The role of tool making in human evolution is undeniable. The question for now is only: how did it get started?

I do not place a great deal of weight on the observation that the driving selection pressure for bipedalism was to 'free up' the hands for tool-making and gesturing, though it is feasible that this was a contributing factor. It is the practical abstraction and practical recursion made possible by bipedal carrying, taken over and expanded in the practice of tool-making, which is most significant in behavioural and psychological terms, and in the formation of language.

3.2 *Gesturing*

I agree with Corballis (2002) that the first manifestation of language properly so-called *must* have been signed language – gesturing with the hands, face and body, miming, pointing and conventionalised hand-signs. The vocalisations of our predecessor species are direct emotional reactions not under voluntary control. Hand use, on the other hand, is already under voluntary control amongst our primate forebears, and the more so if indeed carrying things has driven the evolution of bipedalism, rather than running from predators, or peering over the long grass. So, it is unlikely that, lacking the capacity for articulate, voluntary control of the larynx, hominin vocalisations could have constituted the rudimentary speech which would make the transition to spoken language properly so-called. Nonetheless, it is likely that the earliest gesture and mime would have been *accompanied* by unselfconscious expressive vocalisations.

4   Voluntary Control and Conscious Awareness

At this point a word on 'conscious control' is in order. In general, complex forms of behaviour are composed of *operations* (Leontyev, 1978) which adapt to conditions without conscious awareness. For example, walking requires the angle of the foot and the length of the step to adapt to the form of the ground underfoot, etc. In general, even very primitive animal behaviour entails operations of this kind, which in themselves are not subject to conscious control. The environment provides the stimuli to which the behaviour adapts. Moulding to the conditions is an integral part of the operation itself. Every action is thus composed of a series of operations. Even though the action as a whole is consciously controlled, not every component operation is consciously controlled.

Modern human beings acquire conscious control of their own behaviour in childhood by appropriating (internalising) the means by which their parents have controlled the child's behaviour – that is to say, by using symbols, generally words (Vygotsky, 1934), and these units of action are acquired ultimately in the form of operations. Parents control their children's actions. They use all the means of communication to do so – demonstrating, pointing, scolding, commanding, with or without words. From being commanded by their parent, children learn to command *their own* actions, and thereby become consciously aware of these actions, incidentally mastering the means of communication. But the actions they have learnt to control with conscious awareness are later carried out as operations, without conscious awareness (and without vocalisation), directly in response to conditions (Leontyev, 1978). But this kind of unconscious learnt activity is different from preconscious or 'automatic' responses, 'hard-wired' in biology. If something upsets the course of learnt activity, the operation springs back into conscious awareness and is controlled. Unconscious activity, actions of which the subject is not consciously aware, in this sense, is simply a part of conscious control which has been mastered.

It is neither here nor there whether animals other than humans have the capacity for this kind of culturally acquired conscious control. There have been reports of bands of chimps which have mastered certain tools not used by neighbouring bands, for example, and in such a case, it would have to entail conscious control. But among chimps it is extremely rare and rather inept. Most likely use of culturally acquired tools is not unique to human society. But there is no doubt at all that it is a most important feature of modern human behaviour, a key component of human evolution, and that for us language is an important means of constructing it, and of mastering conscious control of one's own behaviour in general. *Tool use and word use are intertwined.*

It is often argued that animals communicate symbolically: one chimp screams in fright, nearby another chimp runs for cover. Indeed almost all complex natural processes can be viewed as semiotic systems (see Colapietro, 1988 on Peirce's semiotics, for example. The chimp vocalisation is not a symbol, but an index, of a type widely found in nature, even in the plant world). This is not language. Language is the *intentional* use of a *culturally acquired* system of symbols. Language use, as opposed to natural semiotic interaction, begins with effortful, conscious awareness, and as it is mastered, becomes unconscious in the specific sense described above. Language in this sense is not a natural process. It is learned and used with a conscious intention, not spontaneously, for its own sake, not automatically like a reflex.

The question before us – the origins of language – is a question of *this* kind of semiotic activity, qualitatively different from the kinds semiotic processes normally found in nature. Language is consciously controlled, and conversely, is the foundation for a specific kind of consciousness which can be called *verbal intelligence* as opposed to practical intelligence. Language is not just any semiotic process.

Further to this characterisation of modern human consciousness, it needs to be noted that for human beings the perceptual field is structured by symbols. In infancy we learn to pick out objects and processes from their background through interactions with adults, and by the time we reach adulthood, our entire sensory field is structured by the use of words and other symbols. Observations of chimpanzee problem-solving has shown that chimpanzees do not see the world like this. Experiments (see Donald, 1991, and Vygotsky, 1930) with chimp problem-solving show that they respond to their field of vision as a whole, and can only solve practical problems when all of the elements of the puzzle are present within their field of vision simultaneously. Our clever crows are not restricted in this way, but that is another story, not ours.

Not only gathering and carrying things, but also *cooking food*, presupposed the extraction of objects from their environment and their transformation into symbolic, i.e., meaningful *products*. This use of objects which requires their singling out and manipulation according to their properties is the ground on which abstraction can grow. Practical abstraction and psychological abstraction co-evolve with one another. But in the *beginning* was the deed.

4.1   *Gesturing Again*

Gesturing would have been accompanied by a pre-existing range of associated vocalisations which would not have been under voluntary control. The converse applies with the way we modern day humans exhibit facial gestures which are not under conscious control while communicating with speech, some of us even fling our arms around and gesture with our hands, all without conscious control – though of course, if someone complained, we could control it. The anatomical and psychological preconditions for the adaptation of the hands for carrying things had already been provided by the behaviours associated with bipedalism. Foremost among these behaviours is living in collaborative relationships in relatively large bands with all the demands for communicative action which this entails.

It all began with simply carrying things back to camp for later consumption.

It is maintaining these large groups of rather aggressive *hominids*, bound together in collaborative activity enabled by bipedalism, which is the principal condition driving further development of language creation and use. There are other factors facilitating language acquisition and other pressures driving language acquisition, but it is the demand for communicative skill which is most powerful. Maintaining peaceful cooperation in large groups of primates demands a great deal of effort to be expended in communicative action, whether scratching each others' backs, mediating disputes or launching an attack on the neighbours – all of these behaviours are observed amongst bands of our dumb primate cousins, without sharing out food brought back to camp. The power of abstraction already vested in voluntary control of the hands engaged in abstracting things from nature is inevitably going to be brought to bear in communicating abstractions, leaving vocalisation for immediate, uncontrolled emotional responses.

So, carrying things drives bipedalism and gesturing behaviour, while vocalisation remains simply unconscious emotional colouring for gestures. The result is the anatomical and neurological adaptations which mark our species and open the way for language use.

We know from our Deaf communities that signed languages are fully developed languages with the same pragmatic, syntactical and semantic structures as spoken language, and individuals acquire facility in sign language *spontaneously* under equivalent cultural conditions as spoken languages. Should signing be the locally dominant mode of communication, children are driven by the same compulsion to acquire the signed language in their environment as compels children to acquire a spoken language in circumstances where this is possible. That is, so long as the subject has the anatomical equipment required to perceive and use the language, whether naturally or thanks to compensation on the part of the community. The 'language drive' is directed at acquiring the locally predominant language, equally whether signed or spoken, and the evidence is quite clear that this drive is part of our biologically inherited make-up, even though *which* language and *which* mode we use is determined by cultural conditions. (See Chapter 11, this volume.)

5 Speech

The point here is that:

> Language must have evolved before the anatomical prerequisites for speech were in place.

Child-talk, creoles and home-signing aside, there is no such thing as a 'primitive language' in existence anywhere in the world today. There is no reason to suppose that the psychological capacity for language used some hundred millennia ago by the first homo sapiens sapiens was not *already fully developed* in the immediately preceding species, having arisen from a language based on gesture which had *many* hundreds of millennia of cultural development behind it.

Why do I say this?

Phonological analysis of changes in the spoken world's languages has identified uniform tendencies corresponding to the most recent wave of homo sapiens sapiens migration from Africa, and suggests an origin time for spoken language coincident with the origins of homo sapiens sapiens 100,000–170,000 years ago (Corballis, 2002, p. 133). That is, *speech* is no older than homo sapiens sapiens.

That speech is *relatively recent* on the evolutionary time scale, is evidenced by this phonological analysis, but there is no evidence of an increase in the structural complexity of language *over this same time span*. Language itself must be relatively ancient, and comparative analysis of the brain cavity does not indicate significant change of language ability. Over the period during which homo sapiens sapiens spread across the globe, there is phonological change but no further development of structure. This surely indicates that language was already fully developed in mediums *other than* phonology – signs, gesture, facial expression and mime – at the time when speech came to be part of the linguistic mix and homo sapiens sapiens began their final wave of migration out of Africa. Phonology is relatively new, but language is ancient.

The alternative proposition – that a sophisticated anatomical and psychological apparatus enabling voluntary, articulate speech evolved but without being used, and then one day a human *discovered* he or she could speak – is absurd. It takes hundreds of thousands of years for such anatomical and neurological changes to evolve, during which time creatures have ample opportunity to explore the boundaries of their capabilities. Behaviour leads biology.

The ancestors of the Homo species were already using language. Effective, controlled use of vocalisation gradually expanded while the gestural components gradually receded, even though gestures still continue as part of our normal speech to this day. This would be an instance of selection pressures based in behaviour driving the evolution of physiology and anatomy. Behaviour leads biology.

Again, I do not place any weight on the argument that speech 'freed up' the hands for labour, but it could feasibly have been a contributing factor in the gradual transition from signed language to spoken language. This change of behaviour unfolded in the context of collaborative social life, where selection pressure for better communication was forcing the biological change so as to subject the vocal apparatus to better and better conscious control, just as gestures were already doing the same work.

5.1   Music and Dance

The above observations are suggestive of an explanation for the otherwise inexplicable fact that we language-using primates, humans, are also lovers and users of culturally transmitted music and dance. If our evolutionary forebears went through a protracted period of gesturing with accompanying vocalisations, but did not yet have the capacity for *words*, the idea that we sang and danced together seems plausible. It was these singing, dancing and waving hominins who later learnt words to put to the music. But all this is mere speculation and is aside from the central issue here.

5.2   How Did Our Primate Ancestors Think?

We have looked at how practical abstraction could have given our hominin predecessors the capacity to associate general meanings with objects plucked from nature and the tools they fashioned, conditions from which the use of symbolic artefacts like gestures and words could have developed. But what kind of consciousness did they have to begin with? Was there a place in it for symbolic artefacts?

Merlin Donald (1991) has studied the consciousness of present-day apes through what he calls 'ape culture'. Apes have generally proved unable to form psychic representations of symbols when humans have tried to train them in symbol use. It turns out that the basic unit of the ape mind is the *episode* – apes can perceive complex, multi-actor episodes and appear to be able to form representations of such episodes and remember them, and organise their behaviour around episodes. They do have a limited vocabulary of gestures and vocalisations, but do not have the capacity to represent in symbolic form the episodes which make up the ape mind. Their perception of episodes is immediate and context-bound. They cannot abstract from it.

Donald uses neuro-archaeological evidence to suggest that the first break from this limited 'episodic culture', 'mimetic culture', was developed by the *Australopithecus* line, who learnt to mime episodes, that is, to represent and communicate these units of the ape mind. Donald goes on to suggest a series of stages of development from mimetic culture to mythic culture to theoretic culture, in the course of which gestures and speech are successively introduced into mimetic behaviour so as to step by step attain the full range of psychic and communicative capacities of a language-using species. (See Blunden, 2006 for a synopsis).

5.3   Tool Making

Carrying things, facilitated by bipedalism, is, I have suggested, the first behaviour exhibiting practical abstraction and recursion, but next is the manufacture of tools, along with the use of tools, sharing and instruction in the use of tools. This development in behaviour had been prepared for by the pre-existing consciously controlled use of the hands and later on, greatly improved communication, and later still by a growing facility in hands-free communication.

Tool making and tool use is a particularly significant phase in the development of practical abstraction. The rendering of human powers into objective material objects continues to drive the development of language to this day, with new words flowing into the language from the latest products of technology and going on to be normalised in use remote from the institutional and technological context in which the words originated. For example, 'interface' arose in the context of development of new electronic devices in the military industry, but nowadays commonly refers to interpersonal and institutional relations.

Hegel (1804) said: "The word is the tool of Reason." Tool making and tool use, entails a concept, or form of human action, to be given a specific material shape just like a symbol. A tool is a human power reified as a material object. This constitutes practical abstraction, the necessary condition for abstraction in thinking. Today's tool is tomorrow's word. The most impressive proof of this is the history of colour words, which shows that no matter how prevalent a colour may have been in a people's environment, historically, a word for the colour enters the language only when a community had learnt how to *manufacture* the colour.

Speech turns out to be a particularly effective mode of language and once it becomes dominant, drives the evolution of the necessary anatomical adaptations. Gesture can then gradually cede centre stage to speech.

Once speech was dominant, tool-making and social organisation co-evolved with speech.

5.4 Collaborative Projects

Language communicates one's *intentions* and *feelings* to others and makes it possible for individuals to read their conversation partner's readiness for action (their intentions and emotions). How do intention-*expression* and intention-*reading* get started on this co-evolution?

The basis for becoming consciously aware of one's own intentions and being able to perceive the intentions of others is practical participation in collaborative projects. Prides of lions and bands of chimpanzees hunt in cooperative groups without conscious awareness, but relying on instinctual patterns of cooperation. Our hominin predecessors were surely capable of this kind of collaborative activity which already existed among their predecessors. A collaborative project is characterised by a shared object (such as catching the prey) and a diversity of individual goals which together bring about the success of the object. The participants operate with a kind of *practical calculus* of intentions *evolutionarily before* they are psychologically able to form conscious abstractions of the objects and goals of their actions and those of their fellows. But the shared intentional behaviour provides the material foundation for acquiring conscious awareness and control of the motives and goals.

Behaviour leads conscious awareness and control.

There is no need to hypothesise 'mirror neurons' and other such weird and unproven neurological entities. If they exist at all, they must be the evolutionary products of practical collaboration, not accidental products of a biological inheritance.

Chomsky's supposed Language Acquisition Device (LAD) is another unobservable, hypothetical neurological formation which appears to be the product not of biological evolution but of a miracle – it suddenly appeared in one individual who fortunately discovered their newfound capacity for language (despite having no one to talk to or a vocal apparatus to talk with even if they wanted to, or a vocabulary or syntax nor any use for them) and the given individual turns this divine gift to such evolutionary advantage as to ensure that its descendants take exclusive control of the human genome thereafter.

No, if there were such a thing as a LAD, it must have evolved *after* humans were already using language without it. Nonetheless, the urban myth about the existence of the LAD having been empirically proven by the invention of a language *de novo* by illiterate, deaf children in Nicaragua persists. (See Chapter 11, this volume.)

5.5   *Writing*

Tool making co-evolved with signed language in early human evolution as functions of the human hand. But communicative technologies like writing, which could underpin an accelerated development of language and symbolic thinking generally, come *much later*, well after the formation of Homo sapiens sapiens.

Writing is completely different from speech and gesture. The ability to read and write is a *cultural* achievement which even today is far from universally accomplished and there is no drive to learn to write apart from culturally constructed motivations which have appeared only in recent centuries. Self-evidently, the modern human type has always had the psychological and anatomical *capacities* to form hieroglyphics, letters or characters, but for hundreds of thousands of years they did not do so.

Writing was invented independently in Mesopotamia c. 3200 BCE, in China c. 1200 BCE, Phoenicia c. 1000 BCE and in Mesoamerica c. 700 BCE, and spread from there to other societies while some communities remain non-literate to this day, despite evidently having the same anatomical and psychological resources as the people in literate societies.

Writing was not invented in the context of interpersonal communication or the writing of epic poetry. It arose in the context of ancient class societies with bureaucratic regimes and their need to keep accounts of their wealth and its distribution. A specialised class of scribes was trained to keep these records. The scope of writing activity subsequently expanded – and continues to do so. Modern electronic machinery has to be programmed with written scripts no different in principle from the how-to manuals written for people to read.

The main difficulty in writing which even fluent speakers have to overcome, is that writing is a form of language action in which the writer's conversational partner is *not present*. It cannot emerge spontaneously.

Speech is commonly carried on without conscious awareness, springing back into consciousness only when special attention to the words and their delivery is demanded for some reason. Generally speaking, we respond to circumstances and go straight from thought to speech without thinking, that is, without conscious awareness.

Writing on the other hand requires conscious control with the hands, without the aid of sound or the immediate presence of the reader. It is a new level of conscious control of psychological action. Thoughts first have to be silently formed into words and then the words inscribed one by one, holding back the mind so as not to get ahead of the hand. The art of writing can develop up to a facility matching that of speech, but that is generally not universally attained.

The use of what Vygotsky called 'psychological tools' never arises spontaneously. All children learn to speak without any conscious effort on the part of their parents or friends, and deaf children will acquire signed speech in just the same way if their parents use signed language in the home. But learning to write requires specific instruction. There is no innate drive to read and write.

Writing, and psychological tools in general – i.e., the use of maps and diagrams, telephones and emails, mathematical symbols, charts, etc. – develops off the back of the development of technology. As industry moves from earthenware and the production of fabric to mechanical devices like the printing press to electrical devices like the telegraph and telephone to electronic devices like computers, the array of *psychological* tools develops apace.

> Technological development leads the acquisition of psychological tools, but the development of psychological tools leads psychological development.

5.6   Art

Cave paintings, jewellery and burial decorations are frequently cited as evidence of the ability to make abstractions. This makes sense. People who can communicate with gesture and speech, make and use tools, exercise delayed gratification and bring prey back to camp to share with others, can likely learn to manufacture paint and represent their life in cave art.

People who could paint evidently had the psychological and anatomical wherewithal to write. But *they didn't*. Not until large, hierarchical class societies emerged, with their need for accounting. Cave art is evidently expressive, and perhaps instrumental but probably only marginally communicative. Writing is a cultural accomplishment and there is no reason to interpret cave art as rudimentary writing.

On the other hand, there are practical and symbolic uses of artefacts which are not yet writing, but are communicative and not just expressive. The Australian aborigines marked the land with what were, in effect, sign posts. When was property in land first established by marks such as boundary posts? And there are the message sticks apparently used for long distance communication. But none of this is relevant to human evolution is it? It was anatomically fully-modern human beings who did these things.

6   Conclusions

The following principles have been established:
- The behaviour which drives the emergence of a new species, and which is therefore its characteristic feature, must exist in rudimentary form in the predecessor species.
- Behaviour leads biology, so certain absurdities in speculation about human origins can be avoided. Anatomical adaptations are not first evolved and then used. First, inadequate anatomy is used and later, anatomy evolves to become adequate.
- Behaviour leads conscious awareness and control. Behaviour evolves with a logic of its own; once a form of behaviour becomes established it has the potential to be reflected in the psyche.

Following from these principles, the following speculative conclusions may be offered with some degree of confidence:
- Language must have evolved before the necessary vocal apparatus and conscious control of the vocal apparatus had evolved. Language before speech is a necessary premise.
- Collaborative labour provides the basis in behaviour for the need and possibility to be aware of the motives of others and oneself.
- It is not language or tool making which is the original occasion for the development of consciousness, but simply carrying things – the first break from immediate consumption of nature, represented in the human hand.
- Carrying things is the germ cell of human development. Carrying things led to the evolution of bipedalism and signed language and thereby to tool making and speech.

On the other hand, observations of present-day human communicative and cognitive activity tells us little about the origins of language. But whatever capacities we observe in modern human beings must be plausible as outcomes of the phylogenesis of language that we propose. Equally, whatever we find about the origins of language has little to tell us about modern human behaviour which could not be determined more reliably by contemporary observation of behaviour.

Doubtless, we learn more about human behaviour by closely observing how children and young adults acquire language. But nonetheless, the origin of language remains one of the most fascinating and intractable problems of natural science, and we must await the progress of palaeontology, archaeology, genome sequencing, microbiology and neurology before we can be sure about these questions.

CHAPTER 13

Power, Activity and Human Flourishing

Activity theory is a theory of human flourishing. 'Human flourishing' is the usual English translation of the Greek word *eudemonia*, the central concept of Aristotle's ethics. As a current of scientific thinking, activity theory has the great merit that its central concept – 'collaborative project', also often referred to as 'an activity' – is equally a descriptive, explanatory and *normative* concept.

'Human flourishing' refers to the enjoyment of a *good life*, something which bears little relation to the consumption of material goods, and is little concerned with rights, but rather with the expansion of a person's capacity for enjoyment. As Aristotle showed, human flourishing is meaningful only in the context of the *collaborative* creation of a good life for *all* human beings. So activity theory is a scientific theory which is simultaneously an ethical theory. We not only *see* the world as made up of collaborative projects, and *use* collaborative projects to promote human flourishing, but we also *advocate* collaboration as the norm for secular life. The way all people *ought* to deal with one another is to *collaborate* with each other in projects.

What I would like to reflect on in this essay is the question of how we see situations where the norm of collaboration goes wrong, and people find themselves trapped in projects toxic to their own health and that of others. In particular I want to tackle the problem of abuse of power, a topic which cannot even be clearly framed so long as ethical and analytical concepts are at odds with one another.

1   Collaborative Project as a Unit of Social Life

When economists build their science on the utilitarian assumption of an independent, individual economic agent who makes rational decisions to maximise their own utility, they take it that the norms of utilitarianism are universally adhered to by the economic actors. In the event that the subjects of a community do not act as individuals maximising their own utility, then the science fails. Corrections such as allowing for delayed or incomplete information do not change the underlying ethical problem. More importantly, governments and firms which make policy on the basis of economic science, and therefore utilitarian ethics, are acting so as to *foster* this ethos in the community, with all the consequences in terms of inequality and social disintegration.

At the very root of modern society is the ethical principle known as the Golden Rule. This principle is found in all the great religions of the world and was used by Kant in his derivation of secular ethics. This implicit 'social contract' is expressed in the Christian Bible thus:

> Do unto others as you would have them do unto you.
> LUKE 6:31

But the Critical Theorist, Agnes Heller (1987), showed that this maxim is deficient in our postmodern times, for it is based on an untenable presumption of cultural homogeneity. Another person may fairly demand *not* to be treated in the same way you want to be treated. Unless there is some real interaction with the other person, however, this qualification is empty. As Seyla Benhabib (1996) has shown, ethical maxims which treat of relations with an abstract other can offer no real guidance. One's actions in relation to some other have to be taken in connection with the practical relations one has with that other. Activity theory begins from the assumption of collaborative rather than individual action, so in the light of these considerations, the appropriate maxim is:

> What we do, is decided by you and me.

So, in the light of the criticism of the Golden Rule just given, we take this practical relation to be the project in which you and I are, in one way or another, doing something together. The revised Golden Rule then simply reads as the well-known norms of collaboration.

Collaboration is a concrete relation whose norms differ widely according to the kind of project involved, but in every case these norms are robust and well known, and rooted in the self-concept of the shared project. In some cases the norms of collaboration strictly require joint decision-making, in other cases, customer/service provider norms suffice, and in other cases the norms of line management prevail. But it remains the case that the norms of collaboration are facts, norms of modern social life, not just the assumptions of a social theory.

Consequently, by taking collaborative projects as our unit of analysis we can do *realistic* science, and insofar as an object of scientific investigation departs from this assumption, it is to that extent also a departure from the relevant ethical norms. In part, this dependence on the reality of ethical norms is the motivation behind the current reflections on abuse of power.

We also take 'projects' rather than 'social groups' as *units of analysis*. That is, rather than seeing a community as a mosaic of groups of various kinds – ethnic groups, age groups, occupational groups, voters, consumers, etc. – we see the social fabric as woven of *projects*.

This has a number of implications. First, it means we do not take subjects as nonentities with contingent attributes attached (gender, occupation, ethnicity, etc.) by means of which an observer can pigeonhole people into various groups. We see social life as made up of people pursuing common ends, i.e., projects, and the community as we find it is a work in progress. This society, with its laws, customs, land, human beings, etc., is all created and shaped by past projects and kept alive by the projects we pursue today. Every individual human life is itself a collaborative project.

Second, although bureaucrats and statisticians prefer the pigeonholing approach to analysis, the project approach is an eminently suitable lens through which to view society for those of us who are interested in *change* and who are less interested in people as consumers and voters than in people as agents shaping their own lives and the lives of others through participation in projects.

Being a person is not about what you have, or even so much about what you do, but rather what you aspire to do, and especially what you aspire to do with others. So we see a social formation as flourishing more or less successfully, because we understand it through the same norms by means of which people pursue their *own* life projects.

When we talk of projects, however, we do not have in mind only the planned responses to a situation which are normally what is referred to as projects. When a project resonates with a broader community it becomes a *social movement*. And to the degree that a social movement becomes successful, and manages to objectify its aims in the laws and customs of the wider community, it becomes an *institution*. And as an institution makes its way into the language and consciousness of the entire community it becomes simply a *concept* alongside others, an inseparable part of the whole culture. We see all these social formations as stages in the lifecycle of a project and as such we take them all as projects. Things can go wrong in the life of a project where an institution has degenerated to be no more than a vehicle for individual self-aggrandisement, or in a social movement which has failed to embed itself in the broader society and make the transition to institutionalisation. That is, in the case of social scandals, abuse of various kinds and corruption, we are generally concerned with the developmental pathology of projects. It is especially those projects which have embedded themselves and are taken for granted as concepts which are no longer the real motivation of activity, which are the ubiquitous sources of injustice.

From what has been said, it is clear that projects are the *means* for changing the world, as well as being what the human world is made up of – the world process. Projects are the one and only means by which human beings can manifest their will, change the world they live in and attain self-determination. What we and those who have gone before us create in the course of struggling for freedom are concepts, now simply part of the language, and projects which have become institutionalised in the form of routinised practices sustained by both external rewards, such as wages and social status, as well as internal rewards such as self-realisation and promotion of the social good. In the course of the development of these projects, both internally and under the impact of external developments, problems, crises, injustices and conflicts arise. These are not only the inevitable outcome of the institutionalisation of projects, but also the very conditions from which new projects are launched, 'correctives', which modify the innovations made by earlier generations. Further, it turns out that no matter how ossified and bureaucratised a project may have become, there is always at its heart a principle, a *mission* for which purpose it was founded. Although in day-to-day life this mission is usually pushed to the background (and indeed may harbour unresolved contradictions), while decisions are made and motivations derived from regular, well-established subordinate or particular concepts or practices, it remains always there as a kind of court of last resort. A project which has become institutionalised in taken-for-granted, routinised forms of practice can be 'reawakened' when its fundamental tenets are called into question by contradictions and failures in its operation, and challenged by a new social movement. The 'principle' which was championed by a social movement before becoming institutionalised is often objectified in the form of some kind of 'historic compromise', like the constitution of a new nation, a peace treaty or an agreement signed to end a strike. The 'reawakening' of an institution means bringing this principle back into question in the light of new problems. Instances of this process are the intervention of HIV/AIDS activists in the medical research project and the intervention of the Women's Liberation Movements into *all* the institutions of modern society.

2   The Abuse of Power

As remarked above, a social movement is successful only insofar as its mission is objectified; that is, its demands are legislated or simply adopted as custom and practice in the community at large and 'mainstreamed'. If a social movement exhausts its mission, but does not dissolve, then it lives on as a kind of vestige or sect.

A woman may get involved in the women's movement in the first place to get a pay rise or better childcare, but they do not make a lifetime commitment to the women's movement for those immediate motives. Those are privileges that will more likely be enjoyed by her daughter. But if she is lucky enough to reap the fruits of her struggle, it will have been a heavy price to pay. In the main, except at the last moment or where lives are literally on the line, people participate in social movements *on principle*, for the future benefit of others, not themselves, though perhaps others like themselves.

Under these circumstances, a social movement goes awry only when the objective itself becomes malign. For example, when the Communist Party of the Philippines under José Maria Sison turned on itself in a frenzy of witch-hunting, this was the almost inevitable outcome of a much earlier decision of the CPP to leave Manila and go into the countryside to build a guerrilla army of displaced urban intellectuals. Shining Path in Peru, led by Abimael Guzmán (President Gonzalo), is another classic example. Having been established as a peasant-based movement to fight for a revolutionary communist state, Sendero Luminoso degenerated, and ended up murdering the leaders of social movements, farmers and trade unionists of the Peruvian left. In the 1960s, inspired by the Revolutions in China and Cuba but finding the road to socialism by normal political means blocked, a section of the urban intelligentsia in almost every country took this dead-end road. Since 1959, only in Nicaragua and Nepal could this strategy boast some success. This was a project which was appealing in the 1960s. It was an ideal, a concept which seemed to a certain social layer to respond to the injustices of the times. However, it developed through interaction with the unfolding world situation such that it had either to be abandoned as untenable, or adapt itself to the changing situation, as in the case of the Irish Republican Army (IRA) and the Revolutionary Armed Forces of Colombia (FARC). Otherwise, the result was degeneration, isolation and growing irrelevance or pathological dysfunction. No concept can remain as it was at birth; it either grows in response to the experience of its own impact on the world, or it rationalises its difficulties and becomes weaker.

This is the first type of pathology I want to address. The root cause lies in the very founding of the project, in what turns out to have been a misconception. Projects always have a powerful inertia. All blows and sceptical attacks are absorbed by revisions and rationalisations of the basic premise, so far as is possible without a fundamental abandonment of its mission. This resistance to scepticism and criticism is necessary for the maintenance and development of any movement, but can also prove to be its downfall.

The original insight which launches a social movement is always a leap of faith, and its future destiny cannot be predicted. A social movement which has missed a fork in the road is doomed, and if spirited internal critique of the founding principle cannot restore sense, then it is best to get off the bus as soon as possible.

But there is a second type of pathology which is not quite the same. In this case, the project does not so much take a wrong turn, as simply fail to notice when its time has passed and it has outlived itself.

> There is a tide in the affairs of men.
> Which, taken at the flood, leads on to fortune;
> Omitted, all the voyage of their life
> Is bound in shallows and in miseries.
> JULIUS CAESAR, Act 4

Such a project is a halfway house to becoming an institution. Actually, it is neither social movement nor institution. It offers no prospect of resolving the injustice which motivated its founding (the internal rewards offered to those who join a living social movement), and having failed to institutionalise itself, it generally does not have the resources to offer significant external rewards. Being Secretary of the Moe branch of the Australian Socialist League does not attract a wage. As a result, the entire project operates on dreams and various kinds of self-deception. Lacking the resources for real internal or external rewards, such bureaucratised social movements generally offer soft, inessential rewards (friendship, mutual aid, solace, hope, etc.) for the often arduous demands placed upon participants.

The leaders of such projects do not in any normal sense of the word wield power. They have power only in relation to participants of their group for whom the leaders symbolise the ideal to which the project is oriented. The power exerted by a leader over a member of such a project may be nothing or it may be life and death. The mystique by means of which this *puissance* exerts itself is entirely dependent on the subject's commitment to and belief in the project's proximate ideal. By 'proximate ideal' I mean the ideal with which the particular project invests itself, its 'brand', as opposed to the more remote 'abstract ideal' (such as Christianity or Socialism). The moment a participant is 'disillusioned' that power loses its mystique, even while possibly exerting itself indirectly through others. The underlying source of the pathology which is manifested in small religious or socialist sects is the illusory character of the proximate ideal which sustains itself by ever more illusory and erroneous perceptions and rationalisations. Generally speaking such ideals are sustained by a kind of circular logic which can be broken only by trauma. While the logic of a concept has a circular character, for an ideal which has become institutionalised within a community which enjoys openness, this circularity is always infected by the liberalism of the general community. It is not institutionalised, merely ossified. But when a sect becomes *isolated* and then in turn rationalises this isolation ("everyone is against us") the logic becomes a *closed* circle. Its mystique can be broken only to the extent that ties with the community at large continue.

More significant however is the project which has successfully completed its social movement phase, merged itself with the community at large and transformed itself into an institution, whether this is a finite institution such as the Education Department, or a ubiquitous institution such marriage. In general, the rules and norms of an institution are the special or particular principles of the ideal which the institution serves. But on the other hand, being institutionalised means that the project becomes itself a special or particular principle of the self-concept of the community as a whole. Consequently, an institution is able to muster the resources to maintain its activity by external rewards such as the wages upon which its employees rely for a living, lucrative salaries and high social status and privileges for the top dogs. The phenomena which manifest themselves in small sects are then not only normalised, but greatly expanded in scale. Here we can have in mind not only small sects but institutions like the Catholic Church or the Chinese Communist Party.

Institutions therefore become bastions for the inequality and injustices characteristic of the society at large. They also grant themselves and their upper layers immunity from criticism. I recall a recent case of an incompetent surgeon who was killing patients in a Queensland hospital, while nurses were doing their best to steer vulnerable patients clear of him, but were unable to expose him because of his superior status.

The 'thick ethos' which obtains within institutions differs from the 'thin ethos' which pervades the general community. "Equals should be treated equally and unequals unequally" (Heller, 1987). The CEO and the base level worker should deal with each other as equals if they meet in the street, but at work one is paid ten times more than and gives orders to the other, a relationship which could be reversed on the football field. The norms governing these relations in an activity setting are instantiations of the concept upon which the institution was founded. The very idea of a hospital was founded on the principle of the autonomy and moral superiority of a doctor and the traditionally female service role of nurses. When hospitals were created, the concept of health care they objectified took on a great deal of the hierarchical character of the society of that time, and it has been slower to change than the general community. To change this hierarchical ethos requires the intervention of a social movement with a different concept of health care, and which can challenge the basis upon which the institution was founded. A social movement which addressed the ethos within a hospital with an abstract demand for egalitarianism would be unlikely to be successful. To bring about change in an institution, a social movement must address its critique to the institution's core mission, from which its norms and rule flow. The Women's Health Movement and the Consumer Health Movement did so on the basis of a conception of health care in which the carer entered into a collaborative relationship with the patient.

The trade unions are a strange and difficult hybrid of social movement and institution, one could say an 'institutionalised social movement'. Because the conditions of wage labour mean that the conflict between labour and capital is permanent, the mission of the trade unions can never be exhausted short of the socialist utopia, so they can never be merged into the community at large. As Trotsky remarked:

> ... one sees very clearly how absurd it is to oppose as two different principles trade union organisation and state organisation. In England more than anywhere else, the state rests upon the back of the working class which constitutes the overwhelming majority of the population of the country. The mechanism is such that the bureaucracy is based directly on the workers, and the state indirectly, by the intermediary of the trade union bureaucracy.
>
> TROTSKY, 1930

The kind of permanent armistice through which fundamental conflicts underlying the state are contained mean that no institution lacks internal contradictions, and these contradictions break out from time to time. However, the days are long past when the trade unions confronted the state as an alien force. But with a mass membership, the trade unions offer all the 'temptations' of an institution: jobs for the boys, good salaries, and so on, and with the day-to-day business of unions – getting an extra penny on the wage, defending individuals before disciplinary hearings, and so on – the sharp emotions and principles which motivate the new trade union official are soon worn smooth by bureaucratic drudgery, not to mention the experience, novel for the newly elected delegate, of seeing the working situation 'from above', so to speak.

Reflecting on the quandary facing socialist parties and trade unions, and other social movements and semi-institutions defending the interests of the permanently oppressed, we can see the space for a permanent social movement. It is not an impossibility, but such projects can surely only survive by constant renewal, continuously revisiting their guiding principles and finding how to give expression to them in the existing conditions.

2.1   *Institutions*

The Church is an institution which is also not properly either an institution (unless the Church is established) nor a sect (unless it is a marginal religion). The Catholic Church is now 1,700 years old and operates according to rigid norms, up to and including papal infallibility, maintaining its homogeneity despite operating in every country in the world. But the Catholic Church is not a small sect which can isolate its mass membership from the general community. On the contrary, it is deeply embedded in every aspect of social life. Such a contradictory situation obliges the Church to actively defend its privileged position with respect to the norms of the wider communities. The mystique of religion means that the symbolic power acquired by the leader of any institution or social movement is considerably amplified, so the priest wields more than the power of life and death over the most devoted of his flock, and in the case of children, this power is almost unlimited, both because of the reliance of the child upon adult care and the fact that the mystique envelopes the child's family. For this reason, sexual abuse perpetrated within the Church should be categorised as incestuous rape.

The recent exposure of sexual abuse within the Catholic Church has been most intense in countries where the general community enjoys a liberal ethos. This may be the result of the difficulty the Church experiences in insulating itself from the thin ethos of post-industrial liberal societies. The mystique of the Church hierarchy is continuously undermined by the liberal ethos in which members are immersed every day. The clergy itself does tend to be insulated and disciplined against this exposure however. The evidence seems to be that it is by appeal to the norms of the wider community and by invoking its powers (police, courts, welfare services, etc.) that this abuse can be combated. It is unlikely that critique of Catholic doctrine can help. Of course the Church does not directly condone child abuse, but the closed and strongly hierarchical character of its organisation and the powerful mystique of papal infallibility is probably the main reason that systematic sexual abuse has been more pervasive within the Catholic Church than anywhere else. Catholics should be more like Protestants, one might say, but the past 500 years have shown this to be unlikely. In any case, it seems that *wherever* children are cared for by adults, there is abuse. While the Catholic Church has remained meaningful to its flock over millennia, as integral to a moral life, for those who have made their lives within the church hierarchy it is the organisational norms which predominate over the obligation to save souls. Equally, the fine words of the constitution have little practical meaning to the citizen outside of their practical expression in everyday life. Admittedly, wherever there are children there will be sexual predators. The only protection is public visibility.

The other site for the abuse of power in relation to women and children is the family. Families vary widely of course, and child abuse and domestic violence are by no means the norm. But where social conditions support a powerful role for the head of the household, and leave members of a family at the economic and legal mercy of the head of the household without the option of leaving or seeking the help of the police, then the father may acquire a powerful mystique which licenses abuse. Each family is a project, but a project which may be closely tied to the personal project of its head as it was in times when the father enjoyed legal coverture over his wife and children, not to mention servants and tenants. Whether a patriarchal family is mirroring relations in the general community or is insulated from the general community, this little system of activity is for its members a self-concept, in which the subordinate members conceive themselves as subordinate concepts of the concept instantiated by the father figure. In this situation, the wife and children are but the limbs on the body of the father. What enjoys the approval of the father is good. Up to a point this is not in itself pathological. The little boy who works like a Trojan running errands for his father is not necessarily exploited thereby. And what counts as abuse or exploitation is historically variable. The young girl seduced by an older boy may suffer more than a young boy seduced by an older woman, not so much because of the nature of the action itself, but because of the community which stigmatises the girl and lionises the male victim.

In all the above cases, the general rule is that it is only your collaborator who can *really* hurt you. One way or another, the norms of collaboration can be violated by utilising the mystique offered by playing a senior role in a project so as to exploit junior collaborators. Ancient projects like the patriarchy, which are deeply embedded in communities, have sedimented themselves in the form of concepts which normalise that which, when seen from a distance, is obviously exploitative and abusive.

2.2 *Firms*

Turning now to the most characteristic creature which inhabits the terrain of liberal capitalism – the capitalist firm. Although the firm grows in egalitarian liberal soil it is far from liberal or collaborative within its own ranks. A firm is a project whose mission is the expansion of the proportion of social labour (i.e., value) it subsumes and generally operates a regime of uncompromising top-down dictatorship worthy of the most byzantine authoritarian dictatorship.

Although norms of collaboration may apply within the board of directors or among co-workers on the shop floor, these collaborative relations are subsumed within the ethos of top-down direction.

Despite all the efforts of trade unions and socialists down the centuries to inculcate in workers the ethos of *class* solidarity, it is generally the case that employees of a firm to a greater or lesser extent 'identify' with the firm and often the entire industry, enjoying its successes and failure as their own, and take the hierarchy embedded in the firm's line management as legitimate. In this sense a firm is a project like any other.

This fact leads to surprising kinds of pathology. For decades, senior executives of asbestos manufacturers have known full well that their product was killing people, but have lied and fabricated scientific evidence to cover this up. So successful have they been in perpetrating this myth that many of them, together with their wives and children, have themselves fallen victim to asbestosis or mesothelioma. In the overwhelming majority of cases, base level operatives who are daily exposed to lethal doses of fibre have kept on working with the material despite information widely available in the public domain, including TV and newspapers, making it clear that by doing so they were condemning themselves to an agonising death. But these workers *believed* in their firms; they trusted the managers who were lying through their teeth, while regarding medical scientists and their own union representatives, who were telling them the truth, as scaremongers. The same is true of the citizenry in the company towns where asbestos has been mined. It is said that townspeople in the US often regard the Environmental Protection Agency (EPA) as public enemy number one.

Now it is often supposed that monetary interest explains this suicidal blindness. If this were the case then it is a misplaced self-interest, because the price always ends up being far too high. But the evidence of risk-taking behaviour across a range of situations (Lightfoot, 1997) tells us that this kind of utilitarian calculation explains nothing. People on the whole do what they deem to be right and honourable. And what is right and honourable is determined in great measure by the terms of the project they are committed to and their position within that project.

We know that soldiers fight and die for their country, but it is always surprising when we see low-paid manual workers dying for their company. But this is what commitment to a project entails.

Generally speaking, the rights and privileges a person enjoys flow from their social position which may derive from their family and upbringing or may be determined by contingent attributes such as gender, physique or racial type. An individual's fortune and the extent of their freedom and opportunity for self-realisation is determined by those projects into which they are accepted as participants and the *place assigned to them* within those projects. While a person's contingent attributes in themselves pose no barrier to their flourishing, people tend to be judged and assigned to social positions (treated) according to what may be quite inessential attributes. The interpellation of a person to an inappropriate social position is called *misrecognition*. For example, being able to get only a menial manual job is no injustice in itself, but if this restriction is to do with race or gender then this is an injustice, as is the low pay and social status which goes along with performing that menial, poorly paid job.

So there are two issues implicated in the problem of justice outside those problems discussed above in connection with the failure of the norms of collaboration within projects, viz., (1) the mis/recognition of subjects according to contingent attributes, and (2) the maintenance of social positions whose occupants will enjoy markedly different social status and opportunities for self-realisation. The first is the problem of the construction of the human subject and the second is mainly a problem of political economy.

3   The Human Subject

There are in social philosophy two theories of the nature of the human subject. According to the theory credited to Kant, the subject is just a point, a nothing, to which attributes are attached – a person is their gender, age, nationality, occupation, favourite colour, etc., and nothing else beyond. The person has preferences and needs, but they do not exist 'for the sake of' something else (to use Aristotle's phrase). The other theory can be credited to Hegel and sees the subject as a kind of puzzle which is forever seeking to discover and define itself, and change the society in which they live so as to foster human flourishing. Activity theory stands in the Hegelian tradition, and is consistent with narrative and developmental theories of the self. A person is not born a sovereign individual. On the contrary, life is an ongoing struggle for identity and self-determination. So the self is not given at the start, but, to use Aristotle's phrase, is what the individual is 'moving toward'. As to power, the point is this: as a nothing with predicates attached, the subject is at the mercy of their interlocutors – there is nothing underneath those contingent inessential attributes. When they are interpellated into a subject position, they are *subjected* (in that curious, contradictory sense that the English language has preserved). From the Hegelian point of view, essential subject is what the subject is moving towards, and can never be finally and irrevocably determined.

The Kantian subject, on the other hand, can be understood by the methods of Set Theory: labelled and sorted into boxes, as is the routine in political analysis in the US, and institutionalised such as in electoral systems based on large geographical electorates. Kant promoted the ideal of self-determination, but conceived of self-determination in the shape of autonomous individuals.

From the standpoint of activity theory, a subject makes themself by means of activity in projects collaborating with other people. But this is not to deny that misrecognition and interpellation are real phenomena. But they are not actions which are essential to the human condition, they are products of entrenched hierarchical institutions, either as remnants of pre-modern society, or in the form of *bureaucracy* – routinised procedures for dealing with large numbers of impersonal relations in conflict-ridden social situations.

4 Political Economy

According to liberal thinkers like Robert Nozick (1974), inequalities of wealth which are outcomes of the operation of a free market cannot be unjust, any more than someone who dies of an incurable genetic illness can be deemed to have suffered an injustice. It's just the way things are, and for Nozick redistribution is tantamount to theft. He sees no essential difference between progressive taxation and Robin Hood.

But this so-called free market is a myth. Every system of distribution, whether a neoliberal market economy, a regulated welfare state economy or a peasant commune, is a product of human beings collaborating in projects, shaping the mode of their collaboration, just as much as they are shaping the product being distributed and the human beings producing them. No system of distribution and exchange just happens, it is *produced*, just as the legal and political systems which regulate them are produced.

Then there are the questions of justice and power attaching to the *production* of distributive institutions themselves. The moral issue arises in the social and political processes by means of which the relevant mode of distribution is formed and maintained. Injustice is in the first place something inherited from the past, a past to which people are connected through the projects to which they areconnected, including families, nations, professions, and so on. To the extent that collaborators in a project enjoy the benefits of past activity which privilege them to the cost of other collaborators within a wider project (e.g., other citizens of a country who do not belong to a privileged profession), they have a moral obligation to utilise any opportunity which arises within their collaboration to rectify that injustice. Not to do so is an abuse of power.

There can be no doubt that the capitalist economy is the vehicle for the production and maintenance of *puissance*, placing powerful projects into the hands of a few whilst funnelling fortunes into the pockets of a tiny minority. Pierre Bourdieu (1984, see Chapter 24, this volume) has shown that power in contemporary society is a sum of monetary wealth and what he calls cultural capital and social capital. The power and independence a class fraction enjoys thanks to the distinctions it maintains relative to other class fractions is nonetheless 'cashed in' through political economy. James Coleman's (1990, see Chapter 21, this volume) version of political economy, in which the basic value is a promise to return a favour, not necessarily embodied in cash, may be a necessary extension of political economy to encompass such forms of obligation. But either way, within capitalist societies, power is a function of wealth (a broader category than 'money' or 'capital', one which could encompass Bourdieu's and Coleman's concepts of 'capital'), and a considerable portion of that power is utilised to *maintain* a political economy which preserves that concentration of power and wealth. There is no obvious answer to the big question of "What is to be done?" in respect to this situation of self-serving wealth and power. All that can be said is that the institutions which maintain this situation can be changed only by collaborative projects, and it is at least an open question whether such revolutionary projects should constitute themselves as parties or fronts or alliances or any of the various historical forms of radical subjectivity (Blunden, 2009). I tend to believe that there is merit in identifying as a project and being conscious of everything that that entails.

CHAPTER 14

Vaccine Hesitancy

Last year (2014), the rate of measles infections reached a 16-year high in Australia, mainly due to travellers catching measles overseas and passing it on to unvaccinated children after coming home. We are in serious danger of horrible diseases which had been eliminated from Australia making a comeback due to a rapid increase in parents failing to have their children vaccinated.

The conventional term, 'vaccine hesitancy' (VH), implies *hesitancy* in relation to *vaccination*, but some people are not hesitant at all, being *decisive* in refusing vaccination, and some are hesitant about a specific vaccine not vaccination in general. However, the term is accepted as indicating this entire field of activity.

Since the Christian Scientists confirmed that they do *not* have a conscientious objection to vaccination, there is now no basis for objection on religious grounds. The tolerance and legal protection extended to religious orders is firmly established in the principles of secular government. Implicit in this tolerance is the reciprocal obligation on religious orders to conform to the law of the land. Conflicts which have arisen between religious and secular law have been resolved historically by negotiation, and continued tolerance relies on past compromises. Examples include the allowance for religious holidays celebrated by minority communities, and the right of conscientious objection to performing abortion or serving in the army. In the absence of such formal accommodation, the secular law prevails, forbidding genital mutilation and so-called honour killing, for example. Nowhere in this practice is there room for an individual or group to unilaterally declare a conscientious objection on the basis of personal conviction. Such an idea would make a mockery of the very idea of human civilisation.

There remain however a range of reasons behind failure to access available vaccination programs, and different responses by the community are required in each case. The Abbott government's policy to send a 'price signal' by withdrawing welfare payments will work for a minority of those who have not had their children vaccinated but will alienate and harden the resistance of an expanding section of refusers for whom a legal penalty would only confirm their scepticism.

Socio-economic status and level of education have proved to be poor predictors of vaccine hesitancy and the usual empirical-demographic and public

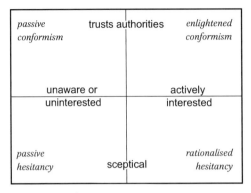

FIGURE 4   The VH Compass

education approaches to public health challenges have proved ineffective. Policy makers do not know what to do to improve the uptake of vaccination.

Peretti-Watel et al. (2015) use the ideas of 'reflexive modernity', 'risk society' and 'life politics' from Ulrich Beck et al. (1992; 1994) and Anthony Giddens (1998) to describe the field of vaccine hesitancy in terms of two dimensions, parallel to the way that Giddens described 'beyond left and right' in the political domain, with his 'political compass'. That is, just as political opinion can longer be mapped on to a single axis, people cannot be seen as simply more or less reluctant to vaccinate.

The horizontal axis (Figure 4 above) measures the extent to which the subject has embraced the modern trends of *risk culture* in which the world is full of unpredictable sources of danger, and 'healthism' in which the subject is someone who takes active responsibility for managing their own health. The vertical axis measures the subject's disposition to trust the entire system of expert culture and established power and authority, or not.

1   Risk Culture and Healthism

On the left of the horizontal axis are people unaware of the severity of diseases like measles, smallpox and rubella, because they have never had any personal experience of them (thanks to the success of past immunisation programs) and are unaware of the need for immunisation.

On the right are people who take an active interest in their own health and that of their children, seek out information and are strongly committed to whatever action they find to be appropriate, positive or negative.

Positioning on this axis is questionably deemed to reflect a *personality trait*. What is characteristic of modernity is the shift towards *individual responsibility*. Typically, people no longer ascribe either their good fortune or their poverty to the prevailing political-economic system nor look to governments and authorities to help them. People tend to accept that problems in their life are the result of their own action. Further, governments actively promote ideologies of self-reliance, and discredit *collective* action, such as by trade unions or other kinds of activism. Governments have changed employment laws, for example, to encourage individual contracts, and reduced welfare payments. Under these conditions, it is questionable to attribute vaccine hesitancy to personality traits, irrespective of quite rational bases for scepticism and customs and norms which force people to accept personal responsibility for their own welfare.

2 Trust

Distrust of public officials is as old as civilisation, but in the past, while people may have distrusted salespeople, police or their boss, they tended to accept the advice of experts. However, the rational scepticism which has been the province of science for 400 years, is now turned back on to science itself and non-scientific people routinely treat scientific opinion with scepticism (This is one of the implications of 'reflexive modernity'. It is 'reflexive' because now people who were formerly merely the objects of social science are now sufficiently educated to see themselves subjects of science, and are aware of the sciences being used to control their behaviour). People don't generally believe advertisements, whose economic interest is undisguised, and nor do necessarily they believe the unbiased, measured but less persuasive claims of scientists and public health officials. Modern egalitarian individualism suggests that every citizen is as qualified as any other to offer an opinion on questions of science.

At the top of the vertical axis are those who still believe that the doctor will generally keep you healthy and that scientists generally understand nature. People who believed that Iraq had weapons of mass destruction and our soldiers are the most courageous in the world would also be found at this end of the vertical axis.

At the bottom of the vertical access are those who presume that genetically modified food is dangerous to world health, the government is probably lying, scientists are motivated by prospects for promotion and whoever is funding their research, while vaccination programs are either a cover for the CIA or a fraud perpetrated by Big Pharma.

What is characteristic of modernity is that rational scepticism is now turned, not just on corrupt or foolhardy officials, but on science itself.

3   The 'VH Compass'

The combination of the two axes produces four archetypes which can be mapped on a 'compass'.

Passive Conformism: in the top-left quadrant are people who take no interest in vaccination issues, believing it to be either unimportant or all taken care of. Unaware of the danger of diseases like rubella and smallpox or their part in eliminating them, they forget to attend clinics for top-ups and ignore news about infectious diseases. But when told that this is what they have to do, they will not suspect any ulterior motive or doubt what their doctor tells them, and will try to comply. These are the people who may possibly respond to 'price signals' or 'No jab no play' rules at childcare.

Enlightened Conformism: in the top-right quadrant are people who generally seek and follow the advice of their doctors and health authorities, closely read the instructions on the packets, check that the local school is doing the right thing and actively support public vaccination programs. These people need neither threats nor propaganda, just reliable and accessible public information and access to the vaccine.

Passive Hesitancy: in the SW quadrant are people who make no effort to inform themselves about vaccine issues but neither do they believe what the government or their GP tell them. They trust information from their friends and neighbours, however, without questioning the source of the advice given. Messages from experts or authorities are liable to be judged politically.

Rationalised Hesitancy: in the SE quadrant we have that group which is truly a product of our times: they take responsibility for their own health, meticulously controlling their diet, avoiding manufactured food and taking an active interest in issues such as contamination of crops and water sources and inform themselves about vaccination issues. However, they do not regard their GP or the government, far less pharmaceutical companies like Pfizer or Roche, as sources of reliable information and believe that university research is subject to malign corporate influence. Because individuals in this group make their own judgments based on evidence, they may refuse one vaccine while accepting another. It is this cohort which is of particular interest, both because it is the quadrant which is growing, and which is most resistant to blunt public health instruments such as Abbott's 'price signal' and dumbed-down public health messages.

'Herd immunity' relies on the number of unvaccinated people remaining below a critical percentage, somewhat like the critical mass of a radioactive material beyond which a nuclear chain reaction occurs. So long as the percentage of vulnerable people is less than some critical level, subject to public health measures, the reproduction rate of the infection will be remain at a level such that the infection will eventually die out. Beyond that level, transmission continues indefinitely, or spreads exponentially. So vaccination is *not* a question of personal choice but of *public safety*, like the fire ban enforced during the summer months, and messages based on 'rational actor' logic are misplaced. Self-interest would advise an individual *not* to get vaccinated, but rely on other people's immunity.

At the same time, rational scepticism is an entirely responsible orientation. There are ample precedents for irresponsible marketing of health products and unforeseen consequences of innovative medical practices. There is no formula or universal criteria by which to judge the safety and efficacy of vaccination which does not rely on *trust*.

The question is always: who to trust and for what kind of advice?

3.1   The 1976 Swine Flu Scare at Fort Dix

In February 1976, hundreds of soldiers at Fort Dix, NJ, contracted a new strain of the H1N1 virus (swine flu). President Ford met with a panel of experts and appeared on TV saying "we cannot afford to take a chance with the health of our nation," announcing an immediate $135 million congressional appropriation "for the production of sufficient vaccine to inoculate every man, woman and child in the United States." A vaccine was fast-tracked past the usual clinical trials, and celebrities, including the president, lined up to get jabbed (Abeysinghe, 2015). As it turned out, the H1N1 strain never made it out of Fort Dix, where only one Army recruit died. But of the 45 million vaccinated, an estimated 450 people developed the paralysing Guillain-Barré Syndrome and more than 30 died, and the government suspended its mass vaccination effort in December.

3.2   Whooping Cough Vaccine Scare in the UK, 1977

In the early 1970s, the whooping cough vaccine was producing some unpleasant but harmless side effects. In 1977, the *Lancet* published an article by Gordon Stewart (1977) suggesting that the risks of this vaccine outweighed the benefits and media coverage led to the coverage rate falling from about 75% to 40%.

Controversy raged in medical press until 1981 and public confidence gradually recovered, coverage reaching 90% by 1992.

During this period there were no active anti-vaccination groups, which only appeared during the late 1980s and the 1990s. In both the above cases, vaccine hesitancy would have been a manifestation of rational scepticism.

3.3 MMR Vaccine Scare in the UK, 1998

In 1998, the *Lancet* published a paper by Andrew Wakefield (1998) claiming that the MMR vaccine – a combination of measles, mumps and rubella vaccines – caused autism and colitis. The claim was completely fraudulent, but it was only in 2010 that the *Lancet* fully retracted the paper and Wakefield was struck off the Medical Register. Epidemiological research conclusively ruled out the claimed association, but the claim was widely reported in the media internationally, and the belief that MMR vaccination can cause autism persists to this day (2015). MMR vaccination rates in the UK dropped from 92% in 1996 to 84% in 2002, as low as 61% in parts of London, and has still not recovered to the 1996 level. By 2006, the incidence of mumps was 37 times higher than 1996 levels, and in 2008 measles was once again declared endemic in the UK, and there were consequent outbreaks in other countries.

In these latter two cases it was the most trusted medical journal in the world which started the scare, but it proved extremely difficult to put the genie back in the bottle.

3.4 Polio Vaccine Boycott in Nigeria, 2003

Between August 2003 and July 2004, there was a boycott of polio vaccinations in five northern states of Nigeria initiated by Muslim leaders who claimed that western powers "deliberately adulterated the oral polio vaccines with anti-fertility drugs and...viruses which are known to cause HIV and AIDS," (Jegede, 2007). In the context of the US invasion of Iraq, a recent case of Nigerian children being used as guinea pigs by Pfizer, and earlier similar claims about vaccination and medical research in Africa, the people were inclined to believe these claims by their religious leaders (see Jegede, 2007). All efforts by the government to verify the purity of the vaccine were rejected and despite the spread of polio and the lack of any evidence of contamination, the boycott continued. The impasse was eventually resolved in July 2004 through dialogue between the religious leaders and the health authorities. In the meantime, polio had infected 1,434 people in Asia, 1,133 in Africa and 25 in Europe before the outbreak was stemmed.

The issue of trust in the pharmaceutical companies providing the vaccine and the health authorities administering it was legitimate. This was combined with the greater trust in religious authorities who unfortunately misused that trust. The religious leaders evidently underestimated the dangers of not vaccinating and acted precipitously in publicising their suspicions. It was these same religious leaders, however, who were able to quell the panic.

3.5 H1N1 Vaccine Dispute in Europe, 2009

In December 2009, Council of Europe parliamentarian and epidemiologist Wolfgang Wodarg presented a recommendation to the Council of Europe entitled 'Faked Pandemics: A Threat to Public Health' claiming that the WHO had over-reacted to the threat of the H1N1 virus in effectively obliging governments to institute mass vaccination programs in readiness for a possible pandemic. After months of debate, the Council of Europe passed a motion decrying WHO's public reaction to H1N1 (see Abeysinghe, 2015). In the event, Britain, which did implement a mass vaccination program, had more cases of infection than Poland, which did not. So subsequent experience tended to confirm that the Council of Europe had been correct. Scientists judged that a pandemic had not developed, there were questions over the efficacy and safety of the H1N1 vaccine and the threat was not serious enough to warrant mass vaccination, which carries its own risks. The anti-vaccination voice proved to be the most worthy of trust in this case, even if one allows that WHO may have legitimately erred on the side of caution. The discrediting of H1N1 vaccination in this instance may have tainted the reputation of vaccination and health authorities in general.

Abeysinghe, who is a discourse theorist, makes the point that decisions on vaccination cannot sensibly be understood as individual decisions. The Council of Europe and *Lancet* are not simply 'sources of information' on which an individual can draw. An individual is a participant or not in a discourse prior to the reception of an argument framed within that discourse, and will accept or reject the argument accordingly. Who to trust? is not a question which can be answered from outside the discourse in which advice is framed. In Abeysinghe's terms, it is always decided *within a discourse*. I understand that a 'discourse' is the linguist's name for a 'project'.

Consider the case of asbestos (Beaton and Blunden, 2014). The entire medical science establishment world-wide, the regulating authorities, unions and media were nobbled for 60 years after the Australian industry, at least, had become convinced that it was killing people and took legal action to defend itself from claims for compensation in 1939. A collaboration between a US medical scientist, a trade union, a legal firm and an ABC journalist eventually brought the issue to public attention and forced the government to take action. Asbestos was banned in Australia in 2003, but it is still used in most countries to this day. And there are great many instances of the corruption of science and public health authorities by capital (see Bell, 1992; Epstein, 1996). No one who was alive in the 1960s can fail to remember the impact of Thalidomide – a medication recommended for pregnant women that produced thousands of terrible deformations, or the bare-faced lying of the tobacco companies who swore that cigarettes promoted health. Who to trust? is not a question which can be answered from outside the networks of trust built around the shared pursuit of common life-goals. It is always decided *within* whatever frame originally produced a person's perception of the safety of medical treatments, be that a religious, scientific, political or cultural discourse.

3.6   *Persuasion and Decision-Making*

In Australia, the average vaccination rate at five years old is 91.5% (NHPA 2014). This leaves 75,000 children vulnerable, with 15,000 of them registering a conscientious objection, distributed across the country. The three postcodes with lowest vaccination rates at 5-y-o are:

- 2481 Byron Bay, NSW North Coast 66.7%
- 2483 Brunswick Heads, NSW North Coast 70.2%
- 2000 Sydney, NSW CBD 72.1%

These areas are well-known for having significant sections of the population which can be described as well-educated, favouring 'alternative' life-styles and distrustful of authorities, squarely fitting the profile of 'rationalised hesitancy'. Areas with the highest numbers of children registering with a 'conscientious objection' (which was possible before 2015) were: North Coast (NSW), Greater Metro South Brisbane, Metro North Brisbane, Sunshine Coast and Gold Coast (Qld), emphasising the same demographic.

The highest rates of vaccination are in far north Queensland, exposed to transmission of diseases across the Torres Strait. In Indigenous communities, rural areas, immigrant and working class suburbs, the 5-y-o vaccination rate is nowhere under 90%. So it is clear that the problem with vaccination levels is with the 'rationalised hesitancy' of the SE quadrant, whether or not living in the 'life-style' postcodes. On the whole, in Australia, working class, immigrant and indigenous communities trust the medical authorities.

So in a modern country like Australia, the analysis offered by the VH compass seems to fit. The types of people described in the low-trust half of the compass are well-known characters. A finer analysis would be required, however, to bring out the influence of place reflected in the marked 'local vaccination cultures' indicated by the postcode data.

On the other hand, the dramatic collapse in immunisation experienced in Nigeria reflected modernity inversely in that Muslim people trusted their religious leaders more than the government in the Christian South, while the Muslim leaders in turn had good reason to distrust the American pharmaceutical companies (*Lancet*, 2014).

In the UK, one could say that the public's loss of confidence in the whooping cough vaccine was a rational reflection of the state of scientific knowledge in the 1970s. But whereas authorities could restore confidence in a vaccine in 1992, a few years later they proved unable to do so, even when confidence had been shaken by a clear fraud rather than by doubt in genuine science.

Modernity has fostered certain social attitudes which colour public health problems in a distinctive way, but the strongly localised concentration of refusal of vaccination suggests that the problem is not one of attitudes and personality types, but that individual responses to modernity are *socially constructed* in definite networks through which attitudes to sources of advice are formed.

Statistical research (Blume, 2006) has shown that being critical of vaccination is correlated with preference for natural childbirth and the use of alternative therapies such as acupuncture, homeopathy and naturopathy. This, combined with correlation with living in the 'life-style' areas or the inner-city neighbourhoods of the major capitals confirms that vaccine hesitancy is part of a *wider* attitude to health.

Giddens and Beck have given us a plausible description of the social conditions which have fostered distrust of experts and individual 'entrepreneurship' – high levels of education, industrial practices with potential for catastrophic impact, ubiquitous media reporting, neoliberal economic policies, the rise of service industries, extreme concentration of wealth, widespread radicalism amongst the middle-classes, etc. However, if anti-vaccination views are taken to passively reflect the conditions of modernity, how could we *change* this situation? Short of a social revolution, these social conditions will continue, and so presumably will the attitudes characteristic of these conditions. However, the 'life politics' of 'reflexive modernity' is not a spontaneous response to modern social conditions but a product of projects which have arisen from modern conditions and together *produced* modernity as we know it.

None of the archetypes represented in the VH compass are actually entirely rational stances, including the 'balanced position' at the centre-point. The WHO, the *Lancet*, the Council of Europe – all paragons of rational decision-making – are also subjects that could be mapped on to the compass. There is no dimension on the compass measuring the *real* level of expertise of the subjects, all of whom are taken to be laypeople, or the *real* efficacy of the relevant treatment. This reduction of the problem to an objective process, a stimulus → response process, leaves no room for a genuinely reflective, human response to real problems. In such a view, 'reflexive modernity' simply reproduces itself like a virus. If we are going to characterise subjects according to dimensions, is it believable that there are only *two* dimensions? For example, isn't trust specific to *who* is trusted – religious leaders, passers-by, neighbours, scientists, pharmaceutical companies, the media, politicians? And is 'entrepreneurship' really so thoroughly individualised, or do some people still seek to control the events affecting their lives collectively, maybe not through governments, but possibly with trade unions, self-help groups, political parties, church groups, and so on? In any case, one and the same person would occupy different positions on the compass in respect to particular vaccines. Rational scepticism discriminates according to the severity of the infection, the efficacy of the treatment and its safety.

As valuable as the insights of 'reflexive modernity' may be, we are still left with a picture of an individual making rational decisions on a background of given social conditions and policy makers have no clue as to how to deal with rationalised hesitancy. Asking sceptics to 'listen to reason' has not worked so far, and legal sanctions will not work either.

Rather than taking the rational hesitancy of a section of the population as an individual response based on personality, we need to know *how* parents actually acquire their opinion of a vaccine, and *how* and *why* the population's trust in the scientific and medical establishments was lost, in order to know if and how it can be restored, while continuing to see to it that scientific, regulatory, corporate, media and political figures act in a way which is worthy of trust and subjecting them to effective oversight.

Stuart Blume (2006) examined the proposition that vaccine hesitancy could be explained as the product of an anti-vaccination social movement. He has assessed data on how parents have formed their attitudes to vaccines, and examined the contribution which the medical profession have made to this loss of trust. The history of earlier health activism such as Women's Health Movement (Nichols, 1999) and the HIV/AIDS movement (Power, 2014) and the Asbestos Campaign (Beaton and Blunden, 2014) make it clear that relations between the medical establishment and the population is actively produced and not a passive, individual reflection of social conditions.

In order to cut through some difficulties of terminology, I will first introduce the concept of 'collaborative project'.

3.7 *Collaborative Projects*

Rather than taking as units of analysis individuals and the discourses or social groups to which they belong, I propose 'collaborative projects', or just 'projects' for short. A project is an aggregate of actions that share a common object, so it is made up of actions not individual people. Individuals participate in various projects through their actions, and their consciousness will vary according to the different action settings and their position in a given project, as a novice or old-timer, more or less committed, etc. Social formations can be seen as bundles of such projects, interacting with one another in changing ways, and changing as the projects themselves develop.

Projects begin as a social stratum that shares some aspect of their social position, but have no collective self-consciousness. As a result of some problem or opportunity that arises for this social position someone launches a project to resolve the problem and others then join that project. That is, you do not just have a lot of people all reacting to their situation in the same way – people collectively commit to a proposed solution. The project begins with some object but in the course of time and the difficulties which arise, that object develops, becomes more concrete and may be subject to radical revision in the light of experience. The project thus takes the form of an evolving social movement, in which there is a shared ideal which usually gives its name to the movement. Around that ideal, a whole 'theory of the world', an ethos and self-consciousness – a discourse – develops. Projects are limited in time as a social movement. They either pass away, or to the extent that are successful in objectifying their ideal, they become institutionalised – their ideal is incorporated in the customs and laws of the community, albeit in a truncated or compromised form. Nation states, religious movements, capitalist enterprises, political parties, sciences, pressure groups and fashion trends – these can all be seen as projects. The world we live in is the product of past projects and the projects of today are shaping the world of the future. The world is a work in progress, we are building the 'plane as we are flying it.

A collaborative project is needed, probably like the HIV/AIDS campaign (see Power, 2014), involving medical professionals and public health officials collaborating with stakeholders in the 'wellness industry', complementary medicine practitioners and leaders in life-style communities to restore trust in vaccines and the people who provide them.

Participation in a project means collaborating with others, and collaboration is governed by norms specific to that project. These norms constitute the fundamental ethical substance of the whole movement. Unlike the assumptions of the rational actor theory which underpins bourgeois economic science, projects are therefore not idealised, but realistic and *normative* for the participants themselves. Because projects of the past underlie the concepts found in a culture and projects of the present provide the motivation for action, analysis by projects not only gives insight into dynamics of a social formation, it also gives insight into the psychology of the individuals.

The conditions which give rise to a project are objective in the sense that they arise from contradictions implicit in a society at a given historical moment. These conditions do not depend on the consciousness of individuals but are objectively given. However, where a person is placed in some kind of predicament by these conditions they are going find a resolution and, finding that others share their predicament, they will collaborate. The project which arises in this way is subjective in the sense that it expresses the standpoint and will of people who have joined together to act in collaboration. Learning takes place collectively in the context of experiencing the reaction to their own collaborative activity. Medical science is a project, and in the context of its interaction with the world it generates and enforces its norms. Individuals within that project are of course also participants in other projects. As a result, the norms which enforce fidelity to scientific practices are under constant pressure from other motivations acting on individual scientists. But on the whole, institutions of this kind develop and learn over time. Corruption comes and goes. Thus the relations which gave birth to the project are reshaped by it; a new objective alignment of relations is the result. Social change is thus viewed as a subjective reaction to an objective situation. The state of affairs at any given moment is conceived of as a process, arising out of objective contradictions.

Even institutions which have become a settled and accepted part of a society remain projects with an object, and a corresponding worldview and norms of collaboration, which underpin not only forms of collaboration, but hierarchy, division of labour, material rewards, training and motivation. Contradictions can arise within projects precisely because they are normative. Such contradictions can have the effect of revitalising a formation that may have had the appearance of a fossilised structure. In response, an institution it can regain properties of a social movement.

Before reflecting on the history of medical science in general, vaccination in particular and how attitudes and practices have been shaped, a couple of observations about a project whose historical development is more well known may be helpful.

One could say that modernity inherited from the past the practices of gender discrimination which provoked the women's movement. One could also say that modern social conditions fostered the emergence of the Women's Liberation Movement in that it provided opportunities which were not previously present and threw light on certain contradictions. It would be untenable, however, to say that the resultant relative equality that women now have in westernised countries (such as equality before the law, the vote, right to own property, etc.) is a 'product of modernity'. No! Women fought for these things and what is more, certain gains, such as equal pay, are still incomplete and constantly in jeopardy and still have to be fought for. And this is an important, practical distinction. Even an institutionalised project, which the Women's Movement now is, is never simply a 'structure' but remains a project at a certain stage in its lifecycle, with its object, its rationality, its ethics and its identity. On the other hand, the ubiquitous fragmentation of social relations characteristic of modernity is probably not a condition anyone ever fought for. It is largely collateral damage pursuant to neoliberal capital accumulation.

Both the trust and the lack of trust in the medical establishment and the popular interest in assessing the evidence for oneself are not simply aspects of the structure of modernity, but the *products* of projects which continue to this day, and which have the capacity to overcome the distrust and harness the interest in science beneficially.

3.8   *The Origins of Vaccine Scepticism*

Blume (2006) says that anti-vaccination social movements first appeared in the 19th century when compulsory mass vaccination programs were first introduced in Europe and America. These movements were generally led by the promoters of alternative therapies whose projects were threatened by mass immunisation. They found allies in both the working class and middle class because of the compulsory aspect of the vaccination programs. Compulsory vaccination was a challenge to the workers' movement, because after the failure of Chartism in 1848, until the successful turn to parliamentary representation in the 1890s, the project of the workers' movement was *independence* from state regulation, welfare and philanthropy. The project of the liberal middle class, on the other hand, was the extension of personal liberty. Without a history of the success of mass vaccination, the procedure did look risky, and there were plenty of adverse outcomes to fuel antipathy to vaccination.

However, with the progress of medicine and the manifest success of public health measures overall, the rhetoric of the snake oil salesmen sounded less convincing while the frequency of adverse outcomes declined. At the same time, Social Democracy began to deliver real benefits to the working class mediated by the welfare state. Independence from the State was no longer a project of organised labour. The anti-vaccination movement disappeared in the first decade of the 20th century and science-based medicine and mass vaccination was generally accepted and welcomed until the 1980s.

Because of this hegemony, the medical establishment suffered from a measure of hubris. Critics of medical science began to appear in the 1960s, such as Critical Psychology which began among psychology students and other critical trends within psychology (Teo, 2012). The natural childbirth movement also emerged *within* the medical profession, and the Women's Health movement of the 1970s involved both medical professionals and patients demanding women have a say in how they were treated (Nichols, 1999), followed by the HIV/AIDS Movement in the 1980s. The AIDS activists (Epstein, 1996) objected to terminally ill people being given placebos in clinical trials, and demonstrated that research could be far more effective if people with AIDS were included as *collaborators* rather than objects of research, and that gay men, drug users and prostitutes were better placed to design and implement public health programs than public authorities. In the US, medical institutions were dragged kicking and screaming into collaboration with their clients. In Australia, the Women's Health Movement had already prepared the ground, and the government of the time initiated what proved to be a successful collaboration along the lines suggested here (Power, 2014).

A rising tide of voices objected to the abuse of research subjects, the marketing of drugs which later proved to be toxic, the corruption of GPs and researchers by drug companies, and dangerous and unethical research practices by the US military. Modern conditions contributed positively to the formation of these opposition projects and the scientific and medical institutions failed to rein in their hubris before these voices were raised. Among the critical voices were a number of anti-vaccination groups, which first appeared in the late-1980s, after the decline of the 'new social movements' and in the wake of the AIDS controversy and the whooping cough scare.

According to Blume, these anti-vaccination groups are predominantly self-help groups of people who have become anti-vaccinationist as a result of adverse experiences that they (rightly or wrongly) associate with vaccination. Their message is promoted over the internet and is easily accessible for anyone who goes looking for them. Only a minuscule proportion of the population would have contact with an anti-vaccination group by any other means, far fewer than the number who exhibit vaccine hesitancy. How many parents actually make their decisions about having their children vaccinated by consulting internet sources? According to Blume (2006), only 2% of parents consult the internet in making their vaccination decision, and only a proportion of these would even have read an anti-vaccination website, let alone trusted it, although this figure probably would be larger nowadays. Only a minuscule proportion of the population would have direct contact with an anti-vaccination group, insufficient to explain the extent of vaccine hesitancy. So vaccine hesitancy is *not* the product of scaremongering by anti-vaccinationists. These groups do indeed propagate misinformation, but according to Blume's (2006) research, their influence is negligible. They are more a *manifestation* than a *cause* of widespread vaccine hesitancy.

The most dramatic collapses of trust in the safety of specific vaccines have occurred in direct response to doubts raised *within medical research itself*. But parents did not get this information by reading the *Lancet*. They received the information mainly through conversations with friends, family and neighbours. A survey showed that 75% of parents who had made a decision on vaccination had had at least one discussion on its advisability with the relevant health professional and 85% had read the literature provided, but 16% felt they needed more information. For the majority it was the information they received from *trusted peers* which was most decisive in forming their opinion. Moreover, the proportion of parents distrusting the information from health authorities is growing. This group is strongly correlated with people using 'alternative' therapies. However, Blume finds that active criticism of vaccination by advocates of alternative therapies is also insufficient to explain the decline in vaccination rates, although such views are finding increased resonance among the population at large.

So the question is: why are increasing numbers of people open to arguments that the medical establishment should not be trusted and accepting advice which contradicts the scientific consensus, even while the days of unchecked marketing of drugs like Thalidomide or practices like shoe shops using X-ray machines, are long gone?

> Most of the parents with whom they spoke, explain these authors, see vaccination as a dilemma for which there is no clear solution. Starting from their own individual perceptions of risk they try to make an optimal, vaccine-by-vaccine choice: decisions for which they are willing to assume responsibility.
> BLUME, 2006, p. 635

One bad experience can sow the seeds of doubt, but this would not be enough on its own for a parent to reject the advice of their doctor. Given that publishing by vaccine sceptics and alternative therapists is not in itself sufficient to explain the extent of vaccine hesitancy and its growth, it seems that it is when parents consult their trusted friends, neighbours and family that doubts become consolidated. Even someone who trusts vaccines may be unwilling to vouch for them for a friend.

Blume claims that the best predictor of vaccine hesitancy is "a general commitment to holistic ideas about health (and to natural child birth and breast feeding) and the importance of life style and environment for a child's well-being."

Information about vaccination from the media, friends and neighbours, alternative health practitioners and health professionals will be framed by this pre-existing view. Most influential in developing this 'holistic' view of medical issues are friends and neighbours, not professionals of any kind. *Local* vaccination cultures form because it is through friends-and-neighbours networks that antivaccinationism is propagated, as an incidental part of interest in 'holistic medicine'. Generally speaking, the original source of a vaccine scare is *genuinely authoritative*, but it is hearing it from a trusted source which is decisive for its acceptance.

Blume claims that the antivaccination movement is not aiming to create or defend a shared identity nor threatening mass mobilisation to defend the interests of any social strata, but according to some theorists, "what binds social movement organisations together is their collective attempt at building an 'oppositional culture' … in a shared project" and it is this conception of a social movement which best describes antivaccinationism. I don't agree that the holistic medicine movement is lacking in an element of identity formation, though perhaps not to the extent that identity formation is central to movements like those representing denigrated groups in a society. *All* projects have an element of identity formation.

Vaccine hesitancy is not the product of an antivaccination social movement as such, but the by-product of a movement *for holistic health*. Science is a hegemonic ideal. Some of the wackiest strands of alternative medicine still *claim* scientific status, even if without basis. In itself, an holistic health movement ought not to be a danger to public health. But because it arose as a critique of institutionalised scientific medicine, holistic medicine is saddled with a fatal contradiction – it excludes the only party capable of producing a genuinely holistic theory of well-being: scientific medicine.

Both the holistic medicine movement and the public health institutions should recognise that they are in the same position as the HIV/AIDS Movement and the medical science establishment was in the mid-1980s – being treated as an irrational pariah by those with whom they needed to collaborate. Instead of treating antivaccinationism as an irrational curse, the medical establishment needs to enter into a collaborative relationship with antivaccinationism as part of a scientific holistic medicine movement, involving activists in clinical trials, inviting consultation over vaccination programs. Critics have to be invited into the tent. This was the outcome of both the Women's Health movement and the HIV/AIDS movement, and in many different contexts, corporations have been dragged into collaborative relationships with their critics, and have ultimately proved invaluable.

Nowadays, people want to make decisions about their own health and that of their children 'for themselves'. In fact such a decision is possible only by weighing up conflicting sources according to the trustworthiness of the original sources of the information. The sources of information themselves – whether neighbours or professionals – and assessment of those sources, is constructed through participation in collaborative projects and generally speaking you trust a collaborator before someone you have never collaborated with. If your doctor has only ever issued instructions, then you are unlikely to trust them. For many people the only collaborative relations they have are with family, colleagues, friends and neighbours.

The brochures provided by the health system supporting vaccination make no pretence at helping you make your *own* decision. They are transparently aimed at *persuading* you to comply.

The medical establishment is part of the problem and the holistic health movement is part of the solution. Only by these two projects collaborating can scientific medicine become genuinely holistic and the holistic health movement become genuinely scientific. 'Science' can be subjected to stereotyping. Most people are unaware that the positivist, narrow and dogmatic style of analytical science and medicine is only *one style* of doing science. Science is, in essence, holistic and collaborative. But science also relies on trust. Science needs to be able to trust its sources, and the elaborate procedures by means of which science verifies its sources is the most essential part of the scientific project. There is no scientific concept which stands up if separated from the narrative about how it was created.

You cannot claim to be holistic if you exclude the most significant source of experience, the scientific establishment. Medical experts have to be *engaged* and drawn into collaboration. People become doctors, public health officials or nurses, because they want a career in promoting health. The departmentalisation of all the relevant institutions militates against a holistic approach, but medicine is in essence holistic. In collaboration with non-experts who insist on taking the idea of holistic medicine seriously, these structural problems can be overcome. Realistically, it probably means forming an alliance with *a section of* the medical establishment, in order to achieve the necessary transformation of the health system. But for this to be possible, the holistic health movement would itself be transformed.

4   Conclusion

The vaccine hesitancy arising from the growing distrust of institutionalised medicine is a serious problem. If it continues to grow, we will eventually learn our lessons in the wake of a global pandemic. Public health authorities must take the holistic health movement seriously and engage them in finding practical solutions in collaboration with the medical profession. 'Representatives' of the holistic health movement are not easily identifiable, but people who may be influential in localities where there is an antivaccination culture, could be engaged in formal deliberative dialogue, not to persuade but to explore solutions. The grievances have to be seriously engaged collectively and not treated as the mistaken opinions of individuals.

5 Postscript 2020

How much this terrain has changed in the five years since an abridged version of this article was published in 2015! Compliance with childhood vaccination regulations has improved to 95% and the seasonal flu vaccine has been accessed by more than 50% of the population, whilst antivaxxers have come to be widely seen as dangerous, albeit marginal, misanthropes and attract the attention of the police. But the wider field, generally characterised as 'conspiracy theorists', has expanded enormously, even in Australia, where the 'First Lady' is a close friend of the leader of the local wing of QAnon and the wackiest conspiracy theories are sometimes promoted from government benches.

The source of this moral pandemic is the United States and its provocateur-in-chief, Donald Trump. If the reader has gained anything from the above article it must have been that *trust is gold*. The only way of restoring trust where it has been destroyed is to 'reach across the aisle' and collaborate to find solutions. Trump himself is beyond any such project of course, and probably the entire leadership of the Republican Party, which has enabled Trump's madness through their own cowardice and complicity. But at 'ground level' there remain surely common projects from defending public schools to restoring normality on the streets of decimated cities where collaboration is both sorely needed and surely possible.

At the time of writing (August 2020), there is no vaccine which has undergone the normal trials and approval processes. Ironically, it is government leaders (Trump, Putin, Bolsonaro) who are promoting the use of unsafe treatments from injecting bleach to hydroxychloroquine and untested vaccines, and the same leaders are spokesmen for anti-science conspiracy theories. This in turn places the medical science establishment and those who take science seriously in the role of sceptics. How ironic! But it was the same with the whole multicultural movement which advocated for cultural and ethical relativism against a conservative establishment – this relativism is now the ideological weapon of white supremacists who claim the victim role and an entitlement to 'alternative facts'. The idea of 'healthism' mentioned above is now coopted by evangelical advocates of injecting bleach. At the same time, it should be recognised that not all conspiracy theories are equal. Some, like QAnon, are vehicles for racism and anti-Semitism, others, like the 5G conspiracy, are terribly misguided but progressive in their intent. Clearly, this is a phase of cultural development beyond the terrain characterised as 'reflexive modernity'. The barbarians are inside the gates.

CHAPTER 15

Something Worth Dying For?

Perhaps the most challenging thing about the foreign fighters – those people who disappear from their suburban homes and reappear on Facebook in Syria or Iraq carrying a grenade launcher or wearing a suicide jacket – is that they evidently have something they think is worth dying for. Probably most of us would lay down our lives for our immediate family. Beyond that, Anzac Day parades and endless military posturing by political leaders notwithstanding, it is difficult to imagine most people in this country genuinely willing to put their life on the line for Democracy, Australia, Socialism, the Liberal Party, Jesus or anything else. Not that people wouldn't fight like hell to hang on to what they have, but willing to put their life on the line for an *idea*?

A society which cannot give its young people an idea worth dying for is what is really shocking. Evidently finding nothing here which they find worth sacrificing their life for, they embrace a cause which seems to have little merit. The suicide bomber may be misguided, but doesn't *finding something worth dying for*, indicate *having found something worth living for*?

I will briefly review the rise of foreign fighters before analysing this phenomenon through the lens of the concept of 'collaborative projects'.

1   Foreign fighters

A *foreign fighter* is someone who participates in an insurgency but has neither citizenship nor kinship links in the war zone and has travelled from afar as a private citizen to fight as an unpaid volunteer. Foreign fighters are quite distinct from both *terrorists* who carry out violent acts outside of any war zone and those who travel overseas to attend a terrorist training camp. Foreign fighters are engaged in conventional warfare.

Before you can become a foreign fighter, someone has to be waging an insurgency that you can join. I will deal with the 'demand side' of foreign fighting first, chiefly relying on the work of Thomas Hegghammer (2011) who has provided the most well-founded and convincing narrative for this issue. I will then turn to the 'supply side', where I will draw on a variety of sources, but with particular critical attention to the theoretical framework and empirical work of Scott Atran (2014) as I reflect on the relevant methodological questions.

1.1 Islamism and the Duty of the Individual Muslim

The Muslim Brotherhood was launched at a meeting on the Suez Canal construction site in 1928 with the aim of ridding Egypt of foreign influence and exploitation and instituting a life-style and government in line with Muslim principles. Their project was not directed against the West as such, but rather against their own corrupt government, although the Brotherhood did later send 10,000 volunteers to fight the Zionist occupation in 1948. The Islamist project at this point, and still largely today (2015), was a domestic project aimed at bringing their own country to an Islamic way of life.

The Brotherhood supported Nasser's secular nationalist revolution in Egypt in 1952, but they were suppressed in 1954 after being implicated in an assassination attempt on Nasser. This was followed in 1958 by their suppression in Syria and Iraq. Those Brothers who escaped prison went into exile to be followed by thousands of imprisoned Brothers released by Anwar Sadat in 1971. These well-educated and highly motivated leaders of the Brotherhood were now stateless and without hope of participation in the political life of their homeland.

Meanwhile the Wahhabi aristocracy in Saudi Arabia were amassing great wealth from their oil revenue and set about building a nation-state on the Arabian Peninsula, and the flood of capital following the Oil Embargo in 1973 created unprecedented opportunities. The Saudis made the creation of an education system a priority and set up a university district in the Hijaz region on the Red Sea coast. All the positions in these universities were filled by exiled Muslim Brothers, who also took up positions in a range of International Islamic Organisations whose mission was purely philanthropic – equivalent to the Red Cross, Oxfam, etc., on the Western side – to spread the benefits (and influence) of the oil wealth across the Muslim world. The Wahhabis did not interfere in the Brothers' activity and every year the Hajj brought Muslims from all over the world to nearby Mecca. With their positions in the charities and the universities, the former Muslim Brothers found themselves at the centre of a well-funded international Muslim network.

The Muslim Brotherhood's project had emerged as a social movement aiming to restore *their own* societies to a religious life. This largely peaceful project had been thwarted by secular nationalist movements which had come to power in their homeland, leaving them no prospect of fulfilling their project as they had initially envisioned it. At the same time they were presented with an opportunity to agitate for their religious ideals on the *international* stage through education and philanthropy. When a project is thwarted, the subject is faced with the necessity of reframing their conception of the object, and re-orienting to a new activity which *sublates* the former object in a new project, like an adventurer who is crippled in an accident and goes on to become a Paralympic athlete. (See Vasilyuk, 1984 and Chapter 10, this volume.)

An important arm of this philanthropic work was providing relief for refugees, initially Palestinian refugees expelled from their homeland by Zionism, and then Afghan refugees fleeing the 1979 Soviet invasion. This included a major refuge located at Peshawar, near the Afghan border in Pakistan. The international Muslim organisations saturated Muslim communities all over the world with well-produced images of women and children bearing the scars of war and desperately in need of aid.

Until the mid-1980s there was no military component to these activities. The key individual in bringing about the change was the Abdallah Azzam, a stateless Palestinian preacher who had been displaced from Palestine and later from Jordan, and taken in and given employment by the Brothers who arrived in Peshawar in 1986. Azzam was particularly well connected as a result of his time in Hijaz, and he was also a substantial Muslim scholar.

Under Islamic law as it was understood throughout the twentieth century, it would be a sin for an individual Muslim to go to fight in a foreign war. While Islam did entail an obligation upon Muslims to come to the aid of fellow Muslims under attack from a non-Muslim country, it was a *collective* obligation, placed upon Muslim communities as a whole. Before an individual could leave the country to participate in a war, he would have to gain the permission of his parents, his creditors and the political authority in his own country. Not only was there no obligation on an *individual* Muslim to go and fight in another country, it was forbidden, and to encourage such actions was a direct affront to the authority of a Muslim community over its own members, contrary to the strong communitarian ethos of Islam.

Individuals volunteering in foreign wars has been a rare phenomenon in the past. The nearest equivalents are (1) the members of the International Brigade and other labour movement groups who went to Spain to fight Franco in the 1930s – but these individuals were members of national sections of international communist organisations, and identified with the Republican cause as their own – and (2) the Jews who went to the aid of the Zionist occupation in 1948, who were organised by the Jewish Agency and identified with the Jewish settlers as fellow members of a Jewish nation. In both these cases there was a deeply felt identification with a transnational quasi-state entity which mobilised for war.

During the 1980s, Muslims were suffering severely under attack from non-Muslims – the massacres by the Phalange in Lebanon, the Israeli incursions and the Soviet occupation of Afghanistan, plus the genocide of Muslims in Bosnia in the early '90s. The representation of Muslims as victims of aggression by

Muslim media was broadly reinforced by the mainstream non-Muslim media in Western countries. A young Muslim would have had the tacit approval of their own community to go and fight alongside fellow-Muslims, but national governments were *not* consenting to such actions, despite the fact that even in predominantly Christian countries the Muslims were widely seen as the innocent victims in these conflicts.

Nation states had never done much for Abdallah Azzam, and nor did the ancient scriptures have anything to say about nation-states, which were an invention of modern times. But Azzam was a scholar and there was considerable weight in his argument that individual Muslims had not only a right, but a *duty* to come to the aid of fellow Muslims under attack from non-Muslims and that they were under no obligation to seek permission of the political authority in their home country.

Islam is a religion embedded in the religious structures of Muslim communities and there is nothing in the religion which speaks of rights or duties of the individual which transcend the authority of local religious leaders. Islam no more allowed for individual jihadis than it licensed hedonism. The appeal to the *individual conscience* over the heads of the religious and political authorities governing the individual was a truly postmodern innovation in Islamic doctrine. But under the conditions of destruction of Muslim states and genocide at the hands of non-Muslim states and the rule of often-corrupt secular-nationalist regimes in the Muslim world, Azzam's doctrine had a strong appeal.

So, the foreign fighter movement grew out of a philanthropic religious movement. Propaganda depicting the plight of Muslim refugees and victims of war which had mobilised Muslims across the world to come to the (nonviolent) aid of fellow Muslims naturally led on to the mobilisation of Egyptian and Syrian Muslim revolutionaries to Peshawar to meet up with the Afghani Mujahideen and go on to fight alongside them. Foreign fighters initially mobilised in the Afghan War continued as the military leadership of a social movement able to intervene in insurgencies in any Muslim land.

1.2 *Who Is Fighting?*

Muslim revolutionaries in predominantly Muslim regions are focused on overthrowing governments in their own territory not on travelling to foreign theatres of war. However, the exile of many of these revolutionaries before their insurgencies became permanent conflicts provided dedicated fighters for the first wave of foreign fighters, and in turn sustained the social movement into the future. Muslim revolutionaries had never previously invited foreign fighters to join them, but they arrived and were put to suitable work, usually as suicide bombers (70% of suicide bombers are foreign fighters), particularly ruthless fighters (foreigners are free from reprisals against their family, and free of the inhibitions that local fighters may have), or in menial tasks. As foreigners they are dependent on whatever group they have joined.

Terrorists, such as Al Qaïda, are a completely different current of ideology. Their attacks are directed against governments and populations in countries where Muslims are in a minority, where there is no prospect of achieving the Muslim regime which Muslim revolutionaries and foreign fighters aim for. Al Qaïda arose out of foreign fighters who had come to Afghanistan to fight the Soviets, but when that battle was over, reoriented from domestic politics to attacking the Western powers. The switch to global terrorism also meant a change in tactics, involving secret conspiracies and individual attacks on civilian populations. People who travel to terrorist training camps are potential terrorists, not foreign fighters. The questionable rationale for international terrorism is for the states being targeted to withdraw from the treasured lands in question, as was the case with the IRA bombings in Britain between 1972 and 1998 in support of a united Ireland.

Muslim revolutionaries and their foreign volunteers, on the other hand, have an Islamic state as their objective. Even when terror is used as a tactic, it has a rational objective – to deter collaboration with an occupying power such as in Iraq, or, like the terrorism of the Zionist Irgun in Palestine, to achieve ethnic cleansing. Here terrorism was subordinate to state-building.

At least 80% of foreign fighters come from Muslim states and often enjoy the active and warm support of their home communities, and have not been the target of overt repression at home.[1] This is not the case for terrorists, who kill people in their own communities just as much as they kill foreigners. There is cross-over between the two movements, and the distinction has become somewhat blurred, but *in their origin* both individually and as movements, the foreign fighter is distinct from the terrorist.

American research based on the memoirs of American soldiers in World War Two and interviews with Americans who fought in Vietnam has found that the principal motivation governing the actions of rank-and-file American soldiers were (1) to survive the war themselves and (2) to look after their immediate comrades-in-arms, believing their comrades likewise bound to them. Asked to characterise what 'democracy' meant to them, soldiers responded 'crap' and 'a joke'. The same soldiers described the selfless bravery of their Vietnamese opponents "because they believed in something" and "knew what

---

[1] The one country where the Arab Spring led to a liberal and secular government, Tunisia, is the largest contributor of foreign fighters.

they were fighting for" (cited in Atran et al., 2014). In keeping with these findings, American military theorists have designed their strategy and tactics on the basis that soldiers act according to their rational interest as individuals, just as they are assumed to act in bourgeois economic theory. The only explanation then for enemies whose soldiers fight with selfless courage and willingly sacrifice their lives is that they are 'brainwashed'. The same explanation is all the theorists of bourgeois society can offer for foreign fighters, who have no rational self-interest served by volunteering for a foreign war. They have been 'indoctrinated' by 'messages' received over the internet or by radical preachers at home. This mistaken view of the motivation of soldiers who are fighting for a cause was on show in the performance of the American-trained Iraqi Army, which fled on sight of their ISIS enemy, while the Kurdish, Shia and even Sunni militias defending their own land and families have proved stalwart against ISIS and in the opinion of this author will ultimately defeat them.[2] I should add however, that for some soldiers, generally elite career soldiers and not volunteer foreign fighters, there is a dedication to the warriors' craft which, in combination with comradeship, can motivate extreme sacrifice. In such cases the motivation arises from what Alasdair MacIntyre (1981) would call the 'internal good' inherent in the soldiers' profession. An established professional army ought to be able to count on its officer class; but if it is to have a rank and file which is prepared to put its life on the line, then something more than army pay and adventure is required.

This raises the question of the motivation of the foreign fighters and in what way they differ from the rank-and-file soldier of an imperialist army.

2 Who Wants to Be a Foreign Fighter?

The first thing to learn about the sociology of foreign fighters is that there are no demographic predictors for who will become a foreign fighter: not social class, education, religiosity, age nor even gender, except that foreign fighters usually volunteer as part of a group of friends and/or follow friends from their home town into service and/or are recruited by friends who have returned home from a conflict zone. This is reflected in that fact that, for example, Portsmouth, Cardiff, Brighton and certain parts of London account for most of Britain's foreign fighters, and almost all of Norway's 60 recruits came from

---

2 This is what transpired in May 2016 when a pincer operation by Kurdish Forces and the Popular Mobilisation Forces led by Qassem Soleimani (later assassinated by the US) recaptured Fallujah. The PMF united Shia and Shiite militias, each fighting under their own leaders.

the *same street* (Neumann, 2015). Hence the idea that people are persuaded to become foreign fighters through the social media is a myth. Overwhelmingly, people are convinced to become foreign fighters by people who were already personal friends before either became a foreign fighter. What social media does is assist foreign fighters in maintaining contact with home while they are away, and this works both ways. Different demographic groups play different roles when they join up, but (within limits) all are equally likely to volunteer.

Countermeasures on social media promoting democracy and exposing the supposed agents of Islamist indoctrination are a waste of time. On the other hand, images of the 'Shock and Awe' wreaked on Baghdad, a modern city in which people live in tower blocks just like in New York or London, must have had a powerful effect. Likewise, everyone knows about Guantanamo Bay where prisoners, many of them sold to US forces for a bounty and none of them convicted of any crime, are kept without recourse to any legal right. The criminal invasion of Iraq and the continued support for the Zionist occupation – these are all *objective facts*. Messages promoting democracy and criticising Muslim fighters are water off a duck's back for the brothers and sisters of Muslims suffering from these appalling, illegal, attacks on Muslim lands. Foreign fighters have been documented whose only knowledge of the conflict they went to join was from the same mass media everyone else was receiving.

How is it that people go, willing to sacrifice their lives, to a conflict apparently so far from their everyday concerns? Scott Atran (2014) conducted face-to-face surveys in a community in Morocco which had provided many foreign fighters, and in Lebanon amongst Shia, Sunni, and Christians. He tested subjects' attitudes, including their willingness to sacrifice themselves in war and their attitude towards others who do so. His research has the merit that he spoke to people who might or might not become foreign fighters but who were acquainted with the practice at first hand.

Atran's hypothesis is that the coincidence of two factors make for the readiness to become a foreign fighter and/or approve of others in the community who do so. These two factors are (1) 'identity fusion' with a larger group whose welfare may be threatened, and (2) holding a relevant 'sacred value'.

A *sacred value* is something that motivates a person's actions, but which transcends any immediate interest, such as King and Country or Socialism. A sacred value is something abstract and remote from the close personal ties which commonly motivate sacrifice of individual material interest. *Identity fusion* refers to a person whose identity is wholly subsumed by a collectivity, whether a nation or religious community or a family or group of close comrades. A subject's identity is fused with a group if the subject cannot see themselves apart from the relevant bonded identity group. According to Atran, the combination of these two factors is involved when the group to which a person's identity is fused is united by a sacred value, when we-all are fighting for the same ideal. Thus, a soldier who sees themself as an Australian, and has no ties to another country, is patriotic and takes Australia as a sacred value, may be prepared to die for their country, if it is genuinely threatened. (As mentioned above, an elite career soldier may be prepared to die in combat on a matter of honour.) Note that a person may have other ties and other sacred values, but in the event that there is a threat to the sacred value uniting the social group to which the person's identity is fused, then that person would be prepared to die defending the interests of that group, even if they are the last one standing.

A person may have a strong personal belief, but so long as that belief is *just personal*, and not an ideal shared by and constituting a community of others, serious mental illness aside, it cannot motivate extreme sacrifice. Many of this author's cohort who took up a cause in the 1960s/1970s as part of a mass movement would have been prepared to die for that cause, and many activists in the Civil Rights and Peace Movements in the US *did* die for their cause. But *now* that that flood has subsided, such a self-sacrifice would be meaningless. So, a transcendent ideal is not enough in itself. Further, a person may identify themself as a member of a social group, such as 'employees of BHP', but no one takes BHP as a sacred value, and they are generally not going to die for the Company.

Atran demonstrated empirically that a person whose identity is fused with a group bonded by a sacred value will be prepared to die in defence of that sacred cause. By 'sacred value' he meant an ideal which motivates action transcending immediate gain, but not necessarily life itself. Identity fusion comes in degrees from slight to total. This offers an explanation of the motive for social action up to and including sacrifice of one's life, and not limited to the scenario of ultimate sacrifice. This constitutes an alternative rationale for social action to the 'rational actor' theory which has proved so inadequate in understanding social movements for which self-sacrifice is a contradiction in terms.

2.1   *Collaborative Projects*

'Collaborative projects' are a unit of analysis which is particularly useful for understanding this phenomenon. Collaborative projects, or 'projects' for short, are entities which people join rather than launch themselves, in the overwhelming majority of cases. A project differs from a group. A group is a collection of people united by some attribute such as ethnicity or beliefs, but a project is an aggregate of actions directed towards the collaborative realisation of some ideal. All those entities which motivate actions which do not satisfy a person's immediate needs are projects. Going along on a project for the ride, so to speak, without any real commitment to the ideal, is something else.

The unity of sacred value and identity fusion is what I call a *collaborative project* (Blunden, 2014). All ideals within a community are constituted by collaborative projects, but the extent of a person's identity fusion with a project may be slight or absolute, and the project may belong to the past, or may be the chief fact of current social life (as when the country is at war). Likewise, all identity groups are constituted by this kind of transcendent ideal. 'Collaborative project' is therefore a unit of analysis for social formations which captures the identity and motivational structure of the community. It not only describes a social formation as it is, but also the pattern of change at work in the community. 'Collaborative project' is a powerful instrument of analysis, but it is also a crucial component of ethical life itself.

It is normal to be committed to collaborative projects and for at least one of those projects to be unified by a sacred value. Such a project I will call a *life-project* as it gives *meaning* to a person's life. Psychological pathology arises through (1) the blockage or destruction of a life-project, (2) a clash between two life-projects, (3) a crisis arising from the failure of a life-project or (4) the lack of any life-project, which is normal for a child but pathological for an adult (see Chapter 10, this volume).

From this standpoint, a substantial proportion of Australians who count as psychologically normal are in that infantile condition of *lacking* a life-project, and from this standpoint, the actions of the foreign fighter seem inexplicable if not insane. But if we accept that commitment to a life-project is psychologically normal and healthy, all that requires explanation is how a person comes to commit themselves to this particular life-project which receives such adverse representation in our mass media, and how that life-project might unfold when they arrive in the conflict zone and when they later return home, if indeed they ever do.[3]

It should already be clear that any person who identifies themself as a Muslim will have received an ample flow of information to demonstrate that Ummah (*Ummat* for Shias), the Muslim world, is under attack and in danger. And you don't have to be a Muslim to have seen the genocidal attacks in

---

3   At the time of writing (2015), the Australian government was wrestling with the problem of a foreign fighter, formerly a Labor Party leader and respected citizen, who has returned from Syria where he went as a foreign fighter to fight with the Kurds (an ally) *against* ISIS, in defiance of a law making him liable to a life imprisonment should he return. And yet, according to everything we saw in the press, his action was honourable, and to imprison him seemed senseless and unjust. The only person who has actually done something to defend values evidently held by his community was deemed to have violated those values and to be a danger to society.

Palestine, Lebanon, Bosnia, Gaza, Mindanao, Rakhine, Uyghur and the repression of Muslims by secular or sectarian governments in Egypt, Syria and Libya for example. But while many non-Muslims see the oppression and injustice which Muslim people have suffered over the past 60 years, it is generally only Muslims who *identify* with this suffering, for whom these attacks are a direct challenge to their life-project. Foreign fighters are invariably motivated by altruism when they set off to travel to the conflict zone. The first foreign fighters to go to Syria were motivated to defend their Muslim brothers and sisters whose peaceful protest had been met with brute violence by the Assad regime. In time, however, this project moved on to the construction of an Islamic State in Syria and Iraq, irrespective of the wishes of the people who live there. This is typical of the development of a project at first focused on a particular injustice but becoming more universal over time. We see the same phenomenon when someone is launched into social activism by a personal experience of social injustice, focusing initially on that particular cause but going on to champion the cause of social justice on a much broader scale, potentially embracing utopian visions of how social justice can be permanently secured.

To be clear: it is not a question of the tenets of the Islamic religion. Neither the Palestinians (who invented suicide bombing in the 1970s) nor the Tamil Tigers (until their final suppression in 2009, also prolific suicide bombers) were motivated by religious doctrine: their sacred value was the *land* of their ancestors. Commitment to a life-project and its implied sacred value presupposes no element of religiosity, no life-after-death.

The flow of foreign fighters to conflict zones in the Muslim world began in the mid-1980s in response to calls by Abdallah Azzam and others. In those days, the foreign fighters in Afghanistan were known locally as 'jihad tourists', because they stayed only for a short time and their death rate was low, only 2–6%. By way of comparison, the death rate in Syria and Iraq is as high as 10% and few foreign fighters who went to Chechnya in the 1990s survived at all. It has only been since the US invasion of Iraq and the Arab Spring that foreign fighting has blossomed. 80% of foreign fighters are citizens of Muslim countries who sometimes have the tacit consent of their governments. The foreign fighters who pose the sharpest challenges are those 4,000 or so from Europe or other Western countries where Muslims are immigrant communities, who have left their homes in defiance of law and social norms, to fight with ISIS or other Islamist forces. Fighters of this type have proliferated in recent times as international travel and international phone calls have become very cheap, and social media makes communication with friends and family at home seamless even from the battlefronts.

Governments have a responsibility to prevent their own citizens from travelling to cause havoc in other countries, but their main preoccupation is not what their foreign fighters do overseas, but what they do when they come back. There are several possible outcomes when someone becomes a foreign fighter: (1) they die in battle, and the death rate is high for foreign fighters these days; (2) they settle down in the country where they have gone to fight; (3) they become a career fighter, moving on from one conflict to another. In all these cases the foreign fighter never returns home. Of the minority who do return home, they are invariably already known to security authorities.

Those returning from a holy war usually fall into one of three categories: (4) the dangerous, (5) the disturbed, and (6) the disillusioned. The disillusioned constitute 90% of returnees and go on to lead a normal life without further involvement in violence (Hegghammer, 2011). Such people are the most likely to be successful in dissuading others from terrorist activity. Those who return traumatised by their experiences need help, not imprisonment. Less than 10% of returning foreign fighters want to bring the jihad home with them, but records show that they are no more effective than those without combat experience – terrorism demands a different skill set than conventional warfare – and have only ever engaged in terrorist acts together with others without foreign fighting experience. In other words, security officials would be better advised to *encourage* the return of foreign fighters, as they will either inadvertently help the security officials locate terrorist plots or actively discourage them. It is well-known that returned soldiers often have difficulty readjusting to civilian life, so governments should approach returned foreign fighters with some sensitivity.

The one condition which is most likely to lead to foreign fighters becoming disillusioned with jihad and dissuading others from joining is the shattering of the myth of Ummah by the reality of *bitter sectarian warfare between Islamic factions*. Foreign fighters are as likely to find themselves fighting other Islamists as they are fighting repressive governments, and 50% of foreign fighters who die in battle, die at the hands of other jihadis.

This fact should be drawn attention to in the mass media. Foreign fighters often discover that they are unwelcome when they arrive; not only are they assigned menial or suicidal tasks but are often treated with particular hostility by the local people. Those coming from the West often lack the language, or at least the dialect of their hosts, and some may feel vulnerable. These problems, which are inherent in the foreign fighters' project, need to be highlighted in the media.

The idea that foreign fighters are people who are *alienated* from the society in which they live is not quite right. They are frequently well-educated, well-paid and well-respected professionals. This is to be expected for people who make a commitment to pursue a sacred value – they are *not* alienated drop-outs! But Neumann (2015) says that foreign fighters are frequently people "who lacked a strong sense of meaning in their own lives in the West." The most well-integrated person may find their life meaningless in countries like Australia.

And we should not be surprised by the inhuman brutality of the actions foreign fighters engage in. Life-projects are what give meaning to our lives and can therefore facilitate great acts of self-sacrifice and virtue. But they also facilitate acts of breath-taking bastardy. We have seen in recent years how the leaders of Catholic churches have thought it appropriate to move priests who abuse children on from parish to parish to avoid their being exposed. The abusive priests themselves felt free to exploit children entrusted to their care. The Directors of James Hardie, whose asbestos has condemned tens of thousands to a slow and painful death from mesothelioma, thought it was OK to move the company offshore to avoid paying compensation. Commitment to a life-project, be that a Church, a political career, a capitalist firm or the army, brings with it an entire ethos, moral code and a theory of the world which may be quite at odds with the loose ethos which pervades public life. That 'loose ethos' (Heller, 1988) cannot give meaning to life however well it supports a liberal, tolerant, multicultural bourgeois society. Our children are more likely to commit suicide if we raise them to be contented shoppers than if we raise them to be passionate idealists likely to do something worthwhile with their lives. But it is always a risk. As Vygotsky (1926, p. 232) said: "People with great passions, people who accomplish great deeds, people who possess strong feelings, even people with great minds and a strong personality, rarely come out of good little boys and girls."

3   Conclusion

There are a number of viable responses to the rise of foreign fighters, not including withdrawing their passports after they have left, or imprisoning them on return. Foreign fighters should be assisted to return, though any government does have an obligation to the international community to do what it can to prevent its citizens from wreaking havoc in other countries, and find another, more productive project. On the international arena, governments should take responsibility for preventing the kind of gross injustices which have inflamed the passions of foreign fighters. And in the domestic arena, we need political leaders who have a vision and a life-project which is worthy of a country where citizens no longer have to struggle daily for the bare necessities of physical existence, political leaders who have a genuine commitment to social justice, capable of inspiring others.

Political leaders need to stop stoking fear and selfishness, and instead of celebrating military adventures, celebrate the numerous altruistic projects which are open to young Australians who wish to give their lives to something worth living for.

CHAPTER 16

Capital and the *Urpraxis* of Socialism

0   Preliminaries

If we are talking about a Marx for our times, then we have a lot of catching up to do. The labour process and the working class of today are *so* different from those which Marx knew!

During Marx's lifetime it was an axiom of capitalism that the number of 'unproductive workers' had to be reduced to a minimum. In 1898, Frederick Taylor promoted 25% of the workers at Bethlehem Steel into supervisory positions with a 30% wage increase, and increased productivity by a factor of ten, while splitting the industrial working class itself into numerous strata.

The truism that the manufacturer made a profit by keeping hours as long as possible and wages as low as possible was turned on its head in 1914 by Henry Ford, who cut one hour from the working day, doubled wages, and made a mint, while creating a corporatist layer within the industrial working class.

Then, in the wake of depression and war, came the welfare state, which John Maynard Keynes rationalised with his macroeconomics. What remains to this day the core of the organised working class in the old capitalist countries, in service sectors – health and education, and building and maintaining infrastructure – apparently spends rather than creates surplus value, but are unionised and socialist-minded nonetheless.

As macroeconomic reform gave way to microeconomic reform, Toyota came along and turned Frederick Taylor inside out, passing the supervision of labour back to the shop floor and bringing the market inside the capitalist enterprise itself.

Now we have Google and Facebook who employ a small crew of so-called symbolic analysts to cream the profits off the unpaid labour of the users of their product. Meanwhile, most of what looks like industrial labour is being done in countries where the labour process and the working class still look much like it did in Europe in Marx's lifetime.

Only two things remain the same: the great stumbling block – capital, and its nemesis, the organised working class. But that working class is *so* different.

1 Goethe, Hegel, Marx, Vygotsky

My talk will be in two parts. In the first part of the talk I want to present a methodological insight I draw from Marx's *Capital*, and then in the second part, use this insight to address current ethical-political imperatives.

Working from the present back into the past, it was Lev Vygotsky's idea of 'unit of analysis' that put me on to the trail. There was a lot of confusion among Vygotsky's followers about what this meant. I came to understand it by tracing it back to its origins in Marx, Hegel and Goethe. I will now tell this story, very briefly, in the traditional way, from the past up to the present.

Goethe, Hegel, Marx and Vygotsky are part of a line of thinkers who, in their own way in their own time, sought to understand processes *as a whole*, and made a conception of the whole the starting point for a reconstruction of the concrete. Easy to say, eh? but how *do* we grasp something as a whole? What form does a conception of the whole take and how is it arrived at? Our task is to place ourselves in that tradition in the fight for socialism.

Goethe's discovery, which he first put forward in 1787, was the archetypal phenomenon, or *Urphänomen* – the simplest observable thing which exhibits the universal features of the whole process.

Hegel described it this way in an 1821 letter to Goethe:

> What is simple and abstract, what you strikingly call the *Urphänomen*, you place at the very beginning. You then show how the intervention of further spheres of influence and circumstances generates the concrete phenomena, and you regulate the whole progression so that the succession proceeds from simple conditions to the more composite, and so that the complex now appears in full clarity through this decomposition. To ferret out the *Urphänomen*, to free it from those further environs which are accidental to it, to apprehend as we say abstractly – this I take to be a matter of spiritual intelligence for nature, just as I take that course generally to be the truly scientific knowledge in this field.

Goethe's insight was realised in cell theory, but modern cell theory developed only in the 1830s. Microscopes were not sufficiently powerful in Goethe's times to reveal the complex microstructure of organisms. It was Goethe's aim to discover the *Urphänomen* by what he called 'delicate empiricism' which entailed training the senses, immersing yourself in the subject matter, withholding judgment or hypothesis, not looking behind phenomena for invisible forces – just the phenomenon itself.

But this kind of intellectual intuition Hegel could not accept. Hegel demanded that development be grasped *rationally*, which entailed grasping the process not as a phenomenon but as a *concept*.

Accordingly, the *Urphänomen*, or archetypal phenomenon, underwent a kind of transformation in Hegel's appropriation in which it became the "concrete simple something," or *Urbegriff* (that's my word, not Hegel's), which develops from the abstract to the concrete in just the way Hegel described in his letter to Goethe.

Marx appropriated this idea from Hegel, but in Marx's hands the *Urphänomen* was again turned inside out. In the passage of the *Grundrisse* known as 'The Method of Political Economy' Marx recapitulates the same process of digging down to the abstract concept, and then rising from the abstract to the concrete, reconstructing the concrete as "the concentration of many determinations, hence unity of the diverse." But there is an important point of distinction to which I must draw attention.

In his Preface (1867) to *Capital*, Marx says that "in bourgeois society, the commodity form of the product of labour – or value-form of the commodity – is the economic cell-form." But he makes an important clarification in his *Notes on Wagner* (1881): "I do not proceed from the 'concept of value' ... What I proceed from is the simplest social form in which the product of labour presents itself in contemporary society, and this is the '*commodity*'," what Hegel called "the One."

So long as wealth presents itself in the form of commodities, people are constrained to exchange commodities in order to live. So Marx gives first place to the mediating *artefact*, the material conditions. But:

> The coincidence of the changing of circumstances and of human activity or self-change can be conceived and rationally understood only as revolutionary practice.
> MARX, 1845

We can see that the *Urphänomen* which became the *Urbegriff* has now been transformed by Marx into the *Urpraxis*, the simplest unit of practice which exhibits the essential features of the whole, bourgeois society – exchanging commodities. Practice changes material conditions, which in turn constrain and enable practice, which in turn transforms the conditions of labour, and so on.

In moving from a theory of the social reproduction of bourgeois society, to a theory for the practical overthrow of capitalism, we require a theory of praxis.

In this spirit, we read *Capital* as making its beginning from the simple, artefact-mediated *practice* of *exchanging products of labour*.

In Chapter 4 of *Capital*, Marx shows how the cell, C–M–C', is inverted into M–C–M' and a new process of ascent from the abstract to the concrete is initiated beginning from the unit of capital, the capitalist firm, buying in order to sell at a profit.

So we have *two* units.

Goethe hoped to determine the *Urphänomen* by means of his 'delicate empiricism', and Hegel hoped to make social practices and history intelligible by means of a logical critique, for example, reconstructing a concrete idea of the modern state on the basis of *freedom*: the simplest social form of freedom, the *Urbegriff* of freedom, is *private property*, and the state is the developed, self-reproducing form of concrete freedom.

Marx made the *Urphänomen* of his science a *real act of social practice*, not an imagined social practice, but one whose norms had *already been* produced by the development of bourgeois society and could be the subject of observation, visceral experience and intervention. By turning Hegel's *Urphänomen* inside out, Marx recovered an important element of Goethe's *Urphänomen*.

2   Projects and Solidarity

Neither Goethe, nor Hegel nor Marx were talking just about a theoretical method to be applied to subject matter. They all claimed that the social process itself worked this way. So a study of the social process, and in particular, participation in the struggle for social change and intervention in social processes should reveal to us the logic of social life, and in particular the *Urpraxis* of social change, and this concept should provide us with the guide for understanding socialism at the current juncture.

My study of contemporary currents of social theory has led me to the conclusion that for the solution of the problem of socialism, it is necessary to choose a unit of analysis and that this unit must be an *Urpraxis*. The usual unit of analysis for social theory – social groups of one kind or another, is good only for describing social reproduction and cannot reveal the dynamics of *social change*. Theories based on the individual as a unit of analysis are not worthy of the name social theory at all. Furthermore, all contemporary human science is affected by the departmentalisation of the academy, which itself reflects the rupture of the modern world view into great societal forces and institutions on one side, and individuals and their families on the other. Social revolution demands that this dichotomy be transcended. As I indicated above, I found what I needed not in social theory but in Cultural Psychology, specifically, the strand of theory founded in the early Soviet Union by Lev Vygotsky.

The unit of analysis I use for understanding social life in general and revolutionary change in particular is the *collaborative project*, or 'project' for short. A project is not an aggregate of people but of actions, explicitly *artefact mediated actions*. So just as Marx used two units of analysis: exchange of commodities (C–M–C) and buying in order to sell at profit (M–C–M'), I use both a molecular unit, artefact mediated actions, and a molar unit, collaborative projects. Cultural Psychology is the science which deals with artefact mediated actions and I don't wish to say any more about that at the moment.

However, what is posed by the adoption of collaborative project as a unit of analysis are two interrelated studies, which alas are hardly even embryonic in their development: the study of the *internal dynamics of collaborative projects*, and the study of the *collaboration between projects*, both conflictual and cooperative. It is upon this problem, the relations between projects, that I believe the future of socialism rests.

'Project' is by no means an esoteric concept these days, in fact it is even fashionable. And my meaning differs from the everyday concept only in that I do not include individual actions as projects, which is part of the reason that I say: *collaborative* projects. Almost invariably people *join* projects, and only rarely have the privilege of launching one. It is by and only by participating in projects that a person effects anything in this world.

Projects are not eternal, but have a lifecycle. They begin with a group of people unconsciously sharing a social position of some kind for which a problem or opportunity arises. A solution is floated which brings people together to participate and it becomes a social movement. Strategies, tactics and aims change and subsequently, the project either withers away or an adequate concept is formed and becomes institutionalised, and the concept around which it mobilised enters into the everyday culture of the given community. Hegel described this process in detail in his Logic.

The relevance of collaborative project as a unit for social change today, at this juncture, reflects the developments in the productive forces themselves. Just as parties have become ineffectual in bringing about social change, capitalist firms have changed their form in ways reflective of the changing demands of our times. The Left itself now already looks like so many independent projects. That's life! The Communist Party which was able to coordinate the activity of millions of members is gone long ago, along with the great capitalist firm which directly employed all the people who worked for it. Projects have *become* the real unit of social formation, not just in theory, but in social reality.

A project is a collaboration. I call projects 'collaborative' because in projects numbers of autonomous agents collaborate towards universal, though ever changing, ends. But the more important aspect of collaboration is that *between* projects. Collaboration *as such* means projects fusing together in a common endeavour and sharing a common identity. Collaboration *between* projects in which the separate identity is maintained include: colonisation (or philanthropy), exchange (or bargaining) and *solidarity*.

I have made a modest study of some collaborations as such. These include the fight against AIDS in Australia, which was a collaboration between the Gay Rights movement (which also mobilised sex workers and drug users), the Medical Science institutions and a group within the Hawke Labor government. It was a successful struggle and an international exemplar, impossible without that collaboration.

Also, the fight to ban Asbestos in Australia. The asbestos industry had nobbled medical scientists, regulatory authorities and government ministers, but this formation was defeated by a collaboration between trade unions and health professionals in the Workers Health Movement which secured the collaboration of some journalists, labour law firms and victim self-help groups. Once again, only such a collaboration could have changed people's minds and rid Australia of this deadly trade. There needs to be more of these studies, but more importantly, more of such collaborative projects.

My point is this: people will participate in projects and give it their best shot. The problem is that we have to *learn* how to collaborate with *other* projects. Above all we have to learn the meaning of solidarity. It is on this alone that the future of socialism depends.

As the Rules of the International Workingmen's Association declared in 1864:

> That all efforts aiming at the great end hitherto failed from the want of solidarity between the manifold divisions of labour in each country, and from the absence of a fraternal bond of union between the working classes of different countries;

The French workers had invented the word *solidarité* on the barricades of Paris in the first working class uprisings against the bourgeoisie. The French had learnt the hard way that without solidarity the army could defeat them one barricade at a time, as they had in 1832. By 1848, the Chartist movement, which had united ⅚ of the population of Britain against the ruling capitalist class had also learnt their lesson the hard way.

'Solidarity' entered the English language from the French at the Chartist Convention in London in April 1848, popularised by *The People's Paper* of

Ernest Jones and Julian Harney – leaders of the left-wing of the Chartists and founders of the Communist League, for whom Marx and Engels wrote the *Manifesto of the Communist Party*.

The Rules of the International Workingmen's Association began with the maxim: "the emancipation of the working classes must be conquered by the working classes themselves." These two principles – self-emancipation and solidarity – together make the irreducible and inseparable foundations of the workers' movement.

That self-emancipation is necessary is almost self-evident. If the working class is to take public political power it can learn and equip itself for that task only through the work of freeing itself and abolishing the conditions of its own exploitation. No one can do that on their behalf. Self-emancipation is self-creation, the way in which working class self-consciousness – in effect, the working class itself – is constructed. Without self-emancipation there can be no working class, only billions of individual wage workers, socially and politically controlled by capital.

The opposite of self-emancipation is attaining freedom as the gift of another party. Such a thing is actually impossible. A class which is freed by the action of another class or group is only thereby subordinated to their liberators, even if these be well-meaning. How then is a socialist group to foster the liberation of the working class if the liberation of the working class is to be *their own* achievement? The answer to this conundrum lies in the principle of *solidarity*.

The need for solidarity arises from the fact that the working class does not come into the world readymade as a single, homogeneous, organised stratum of society. It comes into the world divided into strata, trades, national, religious and ethnic groups, and spread across the globe in numerous cultural and linguistic communities, and as I have remarked, the working class has become more not less diversified since. Energies are dissipated in numerous projects, very many of which contribute in some way to the socialist project, but independently and often in conflict with other projects.

The modern working class can realise its own emancipation only by the collaboration of these disparate projects. The aims and methods of projects will differ, but the autonomy of every project within a broad movement will remain until at some future time, maybe, they voluntarily create and submit themselves to a shared discipline.

When one group finds themselves under attack, *provided they fight back*, then others have a duty to come to their aid. This duty and its practice is called 'solidarity'. The results of solidarity are threefold. In the first place, as a result of the aid received from others the struggling group may survive. Secondly, they learn who their friends are, and coming at their hour of need, they will not ever forget this.

But most importantly, through their struggle, whether successful or not, their collective self-consciousness, agency and self-confidence is enhanced.

However, this is not automatically the case. Sometimes 'helping' someone is a violation of solidarity. If another group comes along and 'saves' them, then the 'rescued' group may be grateful, but their working class self-consciousness is not enhanced but at best subsumed under that of the rescuing party. As often as not, helping someone does more harm than good.

The principle of solidarity, which guides how different sections of the workers' movement come to each others' aid, avoids such dangers and ensures that the self-consciousness of both the struggling party and the party offering solidarity is enhanced in the very process of bringing them closer together.

It is a simple rule:

> when coming to the aid of another party, do so under *their* direction.

You do it their way, not your way. If your own beliefs are such that you cannot place yourself under their direction, if you believe that they are so misguided, then solidarity is impossible. But if they can contribute in some way to socialism then ensuring that they are not defeated is important, and you will surely be able to find *some* way of supporting them according to their own practices. This may be just by donating to their fighting fund or sending a message of solidarity or whatever. But if you are going to participate in the struggle of another section of the workers' movement, then the principle of solidarity demands that you do so *under their direction*. The working class is unified by voluntary association, not by conquest or even persuasion.

The term 'intersectionality' has appeared. This represents an attempt from activists in a world fragmented by identity politics, racism and neo-liberalism to reach out and support each other. It is a step towards solidarity, but still lacks the basic principle which characterises solidarity.

To be clear, I am not making a call for unity on the Left. This is neither possible, nor actually desirable. Preparing and building a movement which can overthrow capitalism and make something *better*, is the most complex task imaginable, and it is not planned or directed. It is diverse, with many centres. But nor am I making a libertarian, anarchist call for self-expression and multiplicity.

People have to learn how to collaborate. It is necessary to help people find how to practice solidarity. People will do what they will. If people are not struggling for social justice, then there is nothing we can do to bring that into being.

We cannot accelerate the *Zeitgeist*. The job of Marxists is to show people how the practice of solidarity builds a movement for self-emancipation.

A world in which solidarity is universal is already Socialism.

To be clear, again, I am not arguing for a loose movement of diverse projects. That is what already exists. I am not arguing against building a party to win seats in Parliament. I am not arguing against building a monthly journal of Marxist theory, or a direct action group opposing evictions or an antifascist group to defend communities against racism, or building a cadre of professional revolutionaries. All these are part of the struggle for socialism. It is not a question of one or the other, but of how to *bind them together in bonds of solidarity*. And at the moment, young people do not even know the meaning of the word.

But it is *solidarity* which is the *Urpraxis* of the socialist project.

CHAPTER 17

Virtue and Utopia

Review of Benjamin Franks' 'Anarchism and the Virtues', in *Anarchism and Moral Philosophy*, Palgrave Macmillan, 2010.

∴

In his elaboration of 'practical anarchism' (i.e., 'ethical anarchism'), Franks draws extensively on the virtue ethics of Alasdair MacIntyre, especially as set out in *After Virtue* (1981), and proposes that:

> anarchism ... and its distinguishing characteristic of adherence to *prefigurative* tactics ... is best considered as a social virtue theory compatible with the format developed by MacIntyre.
> p. 156

I am not an anarchist, but I am interested in the prospects for a united and effective Left, and I think Franks' proposal to found anti-capitalist politics on virtue ethics has much to offer.

Franks accepts MacIntyre's concept of 'practices' which is somewhat like what I call 'collaborative projects'. In particular:

> like MacIntyre, they [anarchists] view the social world as being constructed out of intersecting social practices.
> FRANKS, p. 141

MacIntyre defines a 'practice' as:

> any coherent and complex form of socially established cooperative human activity through which goods internal to that form of activity are realised in the course of trying to achieve those standards of excellence which are appropriate to, and partially definitive of, that form of activity.
> 1981, p. 175

and he goes on to give examples: games like chess or football, professions such as architecture, enquiries such as physics, chemistry or history, arts such as painting and music, and the creation and sustaining of households, cities and nations. All practices are aimed at the achievement of some good. The concept of 'collaborative project' that I rely on broadens this concept of 'practice' by seeing on-going practices of this kind as *one phase* in the lifecycle of projects, which also include social movements and institutions.

In line with MacIntyre, Franks defines a virtue as:

> an acquired human quality the possession and exercise of which tends to enable us to achieve those goods which are internal to practices.
> p. 178

So virtue is *relative* to the practice in which it is realised. No human quality is *absolutely* virtuous, at least for the foreseeable future.

Practices, as MacIntyre sees it, are components of a *tradition*. A tradition is "an historically extended, socially embodied argument, and an argument precisely in part about the goods which constitute a tradition" (p. 207).

1　　Internal Goods

Participants in a practice are striving for some *good* which is intrinsic to that practice. They may be motivated to do so, however, by *external* goods. The distinction between goods internal to a practice and goods external to the practice is crucial. The successful solution of a difficult problem in medical science is an example of an internal good, and the scientist achieving it will feel good about it, while winning the Nobel Prize is an external good. In both cases, the participant may experience pleasure, but only in the case of the internal good does the community (or at least the tradition) as a whole benefit. Practices arise in response to some problem (or opportunity) with the formation of a concept of the problematic situation, the realisation of which is the end at which the practice aims. This concept undergoes development as people learn from the experience of trying to realise it. The enjoyment (and fame) arising from the successful practice of medicine (which is the well-being of patients), for example, is not the end at which medicine aims. Rather this enjoyment *supervenes* upon the successful activity (MacIntyre, 1981, p. 184), that is, it is a by-product of pursuing the good of the practice. The good at which the practice is directed is definitive of the practice even though both the practice and its aim change over time. The practice maintains a narrative unity constituted by continuous collaboration as it undergoes historical development and both its ends and its means change.

What about if the project concerned is to bring about a radical social transformation, rather than simply the perfection of the practice itself? This is problematic because the aim – abolition of capitalism – is, by its nature, *remote*. Pursuit of radical change is not the same as sustaining and maintaining a community or tradition and incrementally improving it, which is the kind of practice that MacIntyre seems to have in mind. Pursuing the overthrow of the existing social orders is not the same kind of practice as improving life under the existing system.

For an action within a practice of radical social change to be objectively successful presupposes a *social theory* by means of which the contribution an action would make to the achievement of that end, if successful, may be assessed as an 'internal good' which the participants are striving for. We are not going to witness in our own lifetime the overthrow of capitalism as the outcome of our action, but some step in that direction would mark the success of an action, and social change activities are always aiming at some step of that kind. How is such a step to be evaluated though? A social change activity which is *not* aimed at taking some small step towards achieving the ideal which motivates it may be a game or a fantasy of some kind, but it is not social change activism. It is the argument about what is or is not a step towards socialism which constitutes the tradition to which anarchists and socialists belong. Franks' answer to this problem is the notion of *prefiguration*. I will return to this later.

MacIntyre distinguished between institutions and practices. Institutions, he says, concern themselves with external goods so as to sustain themselves and the practices of which they are the bearers – good performances are rewarded, and wages are paid for full-time commitment and apprentices are given formal training by old hands. Education systems based on testing regimes are an example of how institutions can undermine the very virtues they set out to sustain. "For no practices can survive for any length of time unsustained by institutions … institutions and practices form a single causal order in which the creativity of the practice are always vulnerable to the acquisitiveness of the institution … without the virtues … practices could not resist the corrupting power of institutions" (*op. cit.*, p. 181).

Elsewhere (2014), I have argued that collaborative projects (practices) rather than individuals or groups should be taken as the units of analysis for social theory, and that institutions be seen simply as part of the *lifecycle* of projects. Given the antipathy anarchists tend to manifest towards institutions, MacIntyre's claim that they are necessary to sustain practices is an issue which Franks could address. Activists often see the institutionalisation of their demand as a failure, as it corresponds to the demobilisation of the social movement. (See my review of Andrew Jamison (1991), Blunden, 2012a.) As Franks would surely agree, we need institutions which sustain virtues without undermining them at the same time by rewarding performance, and aren't they exactly the kind of institutions we aspire to create? But what kind of institutions? Without institutionalisation, how are the practices to be sustained and the virtues fostered and maintained?

In the early days of working class organisation, breaches of union discipline were punished with fines. Gradually, over a period of 100 years, these sanctions faded away as the norms of unionism were internalised by workers and new generations were raised in the necessary virtues. No one would argue that these fines exercised a 'corrupting power', but the point is that the virtue of solidarity took a protracted period of time to become instilled in the broad mass of the working class and where unions are still strong, is maintained to this day by means of other sanctions. *How* this virtue became instilled and maintained in masses of people is a question of great interest.

So where does anarchism, and 'practical anarchism' in particular, fit into this scheme? The currents of activity which co-existed in the First International and later manifested themselves in the various currents of anarchism and socialism constitute a single tradition, and accordingly have been engaged in arguments about the nature and means of achieving socialism for the past 160 years and more. Anarchism and Communism emerged as separate currents only in the early 1870s. Each of the various currents is a *practice*, and it is the continual interaction *between* and immanent self-critique *within* these practices, all part of the same anti-capitalist tradition, which not only makes collaboration possible, but brings about change and development within each of these practices. As the movement experiences its failures and successes, the vision of the ends being pursued changes, as does the conception of appropriate means.

2   Problems with MacIntyre's Virtue Ethics

Modelling an anti-capitalist project on MacIntyre's virtue ethics cannot ignore the fact that MacIntyre himself regarded modernity *in toto* as an unmitigated disaster and the conclusion he drew for himself was a return to the Catholic Church and obedience to its tradition. James Laidlaw (2013) has made a sharp critique of MacIntyre, but I think that Franks' selective appropriation of the MacIntyre of *After Virtue* is not affected by the problems which Laidlaw identifies and even Laidlaw can see a "vague anarcho-syndicalist utopianism" in *After Virtue*. There is no need to accept MacIntyre's analysis of the failure of the Enlightenment project in order to adopt the idea of a world made up of practices and traditions of practice sustained by virtues oriented to the furtherance of goods internal to practices. This is the feature of MacIntyre's virtue ethics which makes it attractive for those of us engaged in social change activism.

Franks sees two challenges to the adoption of MacIntyre's virtue ethics: (1) "MacIntyre's view that the virtues require a consistent adherence to strict social regulation," and (2) "the biologically determined teleology that is the basis for MacIntyre's description of Aristotle's account of the virtues" (p. 151).

(1) he finds to be not problematic on the basis that the tradition to which anarchists belong supports strong social norms, but simply opposes their enforcement by a state or by capital. Whatever MacIntyre's view, it is now at least widely accepted that civil disobedience is a major contributor to social progress – Rawls (1993) and Heller (1987), who are deontologists, both affirm this, and civil disobedience is an exceptionally important arena for the development of virtues. There could be no justification for "consistent adherence to strict social regulation" as a criterion of virtue, in our times at least.

(2) turns out not to be a problem either. A virtue is that which promotes the achievement of the goods which constitute the defining telos of the practice and MacIntyre says that the definition of virtues "does not entail or imply that practices as actually carried through at particular times and places do not stand in need of moral criticism" (*op. cit.*, p. 187). Indeed it is by means of the moral criticisms which take place through the interaction between practices within a tradition, "as components of a shared unifying narrative," (p. 155) that practices are judged. Every practice has a telos, by definition (an aimless practice is a contradiction in terms), but a telos which is forever under revision. There is no requirement in virtue ethics, however, for 'essentialism' or an 'unchanging human nature', something which Franks seems unduly concerned about. The virtue of the practice is guaranteed only by reference to the tradition of which it is a part, ultimately, according to Aristotle, on the basis that "the good life for man is spent seeking the good life for man" (*op. cit.*, p. 204).

I agree with Franks' turn to *virtue* ethics and his rejection of the supposed two alternative theories of ethics, viz., consequentialism and deontology. However, the dispute is over which criterion should be the *final arbiter* of right and wrong and whether the right thing to do can really *ever* be decided either by reference to an abstract rule or to consequences.

3 Consequentialism and Deontology

According to *consequentialism*, the rightness of an act must be judged according to its consequences. There are two difficulties with this: (1) at the time of acting you do not know what could be the consequences of your action beyond the proximate outcome, if at all, and (2) how are all the myriad of outcomes, good and bad to be aggregated and summarily evaluated? The most established version of consequentialism, Utilitarianism, answers that the total utility (usually interpreted in economic terms) summed across all affected persons ought to be maximised. Apart from the implausibility of this calculation, it leads to well-known perverse and unjust outcomes.

However, the rejection of consequentialism does not mean that a person should be indifferent to the consequences of their action, as Franks seems to be suggesting when he says, with reference to prefigurative methods: "the employment of such methods is not justified consequentially." On the contrary, a person is morally responsible for the foreseeable consequences of their action and in the case of reckless action, even unforeseeable consequences. An aimless action, that is, an action indifferent to its consequences, is not only madness, it is a contradiction in terms.

According to *deontology*, the rightness of an action must be judged by its conformity to a set of rules of the form "Thou shalt ..." Foremost amongst these rules is the Golden Rule: "Do unto others as you would have done unto you," and in modern Communicative Ethics (Habermas, 1984; 1987), decisions about how to act must be made according to rules governing how *collective* decisions are made: consulting all those affected, benefiting the most disadvantaged, eschewing domineering or exclusionary speech, etc.

The rejection of deontology does not mean that there are no rules and norms which people ought to have a mind to in deciding how to act. On the contrary, the rules just mentioned by way of illustration most certainly should be attended to in deciding how to act. But *which* rule should one obey when two or more rules are in conflict, and mandate different actions? That is the question.

4 Virtue Ethics

The point is that reflecting against abstract and implausible criteria while carrying out elaborate hypothetical calculations is just not how people actually make decisions. This is not surprising because it would be actually impossible to make decisions in that way and attempts to do so invariably lead to perverse outcomes. It is when two or more rules conflict and we are called upon to decide *which* rule to prioritise or find a creative *via media* that ethics comes into play, and neither consequentialism nor deontology can help us when we are facing these kind of quandaries. The richness of the vocabulary for virtues and vices – prudence, courage, self-respect, humility, intelligence, intuition, firmness, kindness, fairness, empathy, flexibility, consistency, ... versus carelessness, cowardice, hubris, insensitivity, ... – evidences the complexity of the process of determining one's course of action in difficult situations and the depth of personal character that is called upon to act wisely. For correct decisions we must rely upon the judgment of a person in command of the relevant virtues and in possession of all the facts. This is why courts have judges and do not simply appoint a clerk to look up the relevant legal provision and read off the verdict. It always requires *judgment,* and the virtues needed to make a good judgment and carry it through can only be acquired through a moral education in the relevant tradition. Aristotle called the wisdom entailed in knowing how to act in the face of complex and conflicting imperatives *phronesis.*

In exercising phronesis, a judge, for example, takes into account the foreseeable consequences and the possible unforeseeable consequences of their decision, and attends to rules of conduct which ensure justice and fairness in acting. Judges are subject to a protracted education and training in the practice of the law in order to instil the appropriate virtues and develop the capacity for phronesis. *There is no definitive rulebook* for this. But in every case, this judgment entails an indefinitely complex balancing which can never be definitively resolved by rules or a utilitarian calculus. It is the tradition of which the practice is a part and the self-concept of that practice which provides the resources for the exercise of phronesis, the various rules of conduct, concepts and narratives (precedents) which the judge can call upon in determining what to do. And there is no abstract set of procedural rules or decision guidelines which can substitute for the exercise of phronesis by virtuous actors, determining their action as participants along with others in the relevant practice.

It is virtue ethics therefore that offers a *realistic study* of the exercise of phronesis, but virtue ethics does not exclude the need for deontological and consequential considerations, but on the contrary attends realistically to their application. We still need to evaluate our actions in the light of their foreseeable consequences and we need to have norms and rules appropriate to the work of socialists.

5 Practical Anarchism and Virtue Ethics

Franks repeatedly emphasises that 'practical anarchism' rejects consequentialism, for example:

> Anarchist prefigurative methods are identifiable as they are the types of practices that would collectively build up to create their anti-hierarchical version of the flourishing society. However, the employment of such methods is not justified consequentially. Anarchists, for instance, employ anti-hierarchical forms of social interaction (for instance, in their formal methods of organisation) not because they will bring about their ends more quickly than centralised authoritarian political structures, but because they produce the very forms of social relationship, albeit in miniature, that they hope to achieve in the longer term.
> p. 146

The qualification "more quickly" is a red herring. Anyone who thinks that the issue is about how *quickly* socialism can be attained is seriously deluded. If Franks is saying anything at all, he is saying that the employment of anti-hierarchical methods can bring about socialism whereas the employment of hierarchical structures *cannot*, otherwise the whole argument is moot.

Franks says that these practices will "collectively build up to create their anti-hierarchical version of the flourishing society ... albeit in miniature." Now this is not an ethical argument, it is a *social theory*, viz., the theory that by creating a better world in miniature, a transformation of the entire world may be achieved by "contamination," to use the term coined by Maeckelbergh (2009). The general assembly, it seems, can 'build up' to a larger and larger meeting until the entire world is drawn into its anti-hierarchical structure, without the use of delegates or representatives (which anarchists deem to be inherently hierarchical). Franks does not use the rather pejorative word 'contamination', but he does believe that practice of the virtues is 'generative', that is, that practice of the virtues promotes the formation of a virtuous character, and it is more than reasonable to suppose that virtuous practices will serve to generate further such practices. But the fact is that we have not seen the evidence of this in growing numbers of anarchists and socialists in the world. If this is to happen by some kind of moral education, then we need a theory about how this is achieved. It is not automatic.

Although embedded in an exposition of MacIntyre's virtue ethics, the proposal for prefigurative politics is in fact *not an ethical argument* at all, but an expression of a highly questionable, unproven social theory, that of *contamination* – simple force of example. The force of example is not in itself a reason for doing something. An action must first of all be judged on its own merits.

Let us look more closely. Franks argues that prefigurative politics are adopted *not for consequential reasons*. To be fair, Franks *means* "not for consequential reasons alone," but this line of argument, without the qualification 'alone', is so pervasive in anarchist literature that it cannot allowed to pass. Actions are *always* for their consequence. It is just that actions can be subject to constraints, and these can be constraints of justice or fairness, for example. But if there is any *other* purpose to an action, then such other purposes cannot be imported into a collective action without the explicit consent of participants. If an action is to be carried out for the purpose of promoting anarchism or recruiting other participants to the Party, then everyone involved has consented to that.

So for example, if a non-hierarchical structure is adopted for a campaign and as a consequence of this structure, let us say, an important decision is not made in a timely manner, and the campaign fails (the forest is burnt, the refugees remain in detention, the houses are demolished, or whatever) then the argument is that still it was right to adopt the non-hierarchical structure, despite it being the *cause* of the failure of the campaign. Now I have to say that there most definitely *are* circumstances in which it would be correct to eschew a tactic despite the fact that it may be the only way to produce the most desirable outcome. But in general, it is fair to say that the process of contamination is unlikely to be effective in spreading non-hierarchical structures if a non-hierarchical structure consistently leads to the failure of campaigns. However, if participants are consulted, and agree that failure with an inclusive procedure is preferable to success with less exclusive procedure, then the goal of the action is duly amended and that's fine.

Also, to employ a method without seeking to justify it consequentially *in order to* achieve socialism by means of 'contamination' is a performative contradiction, because the reason for doing it was that the consequence would be socialism.

The question which confronts the activist is whether the need to achieve the proximate aim(s) of the campaign is *genuinely* in conflict with the need for a 'horizontalist' organisation. If, for example, a group of workers are engaged in a campaign for a wage increase and a union official is able to convince the boss to grant the increase by spending the day on the golf course with him and making a secret deal, I would say that such a means is corrupt and not justified by the end because of the negative impact it has on union organisation, loss of trust, etc. But Consensus, for example, is not the only way of resolving differences in a campaign and sometimes such processes are *not* the best way of resolving differences. Knowing the best way to resolve differences in a concrete situation in a campaign requires the exercise of phronesis, a capacity that is acquired through long experience in organising and willingness at all times to learn from experience and eschew dogma, and to know when to adopt one means of overcoming differences and when to adopt another.

The point is that the consequences of (for example) adopting a certain structure *are* significant in deciding whether to utilise it, but it takes judgment. One ought to know the proximate outcome of a decision one makes – for example, that the adoption of a 'horizontalist' structure for a campaign will lead to failure of the campaign, and this has to be taken into account and *weighed*. But the tradition of which one is a part and the self-concept of the practice, which includes its social theory and its norms, provide the concepts, rules and inferences which will also guide you in making a decision. For example, whether or not to let the campaign fail in the interests of preserving relationships within the campaign and being able to learn from a failure. To adopt virtue ethics is not to turn a blind eye to the proximate consequences of one's actions and certainly not to ignore the wisdom accumulated by the anti-capitalist movement over the past 200 years, encoded in the founding principles of the First International and the socialist and anarchist literature produced by the movement since. It is to know how to apply it.

Making a virtue ethic the basis for an approach to social change activism means paying attention to cultivating the capacity for ethical judgment, phronesis, among the activists and building organisations which are themselves virtuous, and will not be captive to rigid dogmas and procedural imperatives (deontology).

6 Goals and Motives

I have said that one knows, or ought to know, the proximate outcome of one's decisions, and an organisation bears moral responsibility for those outcomes and other unintended outcomes insofar as they were foreseeable. But socialist society is never such an outcome. On any reasonable judgment, socialist society is generations into the future. No course of action can be judged consequentially on the basis that its outcome will be socialist society. Only a raving idiot could believe that, the more so in the light of the experience of the 20th century.

An action has effects. These effects combine with the totality of conditions at the time and the responses of all the players to produce a new totality of conditions. One can never know the ultimate consequences of one's action. However, history *is* intelligible and the socialist and anarchist traditions have built up a body of social theory over the past 200 years which provides rules of conduct and some capacity to analyse conditions and estimate the consequences of different conditions and events. There is always going to be room for argument about how this struggle may unfold, and most likely this argument will be settled only in some distant time when people are more intelligent than we are now. What ethics can provide however is that which social theory cannot: guidance on how to work together when we do not agree about the efficacy of this or that decision. It is here I believe that Franks' proposal for a politics based on virtue ethics comes into play.

7   Ethics and Utopia

If prefigurative politics is to be justified, it has to be on the basis of virtue ethics, but this does *not* imply that this or that organisational structure is validated *irrespective of consequences*. 'Socialist Society' – the utopian vision we share of a future world after the overthrow of capital – is not a 'consequence'. This is because it is absolutely impossible to predict the arrival of such a society generations into the future, as a result not just of *our* actions, but those of everyone else. 'Consequences' are the proximate and foreseeable outcomes of decisions made and it is these we must take moral responsibility for.

'Socialist society' is a rendering of the ethics of socialism into utopian form.

It is our *socialist ethics*, which determine our actions, supported by the social theory which we have also acquired through the practices of the anti-capitalist tradition. Our socialist ethics must be, as Franks argues, a virtue ethics, which means we pay attention to the moral education of our cadres so that they will be able to exercise wise judgment in the struggle for justice and freedom. It is a fact that there are many differences in matters of social theory within our movement, despite the fact that we share a common vision of socialism, but there is surely reason to believe that we could share an ethic.

From whence does a socialist ethic arise? Not by transplanting a utopian vision of socialist society into the present, in 'miniature'. No. It is more the other way around: the utopian vision of socialist society is a 'projection' of our (somewhat) shared socialist ethic on to an imagined future world. This socialist ethic exists and develops precisely in and through the practices in which we all *collaborate* together (cooperating and conflicting) and work through our differences, make our mistakes and share our successes and failures, and learn together. If Maeckelbergh's idea of 'reciprocal contamination' means anything

VIRTUE AND UTOPIA

it must mean the negotiation and internalisation of shared ethics in the course of collaborating in common projects. If this is the case, then it would be useful to try to elaborate this socialist ethic and discuss it.

This is a very important and concrete task, because as Franks notes, there will never come a time when all conflicts have been resolved. To moderate the differences *within* the anti-capitalist movement is surely the most attractive way to develop the ethics of socialist society in which an even wider range of aspirations will exist.

The mere posing of socialist society as an *end* is misconceived. It is not a question of bringing means and ends into conformity, as many argue, and any attempt to do so can only lead to a barren utopianism by subordinating our means – our organising practices of today – to an imaginary utopia – a world in which the socialist ethic has been universalised. In fact, when I do this, what is actually happening is that:

    I begin with my spontaneously adopted ethics;
    I then (consciously or unconsciously) project them on to a future socialist society, and
    I then deduce the ethics with which I actually began, but now with the illusory justification that it prefigures our shared end, socialist society.

In other words, it is a fraud. (It is somewhat like the argument which projects capitalist competition on to nature, and then claims that competition is natural.) It implies discussing how to collaborate here and now in terms of how we think people living in some imaginary future society would collaborate, when differences in wealth, power, education and welfare have been overcome and no longer have to be taken into account.

No, the socialist ethic has to be justified in terms of the exigencies of organising here and now, in the light of the wisdom we have inherited from our shared tradition. 'Socialist society' has no determinate content other than the generalisation of the socialist ethic. But the socialist ethic is not something for the future: it is now. The means of our activity, including the social consciousness of our activists, are in fact elements of the capitalist society of which we are a part and which is the very object we are trying to change. This is where the identity of means and ends is located, in the subjectivity of the social strata which are thrown into opposition by the development of capitalism itself.

The social structures and forms in which the socialist ethic might be universalised must remain obscure to us for some time. Franks claims (p. 141) that anarchism lacks 'determinate ends' and surely this must be true for all of us in this tradition.

But it is unclear what Franks refers to when he counterposes this indeterminate end to "our goals." His definition of prefiguration as "tactics [which] encapsulate the values desired in [our] preferred goals," comes close to what I am arguing. But virtues are not goals and what are the "values" which have now been introduced? If we are introducing an axiology into MacIntyre's virtue ethics, the kind of ethics in which exchangeable 'values' figure, this needs to be explained. 'Goal' is usually used to denote proximate aims, in contrast to more remote 'ends' which Franks "hopes to achieve in the end" by means of prefiguration (p. 146). The meaning of these terms is not fixed, but in the context of talking about acting without concern for the consequences but hoping to achieve something "in the end," this all needs clarification.

I shall elaborate an approach to resolving this question by means of an innovation in virtue ethics which marks a departure from the concept of virtue used hitherto.

8 The Virtues of Practices

The traditional concept of 'virtue' is intrinsically individuated in that it references an aspect of an individual's character. On the other hand, an aspect of an individual's character is only a virtue if its exercise contributes to the internal goods of the practice of which it is a part, and what counts as the social good is determined by the social practice and the tradition of which it is a part. Further, character is itself shaped by participation in social practices even though character is a psychological formation. Virtue is thus essentially both social and individual in content.

This ambiguity is not unique to the concept of virtue. Knowledge, for example, is not simply an entity attached to an individual. Knowledge can only be realised in the context of some specific social practice and what counts as knowledge depends on the practice in which it is realised, and individuals in general acquire and realise knowledge only through interaction within that practice. Conversely, customs are taken to be attributes of a community, conformity to which is acquired by individuals in the individual's habits and conduct.

I believe it is justified to take virtue (like knowledge and custom) as in the first place *a property of a social formation* or project, evaluated within the tradition of which the project is a part, and only *derivatively* a property of the character of a participating individual. What is taken to be virtuous in a given practice is realised in actions which manifest that virtue. Like custom and knowledge, virtues should be understood primarily as attributes of a project, realised and manifested in the activities of the project and *derivatively* as something acquired by individual human beings in and through their participation in the practice, according to the quality of their participation and position in that practice. We are all familiar with the inclusive social movement, the competitive sports club, the supportive self-help group, the solid union, the egalitarian community, etc.

Virtues are attributes of practices, rather than individuals.

The starting point of the enquiry then is to determine those virtues which we see as characterising anti-capitalist politics and how they are fostered in the practices which make up our tradition. This conception of *virtuous* political activities is our starting point, and it is reasonable to suppose, at least to start with, that individuals will acquire, or at least actualise, the virtues by participating in virtuous political practices. Surely, taking everything into account, the best possible outcome, if not some utopia, will result from the exercise of those virtues.

So this moves the discussion to the *virtues of social practices* ('collaborative projects' in my terminology), over and above the usual vocabulary of individuated virtues. As MacIntyre pointed out, the study of the virtues is fundamentally an *empirical exercise*, not an abstract theoretical speculation. Much of the necessary empirical data is summarised in my book *The Origins of Collective Decision Making* (2015).

Social change practices must be underpinned by the deontological maxim: *we* decide what *we* do. This is the progressive, secular version of the Golden Rule. The virtues of social change activism are developed on the basis of this maxim and the resolution of conflicts which arise in the course of collective decision making. It is these virtues which 'prefigure' the kind of world we are fighting for, not 'in miniature' but concretely, in reality, here and now.

8.1   Anarchism and Mediation

Franks, like all other anarchists, is 'opposed to' mediation. I put the word in quotes because to me this is like being 'opposed to' nature or 'opposed to' social relations. Mediation is ubiquitous. In Hegel's words: "There is nothing, nothing in heaven, or in nature or in mind or anywhere else which does not equally contain both immediacy and mediation" (1816, §92). In a personal communication, Franks explained that this is because "the mediating term, which initially acts as the method to achieve a goal, begins to dominate. So mediation itself changes its meaning, where once it is initially a mode of assistance, it becomes a feature of dependence and domination." I have to say that it is a fact that wherever two terms come into relation with one another, their mediation generates or strengthens a middle term, and that other things being equal that mediating term takes on a 'life of its own', that is to say, develops according to its own logic. So the organiser must always pay attention to the means of mediation. But I see no necessity in mediation becoming "dependence and domination."

Franks further explained to me that:

> Whilst you are right that anarchists are suspicious of representatives, they do not reject them in total, if there is no practical alternative, but they do put additional safeguards, usually rejected by more orthodox socialist movements. Such as limits on time served in posts, and number of times they can re-elected, as well as areas for decision making. Delegates usually have to abide by the decision of the local group.
>
> personal communication, 2016

This is far more rational than simply being 'opposed to' mediation. However, the populist limitation of delegates to the role of messenger is, except in special situations, misconceived. Mediation needs to be enhanced not nobbled. If they are to be authentic, delegates have to have the right to fully participate in rational debate in the forum to which they are delegates, and then report back and explain themselves. Only in this way, can the delegating group fully participate in the debate and learn from it.

8.2 Anarchist Anthropology

Anarchist researchers tend to see their task like that of an anthropologist, and report what anarchists do and what anarchists say, but they never seek to exercise their own critical judgment in relation to these beliefs or practices. If the most thoughtful and reflective representatives of anarchism do not engage in evaluation of anarchist practices and beliefs, then the possibilities for furthering discussion between tendencies within the socialist tradition is curtailed.

I recall from an earlier time in my own life, when I was a trade union activist and not a researcher, being approached by a researcher and questioned about my beliefs. This was not a discussion between two people who each had an opinion. I was acutely aware that I was a research object and it was very alienating and I put an end to the discussion. So I can see the point, and I understand that this is an ethical problem in the relation between researcher and research object.

A reflective socialist who wishes to conduct research into social struggles, is under an ethical obligation to do so as a fully committed *participant observer*, but a truly committed participant has an opinion about the matter, otherwise they are *just* an observer. Every conversation must, like any other action, be in pursuance of a goal agreed by all the participants. No 'hidden agendas'.

9 Summary

Ethical communities are not constructed by moral philosophers or even by revolutionary leaders, police and judges. Ethical communities are constructed by collaborative projects of various kinds, essentially by forms of collective decision making and action. The virtues which are manifested in social life have their basis in the demands of specific modes of collaboration, both forms of collaboration between distinct projects – mutuality, solidarity, philanthropy and collaboration as such, and forms of decision making within collectives of individuals – Counsel, Majority and Consensus (see Blunden, 2016 and Chapter 18, this volume). The virtues we have mentioned above – good faith, care, solidarity, trust, wisdom, attention, equality, tolerance, inclusion and respect and more – all originate in specific forms of collaborative project.

10 The Question of Delegation and Hierarchy

Two problems have plagued social change activism over the past millennium: delegation and hierarchy, with the incipient transformation of delegates into officers.

The tendency of a delegate structure to solidify into a hierarchy does not issue from egotism on the part of delegates, but on the contrary, more often because of the unwillingness or incapacity of other members of a collective to do the work required of a delegate (an incapacity which may be itself a product of dysfunctional delegation). Even in organisations where representation and delegation are absent, there is an incipient tendency for informal roles to fossilise into offices, and representatives to be transformed into managers. Voluntary associations have been aware of this tendency and have struggled to overcome it for at least 500 years. But without the use of delegation it is impossible to organise on a scale larger than the number of people who can meet together in one room. Over the centuries, organisations have used various measures, such as limiting terms of office, mandation of delegates, rotation of positions, etc., to manage this situation. There is however no substitute for the fostering of virtues among all the participants. The internet certainly moderates these pressures but I don't believe it essentially changes the situation.

MacIntyre's advice quoted above is relevant here: "without the virtues … practices could not resist the corrupting power of institutions." The fossilisation of delegate structures into hierarchies is *a symptom not a cause* of the loss of the practical virtues and the degeneration of workers' democracy.

11 Conclusion

The two principal components of Franks' proposal – virtue ethics and prefiguration – are supported in the above reflections. However, in my reading, Franks chose to frame prefiguration not as the practice of virtues, but as a social theory according to which prefiguration is a means to end, which is in turn conceived of in utopian terms.

The utopian conception of 'socialist society' is a projection of socialist ethics on to an imagined future society. The practice of socialist ethics is not 'in miniature' but a fully concrete practice here and now.

Practices and their various projects and campaigns are not aimless, but *always* directed at their consequences. But *which* consequences are aimed at is always a matter of social theory and inevitably subject to on-going argument and reflection.

To answer "why did the chicken cross the road?" by "to get to the other side," is obviously missing the point. Humans, at least, do things for a reason which differs from the immediate goal of the action. Our immediate goals are intelligible in terms of our social theory and our motivation. Our motivation will be consistent with our conception of the good, reflected in our socialist ethics.

Socialists do not need to be lectured on the evil of means-justify-the-end thinking. Our socialist ethics are developed through decades of workers' struggles and they are in accord with the imperative of self-emancipation of the working class through the practice of solidarity. The virtue ethics which socialists embrace does not mandate this or that method of decision making, delegation, representation or structure. Invariably many imperatives come to bear in deciding on these matters and practical wisdom is always required to work out the best thing to do in each circumstance.

CHAPTER 18

The Origins of Collective Decision Making (Synopsis)

1   The Question

Ever since participating in the S11 protests against the World Economic Forum in Melbourne in 2000, I have been intrigued by processes of collective decision making and in particular by the antagonism between the two main paradigms used on the Left, viz., Majority and Consensus. Reading the literature arising from the Occupy Wall Street events in 2011 I became alarmed at the depth of this antagonism and in particular the way the problem was being aggravated by 'histories' of consensus decision making based on hearsay and ill-informed speculation, and the apparent belief that majority decision making does not have a history at all.

Everyone on the Left has some measure of familiarity with both paradigms but the majority of activists are firmly committed to one or the other and this problem has emerged as a significant barrier to collaboration on the Left and the success of our shared project.

Further, because people – not only young people, but even experienced hands – have no idea of the historical origins of these two paradigms, but simply compare and contrast them pragmatically and on the basis of personal experience, the reasons underlying this antagonism remain shrouded in mystery.

In 2014 I set out to trace the origins of each paradigm, hoping that the findings would shed light on the meaning of this antagonism and provide guidance on how to overcome it. Some elements of the history I recovered from historical records made available on the internet and from published books. The mode of decision making, however, was invariably an incidental topic for both the actors themselves and historians, who were concerned with *what* was decided rather than *how* it was decided. The remaining elements, not to be found in any records, I was able to recover by interviewing participants and witnesses of events in the 1950s and early '60s. There is much work to be done, but I know from having spoken to eye witnesses and experts in the relevant periods, that *no one* has asked these questions before. So *The Origins of Collective Decision Making* is the first ever history of collective decision making based on evidence rather than guesswork.

2 Research Methodology

To understand a social practice is to capture its birth, life and death, and to grasp what is *rational* in that development – the good reasons people had for doing what they did in the historical circumstances in which they lived. But a rational history cannot be assembled from snapshots of the past. If someone did something in some past century and someone else did much the same thing today, this is no evidence as to origins. How did it get from there to here? In what sense is it the 'same' practice? Furthermore, without understanding the earlier instance within some continuing practice or tradition, that is to say, in its context, it is most likely going to be misconstrued.

Practices develop and change through the collaboration of people who are struggling in some social situation and drawing on their own and each other's resources. Innovations do not arise because they were 'in the air', even though I was often told this in the early stages of my enquiries. A new practice is 'in the air' because it has been devised and embraced by real individuals already collaborating together in some practice, and responding to specific, shared problems. To write a history of collective decision making meant tracing the real relations of collaborative participation by individuals in social practices such that either through the continuous operation of definite projects and traditions, or in times of transition, through the lives of the individuals themselves, so as to construct a continuous line of collaborative development from some historical moment to the next and up to the present (cf. Ricœur, 1984; Gadamer, 2005).

Faced with potentially thousands of years of world history, I decided at the outset that I would make my beginning with those forms of collective decision making in which I had participated myself and through the proximate origins of those practices, trace back and back to what I could speculatively propose as an origin, and then carefully work forwards again, this time not speculatively, but rigorously. The aim was to see if I could reconstruct a continuous line of collaborative practice from a supposed point of origin to my personal experiences in London and Melbourne, discarding those lines of development which could not be connected into a line leading back to my starting point in the present.

This is an avowedly subjective approach. However, despite my Anglophone, first-world starting point, given that my researches took me back into Anglo-Saxon England following the end of the Roman occupation and into West Africa from where people were taken to the Americas as slaves, and in the course of chasing up loose ends, into several European countries and even Asia, I am confident that what I have discovered is widely applicable. But I must leave it to others to fill in the gaps.

3 Collective Decisions without Voting

I found a number of instances where people assured me that they had long used consensus decision making and that their practice was not derived from the Peace or Women's movements or from the Quakers but had been developed independently. I also found Quakers who regarded consensus as alien to the Quaker way of doing meetings. I found that the Danish belief that their political life is based on Consensus comes from a long history of multi-party legislatures and the eternal need to negotiate compromises. I found labour leaders and educators in the US who called their approach to negotiating labour contracts 'consensus' because they made agreements with the bosses without the use of strike action. All these opinions arose from a mixing up of the concepts of Negotiation and Consensus. I found likewise that Japanese businesspeople who described the way they operated as 'consensus' were referring to negotiation of business contracts not the formation of a *common will*.

As I use these terms, the difference between Negotiation and Consensus is that in Negotiation normally two distinct parties enter into discussion to arrive at an agreement which meets the needs of both parties; but they remain before, during and after the negotiation *separate parties* pursuing separate aims, and are usually represented in negotiations by *delegates*. Collective decision making, on the other hand, involves individuals making a decision together as part of a common project. From time to time, a collective may split and discussions degenerate into Negotiation between mutually independent factions who go their own way as soon as the negotiated agreement is discharged. In such a case, there is no collective decision making because there is no collective subject.

The other problem I came across in research is the presumption that if a group of people make decisions together without voting, then *ipso facto* they are using Consensus. This is false. It is one of the rationalisations for the baseless conviction that Majority is some alien procedure imposed from above on indigenous and working people, and that present day Consensus is the recovery of an historically earlier practice. In fact, Majority is far more ancient than Consensus. But before Majority was invented, there was Counsel.

4   Counsel

Counsel is a third paradigm of collective decision making. I discovered this paradigm when I had worked my way back in search of the origins of Majority decision making in Anglo-Saxon England, that is, the period between the end of the Roman occupation and the Norman Conquest. The most important decision making institution of this period was the Witenagemot, the King's Counsel. Turning my attention to the Church, I came across St. Benedict, who in about 500 AD wrote the Rule which governed life in monasteries. In Chapter 3 of the Rule he codified collective decision making. Later, checking to see if African Americans may have brought Consensus to America with them from Africa in the days of the slave trade, I found what is mistakenly called 'African Consensus', but is more properly referred to by its Southern African name of Lekgotla. All these practices belong to the same paradigm: Counsel. In St. Benedict's words:

> As often as anything important is to be done in the monastery, the abbot shall call the whole community together and himself explain what the business is; and after hearing the advice of the brothers, let him ponder it and follow what he judges the wiser course. The reason why we have said all should be called for Counsel is that the Lord often reveals what is better to the younger. The brothers, for their part, are to express their opinions with all humility, and not presume to defend their own views obstinately. The decision is rather the abbot's to make, so that when he has determined what is more prudent, all may obey.
> ST. BENEDICT, 1949, Chapter 3

Not only is this recognisably the same method as used by the Witenagemot but it is also the same as Lekgotla. A moment's reflection will confirm that this is the same method of collective decision making used in private companies, in traditional patriarchal families and artistic productions – one person, be it the Abbot, the Chief, the CEO or the Director, takes moral responsibility for making the decision, but must consult every one of the group before announcing the decision. Once the decision has been announced there is no dissent.

I once witnessed this mode of decision making in an Executive meeting of an Australian trade union led by Maoists, just as described by St. Benedict, except that at the end, everyone raised their hand to indicate their consent. Isn't it obvious that if a foreigner were to witness Lekgotla in an African village, they would believe that they were witnessing Consensus decision making, because they would be unaware of the complex status relations between the speakers. Likewise, someone who witnessed that union meeting would believe that the decision had been made by Majority, except that there happened to be unanimity.

Further, as Hegel (1821) pointed out, a collective can only achieve sovereignty if it is able to speak through the voice of an individual. Historically this was the monarch, but even a modern social movement has to be able to represent itself through an appointed individual spokesperson, leader or role model, and in that final moment, the mode of decision making would be Counsel. Counsel in fact co-exists with Majority and Consensus.

So it can be seen why it is important to study these practices *historically*, and in *historical* context, otherwise judging by superficial appearances, what is really going on may be misconstrued.

5   Where Did Majority Come From?

To find the origins of Majority I started with my own experiences in unions in London and Melbourne. How long had unions been using these procedures? I had previously transcribed the Minutes of the General Council of the International Workingmen's Association of 1864, and the procedures used there were exactly the same as those I had experienced in London in the 1970s. So it was clear that the English trade unions, to which members of the General Council all belonged, had been using these procedures throughout the intervening century. I found the minutes of a meeting of the London Workingmen's Association in 1837, at a time when such meetings were illegal under the Conspiracy Laws, and if the minutes had fallen into police hands, the members would have been liable for transportation. The procedures were the same.

In 1824 the Combination Laws had been repealed, and a Select Committee of Parliament collected the Rulebooks of 13 British trade unions, before shortly afterwards, following an upsurge of militancy, the Conspiracy Laws were introduced.

These rulebooks were fascinating. On the one hand, there could be no doubt that they were precursors of the rulebooks of modern trade unions, but they were also marked by distinctly antique features, such as fines imposed for transgressions of meeting protocol and a narrow, particularist orientation. On one hand, they all clearly belonged to a family of conceptions reflecting common anxieties and aspirations, with many rules appearing in identical form in different rulebooks or with minor variations, but also differences, sometimes very marked. There could be no doubt that the creators of these rulebooks had a rich palette of rules to draw from, and the participants were all used to such rules. They were neither orchestrated by a single precedent nor invented de novo by each group.

As further investigation revealed, the lives of the poor of early 19th century England were saturated with a spectrum of such local organisations for mutual benefit, insurance, saving and charitable, religious, political and professional functions. With no protection or aid from the state, the poor had long been used to managing their own welfare, and the source of these structures were the *medieval guilds*, to which the unions of 1824 bore an unmistakable family resemblance.

I consulted experts in the field and my intuitions were confirmed: the early British trade unions were the direct progeny of the guilds. But I also found that no one had written or was specialising in the history of the guilds, so my next task was to discover the origin of the guilds. I found a history of the London Companies written in 1838 which extended back to the 12th century and included detailed information about the rules and regulations governing the guilds together with their life histories, and the information that the guilds had existed before the Norman Conquest. I then turned to a study of Anglo-Saxon England.

6   Origins of Majority

It soon became clear that voting was inconceivable in Anglo-Saxon England because there was no notion of *equality*. In fact, every citizen had a *wergeld* – effectively, a price on their head according to their place in the social hierarchy. Not only was there slavery, but Anglo-Saxon England exported English slaves. Decisions were made by Counsel, from the Witenagemot at the top down to the tything, where the senior tythingman was responsible for the other nine members of the tything at the base of the hierarchy. Apart from royalty and widows with property, women had no rights at all. The whole social formation was based on the land and nested relations of tenancy and lordship from serf up to King. Anyone who was not tied to some piece of land and under some lord did not legally exist and could be hunted like a wild animal.

In the year 997, Ethelred II introduced a jury of 12 leading thegns (public servants) for criminal cases and a majority of eight to four was sufficient to make a decision, provided the minority paid a fine! This is the first instance of something approaching Majority in English law (Loyn, 1984, p. 145). This is not the source of Majority decision making, but it may have presaged it. Majority decision making was the creation of the guilds which quietly came into existence during the last century before the Norman Conquest.

During this period, commerce began to eat away at the foundations of feudalism under which all purchases were supposed to be authorised by a court. Towns began to spring up which lay outside the relations of feudal tenancy, and the merchants and artisans who lived there lay beyond the pale of feudal right. Travelling around the country, they had no rights, and could be killed or robbed with impunity. So these merchants and artisans banded together for their own protection and to make arrangements for retrieving their bodies if they died far from home, insurance against fire and provision for the welfare of their families in the event of their death, and sometimes simply recreation. Over time, the functions of these guilds broadened, were eventually recognised by Royal Charters, and the guilds took responsibility for self-government of all the affairs of their trade.

It was in these guilds that strangers came together and made voluntary associations for mutual protection on the basis of mutual autonomy, equality and solidarity, and they made their decisions by Majority. Although qualified Majority voting had been used in Church elections, there was no precedent for general decision making by Majority. Given that guilds were formed by free association between mutually independent equals, bound together by the pressing need for the solidarity of others like themselves, Majority decision making was the logical and probably the only option available to them.

7   The Development of Majoritarianism

Majority was the invention of the guilds, which predated the House of Commons by about 400 years. Working people were apprentices, journeymen and masters, but moved through these categories over their lifetime and there was no sense of class division among the manufacturing and commercial population until the early 19th century. Although the guilds were largely run by masters, they were accepted as representing the whole trade, and even where journeymen set up their own guilds to push for improved conditions, they used the same Majority procedures. I was able to trace the development and propagation of Majority through the centuries and from the guilds into town corporations, universities, the House of Commons, trading companies and the earliest colonial governments in 17th century New England. Gerard Winstanley thought that the guilds provided a "very rational and well-ordered government" (Winstanley, 1642, p. 549).

So, contrary to the widely held view that Majority was imposed from above, and that Parliamentary procedures trickled down from above into the lives of the working masses, the *opposite* is the case. Debates in Parliament could not be published until 1771 and until the 19th century ordinary people would have had no knowledge about how debates were conducted in Parliament. On the other hand, everyone was involved in the myriad of self-help bodies which provided respectability, security and basic welfare to everyday people. Further, every member of the House of Commons would have been a member of a guild up until the time of the English Revolution, and like everyone else would have learnt how to make collective decisions through participation in guilds of one kind or another.

Throughout this development, we see an unceasing struggle to counteract the formation of cliques and bureaucracies. These problems were not 20th century discoveries but were the focus of concern at least as early as the 15th century. No one considered that this was a problem inherent in Majority, but rather arose from the intrusion of *private* relations, that is, from a tendency to degenerate into Counsel. All their efforts were directed towards attaining the most consistent implementation of Majority possible.

The zenith of majoritarianism was in the Chartist movement which united the disenfranchised population of Britain against the ⅙ of the adult male population who had been given the vote by the 1832 Reform Act. The very essence of Chartism was Majority. However, they were dedicated to constitutionalism and faced an implacable bourgeoisie which not only refused to give the working people the vote but used Conspiracy Laws to suppress the internal democratic life of the National Charter Association. After the third great petition was rejected by Parliament in 1848 and the people abandoned hope of a political solution to their situation, the Chartist movement faded and the working people retreated into trade unionism and working class mutual aid to look after their interests without the mediation of the state.

These unions and similar self-help organisations all used Majority decision making. Techniques of self-government developed by the Methodist Church were appropriated to build the kind of national organisations with the more universal spirit introduced by the English Jacobins, transcending the particularism which had marked the trade unions in 1824.

With the great strikes of the 1890s – the Union of Women Match Makers, the Beckton Gasworkers and the Dockers' Tanner strikes – general unions were established with universal membership and dedicated to the fight for socialism and universal welfare. These general unions gave to Majority the classic and universal form in which it was received in the 20th century. But instead of representing the vast majority of the population outside of the small class of landowners, the mass membership of these general unions represented the poor, possibly a minority, in a working population which had been fragmented and stratified. Even the skilled craftsmen – cobblers, tailors, etc. – who had formed the International Workingmen's Association in 1864, were no longer part of the workers' movement. Skilled manufacturing workers, such as the Engineers and Railwaymen, still carried the legacy of particularism which had been regenerated by the refusal of the British bourgeoisie to accept universal suffrage and had driven workers back to the narrower trade bases of their solidarity.

The only instance of an effort to introduce Consensus into the workers' movement, was when the Anti-slavery campaigner, the Quaker Joseph Sturge, called a Conference in 1842 to unite the National Chartist Association with the middle class Complete Suffrage Union. He proposed an equal number of delegates from each party to find a Consensus, rather than by means of a vote which would have given control to the numerically vastly superior Chartists. The Chartists denounced the very idea of one gentleman having an equal vote with 10,000 working people, and walked out.

8   Crisis of Majoritarianism

The crisis for majoritarianism came in the aftermath of the Second World War, when the Soviet Union and the Communist Parties around the world struck a deal with Imperialism under which a majority of the world was excluded. The people of the colonies were left in the lurch. African Americans were left at the mercy of Jim Crow. Women remained excluded from public life. The post-war settlement brought to the organised working class relative peace, prosperity and stability, but the deal done with imperialism left majoritarianism with a bad name in the eyes of those who had been *excluded*. The ethic of *solidarity* was thenceforth gradually supplanted by the ethic of *inclusion*.

At this point I must turn to the origins of Consensus.

9   The Quakers and Consensus

My first contact with Consensus was a book (Coover et al., 1977) which I picked up at the Friends of the Earth bookshop in Melbourne in the mid-1980s. Then in the early 1990s I helped set up an Alliance bringing socialists and anarchists together to work on campaigns. The Alliance broke down quite quickly because the only way it was going to work was by Consensus, and yet my socialist friends would not consent to Consensus decision making under any conditions. It wasn't just a pragmatic question – although it was often expressed that way – but a moral revulsion, much like the reaction of the Chartists to Joseph

Sturge's proposal. So, in setting out on this investigation I consulted my friend, Jeremy Dixon, who had been one of the anarchists in that project. He had learnt Consensus from his American anarchist contacts in 1977, which brought me back to the book I had read which had been published in the US in 1977 by the Movement for a New Society. Indeed, later investigation confirmed that anarchists had learnt Consensus from MNS. But from where had MNS got it?

Founded in 1971, MNS was the direct progeny of A Quaker Action Group. At this point I was faced with the next question – where did the Quakers get their Consensus? The Quakers were founded by George Fox in 1647, in the wake of the English Civil War, with a radical critique of established religion which attracted the most militant elements from Cromwell's New Model Army. The Quakers held that every believer could interpret the Scripture themself if they listened to the voice of Jesus within their own heart. In the wake of a bloody civil war, this religious liberalism, when combined with their uncompromising critique of established religion, led to disaster. In 1656, a leading Quaker, James Naylor, staged a provocative polemical attack on the established Church which triggered the savage suppression of the entire sect.

In 1662, they adopted the uniquely Quaker way of doing meetings which ensured that individuals would be prevented from going off on a tangent, so to speak, but avoided setting up a hierarchy or orthodoxy (see Hill, 1975). Only proposals which met with the agreement of an entire meeting, without persuasion, argument, or negotiation, would be taken to express the Divine Will. This measure ensured that Quakers would always conform to the prevailing intuitions of the social milieu of which they were a part, which in the wake of the Civil War, was a yearning for peace and stability.

Quakers have continued in this way up to the present day. While their opposition to slavery has been absolute, their 'peace testimony' has not. Many Quakers fought in the American Civil War on the Union side and signed up for both world wars like the loyal citizens that they were. Despite this, the Quakers kept the Peace Testimony alive by providing succour to conscientious objectors and pacifists outside their own ranks. This had the effect of providing a steady inflow of Quaker converts who were politically active pacifists. A Quaker Action Group was a group of such Quaker converts who tried in vain to renew the Quaker commitment to the original peace testimony, but ultimately gave up trying and launched the Movement for a New Society in 1971 (Smith, 1996).

However, Consensus had already taken root in the Peace, Anti-War, Women's and Civil Rights movements long *before* this time, a fact I was able to establish by email enquiry amongst veteran American activists. I managed to identify and make contact with activists, such as Casey Hayden, Mary King and James Lawson, who had been present in the earliest days of SNCC (Student

Non-violent Coordinating Committee – 'snick') in April 1960 and Women Strike for Peace (WSP) in 1961. These two events were the two more or less independent points at which Consensus was introduced into social change activism in the US, a decade prior to MSN, and each of these three sources introduced a different style of Consensus, which would merge in the Peace and Women's Liberation movements during the 1970s. But this discovery still left open the question as to how Consensus came to be invented or discovered by SNCC and WSP. What were the conditions which led these groups to adopt Consensus and where did they get it from?

I had to investigate 11 different possible routes to arrive at a conclusion about SNCC. Two individuals must share credit for this innovation, the 'hillbilly' Marxist educator Myles Horton and the Black Methodist theologian, James Lawson.

10   Myles Horton and Consensus in SNCC

In the depths of the Great Depression, Horton set up Highlander, an adult education centre in rural Tennessee, and shortly before the launching of the CIO he began training rank-and-file union members from unskilled trades to build their unions and run disputes. His courses included training in the use of Robert's Rules of Order, the procedures they would need to operate within the labour movement. After the war, as the CIO moved to the right, Horton moved to training poor farmers to prepare them to set up their own cooperatives to free themselves from exploitation by agribusiness. Following the May 1954 Supreme Court ruling on desegregating schools he focused on the embryonic civil rights movement. In August 1954 he launched the literacy program in which hundreds of thousands of Blacks learnt to read so that they could register to vote. Rosa Parks was one of his students shortly before she launched the historic 1955 Birmingham Bus Boycott.

When a group of activists came to Highlander, they were put in charge of running the centre, and projects like the literacy program were put under the control of the participants themselves. Horton absolutely insisted that decisions were made by the students and refused, on one occasion even at the point of a gun, to make a decision for them.

Collective decision making was at the centre of his approach, the means by which his students actually took charge of their lives and emancipated themselves from those who were hitherto running their lives for them. When he turned from the labour Movement, which was built around Majority, to the unorganised poor farmers and Southern Blacks, he abandoned the use of

Majority and used a form of Consensus. The unions used Robert's Rules of Order, but "Negroes have never mastered that way, their churches don't act that way. ... In the mountains poor people ... get together and talk" (Horton, 2003, pp. 180–181).

I have no documented evidence, however, of this process being used outside of Highlander until the founding of the SNCC on 17 April 1960. However, the records of the Highlander show that Horton was training groups of poor people in Consensus decision making from the early 1950s. Horton had no connection with the Quakers, and so far as it is possible to determine, Horton invented an informal consensus decision procedure with no pre-existing model.

11 James Lawson and Consensus in SNCC

James Lawson was a Methodist theologian whose mother was a pacifist and his father a militant, gun-toting NAACP preacher. James embraced nonviolence from an early age and travelled to India in 1953 to study nonviolence under followers of Gandhi, and after returning to the US in 1956 he was invited to join Martin Luther King as an adviser. When the lunch-counter occupations began in 1960, Lawson ran an intensive program of nonviolence training in Nashville and it was this group attending his program which played the leading role in establishing SNCC. Most of the same students had also previously attended Highlander.

The Methodist Church uses a strict Majority system of decision making, devised by John Wesley in the 1780s, later appropriated by the socialist and trade union movements, and use of Majority applied as much to the Black Methodist Church as anywhere else in the segregated Methodist Church in the US. However, Lawson insisted in interviews that in his work with the Methodist Youth, of which he was Vice-President in 1952, and with the young students who formed SNCC, he always worked by Consensus. It was certainly Lawson who was closest to the students and the most significant influence on them when they created SNCC, and it was Lawson who wrote the constitution of the SNCC in April 1960. But Lawson would not have been conscious of the fact that before the students came to his nonviolence workshops, they had already learnt from Horton how to make collective decisions amongst themselves without deferring to their preacher – as was required by the method of Counsel generally practised by the Black Churches, which were the main organising bodies for Black communities in the Southern United States. This was a generation of Black youth unlike any previous generation, a generation which would no longer defer to either their elders or to Jim Crow. Ultimately, it was the young SNCC activists themselves who developed their own intense version of Consensus, but the idea did not fall from the sky. Consensus prevailed in SNCC only until 1966 when Stokely Carmichael was elected chairman, and a military style of command was adopted.

12   Women Strike for Peace

Women Strike for Peace began in Washington on 22 September 1961 at a meeting of housewives (these were often career women, but they all self-identified as 'housewives') who were alarmed by the nuclear arms race and had become alienated from the mainstream peace organisations, such as SANE. In particular they objected to their bureaucratic procedures, their reliance on lobbying rather than public protest and their capitulation to McCarthyism (see Swerdlow, 1993). One of the six founders was Eleanor Garst who had joined the Quakers as a result of their support for her husband as a conscientious objector. Garst taught WSP the Quaker way of doing meetings, but WSP implemented the idea in their own unique way, with kids playing on the living-room floor and pastries being passed around with half a dozen women talking at the same time. But the WSP way of doing meetings also included the periods of quiet reflection, adopted from the Quaker way, which was not at all characteristic of the noisy and intense way the SNCC made decisions.

The women who founded WSP were in their 30s and 40s and had been active on the Left before the War, but WSP was a separatist women's movement which was emphatically *not* feminist. The WSP women were largely the mothers of those young women who went on to create the Women's Liberation Movement, but WSP continued up into the 1980s and played an important, if contradictory, role, in the creation of the Women's Liberation Movement. They embraced their identity as 'housewives' and used this stereotype to advantage in promoting their peace message. But despite their daughters' rejection of their housewifely persona, there is no doubt that their organising methods were a major legacy for the Left.

WSP refused to maintain a membership list, far less collect a membership fee or elect officers. They never voted and only carried out actions which conformed to the well-established stereotype of the peace-loving, middle class, American housewife. This method, sometimes ironically referred to as 'unorganisation', became the subject of fierce arguments (see Freeman, 1970) as the implementation of Consensus was fine-tuned in the development of the Women's Liberation Movement, which in its beginning, was not at all run exclusively by Consensus. Women's groups originating from the labour movement used Majority voting, but over time, a form of Consensus emerged which drew to some degree from each of its three sources, and became the preferred mode of decision making in the women's movement. Having originated in reaction to the exclusion of denigrated and oppressed groups by the Postwar Settlement, Consensus was motivated by the ethos of *inclusion*.

13   1968 and After

The Vietnam War and the events on the international stage stimulated the emergence and expansion of new social movements, mass movements united around ideals such as Women's Liberation, Participatory Democracy, and the Environment. At the beginning, even in the case of the Women's Liberation Movement, both Majority and Consensus were adopted as norms for decision making, because many of the activists had come out of the socialist and labour movements where Majority was the norm, while others had come out of the Peace Movement where Consensus was the rule. In most cases however, the only vote came when disagreements could not be resolved, the Majority ethos could not generate the necessary solidarity, and a group split. The three styles of Consensus that had emerged from the 1950s merged and became the preferred mode of decision making in social movements, except where labour movement involvement predominated, and Majority remained the norm.

Murray Bookchin, whose anarchist ideas about organisation were influential throughout the 1960s and 1970s, confirmed that the organising traditions of 19th and early 20th century anarchism were unknown to the young anarchists of this time, who learnt Consensus from the Movement for a New Society in particular and the social movements generally. European anarchists had used the type of Majority decision making they learnt in the labour movement, except that in action they preferred to work in small affinity groups. Within these small groups of like-minded friends decision making is informal and resembles Counsel more than anything else.

With the rise of alliance politics after 1999, Consensus became essential to the effective collaboration within alliances, and the antagonism between Majority and Consensus became more and more a feature of radical politics.

14   Conclusion

As can be seen, each of these modes of decision making gain their legitimacy from powerful traditions and express the firm moral convictions of their participants. However, none of them can guarantee wholly satisfactory decisions in the face of persistent disagreement. If the Left is to find a shared ethical framework for collaboration, then recognition of the ethical validity of each other's preferred approach is a starting point. It took centuries for Majority to develop procedures which approximate consistently valid outcomes. Consensus decision making has only been on the scene for 60 years and much remains to be done, above all the imperative to transcend the contradictions between the different paradigms of decision making.

Basing ourselves on the principle of "We decide what we do," we need to develop procedures which tell us when Counsel is appropriate, when Consensus is needed and when to take a vote. Within the family, the fostering of the virtues is the responsibility of the parent(s). Beyond the family, in work and social life, it is by participating in collective decision making that the virtues are fostered. In particular, Majority fosters solidarity and tolerance, while Consensus fosters inclusion and autonomy.

15   Postscript

When the book was published in 2016, it was generally well received by activists, who understood the importance of a balanced reflection on collective decision making. It was also well-received by those who understood the scientific principle underlying the study, that is, the identification of the 'germ cell' as the foundation for solving problems arising in political life.

On the other hand, criticism came from some socialists who rejected Consensus out of hand and regarded it as dangerous to even discuss it. Academic historians also largely dismissed the book because they failed to recognise the specific demands of writing a 1000-year long *genealogy* as distinct from the usual work of historians which focuses on specific episodes and generally dives much deeper into the records than was I able to. One criticism which, I confess, left me speechless, was from a young anarchist who told me that she simply found doing Consensus much more fun than doing Majority.

The few academic historians who had approached this question, focused on the history of *theories* of collective decision making, rather than the *practice* of collective decision making. Consequently, their histories leapt from antiquity to Condorcet's Jury Theorem of 1785, ignoring entirely the actual practice of collective decision making and its millennial-long development through the middle ages.

Interest in the topic was also found amongst practitioners in the field of Deliberative Democracy. This is a profession which has made great progress in the practice of collective decision making, but the practice rests on the guidance of a professional, appointed facilitator and the authorisation of the process by some governmental authority, who may or may not promise to implement decisions and sets the parameters of the process. My investigations have always focused on the *self-determination* of *self-organising* groups, so these practices are interesting, but secondary to the core questions. Above all, the practice of Deliberative Democracy faces an ethical deficit inasmuch as the process is always a managed process posing as self-determining, and as such, lacks moral authority.

Finally, psychologists have also been active in this field. Moscovici and Doise, in their *Conflict and Consensus: a General Theory of Collective Decisions* (1994) said that there were three authorities for a collective decision: Tradition, Science and Consensus, and came to the conclusion that Science was the best authority. In this they were essentially in agreement with Gerard Winstanley (1652) who held "government to be by Judges, called Elders, men fearing God and hating covetousness ... to be chosen by the people" but completely missed the ethical problems of collective decision making.

More recently, Sannino (2020) gathered together a group of people and left them in a room until they collectively decided to retire to the cafeteria, having arrived at a kind of 'creeping consensus' as to how to relieve their boredom. Sannino took this as a model of collective decision making. This caused me to reflect that in specifying a group of people in the same room, jointly deciding on a course of action as my unit of analysis or germ cell, I had neglected to specify that the group *gathered itself* together, and did so in response to a shared situation, presumably more pressing than boredom. This is not to deny that work such as that of Moscovici and Sannino is valuable, including as it does close observation of the formation of consensus without the use of a facilitator. But these psychological studies seem marginal alongside the real-life studies by advocates of Consensus and Deliberative Democracy.

CHAPTER 19

False Heroes and Villains

Australia. 2005. The Left is in a disgraceful position really. We have two very different enemies who should be at each other's throats, but we have allowed them to join forces against us.

I refer to the alliance of social conservatives and neo-liberals. Everything the social conservative holds dear is being done away with by the neo-liberals, who are meanwhile promoting everything the conservatives abhor. Neo-liberalism is destroying the family, laying waste to the Church, undermining authority and decimating communities, while channelling commercialism, pornography, homosexuality and hedonism into our own living rooms. While eroding the country's borders, driving people off the land and flooding the cities with foreigners, they have reduced people's lives to meaninglessness, with consumerism and scepticism eclipsing religiosity, cynicism displacing loyalty and patriotism, and greed overshadowing honesty.

And yet, right-wing leaders of the Anglo-Saxon Crusade like John Howard can present themselves as champions of social conservatism while orchestrating the one of the most devastating onslaughts upon traditional forms of life that history has ever known.

How are we letting them get away with this?

1 Villains and False Heroes

Have you ever read a novel or seen a play or a movie in which there is more than one villain? Do you know of a fairy tale, traditional legend or myth in which there is more than one villain? The Devil of course has his minions and hirelings, but no decent narrative has more than one villain. Imagine Superman fighting on two fronts, or Faust making a pact with two different Devils.

According to Vladimir Propp, the seven archetypal characters of any traditional fairy tale include, in addition to the villain, the false hero. The villain struggles with the hero and tries to thwart the hero's efforts to achieve his goal, classically to wed the princess. The false hero, or usurper, claims to be the hero, often seeking and reacting like a real hero, for example by trying to marry the princess. The villain has to be *defeated*, the false hero has to be *exposed*. The villain's motivations are utterly evil and beyond redemption, the false-hero has character weaknesses, even vices, but is not self-evidently evil.

Iago, Richard III and maybe Hamlet's uncle Claudius are among the few out-and-out villains in Shakespeare's plays. Most of his characters are complex personalities led into tragedy by their fallibility. Even Shakespeare's heroes are never just heroes. Shakespeare builds his tragedies through the medium of anti-heroes like Othello, Anthony and Brutus. But characters never end up as villains, or become villains, or are partly villains. A villain is a manifest evil, and the depth of a well-written plot derives just from how the characters *deal with* that, not the complexity of the villain's character.

The point is that the Left will only be clear about its project if we can formulate our analysis in a coherent and convincing narrative, and the evidence from thousands of years of story-telling is that you can't have two villains, but you *can* have a villain and a false hero.

The polemical stance involved in dealing with a false hero is quite different from dealing with a villain. So the Left needs to make a decision to either:

1. attack neo-liberalism as the real enemy and expose the social conservatives, especially the populists, and the fundamentalists as 'false heroes', or
2. attack social conservatism as the real enemy and expose the neo-liberals as 'false heroes'.

I see social conservatism as essentially a reaction to the erosion of traditional relationships by capitalism, and therefore it is neo-liberalism which is the real enemy. The extreme wings of social conservatism, Islamic and Christian Fundamentalism, claim to defend their respective forms of life against the impact of modernity, but each in their own way manifestly fail and betray the values they claim to defend.

There is much in the social conservative agenda which is antithetical to the Left – homophobia, patriarchy, cultural apartheid, religious dogmatism and so on as well as hostility to unions – but as I see it, in today's conditions, the significant support which such old-world attitudes get does not originate from the few old men who directly benefit from them, but rather from the feeling of a need to defend a viable and meaningful way of life which is under attack.

If, on the other hand, we were in a situation where the destruction of an oppressive traditional institution were the principal historical task, such as in countries ruled by a brutal Islamic theocracy, then perhaps one could take the converse option: directing anger against the reactionary regime, and criticising neo-liberalism as a false hero, attacking the oppressive institutions whilst preparing to reinstate the same power relations in a new form. But that is not where we are today in the 'Western' capitalist countries.

The present conjuncture is characterised by the collapse of social cohesion. It is not generally the case that people are suffering because they are trapped within an oppressive system of social relations, but more generally because they are denied a place in any robust and extended system of social relations. The over-zealous assertion of traditional relations is therefore to be understood as reaction in the literal sense of the word. It is an effort to withstand the neo-liberal onslaught. Success by the Left in overcoming the neo-liberal project would be unlikely to reinforce the power of socially dominant groups, such as religious leaders or male business leaders. It is more likely though that a neo-liberal triumph would benefit the most privileged groups in a traditional society, who would easily reposition themselves in the new set-up.

But those layers of the population who are most disadvantaged by traditional relations are among the very people who are being recruited to social conservatism and its fundamentalist troopers. Because it is they who face losing everything.

2   John Howard

How is Howard getting away with this?

The conservative side of politics has long relied on the aura of those 'born to rule'. A business leader is a natural candidate for the CEO of Australia Incorporated, and no one challenges the premise that the task of government is management of the national business. The relation of the voter to government is seen as that of a customer not that of a shareholder or employee to a company.

Since the final failure of macroeconomic policy that came with the Reagan-Thatcher era, the corporate mentality itself has been transformed. In the neo-liberal ethos, not only should government stay out of business, but business should stay out of business. Everything that isn't 'core business' is outsourced, and ultimately even core business is outsourced, via one-line budgets, work teams, outsourcing and franchising; even *Nike* has its sneakers made by someone else. Every relationship of collaboration is broken and replaced with a *commercial* relationship. Car builders no longer build cars, they just purchase and assemble components.

When this ethos penetrates government it has perverse effects. The 'national business' provides a few residual services, but as a business it can have no place for the reproduction of human life. Capital *consumes* human life which is reproduced externally (that is, outside of capital, in domestic relations). When government is run along the same lines, then for example, like corporate profit, a *budget surplus* contributes to *consumption* of the social fabric. A neo-liberal government becomes a *consumer* of the community rather than its representative.

Howard presents himself as the archetypical socially conservative businessman. However, the socially conservative businessman was never in the past a neo-liberal. The old-style conservative business leader was accustomed to command, and his style of management was autocratic. When transferred to the sphere of government this meant that he favoured a strong civil service, meritocracy and paternalism.

Howard is an icon of this kind of social conservatism. He is *also* a neo-liberal. But the social base for neo-liberalism is actually very small. This may be one of the reasons that the devastating impact of neo-liberalism on social cohesion remains one of the best-kept secrets of social science. But have the words of the *Communist Manifesto* ever been more apt? All fixed, fast-frozen relations, with their train of ancient and venerable prejudices and opinions, are swept away ... All that is solid melts into air, all that is holy is profaned, ...

It remains a public secret that Howard and his neo-liberal policies are responsible for destroying community, for creating pessimism, fear and insecurity, and for lending credence to reactionary social attitudes and religious fundamentalism. And the Left is failing to break this silence.

3   The Right-Wing Populist Narrative

The right-wing populist narrative which Howard and company rely on to keep the Left in its place follows the advice we have proposed, that is, of casting a villain and a false-hero. In foreign policy, Terrorists are the villains; those who jump up and down about the Geneva Conventions, the United Nations and the truth are false-heroes who are undermining the safety of the community. In domestic policy likewise. Child-molesters, dole-bludgers and lazy workers are the villain in each campaign; the civil rights and welfare lobby are the false heroes. And so on.

This has been an effective narrative. It has succeeded in creating an amalgam of the hard-working 'battlers', including tradespeople, labourers, managers and businesspeople on one side, and on the other, the idle and privileged do-gooder elite including the social justice community, academics and public servants. A remarkable manoeuvre!

It is much easier to run a polemic against a legitimate political opponent by painting them as an obstructer, a procrastinator, a dupe, a softy, etc., etc., than to give them power by painting them as a villain. Think of it from the third person point of view. If the listener is at all sympathetic to the target of your polemic, and you ascribe evil motives to them, then you have lost the listener. On the other hand, if you cast the target as well-meaning, but misguided or irresolute, the listener can be more receptive. You can tell your listener that you think they are misled, but no one listens to someone telling them that their cause is evil.

The most successful alliance on the left has always been the intelligentsia and the organised working class. The neo-liberals have succeeded in undermining this alliance, weakening the organised working class and isolating the progressive intelligentsia, at the same time appointing themselves as Dracula in charge of the blood bank.

4   An Alternative Left-Wing Narrative

The proposition is that our polemics need to be based on a polemic which goes something like this. By unrelenting commercialism, the economic rationalists are destroying Australian agriculture and industry, trashing the public education and health services, creating economic insecurity and inequality, and undermining the family and community. The conservatives claim to be opposing these processes, upholding family values, calling for curfews on unruly youth, giving more powers to the police, and so on, but this is only treating the symptom not the disease, etc., etc.

This is a different narrative from one which begins from the fact that both the socially repressive agenda and the socially destructive agenda emanate from the same prime ministerial office. But even though John Howard is only one person, he is representing two quite distinct social bases. Which *should* be a problem for *him*.

It is tempting to treat social conservatism and neo-liberalism as 'twin evils', or as aspects of the same anti-union phalanx, but to engage in polemics that accept the identity of social conservatism and neo-liberalism, actually *reinforces* the amalgam of the two social bases. What we really need to do is to separate them and set them against one another.

We have to patiently explain to those who support social conservatives, exactly how neo-liberal policies are destroying family and community. Central to such an explanation I believe is the notion of *commodification*, or what may be better referred to as 'commercialism'. Commercialism replaces an ethic of virtue and duty with the ethic of the market. It transforms the family into a contractual arrangement. Learning becomes purchase of a certificate. Private medicine sells cures for non-existent illnesses rather than keeping people well. Food producers manufacture sweet-tasting poisons instead of food. Culture is reduced to a feel-good vehicle for advertisements; a person's worth is just whatever they have to sell. Career means a big salary, corporate mumbo-jumbo, putting the kids in childcare and being able to purchase useless and expensive consumer goods.

In battles concerning social issues, the Left has largely already *won* and continued prosecution of the war against social conservatism brings collateral damage. We agree with many of the evils the conservatives criticise. The argument we have with social conservatives and religious fundamentalists is they have failed to fix any of what we *agree* are the real evils of modern society.

The argument we have with neo-liberals is that they are the *cause* of the problems in modern society.

PS 2020. In recent times, I have noticed the emergence of stories which have multiple villains – MI5, corporations, criminals, corrupt police ... – all figuring as intangible evils thwarting the hero from the shadows. This genre is perhaps reflective of our times, and conveys a feeling of powerlessness. Also, we have a new array of false heroes today, and complex situations like the people of Iran suffering under an Islamic Republic *and* a US embargo, which deserve a new analysis.

CHAPTER 20

Amartya Sen on Critical Voice and Social Choice Theory

1   The Critique of Distributive Justice

The problem of inequality, and the exclusion of a large proportion of the world's population from a share of enjoyment of the world's products and a share in deciding how the world's products should be distributed, is as great a problem today as it has ever been.

However, movements for distributive justice have been demobilised and even marginalised. Movements for cultural recognition, which have been most prominent in recent decades, seem no longer able to speak to the problems of the most downtrodden sections of the world. A new paradigm of justice centred around concepts of democracy and freedom seems to be emerging but the relation between a number of different paradigms remains unclear.

Amartya Sen is a development economist who has been conducting a relentless 'internal criticism' of concepts of distributive justice and equality over the past 30 years. Whilst retaining the *form* of a distributive theory, he has successively interrogated *what it is* which ought to be distributed more equally, to a point where the *content* is now closer to that of the politics of recognition, than to that of a traditional theory of distributive justice.

2   Amartya Sen

As a youngster in Bengal in 1943, Amartya Sen witnessed India's last famine, during which two to three million people died. He also witnessed the sectarian murder of a poor Muslim labourer, who had been forced to risk death by seeking work in a Hindu area.

Although Sen has lived most of his life in Britain and the US, he has never been away from India for longer than six months, and there is no doubt that the problems and achievements of independent India have been the central concern of his life.

Sen was a PhD student at Cambridge when Kenneth Arrow published his famous theorem on 'social choice' theory in 1951. Sen has remained fascinated with this highly mathematical theory ever since. His academic supervisors at Trinity College, Cambridge however – Joan Robinson and Maurice Dobbs – were not so excited by this theory, and Sen wrote his PhD thesis, *Choice of Techniques*, on the alternative paths of development open to the newly independent former colonies. In this work, completed in only 12 months, Sen advocated that former colonies should use their relatively low labour costs to promote basic health care and literacy, rather than pursuing rapid industrialisation through capital investment. All his subsequent work has continued to focus on these, his "old obsessions," and his other abiding concerns: inequality, the emancipation of women, and democratic government.

Sen claims:

> In line with the importance I attach to the role of public discussion as a vehicle for social change and economic progress ... I have, throughout my life, avoided giving advice to the 'authorities.' Indeed, I have never counselled any government, preferring to place my suggestions and critiques – for what they are worth – in the public domain.
> SEN, 1999, pp. xiii–xiv

I consider Sen's expressed position to be a misrecognition of the actual positioning of his theoretical interventions. In this article, I argue that there is a theoretical tension in Sen's work, reflected in the ambiguity of delivering advice to government via the public domain, speaking both from the standpoint of social movements and from the standpoint of government, a tension between ethical principles which corresponds to two different subject positions. This ambiguity is shown, for example, in Sen's contradictory positions in relation to social choice theory, in his concept of 'comprehensive outcome' in which process is included as part of outcome, in his attempt to introduce agency into the utilitarian conception of the person and an element of consequentialism into otherwise deontological libertarian ethics. I think Sen's ambiguous subject position reflects the contradictory subject positions inherent in a social justice movement which has become the government, and in that sense, is an ambiguity with a thoroughly objective and progressive basis.

I will return to the question of 'social choice' theory and Sen's subject position later. The first issue on which I want to focus is his conception of social justice and human needs.

3 Human Needs and Social Justice

3.1 Wealth

After a period of work on social choice theory, urged by his wife to involve himself in more 'practical issues', in 1973 Sen wrote *On Economic Inequality*. This work focused entirely on real income as the measure of advantage and well-being, examining problems like the setting of the 'poverty line' and measuring degrees of poverty and inequality. Sen's idea here was that if a society was to make a *decision* about the degree of inequality it would tolerate, then it needed a suitable, agreed *measure* of inequality.

In using real income as the measure of well-being, Sen was only doing what everyone else in the field was doing, and in most cases still is doing. Indeed, there can be no escaping the fact that, in societies where most goods are acquired through the market, real income is indeed a good first approximation to social welfare and the freedom a person has in determining their own life.

Sen had taught with John Rawls at Harvard from 1970, and partly in response to the debate over what constituted the 'basic goods' a person needed in order to participate in democratic social life (which Rawls had conceived in terms of basic human needs), Sen set out to more closely investigate the nature of what people really need by way of 'basic goods'.

3.2 Functioning

This led to the seminal paper published in 1980 entitled 'Equality of What?' in which Sen put forward the concept of 'functioning'. The commodities over which a person had command were, after all, only a means to an end, and that end was a level of functioning in life, being able to live the kind of life that one values. This 'functioning' was subject to objective measurement as well: life expectancy, infant mortality, literacy, morbidity, political participation and so on. An example of the indicators to which this approach draws attention was the statistic that the average life expectancy of a resident of a poor neighbourhood in New York was *less* than that of a citizen of Bangladesh, despite the fact that not only incomes, but *real* incomes, were many times higher in Harlem than in Dhaka.

Sen frequently uses the well-being of someone with a disability to illustrate the point that what someone can *achieve* with a given amount of wealth depends on certain conditions, and any measure of inequality has to take these 'conversion factors' into account, focusing on outcomes rather than means.

Further, even though we value real income as a means to overcome challenges, a person who spends money in order to fend off the dangers of rampant crime and endemic disease is obviously less well-off than a person who enjoys good public health and security, and has no *need* for such expenditure. Thus, the perspective of functionings also brings into account the benefits a person receives from *public goods*, not just private labour and the market.

3.3 Capability

However, on closer inspection, the measure of functionings misses an important dimension of well-being, namely freedom. When Gandhi chose to fast, he was clearly not suffering the same level of deprivation as someone starving as a result of poverty, because although Gandhi had the opportunity to eat, he chose to use his freedom to *not* eat. Sen may have also had in mind comparisons between India and China. Even though, overall, China had far surpassed India in its achievements in overcoming illiteracy, ill-health and hunger, this had been achieved at the cost of choice.

Thus, the real measure of well-being had to be not the actual functioning which a person exercised, but *capability* – the set of functionings from which one can choose. So for example, the university graduate who is serving tables has an unmistakable advantage over their uneducated colleague, for they have a *choice*, just as the adventurer who suffers exposure while mountain climbing is more advantaged than the slum-dweller who freezes out of necessity.

How to measure capability? Sen's relentless concern with measurement, even when the problem appears insoluble, is a great strength. Measurement is integral to all conceptions of distributive justice and social choice, and Sen never tires of subjecting the most intractable concepts to quantification and ranking.

There are two basic approaches to measurement of capability. On one hand, the functioning which a person chooses from those available to them can be taken, *ipso facto*, to be the *most valued functioning*, and therefore a measure of the value of the capability set from which it was eventually chosen. However, a person may choose a functioning for all sorts of reasons (for example, a person may *choose* to give up their freedom in order to care for a sick friend, but this hardly proves that such a life is their favoured choice). Consequently, capability needs to be measured as a *set* according to the whole range of functionings it contains. This is a challenging technical task of course, but conceptually it is clear enough: well-being is properly measured neither by *wealth* (which is but a means to an end) nor by *functioning* (which fails to reflect the valued choices which have been *forgone*) but by *capability*.

It is these concepts (functioning and capability) for which Sen is most famous, but in the late 1990s, driven perhaps by his critique of utilitarianism and a growing conviction that women's emancipation is the central issue in development, Sen took this determination of human needs two steps further.

3.4 Voice

Sen's central critique of utilitarianism is that by reducing human motivation to the maximisation of a person's utility (however defined), utilitarianism effectively *eliminates agency*. The capacity of a person to *choose* to do one thing and not another Sen saw as an essential ingredient of well-being. But so long as choice was confined to selection between options determined by others – so long as a person's capability set was determined by social arrangements in which one had no say – then there is no real freedom.

In *Development as Freedom* (1999), Sen further determined advantage from wealth to functioning to capability and now to *voice*:

> ... the general enhancement of political and civil freedoms is central to the process of development itself. The relevant freedoms include the liberty of acting as citizens who matter and whose voices count, rather than living as well-fed, well-clothed and well-entertained vassals. The instrumental role of democracy and human rights, important as it undoubtedly is, has to be distinguished from its constitutive importance.
> SEN, 1999, p. 288

With *Development as Freedom* (1999), Sen moved from including freedom as *instrumental* to well-being, to seeing freedom as an essential *ingredient* of well-being, to conceiving of well-being *as* freedom: freedom to lead a life that one has reason to value, including both positive freedom (real opportunities) and negative freedom (freedom from constraints and interference), actualised as *achievement*.

In *India: Development as Participation* (2002), Sen shows that women's well-being, fertility and child survival all depend on women's agency (which I am taking as synonymous with 'voice' at this point) including access to employment, women's literacy and property rights – independently of the overall level of opulence, industrialisation or literacy. This advantage shows up, for example, in gender differences in child survival and longevity. Women's voice (as for example in the Indian state of Kerala where there is a long tradition of women's education and property rights) proved more effective in lowering fertility than China's one-child policy, and more effective in increasing longevity than the greater wealth and industrialisation of northern India.

Sen shows how those sections of society which have more than their fair share of *voice* in the determination of government priorities (men rather than women, city people rather than rural people, the middle classes and military elite) enjoy capability sets larger than others, because they are able to see to it that social arrangements are geared to meeting their needs and providing them with opportunities. While voice is therefore instrumental in the formation of real freedom, it is also constitutive of freedom, an achievement, an end in itself. We thus have a fourth concept in the series of determination of human needs: *wealth* (or opulence), *functioning* (or real living standards), *capability* (or real opportunity) and *voice* – the say that someone has in determining the social arrangements to which they are subject.

Sen's observation that no people which has had the vote has ever suffered from famine aptly illustrates the point.

3.5 *Critical Voice*

In *India: Development as Participation* (2002), Sen goes one step further as a result of his study of 'son preference'. Son preference is the tendency of people in certain cultures to prefer a son to a daughter, resorting to abortion of female foetuses or simply neglecting the health of young girls. As a result of these practices, India and China are each 'missing' about 40 million women in their current populations. Sen observed that this tendency not only *increases* with industrialisation and rising real incomes, but increased even in those societies where women had a voice. Even educated women and women who have full control over the decision whether or not to abort a female foetus may be active participants in exercising son-preference because they *share* their husband's preference for a son.

> This type of gender inequality [son preference] cannot be removed, at least in the short run, by the enhancement of women's empowerment and agency, since that agency is itself an integral part of the cause of natality inequality. This recognition demands an important modification – and indeed an extension – of our understanding of the role of women's agency in eliminating gender inequality in India. The enhancement of women's agency which does so much to eliminate sex differentials in mortality rates (and also in reducing fertility and mortality rates in general) cannot be expected, *on its own*, to produce a similar elimination of sex differentials at birth and abortion, and correspondingly in the population of children. What is needed is not merely freedom and power to act, but also freedom and power to question and reassess the prevailing norms and values. The pivotal issue is *critical agency*. Strengthening women's agency will not, by itself, solve the problem of 'son preference' when that works through the desires of the mothers themselves.
>
> SEN, 2002, p. 258

> ... the agency of women is effective in promoting those goals which women tend to value. When those values are distorted by centuries of inequality, for example yielding the perception that boys are to be welcomed more than girls, then the empowerment of women can go hand in hand with persistent inequality and discrimination in some fields, in particular 'boy preference' in births (with possibly brutal results in the form of sex-specific abortions). Indeed, the agency of women can never be adequately free if traditionally discriminatory values remain unexamined and unscrutinised. While values may be culturally influenced ..., it is possible to overcome the barriers of inequality imposed by tradition through greater freedom to question, doubt, and – if convinced – reject. An adequate realisation of women's agency relates not only to the freedom to act but also to the freedom to question and reassess. *Critical agency* is a great ally of development.
>
> SEN, 2002, p. 274

To reflect the fact that recognition as an equal participant in the social and political life of a society still leaves the person trapped within dominant customs, beliefs and modes of living, which for example, may include misrecognition of their personhood or unjust constraints on their activity, Sen introduced the term '*critical voice*'.

This concept of critical voice is thus the fifth in a series of determinations of advantage: wealth, functioning, capability, voice and finally, *critical voice*.

Critical voice is the capacity of a person living 'inside' a society to form views available from a position 'outside' that society:

> ... virtually every society tends to have dissenters, and even the most repressive fundamentalist regimes can – and typically do – have dissenters .... Even if the perspective of the dissenters is influenced by their reading of foreign authors, the viewpoints and critical perspectives of these members are still 'internal' to the society.
>
> SEN, 2002, pp. 476–477

Critical agency refers "not only to the freedom to act but also to the freedom to question and reassess." The answer to the question Sen asked in 1980 – *Equality of what?* – seems increasingly to be 'critical voice'. This does not imply that the demand for equality of critical voice necessarily has traction as a normative demand, any more than does equality of wealth. But 'critical voice' does more truly determine the essence of human need and is the true measure of inequality in a society.

Critical voice is both *instrumental*, in that it is needed in order to sustain the other elements of well-being, and *constitutive*, in that only the person with critical voice is truly free.

That which is the means to well-being, not just apparently, but essentially, comes to be an end in itself, *constituent* of well-being. Thus, for example, while education is valued initially for its contribution to job-seeking, over time it comes to be valued for itself.

Conversely, that which is formally the end, can only be real to the extent that it is supported by appropriate means. Thus, for example, even though everyone in a parliamentary democracy formally has an equal voice, without an adequate capability set, without an adequate functioning and wealth, this right is no more than formal.

So it is not a question of Sen having 'changed his mind', and abandoned an economic conception of well-being and a paradigm of distributive justice in favour of a political conception of justice and a recognition paradigm. Each step in the further determination of well-being both *overcomes and maintains* the previous determination, *including* it within a yet deeper determination.

Thus advantage conferred by command over commodities is by no means done away with in the determination of well-being in terms of critical voice. The capability to choose the functioning of one's own choice retains functioning as the substance of well-being. The voice needed to secure an adequate capability for oneself is actualised only in the enjoyment of that capability. And conversely, voice can only be exercised to the extent that a person enjoys a wide capability set, of which the exercise of voice turns out to be the essential component.

Critical voice is the truth of voice: critical voice can exist only in and through voice, but voice proves to be of little value unless it is critical.

Sen's critical examination of *distributive justice* took the form of asking himself the question: "Equality of what?" But equality of 'critical voice' is surely the key claim of the *politics of recognition*.

In arriving at a determination of well-being which is appropriate to the subject position of the representative of a social movement who demands to be heard, Sen retains his concern for the *consequences* of policy for the *majority* and for the need to critically weigh the preferences and well-being of *all* citizens, irrespective of their social position – an ethical concern appropriate for the representative of a democratic government.

Although it is not spelt out at this stage, it appears that Sen has arrived, by means of a successive critique of egalitarianism, at an ethic which places recognition within a paradigm of *distributive* justice.

4   Utilitarianism and Positivism

In the light of this reconstruction of Sen's theoretical journey, we can understand why, as Sen became the dominant figure in welfare economics, utilitarianism became Sen's nemesis and the subject of a sustained critique over several decades. Sen's critical relationship to utilitarianism is quite complex however, and can only be understood in relation to how utilitarianism has changed in parallel with economic science, in response to positivist criticism.

Utilitarianism is political economy translated into the language of ethics. Utilitarianism originated with the 'first positivism' of Auguste Comte, John Stuart Mill and Herbert Spencer, the positivism of law-governed social progress. Accordingly, Bentham formulated the principle of Utilitarianism effectively as an apology for political economy, identifying capital accumulation with social progress.

As Sen points out, the early literature of utilitarianism is replete with careful distinctions between economic and ethical value, but such declarations cannot detract from the factual affinity between utilitarianism and political economy.

For example, the definition John Stuart Mill gives of 'utility' in *Utilitarianism* (1861) is entirely consistent with the definition he gives in his *Principles of Political Economy* (1848). In the chapter on exchange, he demonstrates that every act of free-market exchange increases the sum of utility, thus establishing the fundamental principle of utilitarianism as a *law of political economy*.

From the fact that a dollar makes more difference to a pauper than to a millionaire, utilitarianism perversely advocates a greater and greater inequality of wealth (see Sen, 1987, pp. 19–20), but this is, after all, nothing but what is required by the laws of political economy.

In the late 1860s, a new wave of positivism, the positivism of anti-metaphysics, began within political economy itself, giving rise to the marginal revolution in economics and ultimately the Mach/Einstein revolution in physics. The 'second positivism' banished the concept of 'value' from economic science, confining economics to the phenomenon of *price*. The result was a significant narrowing of the conception of welfare to *real income*.

This was the state of Utilitarianism at the time of the Great Depression when the absurdity of the criterion of the sum-of-utility became starkly obvious. The illusion that the sum-of-wealth could form a valid criterion for welfare economics could not now be harboured even by the most hardened and cynical apologist of capitalism.

John Maynard Keynes (1936) proved the fallacy of the theory of marginal utility as a macro-economic theory and the inadequacy of utilitarianism, as it then was, as the basis for welfare economics. Strange as it would seem, the reaction of utilitarianism in abandoning the interpersonal sum-of-utility, was to take, not an egalitarian turn, but in effect the opposite direction. Rather than querying the sum-of-utility as a criterion of the good, the 'third positivism', Logical Positivism, denied the legitimacy of interpersonal *comparison* of utility altogether – it was declared 'unscientific' to suggest that the well-being of one person could be greater or less than that of any other person.

Economic science overcame the challenge of Logical Positivism by drawing on a mathematical apparatus named after Vilfredo Pareto. This new economic science eschewed reference to utility, basing itself exclusively on acts of exchange and choice. In logical positivist terms, 'utility' can only be defined in terms of each agent's *preference ranking* as objectively manifested in the choices they make.

The crucial concept here is the 'Pareto optimum' – that state of the market where there is no possible exchange, deemed by both parties to be beneficial, which remains to be executed. By this move, a new utilitarianism is established in which the good is a Pareto optimum rather than the sum of utilities. The Pareto optimum could be a universal famine, so long as no mutually beneficial exchange is left unmade. No one owns anything that someone else wants. It is 'the best of all possible worlds' for the Logical Positivist Pangloss.

If I could coin a term, Kenneth Arrow's economics, together with his contributions to complexity theory and social-choice theory marks the beginning of a 'fourth positivism' based on the concepts of information and communication science. And the contemporary form of utilitarianism is what we call neoliberalism or 'economic rationalism'. It is self-evident that this ethic is as different from the utilitarianism of Jeremy Bentham as the economics of Kenneth Arrow is different from that of David Ricardo.

'Critique of Utilitarianism' therefore has to be seen in this sense: criticism which traces the outlines of the development of political economy is what could be called 'internal criticism', whilst only criticism which pits itself as much against political economy as against its ethical expression, could be called 'external criticism'. In Sen, we find essentially internal criticism.

5   Utilitarianism and the Real Ethic of Bourgeois Society

There are more varieties of utilitarianism than there are species of butterfly. However, I believe that the above sketch illustrates the essential development of utilitarianism, reflecting the development of bourgeois science. Utilitarianism expresses the *real* ethic of participants in political economic discourse.

Preferences are accepted uncritically as 'externals'. 'Real' means: within the bounds of the 'assumptions' of political economy.

There are however at least three distinct subject positions from which the ethics of the market can be viewed: (i) that of the economic agent (obeying the law, keeping promises, telling the truth, etc.), (ii) that of a government (regulating market outcomes and legislating), and (iii) that of a participant in a social movement, who could be critical of the very existence of political economy.

Utilitarianism is an ethic of type (i). Historically, utilitarians have been very prominent in advising governments, but this is simply evidence of the capacity of political economy to manage government rather than the reverse.

Egalitarianism, as the ethics of the market regulator, is an ethic of type (ii). A democratic government, which recognises the equal moral worth of all its citizens, must at least to some extent, attend to the demands of egalitarianism. Egalitarianism has a history as well, perhaps most succinctly summed up in Marx's 1844 three-stage schema: primitive or *crude* communism, *political* communism – 'democratic or despotic', and *humanism* as the *transcendence* of private property. The egalitarianism of our age is an 'electoral egalitarianism', and accordingly, Sen formulates the problem for egalitarianism in terms of social-choice theory.

At whatever historical juncture, the ethical dispute between egalitarianism and utilitarianism is a struggle between two different subject positions. Utilitarianism is at best indifferent to equality, but its significance comes from the fact that utilitarianism informs us about the 'real' ethic of the market. The interest that egalitarianism has in utilitarianism is that utilitarianism describes the conditions which egalitarianism aims to overcome. It is from this point of view that egalitarianism is interested in the 'internal' criticism of utilitarianism. The same issue confronts those who address themselves to the ecological and social fallout from the market.

6 Sen's Critique of Social Choice Theory

For more than 50 years, long before the notion of 'critical voice' found its way to the centre of his work, Sen has been wrestling with this paradox in terms of Arrow's social choice theory. Sen tells the story of the origin of Kenneth Arrow's famous Impossibility Theorem as follows:

> In 1948, Olaf Helmer, a logician at the RAND Corporation, wondered about the legitimacy of applying game theory to international relations (the 'players' were countries, not 'individuals'), and asked young Arrow,

> a PhD student, 'In what sense could collectivities be said to have utility functions?' Arrow replied that 'economists had thought about that question and that it had been answered by Abram Bergson's notion of the social welfare function'. As Arrow settled down to writing an exposition for Helmer, he was soon convinced that no satisfactory method for aggregating a set of orderings into one ordering existed. The impossibility theorem and related results and their proofs came within 'about three weeks'. Arrow changed his dissertation topic to reflect the new finding, and sent off a brief exposition of the result to the *Journal of Political Economy* at the request of the editor.
>
> SEN, 2002, p. 330

A union delegate (for example) needs to have some way of knowing the preferences of the group they represent, but it is a big step from this legitimate, if specialised, need to the idea of establishing the principles of justice for a whole society.

> It is already to make some substantive political assumptions to suppose that there is or should be one sovereign decision centre to determine what is right, even within a limited time span, for society as a whole.
>
> SEN, 1999, p. 2

Social choice theory concerns a *group representative* whose task is to determine a *group preference* from the ordered lists of choices submitted by each group member. These 'ordered lists' are supposedly lists held by each individual member of the population in which they have placed every possible state of the world in order of preference. These preference lists are then handed to the 'returning officer' to compute the *group*'s preference list.

Unsurprisingly, only the most abstract imaginable problems find any solution in this theory. The observation, which goes back to the Marquis de Condorcet's (1785) theorem proving that there is no consistent way of deciding between any more than two options by majority voting, already contained the essential truth which is extended and generalised in Arrow's theorem. The 'group preference' is the preference arrived at by *whatever process* the participants submitted themselves to (see Blunden, 2016 and Chapter 18, this volume).

Once we have dispensed with vain hopes for the sovereignty of majorities, the validity of answers to multiple-choice questions as expressions of individual opinion and the mystifications like 'public opinion', there still remains the problem of the possibility, and grounds, for a group representative to determine their own obligations. Sen suffers from none of these illusions about process, but he comes back again and again to Arrow's social-choice theory. In a strong sense, social choice theory is to parliamentary politics what utilitarian ethics is to political economy, and all four are closely tied together.

Like utilitarianism, social-choice theory takes the preferences of the agents as *given*, effectively as 'externals'. Social choice theory concerns itself only with the calculation by which *any* combination of preferences, however absurd or evil, could be processed to produce a group preference. All ideas about agents discussing with one another, changing each other's mind, doing deals, making promises, sympathising with one another, learning, problem-solving, or whatever, lie outside the bounds of and are *irrelevant* to social choice theory.

Social choice theory, which is concerned *only* with the problem of the group representative or 'returning officer', is therefore closely tied to a specific subject position, the same subject position as that of egalitarian ethics. A critique of social choice theory is therefore a critique of parliamentary politics, but with the same qualifications as we made in respect to the critique of utilitarianism. 'Internal criticism' aimed at improving the processing of agent preferences into a group preference is wedded to that type of government which alienates people from government and utilises illusions about parliament and 'public opinion' to maintain the fraud. A *real* critique of social choice theory must be directed at exposing the fraud of parliamentarism, and re-orienting attention to genuine and effective processes of *formation* of a collective will.

Sen holds to the point that *however* people arrive at their preferences, there still remains the problem of processing them into a group preference:

> Analyses of dialogues and exchanges, and of their impact on individual preferences can indeed be important for social choice theory. While there has not been any denial of the importance of such communication in contributions to social choice theory, this has not been a particularly active area of investigation within the discipline. ... As and when the set of individual preferences alters, there would be related alterations in the corresponding social choices, and in understanding this relationship, social choice arguments of the standard kind would continue to be relevant. It should also be noted that the extensions which are called for in investigating preference formation would often require substantive *empirical* presumptions, regarding what can and cannot be plausibly achieved through dialogues or swaps, taking us beyond the thoroughly analytical format of traditional social choice theory.
>
> SEN, 2002

And against James Buchanan's (1962) argument for consensus decision-making, he argues:

> Difficulties in social choice arise precisely because unanimity does not exist on many questions. What do we do then? One answer is to insist on unanimity for a *change*, and if there is no such unanimity for any proposed change, then to stick to the *status quo*. ... Marie Antoinette's opposition to the First Republic would have saved the monarchy in France.
> SEN, 1970, p. 25

Sen continues to look for a process by means of which a returning officer could determine a group preference without troubling the voters to sort things out amongst themselves, but he argues that more has to be taken into account than simply the list of preferences. In arguing against the use of real income as the measure of well-being and for the use of functioning instead, Sen also argued that the former was *lacking in information content*. In the 1999 *Development as Freedom*, Sen sums up his criticism of social choice theory along similar lines:

> The informational base for this class of rules, of which the majority decision procedure is a prominent example, is thus extremely limited, and it is clearly quite inadequate for making informed judgments about welfare economic problems. This is not primarily because it leads to inconsistency (as generalised in the Arrow theorem), but because we cannot really make social judgments with so little information. ... Acceptable social rules would tend to take notice of a variety of other relevant facts in judging the division of the cake: who is poorer than whom, who gains how much in terms of welfare or of the basic ingredients of living, how is the cake being 'earned' or 'looted' and so on. The insistence that no other information is needed (and that other information, if available, could not influence the decisions to be taken) makes these rules *not very interesting* for economic decision making. Given this recognition, the fact that there is also a problem of inconsistency – in dividing a cake through votes – may well be seen not so much as a problem, but as a welcome relief from the unswerving consistency of brutal and informationally obtuse procedures.
> SEN, 1999, p. 252, my italics

and in perhaps the most damning criticism of all, going to the issue of agency:

... in arriving at social choice solutions of diverse views on systemic process concern, preferences cannot do all the work. In particular, rules of aggregation are processes too, and they are needed to do the social choice exercise of combining diverse views (even about systemic processes). Rules that fix the constituent features of the overall arrangement for aggregation are sometimes called 'the constitution' – in terms of which individual preferences are put together to arrive at a social choice. For example, in the Arrovian system, rules such as the independence of irrelevant alternatives and the Pareto principle are not themselves put to a vote. In fact, if these rules themselves were to be determined by a 'prior' voting mechanism or some other social choice process, there would, then, be a need to have *other* rules governing the choice of these 'prior' social choice mechanisms. At some stage or other, some rules would have to come from outside the immediate domain of individual preferences.
> SEN, 2002, p. 626

With these two paragraphs, Sen effectively damns Arrow's social choice theory. This belies the fact the Sen has spent 50 years with this theory, along with entire academic departments, describing Arrow's Impossibility Theorem as 'momentous', seizing every opportunity to virtually canonise Arrow himself, and even the book from which the last quote is taken (written three years after *Development as Freedom*) spends about 500 of its 700 pages eulogising the 'Arrovian' social choice theory.

This is strange indeed, but the contradiction is inherent in Sen's own subject position, a contradiction inherent in a society in which the major decisions affecting everyone's lives are taken not by the person themself, but by governments posing as representatives.

7   Conclusion

Beginning from an immersion in economics, through a painstaking critique of existing notions of utilitarianism and egalitarianism, Sen arrived at the conclusion that the essence of well-being and advantage is not wealth, or functioning, or capability or even voice. The essence of well-being is *critical voice*.

Egalitarianism must therefore address itself to the distribution of voice and critical voice in particular, rather than just real incomes, functioning or even capability. But this does not and cannot produce any kind of magic formula for a just distribution.

The whole point is that to the extent that people have a critical voice in the social arrangements determining their own life, they can determine those arrangements in collaboration with others affected by those same social arrangements. Through his critique of distributive justice, by introducing into the heart of a fundamentally distributive conception, a concept of recognition (critical voice), Sen seems to have transcended the opposition between distributive and recognition paradigms of justice.

The conception of critical voice at which Sen has arrived has only a sketchy, sociological elaboration in Sen's own work, but there does exist a vast literature of social theory and moral philosophy on critical voice.

The result is by no means unproblematic. Equitable distribution of critical voice is a kind of utopian conception akin to the 'withering away of the state'. Indeed, the very idea of 'distribution', as if there were a fixed total of something to be distributed, is called into question by this critique. Nevertheless, the concept can still function as a regulative ideal. The social measures which tend to give people critical voice are well-known – education and literacy, a free press, public broadcasting and communication media, property rights, access to the labour market, freedom of belief and association, freedom to travel, disability support of all kinds, as well as security, public health, food, land and shelter. Each of these factors can be assessed from the point of view: *how does this measure contribute to the distribution of critical voice?*

Perhaps Sen's work points to a new conception of the relation between the politics of distributive justice, the politics of recognition and the new anti-corporate movements? Sen's conception is not just of 'folk paradigms' or social movements which are antagonistic to one another, but rather that the 'new' social movements arose by way of a *critique* of redistribution as a paradigm of justice, and that the notion of 'critical voice' is emerging, again, by way of a *critique* of recognition notions of justice.

The relation between these competing paradigms of justice is therefore one of *sublation* or transcendence, i.e., negation in the *Hegelian* sense, rather than negation in the simple sense of being alternatives.

CHAPTER 21

Comments on 'Social Capital'

The debate currently (2004) going on around the concept of 'social capital' is an arena of struggle in which the Left can learn something – about the world, about ourselves and about others involved in trying to resolve the problems of poverty and exclusion – and in which we can find others with whom we can make common cause. Marxists need to be present in this debate, even while we refuse to accept the validity of the concept of 'social capital'. The central contradiction in this discourse lies in the *quantification* of important, but essentially *qualitative*, information. This contradiction continually rears its head even in the work of the most fervent advocates of 'social capital'.

If we are to participate in the debate while at the same time refusing to join the confusion, then we need to recognise the value of the qualitative data gathered together under the heading of 'social capital'. However, we must have an alternative response to the data – a viable suggestion for how these observations should be conceptualised. Viable proposals are needed about how poverty and exclusion can be alleviated, which in some way responds to the discoveries that theorists in this area have made about the causes of poverty. The point is that people are poor because they have been *made poor* by the existing social arrangements. This is an opportunity to critique these arrangements through an examination of exactly how it is that people are excluded or marginalised and *made poor*.

To designate relationships as a form of money, or for that matter, to determine relationships in *any quantitative* way presupposes that the relationships can be compared with others and exchanged. Quantification of relationships which cannot be exchanged for others is meaningless. Relationships are quantified or exchanged every day in capitalist society through the activity of the economy, but the theoretical abstraction of social relations from their context and their quantification is subject to the same kind of constraints as the practical monetisation of relations carried out in the economy.

The question is: does the specific quantification process carried out in the measurement of 'social capital' correspond to some *objective* process of quantification or exchange? The answer to *this* question is quite complex and is obfuscated by the lack of clarity about the concept by those who use it, most of whom believe that quantification (or abstraction) is a legitimate theoretical exercise whether or not it corresponds to any objective process.

To resolve the problem of quantification, it is necessary to dwell for a moment on the quite different concepts of social capital developed by the originators of the literature. Everyone knows that there are many, conflicting definitions of social capital, but most believe that one day a consensus will be arrived at in terms of some operational definition for the use of statisticians. However, the social capital theorists are generally unaware of how different are the concepts of social capital of the two main originators, Robert Putnam (1993; 2001) and James Coleman (1990). In general all the useful work being done are refinements of Robert Putnam's concept, while the work which is derivative from Coleman is generally of little value. However, Coleman has played an important historical role in giving scientific legitimacy to the quantification of 'social capital', and it is worthwhile taking account of the difference between his conception and the general idea derived from Putnam's work which drives almost all current work on 'social capital'.

Coleman's definition of social capital was intended as an extension of the concepts and methods of economics into broader social theory. It does pass many (though not all) of the tests as a legitimate extension of the concept of capital.

For Coleman, social capital is control over an event in which another subject has an interest. This summation depends on the extent that the other has direct or indirect control over events of interest to the subject itself. Thus, in summation it expresses the extent of control one has over events in which one has an interest, mediated by the wider circle of such relations. This concept is thus all about *power*, as reflected in the title of Coleman's (1968) first paper on the topic: 'The marginal utility of a voting commitment'.

For Coleman, social capital may be the private property of a subject (an individual, company, government, etc.) and may be traded for a profit. A critique of Coleman's concept of social capital cannot simply rely on a semantic dispute over the word 'capital'. Coleman's claim is that someone owing you a favour is a form of capital, something which is easily monetised or exchanged and can be accumulated.

Coleman's conception runs into problems however. The hypothetical society in which 'social capital is complete' – which is *normative* for Coleman – is an even more horrific dystopian vision than the economic rationalists' ideal market, what I call 'Tammany Hall capitalism'. 'Social capital' can be validly conceived as a quantity only to the extent that there exist *objective* processes for the interconvertibility of different *forms* of the entity. However, the convertibility of 'social capital' (including bribery, corruption and blackmail) is not only limited, but it *ought* to be limited, despite the fact that crime *is* a resource for people living in poverty.

Even if social capital *were* extensively convertible and therefore conceivable as a quantity, there is no basis for the proposition that the theory of *linear action* would be applicable to its summation. Thus, the elaborate mathematical apparatus that Coleman erects on his concept of social capital is spurious. But since few understand linear action theory or the conditions of its validity, the exercise serves only to promote the claim that social capital is a legitimate scientific concept.

This opens the way for empiricists like Putnam to apply statistical techniques to measure utterly a *metaphysical* entity, *created* by the process of measurement itself. With the advent of Putnam's statistical investigations, Coleman's rationalistic definition was quietly forgotten, and like with IQ tests, Putnam's questionnaires measure what his questionnaires measure and nothing more, and correspond to no objective process of quantification at all.

Broadly speaking, what Putnam's surveys attempt to measure is a rational disposition towards trusting strangers and forming new social bonds. But it is not quite that or any of the numerous other definitions. The definition of 'social capital' has been *operationalised*, but not for the use of the subjects themselves, or activists or social workers, but for statisticians and government planners.

Another historical legacy which is uniformly overlooked by both the social capitalists and their left critics is that of Jane Jacobs. It was Jane Jacobs who coined the term, though only incidentally, by way of a metaphor, in *The Death and Life of Great American Cities* (1961). Jacobs' conception *least* stands the test of validity as a form of capital, but Jacobs was not an academic or social theorist. She was an *activist*, and she used the word only once and incidentally. The concept that she was describing, however, is something which the Left should be extremely interested in. What Jacobs was concerned with was those social conditions which contributed towards an urban neighbourhood getting into a position to get organised and gain control over their lives and repel the attacks of big business and government. Although she uses the word 'social capital' only once, she frequently refers to the same entity in terms of becoming a 'Thing', (with a capital 'T') or 'self-government'.

The other theorist who deployed a concept of 'social capital' is Pierre Bourdieu (1984) for whom the idea played a subordinate role alongside 'economic capital', 'cultural capital' and 'academic capital'. For Bourdieu, these non-economic forms of capital were personal property, not community resources, and could be exchanged, albeit imperfectly, and therefore implicitly quantifiable.

Forget the words 'social capital' for a moment, and look at the raw data in terms of the capacity of a group of people thrown together by circumstance to get organised, find a voice and make themselves into an historical subject, and it makes sense. Any activist on the Left is interested in those factors which aid or hinder the capacity of a group of people to get organised and intervene in the affairs of the world in which they live. But there is nothing gained by the questionable process of *combining* qualitatively distinct measures. It is *qualitative* data, and from this point of view it seems insane to add it all up into an 'index'. Especially since it turns out that some forms of 'social capital' are 'bad social capital' and have a *negative* value.

Those who conceive of the data in terms of a single quantity are more and more running into the problem that as such it is meaningless. It is meaningless because *objectively* one cannot exchange, for example, 10% of 'bridging social capital' for 10% of 'bonding social capital', or 10 points of 'vertical social capital' for 10 points of 'horizontal social capital', or one boss's worth of vertical social capital for one elected union delegate's worth of vertical social capital. And do you add 'bad social capital' to 'good social capital' or subtract it? At just the time that the statisticians are arriving at a consensus about how to calculate the 'social capital index', the people who are actually trying to use the data to mobilise people in poor neighbourhoods, are trying to *dis*aggregate the data. They need *qualitative* data about the possible barriers to self-organisation and possible levers for self-determination.

'Social capital' data are amenable to a superior interpretation. Taking the data *qualitatively*, they provide a rich source of information about the possibilities for a group of people to create projects and begin to take control of their lives.

In this context, though it is sometimes difficult to express clearly what we want to say without using the word 'community', it should be recognised that 'community' is just about as much of an abstraction as 'social capital'. 'Community' abstracted from the specific way in which it is constituted, the specific relations through which subjectivity is organised and expressed, is an ideological abstraction. 'Individual' and 'community' are, on their own, equally unable to conceptualise the process of consciousness formation. To counterpose 'community' to either 'individual' or 'social capital' can only lead to deeper confusion. If the Left is to intervene in this debate then the notion of 'project' as I have developed from the ideas of Hegel and Marx has to replace the conception of social life in terms of individuals and groups.

There are different ways of proceeding. It has been said that the conception of the data as 'social capital' *naturalises* a neo-liberal approach to poverty – the *subsumption* of everyday life under capital. On the other hand, to conceptualise the data in terms of *social solidarity* (as I propose) as conditions for the development of *self-determination* still leaves open the form in which solidarity and self-determination can be built. If people choose to collaborate for the purpose of building a *company*, then that's their choice. Alternatively, people might choose a residents' committee, or whatever. But practical intervention for the purpose of building solidarity requires *qualitative* data capable of answering the question "What kind of organisation can we build?" The concepts of social solidarity and self-determination make it abundantly clear how to assess data on networks and norms of cooperation, while social capitalists continue to prevaricate about whether 'bridging' and 'bonding', 'vertical' and 'horizontal social capital' should be added or subtracted from one another.

Australian Labor Party leader, Mark Latham[1] (1998), has firmly set his sights on the neo-liberal interpretation, looking to the market as the solution for every ill; likewise, his commitment to 'social entrepreneurship' – a policy which is most likely to exacerbate poverty and exclusion. The Left needs to have an alternative strategy which can be practically embraced by activists and social workers dealing with poverty and exclusion and this debate gives us the opportunity to develop such ideas and collaborate with others.

'Social capital' is an *arena of struggle*. The Left should be in it even while rejecting the way in which the problem is being theorised.

1 Soon after this article was published, Latham resigned from the ALP and from Parliament, and in 2019 was elected to the NSW upper house representing the right-wing One Nation Party.

CHAPTER 22

Nancy Fraser on Welfare Dependency

The concept of 'welfare dependency' is at the centre of right-wing efforts to justify dismantling the welfare system. It is claimed that welfare programs create a dependence on the state which becomes a kind of psychological or personality disorder in recipients which can be cured only by withdrawing welfare benefits or making benefits conditional upon participation in meaningless and humiliating make-work programs under the banner of 'mutual responsibility'.

The Left has failed to find a satisfactory response to this line of attack. Talk of a work-for-the-dole program run not by the state but by "local communities with extensive participation and/or control" (Mendes, *Arena* 69) offers no discernible alternative to the government's policy of outsourcing disciplining of welfare recipients to church organisations and private contractors.

The Left has to work out an effective response to the problem itself, that is, of the existence of a substantial stratum of people denied access to the social labour process and lacking any other means of support, and the moral and political stigmatisation of welfare recipients and those who campaign on their behalf. This will be possible only if we understand the history of the notion of 'dependency' and how it has come to be used to stigmatise those now deemed to be suffering from 'welfare dependency'. Approaches to the problem 'dependency' must show how it is constructed as the psychological and moral character of the welfare recipient. It is not just that relations of dependence themselves are structurally imposed. One and the same relation of 'dependency' may be suffered as a humiliating condition of moral subordination, or as I shall show, enjoyed as a powerful and respected social status, according to its political-ethical evaluation. Dependency is not *just* something to be cured.

Nancy Fraser's 1997 book *Justice Interruptus* contains her article, co-authored with Linda Gordon, tracing the genealogy of the word 'dependency'. Much of what I have to say below draws on insights provided by this article, though I also depart from Nancy Fraser's analysis at times.

Over a period of 200 years the meaning of 'dependency' has moved from the honourable social condition of the overwhelming majority of the population, to a highly stigmatised personality disorder. From beginning to end of the long history of 'dependency', however, the word has contained a curious contradiction.

In pre-modern times, 'dependency' meant being part of a social unit (estate, family, empire) headed by someone else. Dependants (such as servants, retainers and peasants in a feudal estate, wives and children) were 'dependent' in the sense that they had no *legal* status in society at large, and were 'represented' there by their 'master'. But in actuality, the 'master' was 'dependent' on everyone else in the unit for their *material* existence.

The young, single mother is today the icon of 'dependency', and yet it is not she who is dependent in any *material* sense, but the children she looks after. If she did not accept sole responsibility for the child, then she would not need welfare payments. But she raises the children, generally under incredibly difficult conditions, while the father and the state, who are both also responsible for the support of the child, are *free-riding* on her efforts – 'depending' on her in fact – to do what they will not.

The stigma of 'dependency' seems to *rub off* on the people who do the supporting. Being 'independent', on the other hand, is a socio-legal relation enjoyed by people who are supported by the labour of others. But let us follow how the notion of 'dependency' has changed over time.

1   Pre-Capitalist Society

The earliest definition of the verb 'to depend on' in the *Oxford English Dictionary* is consistent with the usage of the word in Hegel's *Phenomenology*, in the section entitled 'Independence and Dependence of Self-Consciousness', more widely known as 'The Master-Slave Dialectic'. "To depend on" meant "to be connected with in a relation of *subordination*"; sub-ordination = lower in a status order. From the 16th century a 'dependant' was one "who depends on another for support, position, etc.; a retainer, attendant, subordinate, servant."

The points to note about the concept of 'dependency' at this time, in pre-capitalist England, are:
- The concept was not differentiated into separate socio-legal, economic and psychological usages, but rather reflected the fusion of various forms of hierarchy in a society in which these forms of subordination were themselves fused and ubiquitous.
- The condition of 'dependency' was perfectly respectable and covered the vast majority of people, excluding only the top layer of the nobility on one side, and vagabonds and foreigners on the other. Everyone was subordinate to someone else but did not thereby incur stigma.

The term 'independence' was at first only applied to *aggregate* entities, not to individuals, 'independence' coming to be used in relation to churches or nations in the 17th century. By the 18th century, an individual could be said to have an 'independency', meaning an ownership of property that made it possible to live without labouring. 'Dependency' by contrast, was characteristic of the condition of the majority, of wage labourers as much as serfs, of men as well as women. Dependency, therefore, was a normal, as opposed to a deviant, condition, a social relation, not an individual trait. According to Nancy Fraser:

> Neither English nor US dictionaries report any pejorative uses of ['dependency'] before the early 20th century. In fact, some leading pre-industrial definitions were explicitly positive, implying trusting, relying on, counting on another, the predecessors of today's 'dependable'.
> Nevertheless, 'dependency' did mean status inferiority and legal coverture, being part of a unit headed by someone else who had legal standing. ... 'Dependency' ... meant being on a lower rung in a long social ladder.
> 1997, p. 125

That is, the notions of independence and dependence have their origins in a hierarchical society in which one subject has *subjugated* other subjects. Although it is true to say that dependence was the condition of the vast majority and carried no special stigma, it *was* always a condition of subjugation.

2 Wage Labour

To be *outside* this system of relations, as was the case for those driven off their land during the Enclosures, was the worst of all possible fates. These paupers and vagabonds were the human dust out of which the modern wage-labourer was fashioned.

While wage labour did exist within the landed estates, more significantly, wage labour grew from this 'human dust' being sucked into the factories. Meanwhile, the formerly independent craftspeople lost their modest 'independence' and were brought down to the condition of factory workers. (In 1776, Adam Smith refers to "an independent workman such as a weaver or shoemaker.") In general, 'dependent' peasantry and servants were *not* in the front ranks of formation of the modern working class; it was a process which was led by the formerly independent tradespeople – outside of the feudal structure based on land ownership, and had its substance in that 'human dust'.

The rise of capitalism made socio-legal or political subordination transparent as a form of subordination, and these meanings of 'dependency' were differentiated from economic dependence, just as within society itself economic activity was differentiated from the family and the state. At the same time as the socio-legal, political and economic meanings of the word began to be differentiated from one another, 'dependency' also first came to be used in reference to a character trait and the moral and psychological meanings of 'dependency' first emerged.

Capitalism did not abolish subordination of women by men and nor did it abolish colonialism. On the contrary. Legal coverture of women, that is the 'representation' of women by their husbands or fathers, and the subordination of the colonies, meant that 'dependency' now took on an *association* with the condition appropriate to women, slaves and 'natives'.

With the delegitimation of socio-legal subordination, workers organised themselves in order to overthrow this condition of 'dependency', – suitable for wives, servants or 'natives', but not for white male workers – and won civil and electoral rights. In turn, and over a period of more than a century, abolitionism, feminism, and unionism abolished slavery and the legal disabilities of women, and brought about a concept of citizenship which rested on the notion of socio-legal independence.

Thus, the distinctively modern relation of wage-labour became 'respectable', and recognised as a form of 'independence', through the battles which created the organised working class as a *subject*. Though 'dependent' for a job on the owners of the means of production, and subordinated to their employer during the working day, workers distinguished themselves from servants and colonial peoples by incorporating themselves into a *new subject*, the labour movement, and this historical fact was objectified in the extension of legal and political rights to proletarians, the legal recognition of the trades unions and so on. It was by means of this achievement that the workers marked themselves off from the paupers, slaves, servants and 'natives.'

The idea that being a member of the retinue of a feudal noble was a form of 'dependency', while being a wage-worker was *not* a form of dependency was therefore not merely the re-branding of a form of dependency – a *real* change in social relations had been achieved. Famously, wage-slavery differed from slavery by giving the worker the freedom to starve, 'freedom' to sell their labour to the highest bidder, and was presaged on separation from one's means of production. That is to say, the worker did not begin from a base of dependency within a feudal estate, but rather from 'independence', that is to say, from being *outside* the relations which guaranteed rights, both material and political, to the peasant or servant, subsumed within the personality of a feudal lord.

Nancy Fraser claims that:

> the language of wage labour denied workers' dependence on their employers, thereby veiling their status as subordinates in a unit headed

> by someone else. There was a sense, then, in which the economic dependency of the white workingman was spirited away through linguistic sleight of hand.
>
> 1997, p. 130

I have to dissent from Fraser here. It is important when looking at the genealogy of a word to recognise that changes in meaning reflect *real* changes in relationships, which is inseparable from the way a relationship is evaluated, as expressed in changes in word-meaning. Wage-labour in the productive economy is a different relationship from being a servant in the master's household, not just a 'redefinition' of what is only formally the same relationship. This is mainly because being a member of the organised working class is materially different from being an isolated labourer, related to other workers only by way of competition, and from being subsumed into the household of one's employer in relations carried over from feudal times. Further, through the process of economic restructuring (outsourcing, commercialisation, franchising, etc.), even this form of hierarchical subordination is being replaced by the one mode of subordination fundamental to capitalism – the exploitation of free wage labour.

The colonised nations, 'dependent' in most cases in the old territorial sense of dependency until after World War Two, did not throw off the mantle of dependency, i.e., legal and political subjugation, by linguistic sleight of hand, but arms in hand in the national liberation struggles of 1945–75. The racist discourse, through which the territorial meaning of dependency became intertwined with the new moral/psychological meanings, cast dependency as a suitable condition for 'natives', could only be exposed as oppressive and overthrown by such a liberation struggle.

3   Domestic Labour

With the separation of economic dependency – now largely replaced by the honourable independence of *wage-labour* – from socio-legal dependency, still appropriate for paupers, slaves and 'natives', came a new kind of 'dependent', invented in the 20th century, the 'housewife'. Even while socio-legal forms of subjugation of women were being battered down by the suffragettes in the early 20th century, new forms of economic subjugation were being put in place through the collaboration of trade unions, the courts and employers, and institutionalised in the 1907 Harvester Decision (in Australia), the gender division of labour and female rates of pay. *Domestic labour* was institutionalised within a new form of patriarchal subjugation. Continuing the pre-industrial assumption that fathers headed households and 'represented' the other members of the household, the now-unsustainable socio-legal forms of 'dependency' were replaced by new forms of *economic* subordination. While wage labour was deemed a form of independence, domestic labour was a form of *dependency*, moreover one deemed appropriate for women.

Thus, with the overthrow of the class connotation of dependency, and any association with employment, 'dependency' now took on a distinctively female connotation, no longer sustainable in its original socio-legal or political forms, but instituted in *economic* form. The *feminisation* of 'dependency', now economic in appearance, accentuated the stigmatisation of dependency already tied up in the racist connotation of dependency.

Fraser shows that the differentiation of 'dependency' into different 'registers' – socio-legal, political and economic, facilitated the shifts in semantic impact. These shifts, of course, reflect changes in real power relations within civil society wrought by social movements. Economic hierarchy as exercised in the employment relationship, was made acceptable in the 19th century – an invisible kind of 'voluntary' subordination, not subsumed under the relation of 'dependency'. Once political and socio-legal dependency had been formally abolished, it appeared that the only barrier to a person's independence could be moral/psychological, a new register of 'dependency'.

Fraser's point is that the worker *remains* economically subordinated by virtue of private ownership of the means of production in what is now a 'respectable' status no longer subsumed under the notion of dependency, while the remaining forms of dependency have been racialised, feminised and – stigmatised. However, I must respond by pointing out that the subordination of the employee to the employer has been significantly undercut by worker solidarity and the legal framework foisted on employers as a result of economic and political pressure brought to bear on them by the workers' movement. Likewise, feminised forms of dependency stigma can and are being undercut by the activity of the women's movement.

Further, the aura of 'independence' for white male workers was built on consent in the economic subjugation of women. Employers backed up the idea by excluding women from well-paid jobs and governments introduced the category of 'dependent' for wage earners to claim tax deductions for 'supporting' a wife – a regime which, by a whole range of economic, legal and moral measures, replaced legal coverture with new forms of 'dependency', that is, *subjugation*.

4 Public Assistance

The next shift in the semantic power of 'dependency' is associated with the rise of the welfare state. Ironically, 'welfare dependency' was a term introduced by Progressive Era reformers of the late 19th/early 20th century in order to remove the stigma of pauperism, but it was the stigma of pauperism that stuck to the status of dependency.

In Australia, old age pensions were introduced in the wake of the depression of the 1890s, and further benefits for the deserving poor flowed over the next 60 years. In the US, it was the New Deal in the wake of the 1930s Depression which introduced these 'respectable' benefits. Old age, sickness, unemployment benefits and so on, aggravated the stigma attached to 'welfare dependency' in direct proportion to how these new benefits were made 'respectable'. By setting up *accounting fictions* to create the appearance that people who received old age, veterans' or unemployment benefits were only getting back what they had put in, they created the *two-track* benefit system. Workers suffering temporary periods of unemployment, veterans and old age pensioners were deemed not to be receiving 'public assistance', but simply receiving their 'just deserts', to which they had contributed through their taxation while they were working. Thus the term 'social insurance'. Company pension schemes in the US, and superannuation in Australia (available only to a relatively elite section of the population, with a life-time of regular employment), have extended this accounting fiction in stronger terms by privatising the financing instruments. But they remain, it must be emphasised, *accounting fictions*. The person who is out of the labour force is being supported by those who remain in the productive labour force, *not* thanks to the share of total capital deemed to be theirs by discriminatory accounting schemes. Meanwhile, those deemed not to have 'contributed' are paid out of general revenue, and subject to means tests, moral supervision and all kinds stigmatising humiliations on top of a miserly level of benefit.

In the US, Blacks and women were deliberately excluded from these 'first-track' schemes, just as in Australia, indigenous people were explicitly excluded, while today's 'self-funded retirees' live off the profits extracted by capital from those still in work, and yet enjoy the honourable status of being deemed to be 'independent'. For selected groups however, the insult of 'welfare dependence' is added with correspondingly greater intensity to the injury of poverty.

The period of the rise of the welfare state corresponded to the institutionalisation of the organised working class movement. The early trade unions were just as much 'friendly societies' as they were class-struggle organisations. The strike fund was an account alongside the distress fund, and the construction of working-class consciousness was just as much tied to the solidarity with members in their times of need as it was to solidarity on the picket line. The objectification of workers' mutual aid in the welfare state meant that these functions were secured as *rights*, at the same time as separating them from voluntary class struggle associations. So long as people enjoyed these benefits as universal rights attached to citizenship, like public education, then this is not so problematic, but this is not always the case. When the worker's own benefits are mediated by the state, the social and psychological impact of this benefit is determined by the relation of the state to the beneficiary. In the vast majority of cases the individual is alienated from the state, and universal suffrage in large geographical electorates secures this alienation just as surely as any bureaucracy or repressive apparatus.

The point is this: the very formation of the working class was bound up in systems of mutual aid. A hundred years ago the workers' movement succeeded in institutionalising these programs as universal rights and benefits provided by the state. The side effect of this institutionalisation, in which workers' mutual aid was now mediated by the capitalist state, was the subjective and objective gutting of the working class as a class for itself. All answers to the problem of 'dependency' have to begin from this historic problem.

5   Universal and Targeted Benefits

Every opportunity for a claimant to qualify as 'deserving' adds stigma to another person thereby deemed 'undeserving'. The point about universal entitlement as opposed to targeted assistance based on either need or desert, is two-fold. From the social-psychological point of view it removes, for some, the stigma associated with singling out a group deemed to be needy and/or undeserving, thus intensifying the stigma for those deemed 'undeserving'. Further, from the point of view of distributive justice, universal benefits ensure that no one slips through the net. And, because every citizen is a potential recipient of a benefit under universal principles, the overall level of social solidarity is enhanced – a person does not resent contributing to a fund supporting welfare recipients if they know that everyone benefits from the system equally.

However, universal benefits entail the illusion that the state has gifted these benefits and that it is the taxpayer who has to be thanked. The majority of the population who see themselves paying the taxes (deducted from the surplus value they generate for their employers) believe that this magnanimity is at their expense, and may come to resent this burden. Universal benefits have a tendency to become very expensive. The other problem with universalist provision is that although it avoids exposing groups to exploitation and stigmatisation, it does not prevent free-riding. But it is not so much the iconic dole bludger, but the men who free ride on the care-giving of women, and the capitalist who free rides on the backs of underpaid workers. The only answer to this is to change the behaviour of those who free ride. It cannot be fixed by any system of payments, even a universal system.

Thus, even the universalist provision of welfare as of right, does not prevent exploitation and stigmatisation so long as a real hierarchy of subordination exists *in society*. Universal welfare can actually *underwrite* exploitation, for example, by allowing employers to use short term, casual forms of employment, in the knowledge that the state will support their employees at poverty rates while they do not have a wage. Also, however, provision of welfare as of right relies on citizenship as qualification for the benefits they receive from the state, so state-provided benefits are only as secure and meaningful as is citizen control over the state. People who cannot exercise political pressure on the state, and cannot see the state as really an expression of their own will, are not only going to *feel* excluded, they are going to *be* excluded. Politically weak sections of the population find their needs consistently overlooked in government budgets.

6   Dependency as a Personality Trait

The idea that welfare may create 'habits of dependency' dates back to the Depression of the 1930s. In the 1950s psychiatrists began to diagnose 'dependence' as a medical disorder, specifically as a form of immaturity among women, particularly among single mothers. These psychological themes are now ubiquitous.

Colette Dowling's 1981 *The Cinderella Complex*, talked of "women's hidden fear of independence" and the "wish to be saved." Melody Beattie's *Co-Dependency No More* set off an avalanche of books blaming carers for the dependency of those they care for, casting it as a form of addiction just like 'drug dependency', ascribed invariably to women and rubbing off in a stigma attached to all the feminised caring professions. In 1980, the American Psychiatric Association officially listed 'Dependent Personality Disorder' (DPD) "apparently common and diagnosed more frequently in females."

In this environment, efforts by pressure groups to establish welfare benefits as rights are pushing uphill to say the least. All the arguments now are about 'incentives': Do child benefits encourage women to have more out-of-wedlock children? Do they discourage them from accepting jobs? Can reducing or withholding benefits serve as a stick to encourage recipients to keep their children in school? 'Dependency' is now a synonym for poverty, with moral/psychological dependency now widely accepted as a personality disorder, whether taken as the cause or the effect of poverty. The relations of subordination hidden within the discourse of dependency have disappeared from view.

On the other hand, there is a sense in which welfare is an instrument used in combination with policing in order to dissuade people from earning a living by crime. Whether we like the idea or not, welfare is part and parcel of the *suppression* of ways of earning a living which the state deems socially undesirable and securing normal conditions of life for the rest of the population.

7   Building Capacity vs. Philanthropy

The welfare discourse has moved on to some extent from victim blaming and overt psychologising and individualisation of 'dependency', even if such improvements haven't yet penetrated some of the offices in Parliament House. Among the more sophisticated experts in poverty, the talk is about 'capacity building'.

The idea here is that welfare dependency cannot be overcome by philanthropy, i.e., by bridging the deficit in wealth, but only by assisting people in building the 'assets' that they need in order to lift *themselves* out of dependency. Without skills (called 'human capital') and social connections or networks of trust (called 'social capital') people have no way of earning a living.

In this discourse, rather than governments providing education and training, grants and infrastructure, the responsibility for 'capacity building' is handed over to capital ('the community'), who are encouraged to fulfil their social responsibilities by entering 'partnerships' with people to build 'social capital'. A central concept for this exercise is 'social enterprise', which means helping people start up small businesses, employ people in their neighbourhood and provide services, usually back into the same community. This is a kind of 'import substitution', especially for localities where poverty has become endemic, which has the by-product of facilitating the accumulation of small-scale capital. The result is a kind of *privatisation* of welfare which has the effect of subsuming people under capital relationships who, to their detriment, have been outside of capital.

The linking of these two concepts, 'capacity building' and 'social enterprise', results from the conception that the 'real' economy is in the private sector and government cannot act in this arena. The state itself is cast in a kind of relation of dependency in relation to the 'real' economy, with its own services cast as *costs* alongside the services of the private sector deemed as *products*. The state it is argued must hand over responsibility for capacity building to those qualified to play in the economy. Government intervention is therefore to be mediated by private companies (or charities) rather than bureaucracies – a kind of 'franchising' of government activity. There is, however, no reason why the 'social entrepreneur' could not be a local person hired by the local government, so as to ensure that they had capital, mentoring, premises, insurance, etc.

The key word for welfare is 'inclusion', inclusion in the labour market. 'Dependency' denotes being outside of capital. 'Independence' is achieved by being subsumed under capital, either as employee or as small-scale capitalist. Capacity building involves assisting 'entrepreneurship' and 'investing in human capital', to facilitate 'inclusion' under capital.

Still, it is better to be employed and exploited than to be unemployed and marginalised. But isn't there something deeply problematic about transforming whatever relations of trust and collaboration exist within a community into relationships of domination (i.e., employment relations)? Both the small-scale capitalist and their semi-marginalised employees remain in a position of total powerlessness in the face of 'market forces'. The formation of companies *is* one possible step towards self-determination, but it is by no means the only one, let alone the best one for impoverished communities.

There is an interpretation of 'dependency' which holds that getting things from government is dependence, while engaging in a business relationship with a private company is being independent, and what people need is the capacity to do business. The kind of 'independence' people get this way is just in proportion to their economic muscle. But what is left out of the picture altogether is the *political and socio-legal muscle* that people have or don't have.

The problem is that it remains the action of capital which separates people from their means of livelihood in the *first place*. For example, when the Aboriginal stockmen at Wave Hill went on strike and were awarded equal pay by Justice Kirby, the station owner simply sacked them all and hired only white stockmen. Noel Pearson (2007) reports that "it had been clear to the Commonwealth Government in the hearings before the Australian Conciliation and Arbitration Commission that a ruling in favour of equal wages would result in the large-scale removal of Aboriginal stockworkers from the stations of northern Australia." The Commonwealth's solution was to make social security available. The Commission ruled: "If any problems of native welfare whether of employees or their dependants, arise as a result of this decision, the Commonwealth Government has made clear its intention to deal with them. This is not why we have come to our conclusion but it means we know that any welfare problems which arise will be dealt with by those most competent to deal with them." So part of the *deal* to *exclude* Aborigines from wage labour on the pastoral properties situated on land stolen from the Aborigines by colonialism, was unlimited access to unemployment benefit.

Independence is far more about empowerment in the social, legal and political domains than it is about capacity on the productive plane or about moral/psychological disability. In fact, dependence is more often associated with being productive than with not being productive, and with being responsible rather than irresponsible. Historically, being *excluded* is usually the precursor to being subordinated, and subordination is the essential condition which underlies dependence.

What is nasty about being a 'welfare dependant' is that you are subordinated to others – bureaucrats, philanthropists, police, landlords. No welfare claimant is going to complain about the benefits they receive. It is the subordination that goes along with getting the benefit which is the problem, and the stigmatisation associated with that subordination. No doubt, a company turning up and offering work in a small community would be welcome. But if the relationship is just a charade, and benefits which belong to the community as of right are being channelled via a company and offered as a private favour, this is a slender basis for overcoming 'dependency'. So long as the differential power between the giver and the receiver of benefits is there – and passing benefits via a company hardly addresses that differential – then subordination is the likely result, even if it is a benign subordination.

To overcome subordination, what is needed is *self-determination*. Self-determination is not an *individual* question. No individual can attain self-determination except by means of participation in a *project*, collaborating with others – be it a company, a self-help group, a social movement or some administrative agency. The difference between 'dependency' and 'independence' is the difference between subjugation or participation in a project which expresses one's *own* subjectivity through some definite organisational link with other people.

The only answer to dependence, welfare dependence or any other kind of subordination, is getting organised.

8   The Ideology of Self-Help

One of the most pervasive ideological prejudices which support the neo-liberal analysis of 'dependency' and their policies for 'welfare reform' is the thesis that 'self-esteem' flows from 'helping yourself'. In this theory, a person sees an image of their own worth in the value of what they have acquired for themselves by their own efforts. Thus the billionaire is the happiest person imaginable, and the welfare claimant, who has been given what they have without any effort on their part, totally lacking in self-esteem. What welfare claimants need, therefore, is a chance to develop self-esteem by working for their dole.

This is an outrageous lie! The origin of self-esteem is the perception of oneself through the eyes of another who esteems you, above all because you have met *their* needs through your labour, not because you have helped yourself.

A caveat has to be added, admittedly, that providing for the needs of your family or contributing to the needs of any larger institution or movement, by *whatever means*, is indeed a source of self-esteem, but this is equally well met by stock market swindling, collecting welfare benefits or crime. What the unemployed person needs, if they are not raising a family or busy with voluntary work, is not a means of acquiring a fortune, but simply some way of making themself *useful* to someone else, something which work-for-the-dole is not likely to provide so long as it is just the hoop through which you must jump to qualify for your pittance.

Further, the origin of virtue is the enjoyment of values intrinsic to social practices, rather than their *external rewards* (MacIntyre, 1981). Once a person finds themself doing something only for the reward they are given for it, rather than the value intrinsic in the practice itself, then their life loses meaning. That this is the condition of millions of wage workers and celebrities alike is no comfort. If someone does 'community work' simply as the hoop through which they have to jump to get their entitlement, then it is hard to see what psychological benefit will flow from this. Actually, it just generates frustration and cynicism.

All institutions have systems of reward and punishment to support the practices which they constitute, inclusive of allowing people to earn a living there. This is the mortar that binds institutions together. But it is the enjoyment of the essential mission of a project which lifts human beings from subsistence and creates a basis for social solidarity. Reward and punishment, far from alleviating the stigma of dependency, are its usual accompaniment.

There is a third way between benefits being mediated by the state, on one hand, or by private saving on the other. Private saving is essentially unequal and entrenches poverty, and this goes for superannuation as well, even so-called 'compulsory' superannuation, because it is only an elite of employees, mostly male, and mostly those working in the public sector or large institutional employers who reach retirement age with a nest-egg. Industry Super, where employers and unions jointly manage funds, have proved to be far more effective and less open to corruption than the retail funds run by banks. Industry Super is essentially a mutualist institution and gives some real meaning to the idea of retirees having funded their own retirement. But it is still only open to a privileged minority of the community. And yet people working in small businesses or the informal sector *by definition* do not have a life-long relationship to their fellow workers which underpins self-determination. This is an outstanding problem. For those who end up in aged-care facilities, the problem of aged-induced poverty is even more acute. Mutualist solutions may prove useful in this area, especially in rural towns where social bonds have a distinctly local character. The government needs to facilitate the collective intergenerational funding of retirement which does not leave women, and those in insecure employment, in stigmatised underfunded schemes, but at a level where there can be some real sense of mutuality.

So, I think the role of the Left should not just be to promote more universal and 'participatory' welfare schemes, but to agitate and work for poor and excluded people to *get organised*, whether as residents, members of an ethnic group, as unpaid carers, does not matter, so long as vulnerable people get organised and fight for inclusion on terms that they can dictate, or at least negotiate, themselves.

CHAPTER 23

Anthony Giddens on Structuration

A review of *The Constitution of Society: Outline of the Theory of Structuration*, Anthony Giddens, 1984, published by University of California Press.

∴

Anthony Giddens' theory of structuration aims to find a 'third way' between two opposing currents in social theory. On the one hand, there are objectivist approaches like functionalism, social systems theory, structuralism, post-structuralism, which emphasise the pre-eminence of the social whole (structure) and the constraints they impose on individual participants whose knowledge about what they do is discounted. On the other hand, we see subjectivist or voluntaristic approaches like hermeneutics and phenomenology, which tend to see the social whole only in terms of the production and reproduction of individual agents who are taken to be essentially autonomous.

Giddens points out that structuralism takes the individual subjects whose activity is being studied to be 'sociological dopes' and simpleton prisoners of ideologies, discounting the knowledgeability of the participants in social processes. A distinctive feature of the theory of structuration is the idea of 'reflexivity':

> There is no mechanism of social organisation or social reproduction identified by social analysts which lay actors cannot also get to know about and actively incorporate into what they do.
> GIDDENS, 1984, p. 284

So when a sociologist describes a social phenomenon they must expect that those whose actions are being described will use the sociologist's sources and ideas to modify what they do. It is for this reason that the 'laws' which are the currency of natural science can never be manifested in social theory because the objects of research do not act independently of the knowing subject. This also implies that all social theorising is itself an intervention in social life and history. Taking object and subject together, to a great extent it can be said that events unfold in a way reflecting reasoned, reflective activity by many different actors.

The predictability manifested in social life is largely *made to happen* by strategically placed social actors, not in spite of them or behind their backs. Far from people being driven to do what they do by remote or invisible 'structural forces', Giddens points out that "there is no such entity as a distinctive type of 'structural explanation' in the social sciences; all explanations will involve at least implicit references both to the purposive, reasoning behaviour of agents and to its intersection with constraining and enabling features of the social and material contexts" (p. 179). The appearance of inevitability in the actions of actors arises from the limited options available to them on condition that they act rationally, and therefore actually rests on the presumption that social actors have good reasons for doing what they do. This is the meaning Giddens attaches to Marx's famous maxim: "Men make their own history, but they do not make it as they please; they do not make it under self-selected circumstances, but under circumstances directly encountered, given and transmitted from the past" (1852).

These reflections draw attention to Giddens' conception of the knowledgeability of social actors, to which I will turn shortly, because this is not purely a sociological question, but is in large measure also a question of psychology.

Giddens makes a devastating critique of functionalism. The principal idea of functionalism is that some event or social process happens because it is necessary to create the observed outcome, in particular the ongoing reproduction of the social system. There is an ambiguity in this claim. A researcher who observes some situation and figures out that this is evidence that some prior action must have taken place which functions as cause of the observed situation may be reasoning correctly. But contra functionalism, it can form part of a valid explanation only to the extent that knowledge of this idea forms part of some strategically placed agents' reasons for doing what they do. The need for the prior action to produce the observed outcome, in particular a stable social formation, is in itself no explanation at all, unless this is the conscious purpose of the agents in question. It was for this same reason that I have called Leontyev's version of activity theory functionalism. Functionalism poses questions, but it does not provide explanations. People have reasons for what they do and any explanation for their actions has to be in terms of their reasons and those of other actors for doing what they do, irrespective of whether the outcome is an expected result or an unintended consequence of all of their actions taken together.

This brings us to Giddens' conception of the knowledgeability of the social actors who are the objects of social theory, and the manner and extent to which the outcomes of their activity are a product of the reasons they have for doing what they do.

1 The Knowledgeability of Social Actors

The limitations imposed on social theory by the segmentation of learning into academic disciplines is on display when Giddens sets out his psychology. Giddens has never participated, so far as I know, in psychological research, so must put together a psychology to underpin his claims for the knowledgeability and motivation of social actors by picking and choosing from what is on offer from psychologists who are unschooled in sociology. His chosen psychologists are Erikson ("my appropriation [is] strictly limited and qualified"), Goffman, to shed light on the motivation of everyday interactions, and Freud. Giddens is to some extent aware of the problems in using Freud, which he hopes to mitigate by substituting id, ego and superego in Freud's 1924 structural model with his own categories of basic security system, practical consciousness and discursive consciousness. This model bears little relation to Freud's, but 'practical consciousness' seems to approximate Freud's concept of the pre-conscious in his 1900 topographical model of the repressed unconscious, the preconscious and the conscious. In Giddens' schema:

> There is no bar between [practical and discursive consciousness], however, as there is between the unconscious and discursive consciousness. The unconscious includes those forms of cognition and impulsion which are either wholly repressed from consciousness or appear in consciousness only in distorted form.
> pp. 4–5

But Giddens still takes an indeterminate slab of Freud at face value, for example, in referring to the 'back regions' (p. 128) where 'backroom deals' are made, and so on, he takes it that Freudian ideas about anal fixation are relevant to understanding these phenomena. Likewise, Freudian slips may provide insight into unacknowledged motives. This really is not good enough. If one wants to create a social theory which genuinely overcomes the dichotomy between the reproduction of agents and structures, it is not good enough to equip a sophisticated social theory with a do-it-yourself bag of borrowed psychological instruments.

The core of Giddens' ideas about agents' knowledgeability is his conception of practical and discursive consciousness. From the point of view of the Vygotskian psychology which I use there are problems with this idea. However, it has to be said that the obvious fact, from which he makes a beginning, that social actors have a relatively sound practical knowledge of the activities in which they are engaged is a vast improvement over structural and functionalist 'explanations' of the activity of social actors. As to the related conception of agents' *motivation*, I will come to this later.

The category of discursive consciousness is relatively clear, and "Every competent social actor ... is *ipso facto*, a social theorist on the level of discursive consciousness" (p. 18). But the key category of practical consciousness is unclear, particularly in terms of its genesis and so far as I know not based on psychological research – it is just consciousness which is not discursive but nonetheless implicated in behaviour. Giddens' use of Freud is most problematic here because he holds that cognition and motivation may also originate from what Freud called the Unconscious, an entirely mythical construction (see Vygotsky, 1928, §7). As Giddens says, there is no barrier between practical and discursive consciousness. When asked to give reasons for what they do, an actor offers what must be taken to be a discursive interpretation of their own practical consciousness, since they are presumed to be unable to put practical consciousness itself into words. Nonetheless, social actors will generally have a far-reaching practical knowledge of their activity and its context and ramifications and use this knowledge in the activity.

This fact – that social actors have good reasons for their actions, based on relatively sound knowledge – together with the fact that actors' knowledgeability and control over the consequences of their actions is *bounded*, constitute the rational core of the theory of structuration.

Undoubtedly, a social actor makes use of resources, whether allocative or authoritative, without necessarily having conscious awareness (see Vygotsky, 1934) of them and their limits. But how does an agent come to know the limits of those resources other than through what is communicated to their discursive consciousness? How do they learn what they can and can't do? This is a problem for Giddens, because the key concept underlying his conception of agents' knowledgeability is *routine*.

His unit of analysis seems to be the individual agent confronting an ongoing practice which, although not created by the individual participant, is continuously reproduced and possibly modified by them through their participation. The underlying vision is one of individuals routinely enacting institutions. These practices are taken to form a *continuous flow*, and in an infinite feedback loop they are creating the conditions, motivations and reasons for their continuation. So people have their reasons for participating, but they do so under conditions already created by the existence of the practice itself and other such practices.

The knowledgeability of agents is finite however and there are unintended consequences for what people do. According to Giddens:

> Every research investigation in the social sciences or history is involved in relating action to structure, in tracing, explicitly or otherwise, the conjunction or disjunctions of intended and unintended consequences of activity and how these affect the fate of individuals.
>
> p. 219

These unintended consequences of a practice form part of the conditions in which a person takes up a practice and thereby sustains it.

2 Routines

Institutions are essentially routines enacted by participants with the aid of *rules* and *resources*. It is in this concept of routine that the subject matter of sociology overlaps with the subject matter of psychology.

> The concept of *routinisation*, as grounded in practical consciousness, is vital to the theory of structuration. Routine is integral to both the continuity of the personality of the agent, as he or she moves along the paths of daily activities, and to the institutions of society, which *are* such only through their continued production. An examination of routinisation ... provides us with a master key ...
>
> p. 60

The point is not routines, but *routinisation*, the *formation* of routines and their acquisition by the individuals who will sustain them. But Giddens has not explained how a practice *becomes* a routine, thereafter taken for granted, or how routines are changed by the very people who apparently require them for their 'ontological security'. Giddens insists that routines are essentially *continuous*, and must be distinguished from acts, and on this basis, he claims that routines are essentially *unmotivated*.

> But it makes no more sense to claim that every act or gesture is motivated – meaning that a definite 'motive' can be attached to it – than it does to treat action as involving a string of intentions or reasons. ... Action ... cannot be satisfactorily be conceptualised as an aggregate of acts. ... [R]ather than supposing that every 'act' has a corresponding 'motive', we have to understand the term 'motivation' to be a processual one. What this means concretely is that the unconscious only rarely impinges directly upon the reflexive monitoring of conduct. Nor are the connections involved solely

dependent upon psychological mechanisms within the personality of the individual actor; they are mediated by the social relations which individuals sustain in the routine practices of their daily lives.

p. 50

It is the sense of 'ontological security' that a person apparently gains from the approval of colleagues and the predictability of day-to-day life which Giddens sees as sustaining practices. It seems to me that instead of the structuralists' 'sociological dope' what we have here is a 'motivational cripple'. But more importantly, I believe that this concept of unmotivated, continuous routines is a methodological error. Surely routines are composed of discrete, motivated actions, each constituting a *unit* of social action each with its own goal? And surely institutions are aggregates of routines, also themselves units of activity, each in turn having their own *motivation* (see Blunden, 2014)? In particular, Giddens' conception makes the genesis of routines mysterious, and therefore prevents the true nature of routines from being revealed.

The Russian drama theorist Constantin Stanislavskii (1936) expressed the opposite opinion in his direction to actors performing a routine series of actions. Action, he says, has a 'channel', the motivation for which flows from the plot, and it this channel which is motivating a whole series of actions (e.g. going home). The channel is divided into separate 'units' (e.g. looking in a shop window, crossing the road) each of which has its particular motive. Cultural Historical Activity Theory (CHAT) agrees with this three-tier structure of motivation, a conception on which its analysis of action is based.

This does not destroy the concept of routine but does suggest that the idea of routine being 'unmotivated' is psychologically false. This issue also sheds light on the relation between what Giddens calls 'practical consciousness' and 'discursive consciousness'.

3   Practical Consciousness

As consciousness which is not discursive but nonetheless is implicated in activity, practical consciousness subsumes several distinct categories of consciousness distinguished by their *genesis*. On the one hand, practical intelligence is the first kind of intelligence acquired by an infant through their handling of their own body and artefacts. Practical intelligence continues to develop through adulthood in the acquisition of practical skills, but also underpins the development of discursive intelligence from when a child begins to master speech and writing. Practical intelligence is indeed the kind of intelligence which is not manifested in words. On the other hand, operational knowledge, exercised in *operations*, routinised and adapted to conditions, is genetically connected with the development of all kinds of skill, whether practical or discursive. The important category which is skated over by Giddens is *conscious awareness*.

Actions/operations, whether of a practical or symbolic character, may be executed either consciously or without conscious awareness. Operational knowledge is the kind of knowledge and skill deployed continuously in carrying out actions. Facility in using some word, gesture or tool, or in acting appropriately in relation to some person or context, is acquired at first with conscious awareness. In time, as we become used to using the action under different conditions we begin to master it, and use it without conscious control – otherwise it would be impossible to type or walk down the street or engage in a conversation without suffering from mental overload! Each such action enacted without conscious awareness, controlled by the conditions and by the goal of the action of which it forms a part, is called an *operation* (think of learning to tie your shoelaces).

Included in operational knowledge are interpersonal skills including everyday language use, the capacity to use and read facial expressions, etc., which are acquired spontaneously. Vygotsky called this kind of knowledge *potential concepts* and it is indeed a kind of knowledge shared with nonhuman creatures.

However, in addition to everyday operations acquired spontaneously when we participate in the activity of an *institution*, we are required to conform to the expectations of the institution and further its aims. Operations are acquired with conscious awareness and generally with a degree of effort. Although operations are executed without conscious control, when something goes awry the action springs back into conscious awareness. When in the course of enacting a practice something goes awry – you inadvertently disrespect a boss or behave too freely with a customer – this has two effects: the operations routinely carried out without conscious control suddenly become part of conscious awareness and are brought under conscious control, and the person concerned suffers a moment of embarrassment of the kind which not only leads to modification of the given routine, to better align it with its motive, but also to learning and personal development. If the operation has been adequately acquired, a moment's attention is all that is required for a subject to know what was wrong.

Another category of action of which the subject may be aware or not arises from the fact that what is taken to be the normal form of action appropriate to a given social position in some institution may in fact be something which is subject to interpretation. Institutions harbour legitimate conflicts over the proper ways to pursue the object of the institution, differences which have a variety of social roots within the institution, and the degree of awareness of these differences will be variable.

Another category of action which could be subsumed under Giddens' concept of 'practical consciousness' arises when people are participating in institutions. In some cases, and always to some extent, a person fully understands and embraces the aims of the institution. But in general people have their own reasons for participating in an institution, such as earning a wage, furthering their career, organising the union or simply to enjoy the social interaction. Such an alternative agenda may or may not be explicit, may be more or less repressed according to the relevant norms, and may be subordinate to the institutional requirements or may actually be, for that individual, the leading activity.

It can be seen that Giddens' category of 'practical consciousness' is quite inadequate to encompass the variety of forms of consciousness and their genesis relevant to acquiring, maintaining or changing routines. So long as routines are understood as unmotivated, continuous processes, it is impossible to reveal the sources of motivation and the potential for social change.

4 Concepts and Motives

Following Stanislavskii, Vygotsky and the activity theorists, I argue that routines are a series of actions each of which has its own goal and is consciously controlled by the subject. However, the goal of an action is not the same as its motive, i.e., the reason for doing it. That is, when we ask "why did the chicken cross the road?" a valid answer must be something other than "to get to the other side" – there has to be a reason. Conscious control is exercised over actions pursuant to the motive of the entire *activity*, what Stanislavskii called 'the channel', which provides the motivation for all the component actions.

An activity is generally made up of many actions which may be carried out by many different social actors, and its object is represented by the actors as the *concept* of the activity, or institution. It is this concept which orients the actions of actors and provides them with a 'channel', and gives meaning to all their actions. This concept is supported symbolically in multiple ways, both through the actions of other people, and in the case of institutions, the built environment, and all manner of 'texts'. The various actions which make up the routines of the institution relate to the concept of the institution in the same way as many different word-meanings are required to constitute a *concrete* concept; an abstract definition is insufficient. Conflicts within an institution manifest the differing nuances and contradictions within the concept, and the ideal culture of a community is found in the constellation of these concepts, reflecting the manifold interconnection of institutions with each other, everyday life and social movements.

This allows us to understand how routine practices are formed, how participants acquire them and learn to operate the prerogatives and obligations appropriate to their social position, and amend these over time in the light of experience and social interaction with others. The concept a person has of an institution within or in relation to which they are active gives them a concrete form within which their knowledgeability of the practices they are participating in is developed.

Institutions are always 'for' something, which contributes no doubt to the appearance of functionalism in people's activity, and the institution's motive is intrinsic to its concept. Understanding what an institution is for is something that can be solved concretely only through understanding the entire history of the institution, with the founding of the institution being a key moment, usually followed by other transformative moments in which the institution may be turned to new motives. Institutions in general *solve some problem* or a complex or series of such problems, and in this sense have to be understood as the continuation of a social movement, or a number of such social movements. The pursuit of a concept which provides the motivation for actors is quite explicit in a social movement, but this does not disappear when it achieves that crucial moment of realisation when it is institutionalised. Concepts likewise have to be understood as capturing the solution of some problem (Vygotsky, 1934, p. 126).

> Awareness of social rules, expressed first and foremost in practical consciousness, is the very core of that 'knowledgeability', which specifically characterises human agents.
> GIDDENS, pp. 22–23

The fact that people are not *consciously aware* of these social rules does not take away from the fact that, insofar as they relate to institutional life, they are invariably learnt through some kind of instruction, whether formal or informal, and generally grasped through concepts, and as soon as any such rule is violated it springs immediately back into conscious awareness.

So people understand what is required of them and are able to problem-solve when contradictions arise. This does not in itself however resolve the problem of an agent's motivation. An individual may not be wholly committed to a project and nor will everyone have the same concept of it. People are always committed to a number of different projects and it is the relation between the various projects which determines the nature of a person's commitment to any one of them. The classic example of this would be the wage earner whose commitment to their employer's institution is purely instrumental, and their leading activity may be raising a family, using their wages for that purpose. This is a limiting case however, and most employees have some degree of commitment to where they work or their profession. The web of commitments which motivates a person certainly cannot be adequately represented in terms of unmotivated routines serving to bolster someone's 'ontological security'.

5   Unintended Consequences and Conceptual Development

Where Giddens' work reaches the limits of psychology and passes over into sociology proper is when he investigates the *limits* of an agent's knowledgeability. While emphasising that social actors generally possess an extensive knowledge about the practices in which they are involved and their ramifications, there is a point beyond which they cannot control the impact of what they do and activity enters into the domain of unintended consequences.

> Every research investigation in the social sciences or history is involved in relating action to structure, in tracing, explicitly or otherwise, the conjunction or disjunctions of intended and unintended consequences of activity and how these affect the fate of individuals.
> p. 219

The important category of *unintended consequences* of participation in a practice are those which form part of the conditions for agents to take up a practice (understood as an *ongoing* practice) and thereby sustain it. Giddens uses some examples such as the fallacy of composition and the tragedy of the commons to show how actions which are rational for each agent may have perverse effects when combined, to illustrate how the unintended consequences of rational practices may form systematic and predictable outcomes. Among such outcomes are the conditions by means of which a practice sustains itself, and make it into a kind of 'living organism'.

Further, the concept of the boundedness of agents' knowledgeability in relation to their own activity encompasses the fact that in relation to social processes lying *outside* the sphere of their own immediate experience people may be profoundly ill-informed and misguided. Vygotsky used the term 'diffuse concept' to indicate the forms of knowledge which are constructed by extending local knowledge beyond the bounds of its validity. Even in relation to unintended consequences there is a psychological component. According to Giddens:

> Homeostatic system reproduction in human society can be regarded as involving the operation of causal loops, in which a range of unintended consequences of action feed back to reconstitute the initiating circumstances.
> p. 27

Nonetheless:

> Specification of those bounds [on agents' knowledgeability] allows the analyst to show how unintended consequences of the activities in question derive from what the agents did intentionally.
> p. 294

This shows how the appearance of functional and purely structural causation – both of which are illusory – can be created by the actions of perfectly rational people who are not 'sociological dopes'. And the reason that the theory of structuration, which has the knowledgeability of agents at its centre, does not descend into the fantasy of societies as intentional communities is because knowledgeability is always bounded.

Agency, says Giddens, is the *capacity* to make a difference, and is not limited to a person's intentions. Holding some social position, such as an office in some institution, and in general participation in some project, does not mean that the agent has to play some *role*, as if acting out a script dictated by structural or functional imperatives, but simply that they have certain prerogatives and obligations, and it is in this that a person's agency resides (for example, the owners of a company producing asbestos can decide to disinvest in it, notwithstanding the 'profit motive'). Some unintended consequences are within the scope of what a person could control, and these are consequences for which they are an agent, and are morally responsible for, whatever may have been their intentions. Some consequences are both unforeseeable and beyond the control of the person who carries out an initial action. In this case the actor should not be seen as the agent for those consequences.

It seems to me, however, that this does not settle the question of agency. Individuals make a difference only by means of collaboration with others, whether that is as an office holder in some institution or as a participant in a social movement. Entering into such collaborations is almost invariably voluntary and done for good reason. Individuals exercise agency and bear moral responsibility for the difference they make *as part of collaborative projects*. It is really only the project that makes the difference, not the individual, but a project is not some ethereal social function or remote and invisible structure, but an aggregate of the collaborative actions of participants, unified by the common object of the project.

6   Institutions and Social Movements

I take it that there is no hard and fast line between an institution and a social movement. A movement's objectification is never permanent but always liable to disruption and reactivation of its aims. At the very least, institutions form an arena in which social movements contest for dominion. It is only by making institutions continuous with social movements that the cultural and conceptual basis for an institution's existence can be grasped. For Giddens, however:

> I shall distinguish two main types of collectivity ... associations and organisations (all reproduction occurs in and through the regularised conduct of knowledgeable agents) ... [and on the other hand] social movements.
> p. 199

This dichotomy is the reason for the conception of institutions as 'routines'. By comprehending both social movements and institutions under a single developmental concept, the motivational springs of institutional life are made visible.

7   Conclusion

It seems to me impossible that social theory can resolve the dichotomy aptly characterised by Giddens as the dualism of structure and agency so long as sociologists continue to rely on Freud or improvised psychological theories. Cultural psychology and activity theory are uniquely placed to overcome the dichotomy which has its roots in the disciplinary structure of the academy.

Two specific methodological defects in Giddens' work: (1) that he makes his unit of analysis a *continuous process*, and (2) that he takes a taxonomic rather than a genetic approach to analysis. The defects have prevented Giddens from achieving his goal of overcoming the dichotomy.

However, the key insights are that (1) social actors must be recognised as having significant knowledgeability concerning their own activity, while this knowledgeability is *bounded*, so that (2) social phenomena must be understood and explained in terms that include understanding the good reasons social actors have for doing what they do.

These insights should dispose of functionalism and structuralism for good.

CHAPTER 24

Bourdieu on Status, Class and Culture

Review of *Distinctions: A Social Critique of the Judgment of Taste*. Pierre Bourdieu 1979, translated by Richard Nice, published by Harvard University Press, 1984.

∴

If social class is defined by one's relation to the means of production, this still does not tell us how classes *constitute themselves as classes*, nor how the complex status hierarchies of capitalist societies are articulated and internalised by individuals or how other systems of status subordination are integrated within a class system of domination. On its own, possession of greater or lesser title to means of production ('economic capital') in fact explains little about the dynamics of bourgeois society.

In the context of 1960s/1970s France, Pierre Bourdieu claims to show at great length and detail how people's knowledge and use of cultural artefacts and their body, and the taste which they develop for culture – everything from food, clothing and life-style to preferences in painting and music – constitute sublimated transformations of a single relation of dominant to dominated class. The resulting 'distinctions' mediate the myriad of struggles between classes and class fractions in modern capitalist society. He shows how people learn to tailor their expectations and their own view of themselves to their place in a hierarchy of political power and their share in the social product, at the same time finding vehicles to contest the place a class fraction has in that hierarchy and the place an individual can lay claim to within a class fraction.

Bourdieu also claims an understanding of how other deep-seated relations of subordination, especially age and gender, merge with economic and cultural relations of subordination in sublimated forms, shedding light on how multiple forms of subordination articulate with one another. However, I find the way Bourdieu tries to turn all these pairs of opposites into a single, universal ordering principle, such that all dichotomous ordering principles are in some sense 'the same', an aspect of his thinking which is best dispensed with. It adds nothing to what he has achieved. Further, his analysis leads to a pervasive structuralism which seems to rule out the possibility of social progress, and a relativism which if taken seriously, would mean that science is impossible.

Let us clarify some of the main concepts Bourdieu uses.

1 Capital

Let us take it as read that the concept of 'economic' capital is understood, and that it can be expressed in ownership of various kinds of artefact – factories, stockpiles, intellectual property, shares, finance capital, and so on, held for the purpose of selling at a profit rather than for the purpose of enjoyment. What is required then, to justify the concept of *forms of capital* which are 'non-economic' is to establish that they can be *converted* into 'economic capital', and thus that everything deemed to be a *form* of capital can be arranged, under some specified condition, along a single axis, i.e., quantified. Here is how Bourdieu deals with this problem.

> Projection onto a single axis, in order to construct the continuous, linear, homogenous, one-dimensional series with which the social hierarchy is normally identified, implies an extremely difficult (and, if it is unwitting, extremely dangerous) operation, whereby the different types of capital are reduced to a single standard. This abstract operation has an objective basis in the possibility, which is always available, of converting one type of capital into another; however, the exchange rates vary in accordance with the power relation between the holders of the different forms of capital. By obliging one to formulate the principle of the convertibility of the different kinds of capital, which is the precondition for reducing the space to one dimension, the construction of a two-dimensional space makes it clear that the exchange rate of the different kinds of capital is one of the fundamental stakes in the struggles between class fractions whose power and privileges are linked to one or the other of these types. In particular, this exchange rate is a stake in the struggle over the dominant principle of domination (economic capital, cultural capital or social capital), which goes on at all times between the different fractions of the dominant class.
>
> 1984, p. 125

Thus, Bourdieu extends the concept of capital according to an underlying concept which only in principle relies on convertibility into capital in the normal economic sense. Bourdieu does not do us the favour, however, of explicitly spelling out what this underlying concept is that maintains itself across different forms of capital. The in-principle convertibility of different forms of capital allows us to surmise from the place of capital in capitalist society a general notion of 'capital' as Bourdieu sees it. Marx's definition of capital in terms of M–C–M' gives us a 'formative' definition of economic capital, but the whole of social theory is required to see the impact of owning economic capital on social life, a 'summative' definition, so to speak. Likewise, the entirety of Bourdieu's work is required to demonstrate the impact of capital in his generalised sense on social life and what it means to a person to own it. A neat definition is not required but an explanation is.

Capital is the resource, command of which enables one to exercise and resist domination in social relations; put another way, to maintain a position in the status hierarchy of society; or to put it more objectively, capital is an 'organising principle'. 'Composition of capital' thus refers to the composition of total capital as cultural and economic capital – with the other types of capital playing a subordinate role. Expressed graphically, instead of a single *line* of dominance rising from poor to rich, we visualise a *plane* across which dominance increases monotonically towards the top-right corner (economic capital +, cultural capital +) with the gradient at every point on the plane subject to contestation.

Thus, 'capital' in this sense, is capable of ordering the relation between any two people. Such an ordering principle, however, does not necessarily produce a *complete* ordering of society, along a single axis of subordination.

I think it is fair to say that this conception marks Bourdieu's concept of capital off from the broader, more intuitive concept of 'wealth'. The use and maintenance of the various forms of capital is not about enjoyment (i.e., of wealth) but of *work* (i.e., of social production), of *using* capital in order to make a gain of some kind.

Conceived in this way, 'capital' seems to span different social formations, not only bourgeois society, representing the degree of command a subject has over whatever it is in a given society or social stratum which confers the capacity to subordinate others. However, this is subject to the important proviso that the relevant entitlement is *exchangeable*. So someone who has cultural capital can *exchange* that for economic capital, for example, by the high price put on their artistic products, and conversely a wealthy person can acquire taste in art by buying access to artistic circles, etc. This exchangeability is not generally found outside of bourgeois society.

Bourdieu accepts 'economic capital' as the pre-eminent principle of domination in capitalist society, but observes that the efficacy of economic capital as a principle of domination is constantly under challenge by fractions of the dominant class (e.g. artists, professionals, academics, etc.) who are relatively poor in economic capital, but who by dint of their social role, wealth in cultural or other forms of capital, strive to enhance their own specific form of capital as a rival principle of domination.

This conception is not dissimilar to the struggles which have gone on down the centuries between landed property, industrial capital, and finance capital. Once it is granted, for example, that possession of the capacity to define what is valid art (or science or body-shape or life-style, or 'connections' for example) is reserved to those capable of elaborating it, it can be seen to be a powerful lever of domination. It seems not unreasonable to designate command of such authority as a 'form of capital'. Thus, struggles in the domain of art (or science or body-shape or lifestyle) take on the appearance of class struggles, just like the struggles between landed property, industrial capital, and finance capital. A social formation is not completely specified by its status order, but awareness of the status order and struggles over it, does shed light on important struggles going on in social and political life.

2   Field and Habitus

Bourdieu sees the social world through the lens of *field* and *habitus*, complementary concepts representing the social and psychological processes which moderate the actions and attitudes of individuals so that stable systems of interpersonal and class relationships spontaneously reproduce themselves.

A *field* is broadly an institution, a normative and evolving set of rules, roles and relationships which determine how various rewards such as status, authority, income, or autonomy are distributed among individuals acting in roles within the field. Examples of fields are the state, academia, the world of romance, the art world, the village, the factory, etc., where different capabilities are rewarded with appropriate roles bringing commensurate rights, recognition, and salary. The field thus motivates participants to carry out the functions of the field as if their welfare depended on it and ensure the maintenance of the field.

The field acts somewhat analogously to an ecosystem or habitat, and *habitus* describes the kind of creatures that live in that habitat. These concepts successfully capture how people apparently occupying disadvantaged positions in a social formation actively seek to maintain that position and 'police the boundaries', so to speak, punishing individuals who stray outside the norms appropriate to the given field by adopting features or practices which are denigrated in that field.

3 Class and Habitus

The concept of 'habitus', borrowed from Aquinas, plays an important role in Bourdieu's theory.

> To reconstruct what has been pulled apart [the various practices performed in different fields] ... one must return to the practice-unifying and practice-generating principle, i.e., the class habitus, the internalised form of the class condition and of the conditionings it entails.
> p. 101

and

> Social class is not defined solely by a position in the relations of production, but by the class habitus which is 'normally' (i.e., with a high statistical probability) associated with that position.
> p. 372

The 'habitus' is the "internalised form of the class condition and of the conditionings" by which a member of the class knows, without thinking about it, just how to react to different cultural stimuli, what he or she finds 'pretentious' or 'vulgar' or 'gawdy' rather than 'attractive' or 'dignified' or 'beautiful'. Habitus is not a direct reflection of the conditions of existence of a class, but a sensibility acquired through a lifetime and an upbringing in those conditions and the possibilities they include or exclude, with a future (including a future for one's children) which offers prospects, or on the other side, a past remembered when things were better or gains were made.

Thus, whether a person *actually* has money, or skills or education or family, in practice turns out to be secondary to the habitus they have acquired, and may, under unusual circumstances, be at odds with the lifestyle and attitudes, the way of using the body, command of language, friends and contacts, preferences in art and aspirations, etc., etc., which are *normally* associated with those conditions. As Marx (1843) said: "Within the credit relationship ... man himself is turned into *money*, or money is *incorporated* in him." The miner's son who leaves town to become a dancer, or the clerk who bluffs his way into being accepted as a well-heeled investor and turns pretension into reality, are possible, but rarities. The wealthy man's son is accepted into a management position despite lacking any real aptitude for the job while the skilled worker waits a lifetime for promotion – that is the norm.

Bourdieu was successful in explaining the stasis and reproduction of cultural and social formations. His study of how mass higher education failed to improve the lot of the millions of lower-class French people who entered university for the first time in the 1960s, was a remarkable achievement for his approach. How the field and the habitus can be *changed* perhaps by individuals who challenge its norms, by changes in technology, or in some other way, is far less clear, however. In reality, fields and their habitus are constantly changing, and I see nothing in Bourdieu's theory which is inherently static. Bourdieu has failed to theorise the *formation and change* of fields and their habitus. But as meso-level concepts which are amenable to theorising the mediation between agent and structure and therefore of social change, field and habitus are an invaluable contribution to the understanding of the possibility for structural change.

4   Cultural Capital and Educational Capital

Cultural capital is the capacity to play the culture game (to borrow a term from Wittgenstein) – to recognise the allusions made in a novel, what is being quoted or refused in a work of art, to know what and how to approve and disapprove, how to avoid the question when necessary, to have internalised appropriate manners and acquired a taste for art, to know the directors (rather than the actors) of films, *avant garde* rather than popular, to know how to make dinner conversation, how to wear clothes, how to occupy space, how to look down your nose, and give or not give someone your time, and so forth. All these infallibly identify you to others as a person of a culture – popular, *avant garde* or legitimate – with a likely trajectory in life (declining or rising), suitable to have access to certain circles or not, and with more or less right to have an opinion on political and other matters.

> Thus ... the social order is progressively inscribed in people's minds. Social divisions become principles of division, organising the image of the social world. Objective limits become a sense of limits, a practical anticipation of objective limits acquired by experience of objective limits, a 'sense of one's place' which leads one to exclude oneself from the goods, persons, places and so forth from which one is excluded.
> p. 471

Bourdieu's research shows that possession of cultural capital is closely predicted by social origins. The bourgeois child knows the price of an Impressionist painting at auction and where it should hang in the drawing room in the same way as the working-class boy knows who won the World Cup and how to change a sparkplug. Professionals know from an early age who is a good director, in the same way a working-class youth knows the actors and actresses of popular cinema.

The educational system offers a way for parvenus to acquire culture and a certificate to prove it, but Bourdieu's research confirmed that 'academic' culture can never quite duplicate the ease and depth of the cultural capital acquired by constant exposure at home. As the educational system was opened to wider and wider sections of the populace, a struggle went on to redefine qualifications and jobs, and create new certificates, and moved the goal posts so as to restore the social order, and on the other hand, to open new doors to young graduates. At the same time, there is a constant struggle going on between *rising* class fractions and those in *decline*, between technocratic executives with degrees in business management and all kinds of cultural mediators revaluing their own life-styles upwards, while the status of shopkeepers and skilled tradespeople, for example, inexorably decline, and so forth. The autodidact meanwhile, according to Bourdieu, enters a race which he has lost from the beginning. Thus, we have the phenomenon which Bourdieu describes as judgments of classification which are themselves classified and classifying acts.

As is well known in respect to all status struggles, no distinction is so important as the distinction between social neighbours. Thus, one has all the acts of *refusal* in which what is valued by one is refused by its neighbour, such as avant garde art versus mainstream 'legitimate' art.

According to Bourdieu, the main axis of these struggles is *within* the dominant class, between those who lack economic capital, against those wealthy bourgeois who, relatively speaking, lack culture, with professionals of various kinds promoting their own status by trying to shift the dominant principle of subordination towards cultural means, distinguishing themselves from the uncultured wealthy by emphasising taste for the refined and offbeat, as against the acquisition of rare and expensive artefacts. And on the other side, among those lacking in economic capital, among the dominated classes, to promote the sensibilities of professional skills acquired by hard work through the public education system or artistic production, to gain entry to the lower ranks of the dominant class. At the same time, the working class, making a virtue of necessity, call to order anyone of their number who gets above themselves and threatens class solidarity by attending the opera in the evening or reading 'difficult' books during lunch break.

Bourdieu thus reduces appreciation of culture to *pretension* – people acquire and express a taste which expresses their pretension to be recognised in a given class fraction, refusing the vulgar or the common, the difficult or the fancy, according to the need for distinction. The whole business of cultural appreciation is reduced by Bourdieu to a status game.

In more recent times, it would seem that the arena where the value of expertise of all kinds is most subject to challenge is not within the dominant classes but through class resentment on the part of those excluded from both economic and cultural capital.

5 Social Capital, Body Capital, Linguistic Capital, Political Capital

Although economic capital and cultural capital constitute the principal axes of subordination within capitalist society, Bourdieu talks of other forms of capital as well. *Social capital* is 'connections' needed, in particular, to make use of one's cultural or *academic* capital (certificates). *Body capital*, both given by nature and that acquired through the socially approved diet and exercise regime and so on, also constitutes a resource which gives an individual leverage in social struggles. *Linguistic capital* is basically a subset of cultural capital contained in an appropriate ease in the command of language and the appropriate dialect. *Political capital* is one's standing in the political world and the ability to command votes and support in political conflicts.

6 Cultural Relativism

At the end of reading *Distinctions* one is left with the impression of an extreme relativism in cultural criticism. Everything, it appears, is appreciated solely for the purpose of establishing markers of one's social status, albeit unconsciously. The book concludes with a critique of Kantian and other aesthetics and Bourdieu comes close to pure relativism. The 'real motives' are everywhere disguised or sublimated. Taste responds to two kinds of stimuli – on the one hand the pleasure connected with basic human needs, on the other, basically 'quotation' and 'association' which refer to other points in the cultural universe in a kind of 'in-group' conversation. This creates distance from the material world and entry to a cultural world structured and populated by cultural references and the social universe of the dominant class.

According to Bourdieu, all the dichotomies of cultural criticism are successive sublimations of one basic distinction between the dominated class and dominant class, beginning with animal nature versus human culture, therefore crude/heavy versus fine/light and so on. These distinctions can undergo inversion when the subordinate fractions of the dominant class use the same contrast to indicate ascetic/serious versus light-weight/frivolous, etc. in distinction both to the culturally poor, economically dominant bourgeoisie, and the simple enjoyments of the unpretentious worker. Bourdieu also finds that the basic dichotomies of gender and age are deployed to express or reinforce distinctions of cultural dominance. So, for example, one sees the contest between immature/mature against youthful/aged, and all the contested markers of subordination which are as ancient as the human species mobilised in the language of cultural subordination.

So, although the dominant class's appreciation of art is sublimated through multiple shifts, it is basically stimulating the same need for a feeling of distinction or distance from the crude necessity of the life of the dominated classes. My appreciation of fine art, just like the smooth skin on my hands, is a marker of my freedom from the daily grind, and thus my high status. My facility in the kitchen marks me off from the working man who expects his wife to cook for him. Through multiple sublimation, culture constitutes itself as a relatively independent domain, but the taste for a work of art can ultimately be traced back to the pleasures of enjoyment or domination.

Thus, we have a window into the class struggles as it is played out in the domain of culture:

> Taste is at the heart of these symbolic struggles, which go on at all times between the fractions of the dominant class and which would be less absolute, less total, if they were not based on the primary belief which binds each agent to his life-style. ... Conflicts over art or the art of living, in which what is really at stake is the imposition of the dominant principle of domination within the dominant class – or, to put it another way, the securing of the best conversion rate for the type of capital with which each group is best provided – would not be so dramatic if they did not involve the ultimate values of the person, a highly sublimated form of interests.
>
> p. 310

People *believe in* their own life and the value of the skills, knowledge, experiences, social bonds, etc., that are attached to their way of living. When movies mock stereotypes of rural bumpkins, more is at stake for rural communities than the price of farm produce.

7 Idealism

Bourdieu could be open to a charge of 'idealism' by virtue of the fact that he has distanced the means of domination from production of the means of material existence. However, this charge does not stick, for he shows well enough that the class habitus is basically making a virtue of necessity. Taste has its origins in the conditions of production of the characteristic modes of life of a class.

He observes that the means of domination has shifted:

> substituting seduction for repression, public relations for policing, advertising for authority, the velvet glove for the iron fist, pursues the symbolic integration of the dominated classes by imposing needs rather than inculcating norms.
>
> pp. 153–154

So, while the mode of domination is connected to the system of needs and the mode of their satisfaction, how this connection is made is often far from obvious.

Reading *Distinctions* leaves the impression of *objectivism*, in the sense that all the social agents are pursuing tastes and desires which derive from *unconscious* internalisations of their social position. People are deemed to be unaware of the real reasons for their own actions. "Culture is the ultimate fetish," he says, and there undoubtedly is such a pessimistic flavour to the work, but it is nuanced.

In his analysis of the French newspapers, Bourdieu shows how the culture addresses itself to the bourgeois as "subjects of history, or at least subjects of a discourse about history," whereas the habitus of the working class centres around the worker as *object* of politics, whose only political voice is that delegated to a spokesperson who speaks in the language of the dominant class.

The social arrangements reflected in Bourdieu's analysis therefore capture the form of rule active in bourgeois society. There is no suggestion, however, of how the working class, acclimatised to subordination and ruling themselves out of matters of state, could transform themselves into subjects of history.

> With mass market cultural products – music whose simple repetitive structures invite a passive, absent participation, prefabricated entertainments which the new engineers of cultural mass production designed for television viewers, and especially sporting events which establish a recognised division between the spectators and the professionals, virtuosos

of an esoteric technique or 'supermen' of exceptional ability – dispossession of the very intention of recognition of dispossession.
   p. 386

This reflects a very pessimistic view of the prospects for social and cultural progress.

8   Political Opinion Formation

Somewhat as an aside from the main argument, as part of a critique of the naïve use of questionnaires to measure political opinion, Bourdieu refers to three modes of political opinion formation:

> First, a *class ethos*, a generative formula not constituted as such which enables objectively coherent responses, compatible with the practical premises of a practical relation to the world, to be generated for all the problems of everyday existence.
> Secondly, it may be a systematic political 'slant' (*parti*), a system of explicit, specifically political principles, amenable to logical control and reflexive scrutiny, in short, a sort of political 'axiomatics' (in ordinary language, a 'line' or a 'programme') …
> Thirdly, it may be a two-stage choice, i.e., the identification, in the mode of knowledge, of the answers consistent with the 'line' of a political party, this time in the sense of an organisation providing a political 'line' on a set of problems which it constitutes as political.
>   p. 418

These lines were written at a time when the powerful French Socialist and Communist Parties had huge bases in the French working class and mediated the political opinion formation of French workers. This is no longer the case. This interaction between the life experiences of the population and their political opinion formation is now mediated without an effective representative voice.

9   Systems of Status Subordination

According to Nancy Fraser (2003), capitalist society is marked by the co-existence of two forms of subordination, "the class structure and the status order," and it is necessary to utilise two different systems of concepts to grasp the two systems of subordination, and understand the interaction between the two.

Bourdieu's approach to subordination along multiple axes is a kind of utilitarian analysis whereby individuals choose a strategy which maximises their benefit for the particular composition of capital that they have command of, in combination with the struggle by classes to valorise their own life-style in competition with others. But Bourdieu treats economic capital as just one measure ordering one of a number of status orders. Cultural capital and economic capital are orthogonal but so also are social capital, body capital, etc.

Thus, Bourdieu observes that (in 1960s France) working-class women don't bother about their appearance and prefer to be home-makers and make their men happy, because the jobs on offer for them are rotten anyway, while the daughters of the bourgeoisie dress up, get educated and corner prestigious jobs as 'cultural mediators' because this offers the optimum route to improving or maintaining their own status.

Bourdieu is also attuned to a lot of the observations found in Fraser's work, such as the deployment of gender stigmatisation on gendered forms of labour, with consequences such as male nurses suffering from low pay and the pay rates of trades falling when they become open to women, and so forth.

There is a sense in which Bourdieu's (mainly) two-dimensional map of social space expresses Fraser's idea of two systems of subordination, and there is quite a lot of overlap between the two different approaches. Bourdieu, however, seems to believe that political economic structures and status orders are mutually equivalent and interchangeable, while Fraser makes no such claim. Bourdieu's demonstration that *exchange* is possible between different types of capital, on which his reductionism depends, has some merit. However, I don't believe that this exchangeability is universal. It is undeniable that no amount of economic capital can absolutely buy you out of gender, race, body-type, linguistic subordination, for instance.

10   Social Capital Theory

'Social capital' plays a secondary role in Bourdieu's theory. Someone who aspires to move up the social hierarchy and has the necessary qualification and taste still needs connections for their qualifications to be translated into admission to a class fraction of higher status. It is hard to see how this concept could be broadened into a 'third dimension', with the kind of weight it has in social capital theory.

The difference between this extension of the concept of capital from that of people like Robert Putnam (1993; 2001) is that Bourdieu brings the economic and non-economic entities into relation with one another through the in-principle convertibility of cultural, social and economic capital, and by means of a broader conception of social subordination, from which both notions of (economic) capital and cultural (or social, etc.) capital can be derived.

By contrast, Putnam et al. take the bourgeois fetishistic theory of capital as a given, and extend the fetishism into non-economic relationships. For Putnam, social capital is like 'natural capital' – something which by its very nature *cannot be acquired as personal property* but is a condition for production and accumulation. For James Coleman (1990) however, social capital is closer to Bourdieu's social capital, being a resource which an individual owns and deploys for personal gain and which can be converted into economic capital.

Bourdieu clearly breaks with Marx's conception of capital, but does so in a way which acknowledges its own break in attempting to take Marx's critique of political economy a step further, and should be appreciated on that basis.

11   Axel Honneth's Criticism of Bourdieu

According to Axel Honneth (1990), Bourdieu's concept of cultural capital suffers from a fatal ambiguity. On the one hand, his empirical research highlights how social groups and individuals cultivate *distinction* for their own life-style and tastes in *contrast* to those of other, lower strata, by making use of whatever social assets they have to make their own life-style take on the aura of exclusiveness. This criticism does not stand up however. Social groups express their own values in terms of distinctive social practices and demand *recognition* from others for the intrinsic worth of these practices from society at large, rather than adopting other tastes and life-styles which may already enjoy more general social appreciation. The strategy of vesting value in something that you monopolise has exactly the same logic. Capital, if it is to underpin a status order, is the value given to one's property by society at large, by *everyone else*. If no one values what you do, you will be poor; being poor *means* that no one values what you do and have, irrespective of the value you vest in it. Recognition and material self-interest are in perfect accord here.

Cultural capital is not portable to the same degree as economic capital, but both have limited portability. Your ability to appreciate artworks doesn't help you in the pub or the supermarket, but still, it does help you in the academic staffroom. A bank account has little worth in the jungle, or a street fight. Capital is always dependent on the social conditions in which it may be exchanged.

12 Subjectivity

As remarked above, Bourdieu was quite pessimistic about the prospects for the working class or any part thereof, transforming themselves from objects into subjects of history. Indeed, he observes that those who act as spokespeople for the working class are forced to adopt the language of the dominant class in order just to express the political demands of the working class.

On the other hand, his description of the class habitus, contributing as it does to the understanding of class consciousness, and his elucidation of the mechanisms of class struggle within the domain of culture, should give clues about a way forward in the struggle against capitalism and the kind of barriers faced by radical politics.

Certainly, Bourdieu provides an impressive exposé of professional and petit-bourgeois claims to high pay and status, as against the under-valued skills and labour of the working-class. There is a sense in which Bourdieu's philosophically inclined analysis expresses in the most cultured possible way, the spontaneous working-class prejudice that bourgeois culture is nothing more than a pretension aimed to make its connoisseurs look smarter and working class people look stupid, demeaning even their body-shape. In that sense his conceptions are egalitarian.

13 Conclusion

One has to appreciate the power of Bourdieu's insight into how an entire social formation, like modern-day capitalism, is internalised in the most intimate feelings and desires of its people.

It is like Kuhn's (1962) sociology of science minus Kuhn's paradigm shifts (which are the really exciting part of Kuhn's theory). Everyone understands nowadays how scientists write papers for recognition, promotion, overseas travel and so on, not just in pursuit of truth. But the fact is that *science gets done,* nonetheless. Anthropogenic climate change is real, not simply a product of competition in the field of science. If Bourdieu's critique applies to art, why not science, why not sociology? All these institutions have an objective basis irrespective of delivering rewards to the participants of the given institution, and the objective basis of an institution also provides motivation for the individual participants in the form of *internal rewards*, not just status.

It is good to have such a rich theory of social equilibrium, but what we need is a theory of social *dynamics*. We need a theory of *movement* for fields. But is 'field' a concept amenable to a theory of change? Do individuals change their habitus or the field through their struggle? Or do fields change objectively in response to the disclosure of contradictions or as a result of interaction with other fields? These are open questions which Bourdieu does not help us answer.

Nonetheless, an analysis of the current assault on expertise and the social status of knowledge workers would surely benefit from a consideration of Bourdieu's ideas.

CHAPTER 25

The Coronavirus Pandemic Is a World *Perezhivanie*

The Black Plague which swept across Eurasia in the 1340s created a labour shortage. This labour shortage set off a process which over the next 300 years brought an end to feudalism as the dominant social system across Europe.

By the time of the First World War, bourgeois development had created a world market, tying almost every corner of the world into a unified system of needs and labour. At that point, a world subject was implicit. It could be said to be 'in itself'. That is, a 'world subject' did not yet exist but a sufficient objective unification of the world had been achieved such that the potential for a world subject existed.

The First World War gave us the 1919 Flu pandemic and the Russian Revolution. Relations between the classes were changed forever. The Second World War not only set off world-transforming events such as rolling National Liberation Movements, the Civil Rights and Women's movements. Transnational institutions such as the United Nations, WHO, GATT, the World Bank, the European Union, and so on, were created. Their authority may be constantly under challenge, but nonetheless they continue to exist.

Both world wars are exemplars of world-transforming events, what I will call world *perezhivaniya*. Events such as the 9/11 attacks together with the US responses to it, and the GFC (Global Financial Crisis) together with the responses to it, also produced important changes in how the world works, albeit incomplete and overwhelmingly negative in their immediate impact on the lives of billions of ordinary people. 9/11 and the GFC were not in themselves world-transforming, but were triggering events. The transformation came in the *responses* by governments and other actors to the initial events. Events like the 9/11 attacks, are not properly called 'events' (like a volcano or a traffic accident) because they were *activities*, things people *did*, not things which simply *happened to* people. Likewise, the aftermath was not a mere *effect* but the active *response* of people to the foregoing events, by means of which the existing institutions processed and 'dealt with' what had been done.

I am convinced that the coronavirus pandemic – understood together with the various responses both immediate and in the aftermath, if indeed there comes a time which could be called an 'aftermath' – is such a world-changing experience. In particular, I see this experience as a *perezhivanie* (see Chapter 4, this volume).

Formally speaking, *perezhivanie* means 'an experience'. But *'perezhivanie'* is a Russian word which has no English equivalent which fully conveys the breadth and depth of its meaning in Russian language and culture. There are two things about how this is understood in Russia generally, and in Vygotsky's Cultural Psychology in particular, which are not conveyed in the English expression 'an experience'.

Firstly, etymologically, *'perezhivanie'* is equivalent to 'survive' in English. When people write their autobiography, they pick out from the hundreds of thousands of hours of their life certain moments or episodes (sometimes very extended ones) which they survived, times when they made life-changing, personality-forming choices, situations which they handled (or failed to handle) and which forever changed not just how they saw the world but (and this is important) *how the world saw them*, or when a parent or significant other (especially in the case of children) or maybe the justice system confronted them with something they had done and forced them to reflect on it. Those experiences which *changed* them and made them who they are.

Secondly, as the ancient Greek dramatists knew, it is not the experience as such which changes the person. As John Dewey (1939) explained, 'an experience' is an *active* episode of a person's interaction with a challenging situation. It is well-known that the most traumatic events, such as early childhood abuse, can be 'repressed' or passively accepted. Some people pass through a war and remember only the comradeship and solidarity. But in general, after the situation has passed, people reflect on it, maybe on their own in periods of quiet reflection, or together with a trusted other. However, *perezhivanie* always entails the subject changing their relationship with the world. Freud called this process 'catharsis' by analogy with watching a drama on the stage as a means of reflecting on one's own experience, and the medical practice of purging poison from the body. Catharsis is the active process of observing, working over, reflecting upon, processing and 'absorbing' an experience. It is the actual *work* of dealing with what happened and how you responded. It is through the catharsis that the person is transformed, rather than the event itself. The event may be momentary, but the catharsis may take years. This is what *perezhivanie* means: the *perezhivanie* is this whole process. It has a beginning, a middle, and an end. It is a single whole. It is the series of such *perezhivaniya* which makes the person.

Life is a series of *perezhivaniya* with long periods in between of gradual adaptation to the new you, solving the problems that life is throwing up, until the next *perezhivanie* changes your relation to the world.

Perezhivanie entered the English language through the study of Vygotsky's Cultural Psychology and correspondingly, it is associated with the study of personal development in both adults and children. Through this study a lot has been learnt about the formation of the personality and the various aspects of *perezhivanie* relevant to personal development. But it is not essentially a concept limited to personal development. It is the process of *subject formation*. In this case, we are talking about the development of a world subject.

As Hegel (1821) said: the person is the series of their actions. A.N. Leontyev studied the formation of the personality in terms of commitments to practices (activities) among which different life-projects take a leading role at different life stages, as the personality passes through critical periods. We could express this to say that the development of the person is the *work* of making the person, the self-transformation of human activity. And the same applies to any project, a.k.a., self-conscious social practice or activity.

A subject (be that a person or a project, movement, enterprise or institution) does not come into being and mature *gradually*. It goes through periods of effectively gradual development in which it adapts to its situation, but such periods of gradual adaptation are punctuated by periods of crisis which are relatively sudden and in which the subject does not simply adapt to their situation, but actively *transforms* their *situation*. It is in such critical periods of development that the work of self-creation is done, by changing themselves and their place in the world around them. There comes a time in every life when you simply cannot go on living in the old way. In this case, we are talking about a complete realignment of the world system. It must be said though that *perezhivanie* is *work* because the outcome is indeterminate. The dramatic experience which may lead to development, may also destroy the subject forever. Survival and a life-affirming recovery is not guaranteed.

I am not here making a *metaphor* from personal development up to sociocultural development. Both are instances of the same human process. Group *perezhivaniya* have been studied in classrooms, for instance. But personal development gives us the opportunity to study subject formation in a way which is easier than when the subject in question is an institution or an entire world-historic formation.

It has been objected that the coronavirus cannot be a *world-perezhivanie* because every country, every social class, every ethnic group, every person, experiences covid *differently* and will process it differently. This is not an objection but simply a characterisation of the work at hand. In the infant child, each of the basic psychological functions is located in a biologically fixed neurological apparatus. But in the process of subject formation, these separate functions are combined into new 'higher' psychological functions which mobilise the entire body and the surrounding culture to boot. The bundle of flesh with its various reflexes is not a subject, but by virtue of its human body and being treated as a human being by those around it, the infant grows into a subject, makes itself into a person. Likewise a world.

My claim is that this pandemic may be the traumatic experience in which the potential for a world subject is realised. Just as a personality not only shapes itself but comes into being through the work of surviving these challenging experiences, the world-subject, at the moment still only a potential, can give birth to itself in the time ahead – solving the existential problems facing the whole world with the participation, in one way or another, of everyone. Because the world cannot survive any other way now.

What is unfolding around us is an array of separate activity systems – the social practices of the various nations, classes and communities are all subject to the same pandemic. But we all *see* and learn about how the pandemic is going in other countries and in neighbouring suburbs and in the homes of our neighbours. And we learn and act accordingly, and where possible collaborate.

Neoliberal governments are handing out tens of billions of dollars, some approaching a Universal Basic Income, nationalising health facilities and some ending the disciplining of welfare recipients. Some progressive leaders are acting like military commanders, and people can no longer take a stroll in cities which have been Meccas of freedom. Our heroes, our essential workers, are nurses, teachers, hospital cleaners, delivery drivers and supermarket check-out workers. And this while the interbank lending rate in the OECD countries is zero or 0.1% p.a., access to the proceeds of capital is limited to those who are already wealthy – in the absence of new investment opportunities, existing stocks are simply up-valued. Governments in these countries can afford to pay everyone's wages for a year at a cost of a couple of dollars a week in interest. It's the world turned upside down.

And at the time of writing, scientists never have developed a vaccine for SARS or MERS, and no one knows if the vaccine will prevent transmission or how long immunity will last. Only 1% of the world's population has yet had COVID-19, and the loss of trust in authority will mean that millions will not take the vaccine when it comes, and some will never get access to it. And as soon as lockdown measures are removed, a single case can generate an exponential growth of infection. And if we are still in a pandemic in a year's time, the virus might well have mutated enough to re-infect those who have had it and acquired natural immunity, and we still *don't know* what the long term effects of COVID-19 are going to be. And there will undoubtedly be more pandemics to come.

We cannot go on living this way. Liberal freedom is as bankrupt as authoritarian, anti-science populism. The world is sick and needs fixing. The reality show is over. The fragile global climate has been given a slight reprieve by the termination of air travel, but it cannot escape notice that the people who were warning us about the climate emergency – the scientists – are the people we turned to when our lives were put in *immediate* risk. In fact, it is the same uncontrolled destruction of nature which is at the root of the pandemic, and which is destroying all the conditions for human life.

The world subject just barely exists at the moment, but the global means of communication, travel, food supply and virus transmission and the climate emergency remind us that we share *one world*. We have every reason to expect a world transformation in the months and years ahead. Thousands of formative experiments are underway. I have no idea what the future will bring. All the myths of 21st century capitalism have been exploded. But there is every reason for optimism, and the world is crying out for Science and an end to bull-shit jobs and bull-shit leadership.

Don't expect a fully mature socialist world government to emerge from this chaos. Let us just hope that this infant world-subject can enter its childhood, with many difficult experiences ahead, and in need of a self-education.

This is my conclusion: like life, history is a series of upheavals in which we remake ourselves all over again. The world is much more grown up than we were after World War One and World War Two. We are like the stroppy 13-year-old who doesn't really know much but is discovering her/his new body, how little the adults seem to know and ready to take on adult responsibilities. So turbulent times lie ahead. But the world is simply going to have to learn, and change how things are done. The pandemic is already rewriting every rule book we have.

CHAPTER 26

As of 2020, the American Century Is Over

Once the American[1] voters elected the amoral, narcissistic reality TV star, Donald Trump as President, the writing was on the wall. Racist and xenophobic, Trump explicitly promised an isolationist foreign policy, getting out of 'endless wars', making America's allies 'pay their share' and ending conflict with America's long time rival, Russia.

The term 'American Century' was coined in 1941 by the American publishing tycoon, Henry Luce. According to Luce, the British Century had stretched from the 1815 defeat of Napoleon at Waterloo to the quagmire of World War One. America had resisted entering the War, but when it did it tipped the balance decisively.

Once the boots of American youth landed on French soil in April 1917, the War was indeed brought to a rapid end, an event also marked by a flu epidemic which would take 50 million lives. And just as America stepped up to its world-historic role, its nemesis was born in the October 1917 Russian Revolution.

Luce was one of those urging that the US enter the Second World War on the side of the Allies before the Japanese settled the question by attacking Pearl Harbour. He urged America to enter the War for the "triumphal purpose of freedom," and to go on to "create the first great American Century."

Throughout the English Century, America had extended its influence over Latin America and at the end of the 19th century began to intervene directly in the Caribbean and across the Pacific, booting Spain out of its territories. Having built up its formidable industrial might while protected from European invasion by the Atlantic and Pacific Oceans, America stepped on to the world stage in 1917 with the youthful arrogance which would characterise its entire century of dominance of world affairs.

It is easy to forget that until the 1950s, America was widely seen as a liberator by the peoples of the colonised world. Ho Chi Minh, for example, looked first not to Mao or Stalin but to Truman to guarantee the independence of a post-colonial Vietnam. It was Kwame Nkrumah in 1963 who coined the term 'neo-colonialism' for the American road to global hegemony. While possessed of unconquerable military might, America no longer tried to displace the European powers from their colonies by force of arms, but used their economic

---

[1] Throughout this article I will use the word "America" to refer to the USA, for the sake of style.

power to undermine their rivals and foster allies amongst the local people. But unlike the old colonial powers, instead of installing their own direct control (or by moving populations, like the British), America promoted corrupt strong men or other forces within the country with economic, political and low intensity armed backing. This did not exclude the use of armed force. Indeed, there are few countries in the world that have not at one time or another been subject to American bombing and invasion. Nonetheless, the Americans normally relied on their economic might to maintain their domination and in more recent times avoided the need for 'boots on the ground' so far as possible.

By the end of World War Two, all the old colonial powers and the Soviet Union had been devastated and bankrupted. At Bretton Woods, America launched a set of institutions – the International Monetary Fund, the World Bank, GATT and the US Treasury Department. The US dollar was made the reserve currency of the world, and the US held almost all the world's gold, industrial power and military might, not to mention the first atomic bombs and the right to print as many dollars as they liked. The United Nations was created under conditions where the US believed it could control it, and America reshaped the world to a great extent just as America saw fit.

Not only did America dominate the world by its economic and military might, but its music (largely the product of African Americans), its movies, its fashion, its literature and so much of its ways of everyday life penetrated all strata of society across the world. Rock bands and hamburgers became subversive weapons.

From when do we mark the decline of American power? From 1957, when the Soviet Union beat the US into orbit with Sputnik? the partial collapse of the Bretton Woods arrangements in 1968–1973? defeat in Vietnam in 1975? the Iran hostage crisis in 1978? the failure to overthrow Saddam Hussein in 1991? the 'endless wars' launched by George Bush in 2001–2003?

It could be argued that it was the collapse of the Soviet Union in 1991 which marked the beginning of the end. From 1948 to 1991 we had a bipolar world, and when one power collapsed the entire system of shared hegemony was destabilised. Always unable to directly rule the nations it dominated, the USA relied upon the competition first with the old colonial powers, and then with the 'Communist Bloc', to stabilise their domination in their own sphere of influence.

Whether or not there is a critical event, America faced ever increasing difficulty and costs, not to mention insults and humiliation, and increasingly lost the confidence and the will to carry on as before. Isolationist sentiments were encouraged by the stagnation of living standards at home, ever-growing economic inequality and poverty, generating downward class resentment directed against the most recent waves of immigration.

Ever since its founding fathers arrived as refugees from religious persecution in 17th century England, America was populated by wave after wave of refugees fleeing war and religious persecution, landing in dire poverty, mostly facing a hostile reception from the generation of settlers who had preceded them, and in legendary fashion hauling themselves up and making a life in the New World. Long after slavery had been eliminated in Europe, it continued in the American South where fortunes were amassed. Like the plebeians of ancient Rome, the 'white working class' mediated between the Southern Aristocracy and the Slaves. This class survived the Abolition after the Civil War and institutionalised racism in America. Even after Jim Crow's back was broken by the Civil Rights Movement, all politics in America has ever since been *racialised* by the experience of slavery. Along with American individualism, this is the main reason that America never managed to build a Labor Party and lacks the kind of Welfare State which European workers have achieved. Since Ronald Reagan invented his 'trickle-down economics', real wages for American workers stagnated whilst the concentration of wealth in the billionaire class accelerated. The standards of housing, education, health and public safety experienced by the poorer half of America remains that of a 'third world' country.

Donald Trump was elected President on the back of class resentment and resentment directed against the rest of the world. "Why should we try to help these people? What thanks have we ever got?"

When Trump won the 2016 election, much to almost everyone's surprise and probably his own, some people may have thought that this was it. America was done for. But most of us, I think, were prepared to watch and see. As soon as he was elected he tried to ban anyone from a list of Muslim countries from entering the US – a clear message to billions of people that they were not wanted, antagonising allies and enemies alike, but applauded by his domestic base.

Heads of State around the world wondered how they should deal with him and his bizarre behaviour alarmed political leaders among both America's allies and their erstwhile enemies. But just like many people within the US, we could comfort ourselves with the certainty that America has a long and unshakeable institution of Presidential elections on a Tuesday in November every fourth year, and if we could only hang on until November 2020, a 'normal' US President would replace Trump and we could all return to the how things were before.

But then Trump's behaviour on the international arena became more and more feral. He abused NATO, thwarted agreement on climate action in Paris, launched a trade war with China and imposed tariffs on supposed allies supplying US industry and agriculture, and allowed himself to be humiliated by the North Korean leader. Trump unilaterally reneged on a Treaty with Iran and other world powers and placed sanctions on Iran and then placed sanctions on European governments who attempted to honour the agreement. Then he placed sanctions on German companies who worked on a gas pipeline vital to Germany's economy, and Germany responded by making arrangements for European companies to avoid US sanctions

America's weaker allies were fed to the lions. The handful of American troops who provided a largely symbolic thin red line between Turkey and America's Kurdish allies in Syria was peremptorily withdrawn leading to an immediate Turkish invasion and leaving US soldiers wandering aimlessly in hostile territory.

And then there was Ukraine, on the Eastern borders of the EU, with half its territory already occupied by Russia. Trump withheld $500m of US military aid until their President agreed to help him frame up a domestic political opponent.

The message was clear: no America ally, be it a vulnerable national movement or a nuclear armed European ally, could rely on American support when the chips were down.

And America's enemies? Who can forget the humiliating display of Kim Jong Un playing Trump for a fool, getting him to run around the world to meet him in the DMZ and then Singapore, with ludicrous banter about who had the bigger button, while North Korea finalised their membership of the Nuclear Club. Vladimir Putin, Kim Jong Un, Xi Jiping, Recep Tayyip Erdoğan, Narendra Modi, Jair Bolsonaro and other authoritarian leaders, formerly seen as representing the opposite of America's objectives, were praised as 'great leaders'. Not that America had not *always* supported dictators from petty Latin American puppets to the mediaeval Saudi king. But Trump was holding these authoritarian leaders up as role models. America was no longer on a mission to bring democracy and freedom to the world (as it had thought) but rather sought to emulate everything in the world that was not freedom or democracy. But even America's supporters in Latin America could expect no help from America. They were on their own.

Trump's call to follow up his rejection of the Paris Climate Agreement with the withdrawal of US Funds from the World Health Organisation in the middle of the worst pandemic since 1919 was the decisive proof that America had departed from its world role. America had lost the respect of its allies, the fear of its enemies and the leadership of international institutions. Given the continued domestic support for Trump, allies and enemies alike could not count on a return to normal in 2021. American hegemony had been broken already.

International financial and diplomatic organisations had already built workarounds for the boycott or sabotage by America and these would remain in place. The prospect of a 77-year-old Joe Biden in the Oval Office was not sufficient grounds for world leaders to hang out for a return to *pax Americana*. America was no longer feared by its enemies or trusted by its friends, and indeed no one was sure any more who was friend and who was enemy. Israel knew it was a friend, but once America had thoroughly and finally alienated the Palestinian cause, it could actually offer little to Israel that Israel could not do perfectly well for itself. In any case, no Arab country harboured any fear of America.

In terms of global institutions and diplomacy, America is now effectively absent from the international scene. It has more than enough nuclear weaponry to annihilate life on Earth, but this is of no practical use. But to declare an end to the American Century says more than the absence of America. A world can continue on for a time in the absence of its hegemon. What the 'end of the American Century' implies is a transformation and re-alignment of the world system and a discontinuity in the direction of world history.

The Napoleonic Wars and the two World Wars marked such discontinuities, though the first was limited to the European continent. The COVID-19 pandemic constitutes such a moment of world crisis which will bring about a reset in world history. It is the absence of America just at a time when the world system is being reordered, which will mark the end of the American Century.

The pandemic is being experienced differently in different countries. Populations are experiencing the strengths and (mostly) weaknesses of their own leaders and their own polity in intense circumstances. The neoliberal orthodoxy which has governed economic life since Thatcher and Reagan is publicly exposed as hogwash. When the shit hit the fan the market was caught with its pants down and all the most powerful corporations rushed to the state for assistance. Paragons of liberal economics were drafting up laws for a Universal Income (while making sure to victimise this or that marginal group); 'fiscal discipline' turned out to be a hoax. Those who formerly saw themselves as 'strong leaders', having achieved power by dividing the nation and managing to corner 51%, could not unite the nation; leaders who had lied and lied, now found that trust was gold and they had none. Those who had poo-pooed science in the service of the fossil fuel industries now begged the 'so-called experts' to share the platform with them and lend them some of the credibility that they lacked. The 'national heroes' and 'essential workers' turned out to be not soldiers, police and sporting stars, but nurses, doctors, carers, delivery drivers, supermarket workers and cleaners – including some of the lowest paid and formerly least respected workers in the economy. Meanwhile, bankers, hedge fund operators, administrators, accountants and 'symbolic analysts' of all kinds could 'work from home' and no one noticed their absence.

At the time of writing, just about the only economy which is anything like fully functioning is China – now the workshop of the world. Europe and America have gone begging to China for medical equipment they are no longer capable of producing themselves. And not only China, Bangladesh, India and other Asian countries where Western manufacturing has been off-shored are now being begged for assistance. Different countries are having different experiences with COVID-19, but being a wealthy, post-industrial country has been far from a security against the virus. It is early days at the moment (April 2020) and barely 1% of the world has yet had the virus and it seems likely that the virus will eventually infect most of the population of the world. A vaccine will eventually be found but it is unlikely to arrive soon enough to mitigate this trauma. Treatments will be developed and the death rate will lessen, but in the meantime millions will die and everyone is rethinking what kind of world they want to live in. It turned out that there was a hell of a lot more choice about how a country can be run than had been admitted. It turned out that governments have a lot more power to do things if they chose to use that power than we have been led to believe.

The coronavirus is a *world perezhivanie*, that is to say, it is an experience in which the entire world is actively participating and which the world will process and overcome together in a collective *catharsis*. The fact that it will be experienced differently in different countries and by different classes and social groups does not detract from this. On the contrary. There will be a thousand formative experiments under way, and everyone will be watching each other and learning from each other.

It is ironic indeed that this will all take place behind quarantine walls, because in a pandemic this is not a left-right issue. Only a mad person (or the WHO) wants to open the borders in a pandemic, so the liberal refugee advocate has for the moment to agree with the xenophobe that the borders have to be closed. We will all be walled up in our separate cantons but we will be looking over the fence with intense interest. And as bad as things may get, generally speaking we are going to get to solve things on our own. If are lucky and we ask nicely, China might send us some ventilators and India might send us some PPE. But we are also thinking that all that off-shoring and just-in-time delivery was the load of dangerous nonsense we always said it was. Maybe it doesn't matter if we have to pay a liveable wage to have medications made here? Maybe it would be better to give everyone a basic income and let anyone who is available and wants to, do some essential work for more money? Maybe forcing people to work six different jobs to earn a living is not a good idea?

And until a few short months ago we were being told that the very conditions for life on Earth were being eroded by the burning of fossil fuels and other unsustainable practices and that crisis has not gone away. When it came to the crunch, it turned out that even our political leaders turned to the 'so-called experts' when we were faced with an *immediate* threat from the natural world. Isn't it likely we should listen to what these 'so-called experts' have been telling us about the sickness affecting the entire world?

In short, there is going to be a lot of rethinking going on and a lot of trial and error, real life experimentation. It is not the event itself which shapes the future, but the response. And it may not be the first response which turns out to be decisive. But at some point in the months and years ahead a new direction will be settled upon.

As things stand at the moment in America, the Divider-in-Chief has split the country in two just at the moment when national unity is needed like never before. The President who has lied more than 14,000 times since taking office now needs to ask people to sacrifice for the public good. Public trust – trust in government and trust in strangers – has been in decline for decades in America but has now been destroyed entirely. The President openly encourages his supporters to defy the law and make themselves into superspreaders of the virus to boot. As the pandemic has peaked in New York, it is just taking off in the South and this virus will wash back and forth across the continent in successive waves. At the moment, outside of some big cities, people are still largely in denial, but so long as people realise they are going to get sick by going to work or shopping or to a movie or a bar, the economy is not going to pick up. There will be no economic revival until the virus is under control and there is absolutely no sign of that happening. What this means is that the seemingly insatiable capacity of the American consumer to buy whatever the world could produce and generate the demand which has kept the world working, is over.

Suddenly the ever-growing multi-trillion dollar US government debt is thrown into question. So long as America could buy everything the world could produce and was willing and able to tax its citizens, then their debt was safe, but once America can no longer back up that debt with productive power, purchasing power and a compliant tax base, then that debt threatens to crash. Likewise the relation with China depends on the ability of America to buy what China produces, and if this is threatened then the entire world system is in danger.

As leader, policeman, moderator, style-setter and buyer America has left the field at just the time when the world is rethinking itself and reorganising. Who knows what's coming next, but whatever it is, will not be decided by America.

22 April 2020

References

Abeysinghe, S. (2015). Vaccine Narratives and Public Health: Investigating Criticisms of H1N1 Pandemic Vaccination. *PLOS Currents: Outbreaks*.

Abidor, M. (2018). *May Made Me. An Oral History of the 1968 Uprising in France*. Pluto Press.

Arthur, C. (2005). The Myth of 'Simple Commodity Production'. https://chrisarthur.net/.

Arthur, C. (2011). Towards a Systematic Dialectic of Capital. https://chrisarthur.net/.

Arthur, C. (2015). Marx, Hegel and the value-form. In *Marx's Capital and Hegel's Logic. A Reexamination*, ed. by Fred Moseley and Tony Smith, pp. 265–291. Chicago, IL: Haymarket Books.

Atran, S., Sheikh, H., and Gomez, A. (2014). Devoted actors sacrifice for close comrades and sacred cause. *Proc. National Academy of Sciences of the USA* 111(50): 17702–17703.

Beaton, L. and Blunden, A. (2014). The miracle fibre exposed as a deadly threat. Some Moments in the Battle to Have Asbestos Banned from Use in Australia. In *Collaborative Projects: An Interdisciplinary Study*, ed. by Andy Blunden, pp. 261–281. Leiden: Brill.

Beck, U. (1992). *Risk Society. Towards a new modernity*. London, UK: Sage.

Beck, U., Giddens, A., and Lash, S. (1994). Reflexive Modernization: Politics, Tradition and Aesthetics in the Modern Social Order. Stanford, CA: Stanford University Press.

Bell, R. (1992). *Impure Science. Fraud, Compromise, and Political Influence in Science Research*. New York: John Wiley.

Benhabib, S. (1996). *Democracy and Difference. Contesting the boundaries of the Political*. Princeton, NJ: Princeton University Press.

Blume, S. (2006). Anti-Vaccination movements and their interpretations. *Social Science & Medicine* 62(3): 628–642.

Blunden, A. (2006). *Phylogeny*. https://ethicalpolitics.org/ablunden/.

Blunden, A. (2009). Forms of Radical Subjectivity. *International Critical Thought* 4(4): 418–432.

Blunden, A. (2012). *Concepts. A Critical Approach*. Leiden: Brill.

Blunden, A. (2012a). *Andrew Jamison: the life and death of social movements*. https://ethicalpolitics.org/ablunden/.

Blunden, A. (2014). Introduction. *Collaborative Projects: An interdisciplinary study*, ed. by Andy Blunden. Leiden: Brill.

Blunden, A. (2014a). *The Problem of the Environment. A Defence of Vygotsky*. https://ethicalpolitics.org/ablunden/.

Blunden, A. (2016). *Origin of Collective Decision Making*. Leiden: Brill.

Blunden, A. (2016a). Capital *through the Hegelian looking-glass*. https://ethicalpolitics.org/ablunden/.

Blunden, A. (2016b). *Response to Heikki Ikäheimo on 'Normative Essentialism'*. https://ethicalpolitics.org/ablunden/.

Blunden, A. (2018). Goethe, Hegel and Marx. *Science and Society* 82(1): 11–37.

Blunden, A. (2020a). Ontogenesis, Ethnogenesis, Sociogenesis and Phylogenesis. *Human Arenas* 3(4): 470–474.

Blunden, A., et al. (n.d.). *Notes on Perezhivanie*. https://ethicalpolitics.org/seminars/perezhivanie.htm.

Bourdieu, P. (1984). *Distinctions. A Social Critique of the Judgment of Taste*, translated by Richard Nice. Cambridge, MA: Harvard University Press.

Bozhovich, L.I. (2009). The social situation of child development. *Journal of Russian and East European Psychology* 47(4): 59–86.

Buchanan, J. and Tullock, G. (1962). *The Calculus of Consent: Logical Foundations of Constitutional Democracy*. Michigan: University of Michigan Press.

Centre for Activity Theory and Developmental Work Research (CAT&DWR). (2003). *What are CHAT & DWR*. http://www.edu.helsinki.fi/activity/pages/chatanddwr/.

Clarà, M. (2016). Vygotsky and Vasilyuk on *Perezhivanie*: Two Notions and One Word. *Mind, Culture, and Activity* 23(4): 284–293.

Colapietro, V.M. (1988). *Peirce's Approach to the Self: A Semiotic Perspective on Human Subjectivity*. Albany, NY: SUNY Press.

Coleman, J. (1968). The marginal utility of a vote commitment. *Public Choice* 5(1): 39–58.

Coleman, J. (1990). *Foundations of Social Theory*. Cambridge, MA: Harvard University Press.

Coover, V., Deacon, E., Esser, C., and Moore, C. (1977). *Resource Manual for a Living Revolution. A handbook of skills & tools for social change activists*. Philadelphia, PA: Movement for a New Society.

Corballis, M.C. (2002). *From Hand to Mouth. The Origins of Language*. Princeton: Princeton University Press.

Davydov, V.V. (1990). *Types of generalisation in instruction: Logical and psychological problems in the structuring of school curricula*. Reston, VA: National Council of Teachers of Mathematics.

De Saussure, F. (1911/1993). *Third Course of Lectures on General Linguistics*. Oxford, UK: Pergamon Press.

Dewey, J. (1929). Experience and Philosophic Method. In *The Philosophy of John Dewey, Two Volumes in One*, ed. by John J. McDermott, pp. 249–277. Chicago, IL: University of Chicago Press.

Dewey, J. (1938). The Pattern of Enquiry. In *The Philosophy of John Dewey, Two Volumes in One*, ed. by John J. McDermott, pp. 223–239. Chicago, IL: University of Chicago Press.

REFERENCES

Dewey, J. (1939). Having an Experience. In *The Philosophy of John Dewey, Two Volumes in One*, ed. by John J. McDermott, pp. 554–573. Chicago, IL: University of Chicago Press.

Donald, M. (1991). *Origins of the Modern Mind. Three stages in the evolution of culture and cognition*. Cambridge, MA: Harvard University Press.

Engels, F. (1875/1991). Letter to Pyotr Lavrov. 12 November 1875. In *Marx and Engels Collected Works*, vol. 45, pp. 106–109. London: Lawrence & Wishart.

Engels, F. (1875a/1987). Old Introduction to 'Dialectics of Nature'. In *Marx and Engels Collected Works*, vol. 25, pp. 318–335. London: Lawrence & Wishart.

Engels, F. (1876/1987). The part played by labour in the transition from ape to man. In *Marx and Engels Collected Works*, vol. 25, pp. 452–464. London: Lawrence & Wishart.

Engeström, Y. (1999). Innovative Learning in Work Teams: analysing cycles of knowledge in practice. In *Perspectives on Activity Theory*, ed. by Y. Engeström, R. Miettinen, and R.-L. Punamäki, pp. 377–404. Cambridge, UK: Cambridge University Press.

Engeström, Y. (2015). *Learning by Expanding*. 2nd edition. Cambridge, UK: Cambridge University Press.

Epstein, W. (1996). *Impure Science. AIDS, Activism, and the politics of knowledge*. Berkeley and Los Angeles: University of California Press.

Ferholt, B. and Nilsson, M. (2016). Perezhivaniya as a Means of Creating the Aesthetic Form of Consciousness. *Mind, Culture, and Activity* 23(4): 294–304.

Franks, B. (2010). Anarchism and the Virtues. In *Anarchism and Moral Philosophy*, ed. by B. Franks and M. Wilson, pp. 135–160. Basingstoke: Palgrave Macmillan.

Fraser, N. (1997). *Justice Interruptus: Critical Reflections on the "Postsocialist" Condition*. Abingdon: Routledge.

Fraser, N. and Honneth, A. (2003). *Redistribution or Recognition? A political-philosophical exchange*. London and Brooklyn: Verso.

Fraser, N. and Gordon, L. (1997). The Genealogy of 'Dependency': Tracing a Keyword of the US Welfare State. In *Justice Interruptus. Critical Reflections on the "Postsocialist" Condition*, pp. 121–150. Abingdon: Routledge.

Freeman, J. (1970). *The Tyranny of Structurelessness*. https://www.jofreeman.com/joreen/tyranny.htm.

Freud, L. (1914). Remembering, Repeating and Working-Through (Further Recommendations on the Technique of Psycho-Analysis II). In *The Standard Edition of the Complete Psychological Works of Sigmund Freud, Volume XII (1911–1913): The Case of Schreber, Papers on Technique and Other Works*, pp. 145–156.

Gadamer, H-G. (1960/2005). *Truth and Method*. London, UK: Continuum.

Giddens, A. (1984). *The Constitution of Society*. Berkeley and Los Angeles: University of California Press.

Giddens, A. (1998). *Beyond Left and Right: The Future of Radical Politics*. Cambridge, UK: Polity Press.

Goethe, J.W. v. (1827/1996). *Goethe on Science: An Anthology of Goethe's Scientific Writings*, selected and introduced by Jeremy Naydler, with a foreword by Henri Bortoft. Edinburgh, UK: Floris Books.

Goethe, J.W. v. (1795/1988). Outline for a General Introduction to Comparative Anatomy. In *The Collected Works*, Scientific Studies, Volume 12, edited and translated by Douglas Miller.

Goethe, J.W. v. (1787/1962). Goethe To Herder, 17 May 1787. In *Italian Journey, The Collected Works*, Volume 6, pp. 298–299. London: Collins.

Goldin-Meadow, S. (2005). *The Resilience of Language. What gesture creation in deaf children can tell us about how all children learn language.* Hove, UK: Psychology Press.

Goldin-Meadow, S. and Feldman, H. (1977). The Development of Language-Like Communication Without a Language Model. *Science* 197 (4301) (July 22, 1977): 401–403.

Goldin-Meadow, S., Mylander, C., and Franklin, A. (2006). How children make language out of gesture: Morphological structure in gesture systems developed by American and Chinese deaf children. *Cognitive Psychology* 55 (2007): 87–135.

Habermas, J. (1984). *Theory of Communicative Action, Volume One: Reason and the Rationalisation of Society*, translated by Thomas McCarthy. Boston, MA: Beacon Press.

Habermas, J. (1987). *Theory of Communicative Action, Volume Two: Lifeworld and System: A Critique of Functionalist Reason.* Boston, MA: Beacon Press.

Hegel, G.W.F. (1802/1979). *System of ethical life* [1802/3], and *First Philosophy of Spirit* [1803/4], translated by T.M. Knox. New York, NY: State University of New York Press.

Hegel, G.W.F. (1816/1969). *The Science of Logic*, translated by A.V. Miller. London, UK: George Allen & Unwin. §s refer to http://www.marxists.org/reference/archive/hegel/works/hl/hlooo.htm.

Hegel, G.W.F. (1821/1952). *Hegel's Philosophy of Right*, translated (with notes) by T.M. Knox. Oxford, UK: Oxford University Press.

Hegel, G.W.F. (1830/1971). *Hegel's Philosophy of Mind*, Part Three of the Encyclopædia of the philosophical sciences, translated by Wm. Wallace. Oxford, UK: Oxford University Press.

Hegel, G.W.F. (1831/2010). *Encyclopaedia of the Philosophical Sciences in Basic Outline. Part I: Logic.* Translated by K. Brinkman and D. Dahlstrom. Cambridge, UK: Cambridge University Press.

Hegel, G.W.F. (1837/1902). *The Philosophy of History*, translated by J. Sibree. New York: American Home Library Co.

Hegghammer, T. (2011). The Rise of Muslim Foreign Fighters. Islam and the Globalisation of Jihad. *International Security* 35(3) (Winter 2010/11): 53–94.

Heller, A. (1987). *Beyond Justice.* Oxford: Basil Blackwell, Pty, Ltd.

Heller, A. (1988). *General Ethics.* Oxford: Blackwell.

Herder, J.G. (1774/2004). *Another Philosophy of History and Selected Political Writings*, translated by I.D. Evrigenis and D. Pellerin. Indianapolis: Hackett Publishing Company.

Hess, M. (1843/1964). The Philosophy of the Act. In *Socialist thought. A documentary history*, ed. by Albert Fried and Ronald Sanders. Chicago, IL: Aldine Publishing Co.

Hill, C. (1975). *The World Turned Upside Down: Radical Ideas During the English Revolution*. London: Pelican Books.

Holland, D., Skinner, D., Lachicotte, W., and Cain, C. (1998). *Identity and Agency in Cultural Worlds*. Berkeley and Los Angeles: Harvard University Press.

Holodynski, M. (2013). The Internalisation Theory of Emotions: A Cultural Historical Approach to the Development of Emotions. *Mind, Culture, and Activity* 20(1): 4–38.

Honneth, A. (1990). *The Fragmented World of the Social. Essays in Social and Political Philosophy*. New York, NY: State University of New York Press.

Horkheimer, M. (1932). History and Psychology. In *Between Philosophy and Social Science: Selected Early Writings*, ed. by G.F. Hunter, pp. 111–128. Cambridge, MA: MIT Press.

Horton, M. (2003). *The Myles Horton Reader. Education for Social Change*, ed. by Dale Jacobs. Knoxville, TE: University of Tennessee Press.

Ilyenkov, E.V. (1960/1982). *The Dialectics of the Abstract and the Concrete in Marx's Capital*. Moscow: Progress Publishers.

Ilyenkov, E.V. (1977). The Concept of the Ideal. In *The Ideal in Human Activity*. Kettering, OH: Marxists Internet Archive Press.

Inwood, M. (1992). *A Hegel Dictionary*. Salisbury, UK: Blackwell Publishers.

Jacobs, J. (1961). *The Death and Life of Great American Cities*. New York: Random House.

Jamison, A. and Eyerman, R. (1991). *Social Movements. A Cognitive Approach*. University Park, Pennsylvania: Pennsylvania State University Press.

Jegede, A.S. (2007). What Led to the Nigerian Boycott of the Polio Vaccination Campaign? *PLOS Medicine* 4(3): e73. https://doi.org/10.1371/journal.pmed.0040073.

Kant, I. (1787/2007). *Critique of Pure Reason*, translated by Norman Kemp Smith. New York: Palgrave Macmillan.

Kaptelinin, V. (2005). The Object of Activity: Making Sense of the Sense-Maker. *Mind, Culture, and Activity* 12(1): 4–18.

Keynes, J.M. (1936). *The General Theory of Employment, Interest and Money*. London: MacMillan & Co.

King, M. (1999). *Mahatma Gandhi and Martin Luther King Jr. The power of nonviolent action*. Paris, France: UNESCO.

Kotik-Friedgut, B. (2007). Email to xmca listserv, December 2009. In Blunden, et al. (n.d.).

Kozulin, A. (1991). The Psychology of Experiencing: A Russian view. *Journal of Humanistic Psychology* 31(3): 14–19.

Kübler-Ross, E. (1969). *On Death and Dying. What the dying have to teach doctors, nurses, clergy and their own families.* New York: Macmillan.

Kuhn, T. (1962). *The Structure of Scientific Revolutions.* Chicago, IL: University of Chicago Press.

Laidlaw, J. (2013). *The Subject of Virtue. An Anthropology of Ethics and Freedom.* Cambridge, UK: Cambridge University Press.

Latham, M. (1998). *Civilising Global Capital: New Thinking for Australian Labor.* Sydney: Alan & Unwin.

Le Guin, U. (2017). *The Carrier Bag Theory of Fiction.* Talk at Kunsthalle Zürich.

Lenin, V.I. (1920). *Left-wing Communism: An infantile disorder.* Progress Publishers.

Leontyev, A.N. (1977/2009). Activity and Consciousness, pp. 395–409. *The Development of Mind.* Erythrós Press and Media.

Leontyev, A.N. (1978). *Activity, Consciousness and Personality.* Moscow: Progress Publishers.

Leontyev, A.N. (1978/2009). *The Development of Mind.* Pacifica, CA: Marxists Internet Archive Publications.

Leontyev, A.N. (1981/2009). Problems of the Development of Mind, pp. 1–398. *The Development of Mind.* Erythrós Press and Media.

Leontyev, A.N. (2005). Study of the environment in the pedological works of L.S. Vygotsky. *Journal of Russian and East European Psychology* 43(4): 8–28.

Leontyev, A.A. (2006). 'Units' and Levels of Activity. *Journal of Russian and East European Psychology* 44(3): 30–46.

Lightfoot, C. (1997). *The Culture of Adolescent Risk-Taking.* New York: Guilford Press.

Loyn, H.R. (1984). *The Governance of Anglo-Saxon England, 500–1087.* Chicago, IL: Stanford University Press.

Luria, A.R. (1928/1994). The problem of the cultural behaviour of the child. In R. van der Veer and J. Valsiner, eds., *The Vygotsky reader*, pp. 46–56. Oxford: Blackwell.

Luria, A.R. (1979). Cultural Differences in Thinking. Chapter 4 of *The Autobiography of Alexander Luria. A Dialogue with The Making of Mind.* Mahwah, NJ: Lawrence Erlbaum.

MacIntyre, A. (1981). *After virtue.* Notre Dame, IN: University of Notre Dame Press.

Maeckelbergh, M. (2009). *The Will of the Many.* London, UK: Pluto Press.

March, S., and Fleer, M. (2016). *Soperezhivanie*: Dramatic events in fairy tales and play. *International Research in Early Childhood Education* 7(1): 68–84.

Marx, K. (1843/1970). *Marx's Critique of Hegel's Philosophy of Right.* Edited by Joseph O'Malley. Cambridge, UK: Cambridge University Press. Page numbers from MECW, vol. 3, pp. 3–129.

Marx, K. (1843/1975). Comments on James Mill. MECW, vol. 3, pp. 211–228. New York: International Publishers.

Marx, K. (1845/1976). Theses on Feuerbach. *MECW, vol. 5*, pp. 6–8. New York: International Publishers.

Marx, K. (1845a/1976). Theses German Ideology. *MECW, vol. 5*, pp. 15–539. New York: International Publishers.

Marx, K. (1845b/1975). The Holy Family. *MECW, vol. 4*, pp. 5–210. New York: International Publishers.

Marx, K. (1852/1979). The Eighteenth Brumaire of Louis Bonaparte. *MECW, vol. 11*, pp. 103–197. New York: International Publishers.

Marx, K. (1858/1973). The Method of Political Economy. *The Grundrisse*, translated by M. Nicolaus, pp. 100–111. London, UK: Penguin Books.

Marx, K. (1857/1986). Economic Works 1857–1861. *MECW, vol. 28*. New York: International Publishers.

Marx, K. (1864/1994). Economic Works 1861–1864. *MECW, vol. 34*. New York: International Publishers.

Marx, K. (1867/1996). Capital. *MECW, vol. 35*. New York: International Publishers.

Marx, K. (1873/1996). Afterword to the Second German edition of *Capital*. *MECW, vol. 35*, pp. 12–22. New York: International Publishers.

Marx, K. (1881/1989). Marginal Notes on Adolph Wagner. *MECW, vol. 24*, pp. 531–559. New York: International Publishers.

Marx, K., and Engels, F. (1844/1975). The Holy Family or Critique of Critical Criticism. *MECW, vol. 4*, pp. 5–211. New York: International Publishers.

Marx, K., and Engels, F. (1871/1989). Circular Letter to August Bebel, Wilhelm Liebknecht, Wilhelm Bracke and Others. *MECW, vol. 24*, pp. 253–269. New York: International Publishers.

Meshcheryakova, I.A. (n.d.). Переживание, Entry in *Dictionary of Psychology*, http://www.b17.ru/dic/perejivanie/.

Mill, J.S. (1848). *Principles of Political Economy*. London, UK: John W. Parker.

Mill, J.S. (1861). *Utilitarianism*. London, UK: Parker, Son, and Bourn.

Meir, I., Sandler, W., Padden, C., and Aronoff, M. (2010). Emerging Sign Languages. Oxford Handbook of Deaf Studies, *Language, and Education, Volume 2*.

Moscovici, S., and Doise, W. (1994). *Conflict and Consensus: a General Theory of Collective Decisions*. Sage.

Neumann, P. (2015). *Foreign Fighters in Syria and Iraq: Motivations and Implications*. Speech at LSE, London, January 2015.

Nichols, F.H. (1999). History of the Women's Health Movement in the 20th Century. *JOGNN* 29(1). DOI: https://doi.org/10.1111/j.1552-6909.2000.tb02756.x.

NHPA (2014). *Healthy Communities: Immunisation rates for children in 2012–13*. National Health Performance Authority.

Nozick, R. (1974) *Anarchy, State, and Utopia*. Basic Books.

Padden, C. (2005). *Inside Deaf Culture*. Kindle Edition, Amazon.com.

Pearson, N. (2007). Pearson's crucial role for Howard. *The Age*, 3 July 2007.

Peretii-Watel, P., Larson, H., Ward, J.K., Schulz, W.S., and Verger, P. (2015). Vaccine Hesitancy: Clarifying a Theoretical Framework for an Ambiguous Notion. *PLOS Currents: Outbreaks*.

Polich, L. (2005). *The Emergence of the Deaf Community in Nicaragua*. Washington, DC: Gallaudet University Press.

Postone, M. (1993). *Time, labour, and social domination: A reinterpretation of Marx's critical theory*. Cambridge University Press.

Power, J. (2011). *Movement, Knowledge, Emotion: Gay Activism and HIV-AIDS in Australia*. Canberra, Australia: ANU E Press.

Power, J. (2014). Change through Collaboration: Gay Activism and HIV/AIDS in Australia. In *Collaborative Projects. An interdisciplinary study*. Leiden, Netherlands: Brill.

Putnam, R. (1993). *Making Democracy Work: Civic Traditions in Modern Italy*. Princeton, NJ: Princeton University Press.

Putnam, R. (2001). *Bowling Alone: The Collapse and Revival of American Community*. London, UK: Touchstone Books by Simon & Schuster.

Rawls, J. (1993). *Political Liberalism*. New York, NY: Columbia U.P.

Ricoeur, P. (1984). *Time and Narrative. Vol. 1*. Chicago: University of Chicago Press.

Robbins, D. (2007). Email to xmca listserv, December 2009. In Blunden, et al. (n.d.).

Rugg, S. (2019). *How Powerful We Are. Behind the scenes with one of Australia's leading activists*. Sydney, Australia: Hatchett.

Saint Benedict (1949). *The Holy Rule of St. Benedict*, trans. Rev. Boniface Verheyen.

Sannino, A. (2020). Enacting the Utopia of Eradicating Homelessness: Toward a New Generation of Activity-Theoretical Studies of Learning. *Studies in Continuing Education* 42(2): 163–179.

Sen, A. (1960). *Choice of Techniques*. Oxford, UK: Basil Blackwell.

Sen, A. (1970). *Collective Choice and Social Welfare*. San Francisco, CA: Holden-Day Inc.

Sen, A. (1973). *On Economic Inequality*. Oxford, UK: Clarendon Press.

Sen, A. (1980). *Equality of What?* First published in S. McMurrin (ed.), *Tanner Lectures on Human Values*. Cambridge, UK: Cambridge University Press.

Sen, A. (1981). *Poverty and Famines. Essay on Entitlement and Deprivation*. Oxford, UK: Clarendon Press.

Sen, A. (1987). *Commodities and Capabilities*. Oxford, UK: Oxford University Press.

Sen, A. (1992). *Inequality Re-examined*. Oxford, UK: Oxford University Press.

Sen, A. (1997). *On Economic Inequality*, Enlarged Edition. Oxford, UK: Oxford University Press.

Sen, A. (1998). *On Ethics and Economics*. Oxford, UK: Oxford University Press.

Sen, A. (1998a). *Autobiography*. Les Prix Nobel 1998.

Sen, A. (1999). *Development as Freedom*. Oxford, UK: Oxford University Press.

Sen, A. (1999a). Introduction in *Utilitarianism and beyond*. Cambridge, UK: Cambridge University Press.

Sen, A. (2002). *Rationality and Freedom*. Cambridge, MS: Harvard University Press.

Sen, A., and Drèze, J. (2002). *India: Development and Participation*. Oxford, UK: Oxford University Press.

Smith, A. (1996). The Renewal Movement: The Peace Testimony and Modern Quakerism. *Quaker History* 85(2): 1–23.

Stanislavskii, C. (1936). *An Actor Prepares*. New York, NY: Routledge.

Swerdlow, A. (1993). *Women Strike for Peace: Traditional Motherhood and Radical Politics in the 1960s*, Chicago, IL: University of Chicago Press.

Teo, T. (2012). Critical psychology. In R. Rieber, ed., *Encyclopedia of the history of psychological theories*, pp. 236–248. New York: Springer.

Trotsky, L.D. (1930). The Fundamental Principle. Errors of Syndicalism. *Marxists Internet Archive*. https://www.marxists.org/archive/trotsky/1930/02/syndicalism.htm.

Vasilyuk, F.E. (1988/1984). *The Psychology of Experiencing. The Resolution of Life's Critical Situations*. Progress Publishers Moscow. English translation (1988), Hemel Hempstead, UK: Harvester-Wheatsheaf.

Veresov, N., and Fleer, M. (2016). Perezhivanie as a Theoretical Concept for Researching Young Children's Development. *Mind, Culture, and Activity* 23(4): 1–11.

Vygotsky, L.S., and Luria, A.R. (1930/1992). *Ape, Primitive Man, and Child: Essays in the History of Behaviour*, translated by Evelyn Rossiter. Published by Paul M. Deutsch Inc.

Vygotsky, L.S. (1924/1997). The Methods of Reflexological and Psychological Investigation. LSV CW, vol. 3, pp. 35–50. New York: Plenum Press.

Vygotsky, L.S. (1926/1997). *Educational Psychology*, tr. Robert Silverman. Boca Raton, FL: CRC Press.

Vygotsky, L.S. (1928/1993). The Dynamics of Child Character. LSW CW, vol. 2, pp. 153–163, Dordrecht, Netherlands: Kluwer Academic Publishers.

Vygotsky, L.S. (1928a/1994). The Problem of the Cultural Development of the Child. In R. van der Veer and J. Valsiner, eds., *The Vygotsky reader*, pp. 57–72. Oxford, UK: Blackwell.

Vygotsky, L.S. (1928b/1997). Historical Meaning of the Crisis in Psychology. LSV CW, vol. 3, pp. 233–344. New York: Plenum Press.

Vygotsky, L.S. (1930/1992). Primitive Man and his Behaviour. *Ape, Primitive Man, and Child: Essays in the History of Behaviour*, translated by Evelyn Rossiter. Published by Paul M. Deutsch Inc.

Vygotsky, L.S. (1930a/1997). The Instrumental Method in Psychology. LSV CW, vol. 3, 85–90. New York: Plenum Press.

Vygotsky, L.S. (1930b/1994). The Socialist Alteration of Man. In R. van de Veer and J. Valsiner, eds., *The Vygotsky Reader*, pp. 175–184. Oxford, UK: Blackwell.

Vygotsky, L.S. (1930c/1994). Tool and Sign in Child Development. In R. van de Veer and J. Valsiner, eds., *The Vygotsky Reader*, pp. 99–174. Oxford, UK: Blackwell.

Vygotsky, L.S. (1931/1997). Self-Control. *LSV CW*, vol. 4, pp. 207–220. New York: Plenum Press.

Vygotsky, L.S. (1931a/1997). Genesis of Higher the Mental Functions. In *LSV CW*, vol. 4, pp. 97–120. New York: Plenum Press.

Vygotsky, L.S. (1931b/1997). Research Method. *LSV CW*, vol. 4, pp. 27–64. New York: Plenum Press.

Vygotsky, L.S. (1931c/1997). The Structure of the Higher Mental Functions. *LSV CW*, vol. 4, pp. 83–96. New York: Plenum Press.

Vygotsky, L.S. (1931d/1997). The Development of Speech. *LSV CW*, vol. 4, pp. 121–130. New York: Plenum Press.

Vygotsky, L.S. (1934/1987). Thinking and Speech. *LSV CW*, vol. 1, pp. 39–285. New York: Plenum Press.

Vygotsky, L.S. (1934a/1994). The problem of the environment. In R. van de Veer and J. Valsiner, eds., *The Vygotsky Reader*, pp. 338–354. Oxford, UK: Blackwell.

Vygotsky, L.S. (1934b/1998). The Problem of Age. *LSV CW*, vol. 5, pp. 187–205. New York: Plenum Press.

Winnicott, D. (1971). *Playing and Reality*. New York: Routledge.

Winstanley, G. (1642/1941). *Works*, with an introduction. Edited by G. Sabine. Ithaca, NY: Cornell University Press.

Index

1968 95, 330

Abeysinghe, S. 263, 265
Abidor, M. 95
Abstraction 233–234
Activities
　and concepts 26–27
　as units 54
　in Leontyev 173–174
Age levels 150–151
Agency 98–112
Alliance politics 110–111
Anarchism 300–316
　and anthropology 314–315
　and mediation 313–314
　practical 300–301
Arbeitsgegenstand 161–162
Art 243
Arthur, C. 29, 66
Atran, S. 278, 283, 284, 285

Beaton, L. 265, 268
Beck, U. 260, 267
Behaviour and biology 226–227
Bell, R. 266
Benhabib, S. 246
Bipedalism 227, 230
Blume, S. 267, 268, 271, 272, 273, 274
Bourdieu, P. 176, 258, 357, 387–401
　capital for 388–390
　idealism of 396–397
Bozhovich, L.I. 93
Buchanan, J. 352

Capability 342
Capacity building 369
Capital 291–299
Carrying things 230–231
CAT&DWR 162
Catharsis 82–84
Cell
　and unit 29–30, 34–60
　as capital 31–33
　as commodity 28–29
　Hegel's idea of 35–40

　Marx's idea of 40–43
　origins 34–35
Clarà, M. 84
Colapietro, V.M. 236
Cole, M. 57, 90
Coleman, J. 258, 356, 399
Collaborative projects. *See* Projects
Commitment 84–85
Concepts
　and motives 366–367
　as units 48
　formation of 48–50
Concrete historicism 61–77
Conscious awareness 235
Consequentialism and deontology 305
Continuity and discontinuity 85
Coover, V. 325
Corballis, M.C. 228, 234, 238
Counsel 320–321
Crisis periods 151
Cultural capital 392–394
Cultural relativism 394–395

Davydov, V.V. 140
De Saussure, F. 61
Deaf
　in Nicaragua 207–208
Deaf organisations 211–213
　influences on 213–215, 219–220
Decision making 268–271
　collective 317–332
　crisis of majority 325
　development of majority 323
　majority 321–322
　origins of majority 322–323
　without voting 319
Defect-compensation 53
Delayed gratification 231–233
Delegation and hierarchy 315
Dewey, J. 80, 81, 82, 84, 87, 403
Distributive justice 339
Dogmatism 187–188
Domestic labour 364–365
Donald, M. 236, 239

Engels, F. 7, 46, 113, 119, 128, 134, 142
    and Vygotsky 140–142
Engeström, Y. 57, 137, 140, 162
Episodic culture 239–240
Ethics
    and Utopia 310–312
    of collaboration 245–246
    of solidarity 298

False heroes and villains 333–338
Ferholt, B. 90
Feuerbach, L. 159–161
Fighters
    motivation of 278–281
    recruitment of 281–285
Firms 254–256
Fleer, M. 84, 96
Foreign fighters 278–290
Franks, B. 300–316
Fraser, N. 360–373, 397, 398
Freeman, J. 329
Freud, L. 81, 82, 84, 91, 376, 377, 385
Functionalism 188–189
Functioning 341–342

Gadamer, H-G. 169, 318
Germ cell. *See* Cell
Gestalt 31
Gesturing 234, 236–237
Giddens, A. 188, 260, 267, 374–386
Goethe, J.W. v. 13, 25–33, 34, 35, 40, 41, 42, 51, 55, 74, 75, 89, 113, 130, 292, 294
    and Hegel, Marx and Vygotsky 292–294
Goldin-Meadow, S. 208, 220–225

H1N1 vaccine dispute 265–266
Habermas, J. 305
Habitus
    and class 391–392
    and field 390
Healthism 260–261
Hegel, G.W.F. 7–33, 34–60, 61, 66, 67, 68, 74, 98, 131, 137, 142, 157, 159, 160, 161, 240, 256, 292–294, 295, 313, 321, 404
    logic and history in 63–66
    on free will 100–101
    on freedom and state 108–109
    on mediation 42–43
    on natural will 101–103
    on *Objekt* and *Gegenstand* 157–158
    on participatory democracy 16–17
    on the One 39–40
    on the state 8–11
    on universal suffrage 8–11
    on value 14–16
    relation to Marx 7–33
    turning on head 24–25
Hegghammer, T. 278, 288
Heller, A. 246, 251, 289, 304
Herder, J.G. 25, 34
Hess, M. 30
Hill, C. 326
History and evolution 116–117
Holland, D. 176
Holodynski, M. 54
Honneth, A. 399
Horton, M. 327–328
Howard, J. 335–336
Human subject 256–257

Idealism 17–24
Ideology 181–183
Ilyenkov, E.V. 29, 61, 71, 74, 75
Institutions 253–254
    and social movements 368–369
Internal goods 301–303
Inwood, M. 156
Islamism 279–281

Jacobs, J. 357
Jamison, A. 303
Jegede, A.S. 264
Just So stories 134–135

Kant, I. 7, 17, 43, 52, 80, 156, 157, 224, 246, 256, 394
Kaptelinin, V. 171, 174
King, M. 92, 93, 326
King, M.L. 92, 328
Knowledgeability of actors 361–362
Kotik-Friedgut, B. 82
Kozulin, A. 195
Kübler-Ross, E. 81, 83, 91
Kuhn, T. 400

Labour and language 135–137
Laidlaw, J. 303
Language
   acquisition of 215–216
   evolution of 226–244
Latham, M. 359
Lawson, J. 93
   and consensus 328–329
Le Guin, U. 230
Leading activity 152–155
Lenin, V.I. 38, 61
Leontyev, A.A. 171, 174
Leontyev, A.N. 32, 54, 57, 85, 94, 99, 101, 102, 106, 107, 108, 126, 127, 142, 163, 164, 168, 171–194, 196, 199, 235, 375, 404
   on operations 138–140
   on tools and labour 137–138
Leontyev, D. 171
Life world 197–199
Lightfoot, C. 255
Lines of Development 149
Lived experiences 88
Loyn, H.R. 322
Luria, A.R. 44, 114, 117, 122, 123, 124, 135

MacIntyre, A. 283, 300, 301, 302, 303, 307, 312, 313, 316, 372
   critique of 303–304
Maeckelbergh, M. 307, 310
Marx, K. 7–33, 47, 50, 51, 55–57, 61, 63, 70, 72, 74, 75, 92, 102, 119, 131, 134–135, 136, 137, 159–161, 291, 292–294, 349, 375, 388, 391
   Capital 55–57
   logic and history for 66–69
   on Hegel 159–161
   on participatory democracy 16–17
   on the state 11
   on the State 8–11
   on universal suffrage 8–11
Meir, I. 216, 219, 225
Method of political economy 27–28
MMR vaccine 264
Moscovici, S. 332
Motivation 174–177
Motive
   and goal 309–310
   objective 163
Music and dance 239

Neoformation 147–148
Neumann, P. 284, 289
NHPA 266
Nicaraguan Revolution 208–211
Nicaraguan Sign Language 203–225
Nozick, R. 257

Object 156–170
   and aim 162–163
   and objective 178–179
   boundary 167–168
   -concept 165–166
   consumption of 164–165
   etymology 156–157
   for Hegel 157–158
   for Leontyev 195
   of project 168–169
Objective and universal 158–159
Objectivism 177–178
Otnosheniye 196–197
   in social theory 201–202

Padden, C. 210, 216, 217, 218
Particularity 183–187
Perezhivanie 52–53
   and development 89–91
   and reflection 91–92
   critiques of 93–94
   etymology 81–82
   examples of 92–93
   for Vasilyuk 108, 199
   on historical plane 94–96
   types of 199
Periodisation
   of child development 143–144
   of intellect 117–118
   of tools 118
Personal sense 179–181
Personality 190–192
Polich, L. 207, 210, 211, 212, 215
Polio vaccine boycott 264–265
Political economy 257
Political opinion 397
Populism 336–337
Postone, M. 160
Power 245–258
   abuse of 248–253
Power, J. 268, 269, 272

Practical anarchism   307
Practical consciousness   364–365
Pre-capitalist society   361–362
Prefiguration   302, 312, 316
Productivism   189
Project   245–258
   and ethics   245–246
   as unit   245–248
   versus 'activity'   193–194
Projects   241–242, 271–275, 285
Psychology
   instrumental   126–128
   instrumental method in   128–130
Public assistance   366–367
   universal or targeted   367–368
Putnam, R.   356, 357, 399

Quakers   325–327

Rawls, J.   304, 341
Reification   55
Ricoeur, P.   318
Risk Culture   260–261
Robbins, D.   81
Routines   362–364
Rugg, S.   93

Saint Benedict   110, 320
Sannino, A.   332
Self-control   105
Self-help   371–373
Self-relation   152t.1
Sen, A.   339–354
   biography   339–340
Sign languages
   deaf community   217–219
   personal   220–225
   village   217
Smith, A.   326, 362
Social capital   355–359, 398–399
   in Bourdieu   394
Social choice theory   349–353
Social situation of development   53–54, 144–147
Solidarity   294–299
Speech   130, 132, 238–239
Stalin, J.   171, 407
Stanislavskii, C.   89, 379, 381

Status subordination   397–398
Structuralism   61–62
Subjectivity   400
Swerdlow, A.   329
Swine flu scare   263

Tools   240–241
   and operations   138–140
   technical and psychological   120–121
Trotsky, L.D.   252
Trump, D.   276, 407, 409, 410
Trust   261–263

Unintended consequences   367–368
Unit   88–89 *See also* Cell
   as capital   41–42
   Vygotsky on   43–54
Unit of analysis   34–60
Unity   86–87
Urpraxis   30–31
   of socialism   291–299
Utilitarianism
   and political economy   348–349
   and positivism   347–348
Utopia   300–316

Vaccine hesitancy   259–277
   origins   271–275
Vasilyuk, F.   83, 84, 90, 96, 99, 106, 107, 108, 171, 174, 175, 176, 177, 192, 195–202, 280
   Kozulin on   195
Veresov, N.   84
VH Compass   262–263
Virtue   300–316
   of a practice   312–313
Virtue ethics   305–306
Voice   343–344
   critical   344
Voluntary association   109–110
Voluntary control   235
Vygotsky, L.S.   31, 60, 69–70, 72, 73, 74, 78, 79, 80, 84, 85, 86, 87, 88, 89, 90, 92, 93, 94, 97, 98, 99, 100, 102, 103–105, 113–142, 143–155, 165–166, 171, 189, 192, 197, 201, 203, 204, 205–206, 210, 223, 225, 228, 235, 236, 243, 289, 292–294, 295, 377, 380, 381, 382, 383
   and Engels   140–142

Ape, Primitive Man and Child 128
five units of analysis 52–54
History of Development of Higher Mental Functions 130–132
importance for social theory 55
on "primitive man" 114n1, 121–123
on child development 143–155
on double stimulation 43
on ideal form 205–206
on lines of development 125–126
on word meaning 45–47
Thinking and Speech 57–60, 132–134
tool and sign in 113–142

Wage labour 362–364

Wealth 341
Welfare dependency 360–373
   as personality trait 368–369
Whooping cough 263–264
Will
   development 103–105
   free 100–101
   natural 101–103
Winnicott, D. 81, 91
Winstanley, G. 323, 332
Women Strike for Peace 329–330
Working class 291
Writing 115–116, 117–118, 125–126, 243

Zone of proximal development 152–155